Knightmare on Wall Street

Also by Edgar Perez

The Speed Traders
An Insider's Look at the New High-Frequency Trading
Phenomenon That is Transforming the Investing World

交易快手
透视正在改变投资世界的新兴高频交易,

Investasi Super Kilat
Pandangan Orang dalam tentang Fenomena Baru Frekuensi Tinggi
yang Mentransformasi Dunia Investasi

The Speed Traders Workshop DVD Video Package
How Algorithmic and High Frequency Traders Leverage Profitable
Strategies to Find Alpha in Equities, Options, Futures and FX

Available at www.MrEdgarPerez.com

KNIGHTMARE
ON WALL STREET

THE RISE AND FALL OF KNIGHT CAPITAL AND THE BIGGEST RISK FOR FINANCIAL MARKETS

Edgar Perez

www.KnightmareonWallStreet.com

This book is available at special discounts for bulk purchases for sales promotions or corporate use. Special editions, including personalized covers, or books with corporate logos, can be created in large quantities for special needs. For more information, contact info@knightmareonwallstreet.com.

Library of Congress Cataloging-in-Publication Data
Perez, Edgar, 1974-
Knightmare on Wall Street: The Rise and Fall of Knight Capital and the Biggest Risk for Financial Markets / by Edgar Perez

ISBN: 978-0-9896577-0-9

Cover design: Jason Alexander, Expert Subjects, LLC.

First Edition

THE SPEED TRADERS WORKSHOP ON DVD

How High Frequency Traders Leverage
Profitable Strategies to Find Alpha
in Equities, Options, Futures and FX

DVD VIDEO PACKAGE (4 DISCS)
THESPEEDTRADERSWORKSHOP.COM

Golden Networking

THE **SPEED**

TRADERS

WORKSHOP

EDGAR PEREZ

Golden Networking, The Premier Networking Community in Business and Finance

THE SPEED TRADERS

How High Frequency Traders Leverage Profitable Strategies to Find Alpha in Equities, Options, Futures and FX

THESPEEDTRADERSWORKSHOP.COM   Course Director: Edgar Perez

The Speed Traders Workshop DVD Video Package opens the door to the secretive world of high-frequency trading (HFT), the most controversial form of investing today; in the name of protecting the algorithms they have spent so much time perfecting, speed traders disclose as little as possible about how they operate.

DVD 1: Understanding High Frequency Trading in Equities and other Asset Classes
  The need for speed and sophisticated computer programs in generating, routing, and executing orders
  Co-location and individual data feeds to minimize latency
  Time-frames for establishing and closing highly-liquid positions
  Review of the most important strategies: market making, trend following, value arbitrage and others

DVD2: Key Enablers for High Frequency Trading
  Technological innovation: computing power, complex event processing, and low-latency bandwidth
  Shift to electronic trading and the rise of alternative trading systems
  In-depth look at strategies high frequency traders leverage to find alpha in equities, options, futures and FX
  The profitability of typical high frequency trading strategies and its evolution

DVD 3: Global Regulatory Overview: from the U.S. and Europe to China and Brazil
  Regulations in place before the "flash crash"
  Proposed regulatory initiatives after the "flash crash" in the U.S. and Europe
  High frequency trading in Asia, from Japan, Singapore and India to Hong Kong and China
  Regulating speed trading to samba beats: Brazil and Mexico

DVD 4: The Future of High Frequency Trading
  Enhancing profitability: from equities to FX to cross-asset trading
  High frequency trading in the world: from the U.S. and Europe to China and Brazil
  Adding ammunition to the high frequency trader toolkit, FPGA, GPUs and enhanced technologies
  Turning the tables on high frequency trading: the transparency challenge for the buy-side

EDGAR PEREZ is widely regarded as the global preeminent speaker in HFT. He is author of The Speed Traders, published by McGraw-Hill, and Adjunct Professor at the Polytechnic Institute of New York University. Mr. Perez has been featured on CNBC, BNN, Channel NewsAsia Asia, The Street.com, NHK World, iMoney, The Wall Street Journal, The New York Times, Dallas Morning News, Los Angeles Times, TODAY Online, Oriental Daily News and Valor Economico. He has been engaged as speaker at Harvard Business School's Venture Capital & Private Equity Conference, High-Frequency Trading Leaders Forum, Global Growth Markets Forum, TradeTech, FIXGlobal Face2Face, among other global forums. He was a vice president at Citigroup, a senior consultant at IBM, and a consultant at McKinsey & Company in New York City. He has an undergraduate degree from Universidad Nacional de Ingeniería, Lima, Peru (1994), a Master of Administration from Universidad ESAN, Lima, Peru (1997) and a Master of Business Administration from Columbia Business School, with a dual major in Finance and Management (2002).

Contents

For Olga,
Who made me the happiest man when she said yes

Acknowledgments

This book is the result of many months of thinking, interviewing and networking. I was drawn to Knight Capital by the extraordinaire example of entrepreneurship and innovation ultimately brought down to its knees by a risk that was not in its priority radar.

Because of widespread misunderstanding of what really happened with Knight Capital on August 1, 2012, it occurred to me that a book telling the real story would be an appropriate way for financial firms to bridge the gap between the theory and the practice of responding to operational risks.

I would like to gratefully acknowledge the willing participation and helpful insights of the hundreds of interviewees whose quotes and comments appear interspersed liberally throughout the book.

Writing this book would not have been possible without the continuous interaction I had with executives, founders, traders, quants, managers, technologists, academics, journalists, consultants, and investors. I particularly would like to acknowledge the organizers and attendees to my presentations and workshops in Beijing, Chicago, Hong Kong, Kiev, Kuala Lumpur, London, Naples Beach, New York, Sao Paulo, Seoul, Shanghai, Singapore, Warsaw and Washington D.C. I am looking forward to discussing *Knightmare on Wall Street* with you.

I owe particular thanks to my staff that had the vision to see this book as a contribution both to the practice and to the public debate. They have continually challenged me and helped me come to new insights as we have grappled with making a very complex narrative easy to read and understand. Special thanks go to Alina Abazova, An Soyoung, Beatriz Cuevas, Byun Jihye, Claire Wei, Clark Sacktor, Edward Westerman, Ivana Tong, Jake Dalaya, April Zhao, Jane Yan,

Jeanne Qiu, Kim Jiyoung, Michael Innocenzi, Murli Nagori, Roh Eun Kyung, Sean Grant, Shane Sethi, Steven Wong and Ziwei Yao.

Finally, eternal thanks to my parents, Saturnina and Felipe, for their dedication, responsibility, and encouragement, to my brother, Guido, for being so loyal and supportive, and to Olga, the love of my life. They know more than anyone in the world about the late nights and long weekends that, in lieu of hustle dancing, were spent writing *Knightmare on Wall Street.*

Cast of Characters

Once upon a time, an enterprising knight capitalized on the retail investing revolution. That knight is no longer with us...

Knight Insiders

The Founders

Walter Raquet, Executive Vice President, the genius behind Knight's trailblazing idea

Kenneth Pasternak, Chief Executive Officer, the ultimate trader that led through Knight's initial years

Steven Steinman, Founder, Trimark Group

Robert Lazarowitz, Chief Operating Officer, Trimark Group

Management Throughout The First Years

John Hewitt, President, Knight Securities

Peter Hajas, Chief Executive Officer, Arbitrade, and later Chief Executive Officer of Knight Financial Products

Robert Turner, Chief Financial Officer, Executive Vice President, Treasurer and Director

Irv Kessler and Efi Gildor, Co-founders, Arbitrade, acquired by Knight

David Shpilberg, Executive Vice President, Chief Operating Officer

Diego Baez, Senior Vice President, Electronic Trading

Anthony Sanfilippo, President and Chief Executive Officer of Knight Capital Markets, and later interim Chief Executive Officer

John Leighton, Head of Institutional Trading

Robert Stellato, Head of Institutional Trading and former leader of the NASDAQ sales team at Goldman Sachs

Management when the trading incident happened

Thomas Joyce, Chairman and Chief Executive Officer

Steven Sadoff, Executive Vice President, Global Head of Operations, Services, and Technology

George Sohos, Head of the Electronic Trading Group (ETG)

Joseph Wald, former EdgeTrade's Chief Executive Officer, Head of Institutional Electronic Trade Execution Services

Kara Fitzsimmons, Managing Director of Media Relations

Meaghan Mullins, Managing Director, Electronic Services, global voice and electronic access products

Tara Muller, Managing Director, Electronic Trading, Knight Link

Erica Attonito, Managing Director, Knight Link and Knight Match

The Technology Team

Michael Strashnov, Managing Director

Milind Deshpande, Director

Kok Sang, Director and SMARS leader; ultimately, directly responsible for the August 1 glitch

Knight Suitors

The Rescue Investors

Richard Handler, Chief Executive Officer, Jefferies

Ronald Kruszewski, Chairman, Stifel Financial

Curt Bradbury, Chief Operating Officer, Stephens

Laurence Tosi, Chief Financial Officer, Blackstone

Joe Moglia, Chairman, and Fred Tomczyk, Chief Executive Officer, TD Ameritrade

The Winning Suitor, GETCO

Stephen Schuler, Co-founder

Dan Tierney, Co-founder

Daniel Coleman, Chief Executive Officer
Bill Ford, Chief Executive Officer of General Atlantic, GETCO's biggest investor

The Losing (yet Profitable) Suitor, Virtu Financial
Vincent Viola, Founder and Chief Executive Officer
Chris Concannon, Partner
Dick Grasso, "unofficial adviser", and former Chairman of the New York Stock Exchange

The Spurned Suitor, Citadel
Ken Griffin, Founder and Chief Executive Officer
Tom Miglis, Chief Information Officer
Jamil Nazarali, Senior Managing Director, Head of Citadel Execution Services
Matt Cushman, Senior Managing Director
Noel Dalzell, Vice President, Head of Strategy and New Product Development
Matthew Taback, Mark Stehli, John Kane and Michael Donofrio, Trader, former Knight employees
Kristen Benza, Vice President

Knight Observers

Securities and Exchange Commission
Mary Schapiro, Chairman
Mary Jo White, upcoming Chairman
Troy Paredes, Commissioner
Robert Cook, Director of the Trading and Markets Division

New York Stock Exchange
Duncan Niederauer, Chief Executive Officer
Larry Leibowitz, Chief Operating Officer

John Phelan, Former Chairman and President

NASDAQ

Robert Greifeld, Chief Executive Officer
Hardwick "Wick" Simmons, former Chief Executive Officer

The Experts

Rich Repetto, Principal, Equity Research, Sandler O'Neill
Eric Hunsader, Founder, Nanex
Christopher Nagy, former Head of Trading, Ameritrade
James Angel, Associate Professor of Finance, McDonough School of Business, Georgetown University
Joe Saluzzi and Sal Arnuk, Partners, Themis Trading

The Advisors

Brian Sterling, Co-head of Investment Banking Group, and Jimmy Dunne, Head of the Executive Committee, Sandler O'Neill (for Knight)
Edward Herlihy, Partner, Wachtell, Lipton, Rosen & Katz (for Knight)
Joel Fleck, Managing Director, Barclays Capital (for TD Ameritrade)
Ronald Brody, Colin Diamond and Jill Falor, White & Case (for Jefferies)
Patrick Daugherty, Partner, Foley & Lardner (for TD Ameritrade)

The Insiders

Stephanie Ruhle and Erik Schatzker, Anchors, Bloomberg Television's *Market Makers*
Charlie Gasparino, Senior Finance Correspondent, FOX Business Network
Bob Pisani, Reporter, CNBC

Introduction

Founded by Ken Pasternak and Walter Raquet in 1995, Knight Capital was one of the companies whose fortunes had risen as well as fallen as U.S. regulators made a series of changes in the structure of financial markets over the course of 15 years. The top U.S. regulator, the Securities and Exchange Commission, had grappled for years with ways to create a national market system which used technology to ensure that orders to buy and sell shares were sent to the best possible venue, either on-exchange or off-exchange such as broker-dealer internalization platforms and dark pools (trading systems that let investors anonymously buy or sell larger blocks of stock without tipping their hand to a wider market).

New developments opened up the markets to new exchanges and high-frequency trading firms that used algorithms to execute up to millions of trades per second. These high-speed firms used those algorithms to make money from small discrepancies in stock prices (or other listed instruments) and their activity rapidly came to account for more than half of all stock trading in the United States.

The increasing influence of electronic trading and the proliferation of widely covered trading disruptions led some to recognize deep fault lines in financial markets increasingly dominated by sophisticated automated trading systems. These wonders of high technology were able to handle massive volumes of transactions in microseconds (even nanoseconds), a feat human traders could never achieve. But the benefits of technological innovation came at a cost: equity markets had become a jumble of exchanges, market makers, dark pool operators, high-frequency traders, and investors using customized systems that could interact in unexpected ways.

The Flash Crash, the infamous 1,000 point drop the Dow Jones Industrial Average suffered on May 6, 2010 (the largest one-day point decline in history), illustrated how technological problems could cascade from one market participant to the rest. Regulators went into overdrive after the Flash Crash to implement a number of rules designed to prevent such an incident from happening again. At the same time, a number of embarrassing and costly technology issues cropped up. These issues illustrated an equity market worlds away from the "good old days", times when human traders, known as "specialists", worked on the floors of stock exchanges, such as the New York Stock Exchange, to match buyers with sellers and completed trades themselves if matches couldn't be made.

Over the period of a decade, automated trading systems had taken their place and much of the trading volume had moved away from exchanges and into electronic venues such as dark pools.

As off-exchange trading became increasingly more pervasive in financial markets, proponents of traditional exchanges grew significantly more vocal in their criticism of these alternative trading systems. Critics argued, for instance, that dark pools degraded current market structure and wreaked havoc on investor confidence. However, trading volume indicated that more and more financial institutions were turning to dark pools such as Knight Capital-owned Knight Link and Knight Match to execute their trades.

Thomas Joyce, chief executive officer of Knight Capital since 2002, was one of the biggest critics of NASDAQ for the irresponsible way how it had handled Facebook's initial public offering. Joyce had made his name at Merrill Lynch and Sanford C. Bernstein & Company. An unapologetic proponent of electronic trading, he had been scornful of those companies that were challenged by ever-changing financial markets. By contrast, Knight Capital was apparently a combat-tested investing firm with trading systems that had performed dependably through a number of incidents since the late 1990s. Unlike Bear Stearns and Lehman Brothers, it was not the type of firm which took on too much leverage to acquire securities that could later dramatically decline in value; its operating model from the very beginning was to quickly and efficiently match buyers and sellers of instruments. None saw it as a company that indulged in potentially value-destroying risk-taking.

So it was certainly shocking that at 9:30 A.M. on Wednesday, August 1, 2012, right after the markets opened for the day, Knight Capital began issuing an unprecedented number of erroneous orders into the market, due to an error in installing new software. The firm rapidly moved the stocks of 148 companies by automatically sending orders it did not plan. The trades pushed up the value of these stocks, and the company was later forced to sell part of the overvalued shares back into the market at a lower price and the rest to Goldman Sachs for a five percent commission.

Knight Capital announced later that they had lost an estimated $440 million. The losses uncovered a surprisingly weak standing for Knight Capital and threatened the survival of the firm. These losses were greater than the company's cash and cash equivalents position by the end of the second quarter of 2012 when it held $365 million. This was only slightly more than the $350 million it held by the end of the same quarter in 2002, when Joyce became chief executive officer.

What followed this shocking announcement were several rounds of desperate conversations with a number of vulture players who had smelled opportunity and were readying themselves to pick up bargain-priced pieces. As time was running out, Joyce had three choices: take an offer from a group of clients and others that would dilute current shareholders' equity, accept a $500 million bailout from his biggest competitor, Citadel, or go bankrupt.

Joyce and Richard Handler, chief executive officer of Jefferies, were able to assemble a rescue team that included TD Ameritrade, Blackstone, GETCO, Stephens, and Stifel Financial. On Monday, August 6, 2012, Joyce confirmed that Knight Capital had struck a deal with this group of investors, staving off collapse days after the trading mishap, even as the New York Stock Exchange temporarily revoked the firm's market-making responsibilities.

While Knight Capital was back in the game, its limping recovery quickly prompted competitors to bid for the entire company. One of the vultures, the most dangerous of all, was its own investor, Chicago-based GETCO, which had started salivating the moment it inspected the firm's books in early August. The other one was Virtu Financial, a firm founded by Vincent Viola that had quickly become a market-making powerhouse.

Ultimately, on December 19, 2012, the board decided to take the Chicago route. For GETCO's enterprising chief executive officer Daniel Coleman, acquiring Knight Capital represented a gigantic fast-forward step. For Knight Capital, it was the end of its existence as an independent entity.

Knightmare on Wall Street is a behind-the-scenes look at the rise and fall of Knight Capital. It provides a comprehensive account of what it took to elevate the firm to the cusp of the investing revolution of the late 1990s, to struggle through booms and busts, and to bring the firm down, to end up ultimately being ignominiously bought up by a competitor.

Chapter One

The Lazy Morning that Wasn't

9:30 A.M. *Ringing the virtual bell*

On an unseasonably cold day at 84 degrees in New York City for the waning days of summer, trading was supposed to start with no apparent complications for all market participants; by the end of the day, six billion shares were expected to change hands.

At the storied balcony overlooking the historic floor of the New York Stock Exchange, executives and guests of Vringo, a provider of software platforms for mobile social and video applications, celebrated the company's merger with Innovate/Protect by ringing the opening bell. It was the Wall Street rite of passage that in the past had seen the likes of numerous business tycoons, powerful politicians, famous athletes and TV celebrities; among these were former California governor Arnold Schwarzenegger, legendary Yankee hall of famer Joe DiMaggio, Olympic swimmer Michael Phelps, rapper Snoop Dogg, actress Sarah Jessica Parker of Sex in the City and actor Robert Downey Jr. There had also been several famous non-people that had rung the bell, including Mickey Mouse, the Pink Panther, Mr. Potato-Head, the Aflac Duck and – perhaps most ominously in this electronic trading era – Darth Vader.[1]

Because of the flip of the configuration in two internal systems, the orders that Knight started sending at the opening, intending to be peg orders, were immediately becoming marketable. Peg orders were designed to maintain a purchase price relative to the national best offer (NBO) or a sale price relative to the national best bid (NBB). Depending on the width of the quote, these orders could be passive or aggressive. A trader could create a peg order by entering a limit price which defined the worst limit price that they were willing to accept. Next, the trader entered an offset amount which computed the active limit price for the sell order as the bid price plus the offset amount; in case of a buy order, the limit price was the offer price minus the offset amount. For instance, a peg order to buy with an offset amount of 0.125 meant that the trader was effectively posting a limit order that would at all times remain 1/8 less than the best offer price.

Peg orders acted very much like limit orders, where the limit prices changed to match the best offer if buying, or best bid if selling. Often this would have an effect similar to a market order. Certainly, most traders wanting a guaranteed execution wanted a market order, not a peg order. However, when they wanted a peg order, traders didn't expect immediate execution.

Traders submitting these orders were initially pleased, as they were seeing their peg orders immediately executed. These orders were being executed because they were crossing the market; inadvertently, Knight traders were moving the market.

9:31 A.M. More volume than anybody can handle

After just one minute of activity, traders on the floor were able to see that there was a hefty 12 percent more trading in all stocks than there had been on average during the previous seven days. Worried and looking for insight, they turned to CNBC only to read an optimistic headline, "Dow, NASDAQ, Start August in Green After Posting 1-Month Gains in July."

Floor traders at the Big Board who had dwindled in number with the rise of electronic trading, attributed the emerging issue to a glitch in an electronic trading algorithm. The Big Board, the famous nickname for the New York Stock Exchange, was seen as one of the last of its breed with floor traders trafficking shares, in contrast to automated exchanges where trading existed only in computer networks.

CNBC's Bob Pisani would later report the initial reaction on the floor. "What we have is that there was massive volume at the open. I mean, people started yelling and screaming within 30 seconds of the open because some stocks did 30 days' volume in literally a couple of minutes. So something went wrong with the interface. Some massive amounts of orders came through. I find it hard to believe that it was deliberate."

"From the buzz on the [trading] floor, it was clear something was up," said Mike Shea, managing partner with Direct Access Partners.[2] "We were surprised to see that amount of volume so early in the session, given how much volumes have continued to decline," said Ryan Larson, the head stock trader at RBC Global Asset Management.

"Really, everybody noticed," Doreen Mogavero, president of Mogavero Lee & Co., said. "It wasn't two seconds before I was running around, saying, 'What is going on with these stocks?'" Almost forty years before, Mogavero had decided to transform her summer job working on the American Stock Exchange into a permanent position; this circumstance would lead her to found later the Big Board's only brokerage firm managed exclusively by women. Mogavero said that by the time she made it over to ask exchange officials what the problem was, they were already working on a solution.[3]

Jason Weisberg, managing director with Seaport Securities, said the exchange was quick with a response. "First thing, at the opening, they said, 'Slow down, there might be some errant orders that are floating into the system,'" he said. "They'd trade, and then they'd stop trading, and then they'd trade again, then they'd stop again," said Ken Polcari, managing director at ICAP Equities. "The guys are down here on the floor so they were just as caught off guard because they were actually suffering some of the consequences of the failure of their own technology," he added referring to the Knight traders on the floor.

9:33 A.M. Not providing liquidity but taking it

By the third minute of trading there was a massive 116 percent more trading activity than the previous week's average. The Knight code that was supposed to direct the firm's computers to react to trading was instead placing runaway offers to mostly buy shares of companies, quickly driving up the volume of trading to these suspicious levels. The orders were causing wild swings which affected the shares of a large and growing number of companies, including Ford Motor, RadioShack, American Airlines, and more obscure names like China Cord Blood Corp. and Wizzard Software Corp.

9:34 A.M. The Knight who messed up this time

Some Knight employees and New York Stock Exchange officials noticed the blizzard of erratic orders in the minutes after trading started and sent alarmed messages to the firm's managers.

The regulatory authorities traced the problem to Knight Capital. Duncan Niederauer, the NYSE's chief executive officer, noticed the problem and tried to contact Thomas M. Joyce, Knight's chief executive officer, known as T.J. in the business. Niederauer and Joyce had been personal friends for years yet lately they were falling into opposite camps.

Settling into his seat at the witness table in a congressional hearing room just six weeks before on June 19, Joyce leaned toward the man on his left. "Don't elbow me," he said. Joyce was warning Niederauer to brace for a squabble over the future of the U.S. stock market. "Likewise", Niederauer shot back. Both powerful men grinned at each other.[4]

Internalization, the process which allowed brokers to get better prices for clients of discount firms and helped them keep trading costs low, was playing into Joyce and Niederauer's frayed friendship and the broader increase in the amount of stock trading going on away from public exchanges in the so-called dark markets; since 2008, the portion of all stock trades in the United States taking place away from the exchanges had risen from 15 percent to nearly 35 percent, according to the brokerage firm Rosenblatt Securities.

Did Joyce and Niederauer know that Tuesday was Schapiro's birthday? Perhaps a cake prepared by Knight's pastry chef Meaghan Mullins with a "Dear Mary Lovelace" card and fifty seven candles, delivered personally by Joyce at the SEC's headquarters by Union Station, would have opened her heart for a time like this when Knight needed her support the most.

While the trading in the affected 148 stocks was so extreme that it was visible in the volume of trading in all stocks, the NYSE had limited authority to take action. Circuit breakers that curb erratic trading were tied to wild swings in stock prices, whereas the problem at Knight was initially tied to the volume of trading and not necessarily the price of shares. In addition, circuit breakers that halt individual stocks would not work during the first 15 minutes of trading.

9:35 A.M. Enormous spike in volume

Officials at the New York Stock Exchange had begun noticing an enormous spike in volume shortly after the opening bell and were now in touch with the Securities and Exchange Commission (SEC) in Washington D.C., where an internal e-mail system alerted regulators to the problem. A regulator stationed in the agency's market watch room was sending out regular alerts to senior agency officials. Volume was already 30 percent above the day before.

Realizing the urgency of the situation, the notified Knight Capital team placed phone calls to all the teams in charge of the systems, in particular, BRASS and SMARS. They found out the trades were coming from Knight's crown jewel, the Electronic Trading Group (ETG), led by George Sohos since the departure of superstar Jamil Nazarali to Citadel.

In the past years, Knight's ETG had enjoyed immense success in U.S. equities and was expanding internationally and across asset classes. In 2008, Knight had launched ETG Europe and continued to grow the business and market coverage. Knight had committed significant technological and intellectual capital to capture the nuances of both the European marketplace as a whole and the complex microstructures of each country's individual markets, a feat that eluded founder Kenneth Pasternak and president John Hewitt more than a decade before. Building on the success of ETG's U.S. equities business, Knight had quantitative models and strategies to trade futures, options, and foreign currencies, which would prove pivotal in powering Knight's record profits in 2008. Joyce couldn't have been more proud when presenting at Knight's third quarter earnings conference call.

"The third quarter of 2008 was certainly a period of historic turmoil in the global capital markets and sweeping transformation on Wall Street. The ever increasing scale and duration of the mortgage lead crisis was, or rather is, startling. The efforts to date of the U.S. Treasury and the Federal Reserve's officials to contain the crisis have been nothing short of extraordinary. So, it almost goes without saying that the events produced periods of extreme volatility. The VIX index measured volatility averaged 24.4 in July, 20.7 in August, and 30.2 in September with a then inter-day all time high of over 48 on September 29.

"During this period, our hybrid market model allowed us to take in more order flow across multiple voice and electronic channels from buy and sell side firms of all categories and sizes. Our reliable and efficient and scalable trading technology with current capacity of close to 20 million trades per day in 99.99% uptime smoothly processed order flow while traders provided clients with market insights.

We've been aggressively deepening liquidity across the entire equity market through broker-dealer electronic market making which provides instantaneous trade execution. Given the execution speed, often in milliseconds, this usually involves committing our own capital to complete a trade on behalf of our client. Among broker-dealers execution quality is both a competitive and regulatory imperative. We consistently lead the industry in providing broker-dealers with industry leading execution quality according to SEC rule 605 mandates governing speed, effective over quoted, price improvement, and add or better. Further, we employ sophisticated algorithms to optimize the execution of each client's over flow. And we also have cash traders, for oversized or difficult to handle orders. All of this is especially important considering we don't have captive order flow."

Knight's remarkable performance during a slipping market caught the attention of the editors at *Los Angeles Times* so much that they decided to send reporter Walter Hamilton and photographer Carolyn Cole on December 11, 2008. Hamilton would write about Peter Kenny, one of Knight's legendary traders:

"Although the market already has been slipping for about 30 minutes, that's little comfort, given that the last hour of the day has become enormously volatile during the market turmoil of the last. For Kenny, it's a time to either shine or fall flat.

The market's meltdown and last-hour somersaults have made this one of the most adrenaline-filled, nerve-racking stretches ever for the Wall Street traders who are paid to divine the gyrations. The traders at Knight have been like play-by-play announcers chronicling the decimation in the stock market."

Hamilton was impressed with how fastidiously neat looked compared with the messy desks of most traders, "The few objects in view include a pair of pocket-size books -- one of Buddhist teachings and the other of Catholic novenas with which Kenny starts each day with a prayer." Cole, instead, was impressed with the firm's trading floor, pictures of which accompanied the article published on January 8, 2009.[5]

Knight's trading Disneyland was located across the river from the storied New York Stock Exchange floor on 545 Washington Boulevard, Jersey City, New Jersey, at the Insurance Services Office Building, part of the Newport Office Centers complex.

The splendidly radiant blue building, opposite to a Courtyard by Marriott, exhibited nearly 900,000 square feet on its 22 stories, and included tenants such as Insurance Services Office itself, HSBC, financial technology vendor SunGard Data Systems, and affiliated exchange Direct Edge. Knight had occupied 266,000 square feet in the building since 2001 when it moved from its previous headquarters in the adjacent building down the road.

Top Knight executives who were sitting on the third floor in rooms with glass windows, almost as if they were at a pet store, included Joyce, Sohos, global head of operations, services and technology Steven Sadoff, and general counsel Thomas Merritt;

human resources head Bronwen Bastone and her team shared the floor with them. Bastone had started out at Merrill Lynch as a sales assistant in her native U.K. and soon learned that there were many opportunities to be had in such a large global company. Still at the firm, she moved to Australia where she earned her master in business administration (MBA) at the University of Technology in Sydney. After completing this degree, she relocated to the U.S., where she learned about an opportunity away from the front-office business; that's where she started her career within the human resources field.

Knight's data center was hosted on the fourth floor, including the "demark room", the entrance point of all data and voice providers' circuits; it was common for a demark room to have extra security (the cage) in part because vendors would come on site and Knight wanted to limit their access to other parts of the data center. Half of the fifth floor hosted the ETG while the other half was still being deployed.

On the second level was Knight's trading floor, heavily adorned with ubiquitous screen TVs and a gigantic American flag; "a very attractive trading floor," Joyce would say. This was a massive, custom-built trading floor with private elevators; it was designed to seat more than 1,000 equities and options traders and featured expansive viewing galleries to accommodate broadcast media. It had been featured prominently during the movie *Wall Street 2: Money Never Sleeps*, directed by Oliver Stone. The company became so proud of its fictitious Keller Zabel Investments role that it was mentioned in Knight's 2010 annual report for shareholders.

Stone was an American film director who had come into public attention in the mid-1980s for writing and directing a series of films about the Vietnam War, in which he had participated as an infantry soldier. He won even further attention and controversy with the films *JFK*, *Natural Born Killers*, and *Nixon*. Stone was famous for his relentless criticism of right-wing ideology; he had made movies exploring the darker side of the lives of Republican presidents and the deaths of Democratic office-holders such as JFK.

"When Oliver called, I'd heard about the Hugo Chavez stuff," said a Knight executive to Vanity Fair's Michael Lewis. "I thought, oh, here we go again."[6] He was referring to Stone's friendly relations with Cuban legendary leader Fidel Castro and Venezuelan president Hugo Chavez. Stone had completed in 2009 a feature length documentary, "South of the Border", about the rise of progressive, leftist governments in Latin America, featuring seven presidents, including Chavez, all democratically elected and all holding negative views of U.S. manipulations in South America. Chavez, who would lose his battle with cancer in early 2013, later joined Stone for the premiere of the documentary at the Venice International Film Festival in September 2009.

"The stuff they did here that I saw was sort of straightforward," said the Knight executive sarcastically about Stone's take on the financial crisis. The movie starred Michael Douglas, Shia LaBeouf, Josh Brolin, Carey Mulligan, and Frank Langella. The film took place, in New York, 23 years after the original and revolved around the 2008 financial crisis. Its plot centered on a reformed Gordon Gekko, played by Michael Douglas, acting as an antihero rather than a villain, and followed his attempts to repair his relationship with his daughter Winnie Gekko (Carey Mulligan), with the help of her fiancé, Jacob Moore (Shia LaBeouf). In return, Gekko helped Moore get revenge on Bretton James (Josh Brolin), whom he blamed for the death of his mentor Louis Zabel, played by Frank Langella.[7]

One of the location scouts for Stone saw the pictures and liked what he saw. When consulted, Stone thought the location was terrific too and contacted Joyce to meet for dinner. A few days later, Joyce was meeting with friends at "The Capital Grille", a restaurant located a mere few blocks from Knight's downtown office at Exchange Plaza.

"Guess who I had dinner with last night?," he asked them.

Jokingly, one of them replied, "Al Gore?"

Joyce answered, "Very close; it was Oliver Stone," before he demurred at the next question:

"What was he talking about with you?"

While Stone was using the dinner to continue doing his due diligence to pick the ideal trading room for the movie, Joyce was savoring the moment like a kid in candy land.

Stone and Joyce hit it off. Ultimately, Joyce authorized using Knight's trading location. The filming was completed over the course of a weekend in the fall of 2009.

Knight employees would have the opportunity to interact with the cast and help them prepare for their roles. The cast did need all help they could get.

LaBeouf was to play the role of proprietary trader Moore. When he got the call telling him he had a shot at a part, he freaked out and raced down the block to the local Charles Schwab office.

"I ran down the street to this big-ass green building."

At the Encino branch of Schwab, LaBeouf found a stockbroker and pleaded to teach him how financial markets work.

"I had to get my shit together," said LaBeouf, "because I'm just this dude from Transformers. So I opened an account with 20 grand and started trading. I figured, fuck it. If I lose it, I can deduct it, because I'm preparing for a movie."

LaBeouf had to look believable operating his powerful computers with multiple screens. Knight employees were handy at the moment to show him their tricks; they had him sitting with traders to learn how to trade for a couple of days.

Around a hundred of Knight's employees spent Saturday and Sunday working as extras in the floor scenes. The scenes came out very exciting and lively. As Moore walked and a bell rang, a voice could be heard, "Let's go! Let's go! Let's make some dough!" Desks were all closely connected, multiple screens on each of them showing the few ups and many more downs of the stock market in 2008. Traders frantically yelled on their telephones as they nervously stared at their monitors and desperately typed into their computers. Some were yelling into the receiver to get their opinions across. Moore walked through confidently, greeting people with fist bumps and pats on the shoulder, as he made his way through the sea of energetic traders desperate to make money as the NYSE opened.

One of those energetic paladins of capitalism said, "The filming took the whole trading floor. It was a lot of fun. It was probably the first time in years that there was some real comradery on the floor, some real excitement. It was rare for traders, salespeople and everyone to hang out together. You know, we were making a movie! Lots of fun. Great time."

Joyce himself was featured in the movie and therefore earned an entry into the Internet Movie Database (IMDb), the online database of information related to films, television programs, and video games.

"Tom had once nonchalantly said that they were filming a movie at Knight. A year later, my wife and I went to see the movie and Tom was there playing himself. We were laughing. That is what speaks to his character; a very humble man," a close friend would remember.

Joyce's scene was timed just after Zabel committed suicide jumping in front of a subway train. Moore was watching CNBC's *Squawk Box* as the network was collecting reactions from Wall Streeters who knew Zabel. Joyce was interviewed by Becky Quick, both characters playing themselves. Throughout the brief interview Joyce did a superbly convincing job displaying the appropriate set of emotions following the dramatic sequence of events.

"Tom, this news about Louis Zabel comes as a shock to everyone, but, how are you holding up there?" asked Quick.

"The guy was an icon on Wall Street. I always thought of him as a mentor to me. So, to see this happen under the circumstances that it did happen, it's upsetting," replied Joyce, on the verge of tears.

"What does it mean to the employees at Keller Zabel?"

"I think it's the loss of their leader; they are going to be, quite frankly, financially badly hurt on many fronts."

The movie, released at the worldwide famous Cannes Festival on May 14, 2010, and theatrically worldwide on September 24, 2010, by 20th Century Fox, turned out to be polarizing for critics, who generally praised the acting (Joyce's included), but considered it an unnecessary sequel; however, the film was successful at the box office and an unforgettable experience for Knight employees, some of whom attended the premier and got to hang out with the Hollywood crowd.

9:35 A.M. Everybody in the data center

While the team knew that a mind boggling number of orders was being sent to the NYSE without explanation, it wasn't clear at the beginning what or who was generating the orders. Knight's chief information officer Michael Tobin, was the ultimate responsible for all algorithms, DMA, EMS, OMS and listed derivatives technology. He pulled Sohos to his desk as he was working from another floor. Dealing with low-latency communications of millions of messages per second was Tobin's specialty for which he led a 100-person team. Tobin's team included project managers, business analysts and software developers that were building front office, middle office and back office systems to support the trading, settlement and clearing of global equities, fixed income, options, futures, and mortgage securities. For Sadoff though, low latency was just the most overhyped concept in the financial technology space. "If you count the number of people who really care about ultra-low latency, and you count the number of vendors pushing low latency, it is not a good ratio if you are a vendor," he commiserated.

Using every piece of their brains to the fullest, everybody who mattered was in the data center with the exception of Joyce. This wasn't unusual, as trading room inhabitants had known for years. Even if Joyce was in the office, and that was a bigger 'if' than his Darien estate, he preferred not to show up when technological issues popped up; that was Sadoff's responsibility. He reported directly to Joyce; they had known each other since their times at Merrill Lynch, where Sadoff spent five years.

Sadoff had come to Knight after a stint as chief technology officer at Bondbook, an electronic platform that was created by eight of the world's largest broker-dealers (Credit Suisse First Boston, Deutsche Bank, Goldman Sachs, Lehman Brothers, Merrill Lynch, Morgan Stanley, Salomon Smith Barney, and UBS Warburg) to serve as a centralized anonymous exchange-like marketplace open to all institutional participants. Prior to that, he had been a computer scientist at the Central Institute for the Deaf in St. Louis, a vice president at Lehman Brothers, and a technology manager in Japan and New York City for Merrill Lynch.

Born on October 23, 1963, he went to Beverly Hills High School (famous for its unique "Swim Gym", the only gymnasium that had a basketball court that could split open to reveal a recreational-sized, 25-yard swimming pool) and later decamped to Missouri to attend Washington University in St. Louis, where he received a bachelor in computer science in 1985, a master's degree in electrical engineering in 1987 and a doctorate in computer science in 1990.

Sadoff would ultimately bear responsibility and pay dearly for the trading glitch; remembering these stressful days, he would later comment to a friend after Christmas, just days before going with the family to Riviera Maya for a week, "Not sure why, but I'm not missing work..."

Reporting to Sadoff was Michael Strashnov, managing director, who graduated from New York University with a bachelor's degree in computer science in 1994. He was well regarded on the Street; he was invited to speak about Regulation in the Electronic Marketplace at Markets Media's 2nd Annual Summer Trading 2011. He had contributed to Knight Capital Group's Good Government Fund PAC. Under his authority were the BRASS and SMARS teams.

Strashnov had two key individuals in his team. One of them was director Milind Deshpande. An Indian national, he had come to North America to attend the University of Saskatchewan in Canada where he received a master's degree in computer science in 1985. After stints at AT&T Bell Labs and Citigroup, he joined Knight in May 2005. Along with many Knight colleagues, Milind supported worthy causes including the Staten Island chapter of the American Cancer Society Making Strides Against Breast Cancer. He was directly responsible for BRASS and was the first to face questions following the massive amount of orders, after it was found out that the orders hitting the market didn't belong to the NYSE's brand-spanking new Retail Liquidity Program (RLP) implemented that very morning.

Deshpande quickly went through his notes and recounted that none of the proposed modifications to his systems were being implemented. When pressed by Strashnov on who else wanted to bring updates to production, his attention turned to the SMARS leader, Kok Sang. Like Deshpande, Sang had demonstrated a social sensibility that had encouraged him to participate at the JPMorgan Chase Corporate Challenge at Central Park every year; in 2010, he completed a 3.5-mile road footrace in 30:31; in 2011, 33:28.

This time, Sang was too busy to recount his charitable initiatives. Of the five people who reported to him, all of them with an average of 15 years at the firm, two were involved with rolling back the proposed changes to the system started by BRASS. It was then when they realized their mistake: one of the servers was running in production with an unauthorized update, which converted the market-maker peg-orders to executable orders, now in the range of hundreds of thousands.

Nanex Research would later conclude that Knight was buying at the offer and then, almost immediately, selling at the bid, then buying at the offer, then selling at the bid and so forth. Almost all trades alternated between buying at the offer and selling at the bid, which meant losing the difference in price. In the case of Exelon Corporation (EXC), for instance, that meant losing about 15 cents on every pair of trades. "Do that 40 times a second, 2400 times a minute, and you now have a system that's very efficient at burning money."[8]

Employees across the firm wondered what had happened, who was responsible, and who was going to stop it. "Everyone was like, not to say pointing fingers at each other, but like 'Who's doing this?' kind of atmosphere," said a trader. "It ain't me. I'm on the program desk. It's not me, I can assure you of that." Former Knight employees, alerted of the firm's ongoing troubles, were making themselves available on the phone to help.

"It wasn't any single trader, it wasn't ETFs (exchange-traded funds), it wasn't [the algorithmic trading group]," said another

Knight trader. "It really left only one group, which was the market-making group." In just a short time, Sang's name was in everybody's mouth. Sang's lips were doing their best to hide behind his moustache, to no avail; his eyes were not faring well either behind his thick glasses.

Employees had been asked not to speak with anybody outside. All questions started being referred to Kara Fitzsimmons, managing director of media relations. Fitzsimmons was a veteran at Knight. She had joined in June 2001 as vice president of corporate communications; in July 2007 she had been promoted to managing director. In March 2012, Fitzsimmons had replaced Margaret Wyrwas as the top spokesperson for the organization, as she was to become chief marketing officer at AQR Capital Management.

Fitzsimmons, originally from Fairport, New York, had traveled eighty miles east from home to attend Syracuse University, where she received a bachelor of science in magazine journalism in 1994. She worked stints as a reporter at Rochester Business Journal and Dow Jones, and director at Clark and Weinstock, a small, high-level communications consulting firm for companies going through crises as well as business opportunities.

Fitzsimmons had participated in the JPMorgan Chase Corporate Challenge at Central Park first in 2005 and without interruption since 2010. A Pearl Jam fan, Fitzsimmons lived in Montclair with husband Michael Fayne (who also graduated from Syracuse the same year) and children Henry Alexander and Veronica Violet. She didn't imagine she wouldn't see much of them in the forthcoming days.

9:48 A.M. The first restart

When computerized stock trading ran amok, the firm responsible could typically jump in and hit kill switches. These could be implemented both at the software level and at the hardware level and allowed firms to pull the trigger and get out of the markets completely, either in select market or all markets; if managers had to hit a kill switch, they could do it within a number of minutes. Firms also had network monitoring and order monitoring tools that could tell them all destinations and trades routes of any and all orders going to the market. It would have been very unusual if Knight were unable to get that information immediately. Wasn't Knight one of the most sophisticated trading outfits on Wall Street? Wasn't Sadoff overseeing 475 people and a budget exceeding $100 million, sufficient to make sure Knight's systems were indestructible? It was just not enough, as it turned out.

As the torrent of faulty trades spewed from a Knight Capital trading program, no one at the firm managed or wanted to stop it until an explanation could be found. They did however restart their system as there was a sudden drop in trading. However, nothing was working yet; more agony was still to come.

9:52 A.M. The second restart

After having apparently identified the source of the problem, Knight Capital restarted its systems again. For 40 seconds it seemed as if Knight had got everything under control. But there was no such luck; the system continued sending orders.

9:53 A.M. First circuit breaker

Despite the torrent of orders that hit the market starting at 9:30 A.M., none of the trades after 9:45 A.M. had triggered circuit breakers. Under new rules implemented on September 10, 2010, four months after the Flash Crash, a U.S. stock exchange that listed a stock was required to issue a trading "pause" if the stock price moved up or down by 10 percent or more in a five-minute period. After five minutes, the exchange that had issued the pause might extend it if there were still significant imbalances between orders to buy and sell shares of the affected stock. After a ten-minute pause, other exchanges were free to resume trading in the stock, and once that occurred, trading might resume in the over-the-counter markets (OTC).

It wasn't until 9:53:20 that Molycorp Inc. (MCP), a rare earth oxide (REO) producer in the Western hemisphere, triggered the first circuit breaker. Not to be outdone, MCP was followed by Corelogic Inc. (CLGX) at 9:55:53, Kronos Worldwide Inc. (KRO) at 9:56:23, China Cord Blood Corp. (CO) at 9:56:33, and Trinity Industries Inc. (TRN) at 9:59:48. Corelogic Inc. and China Cord Blood Corp. would be halted again later at 10:04:17 and 10:04:46, respectively.

9:55 A.M. Stocks moving for no reason

Speaking on CNBC's *Squawk on the Street* about Avon, the door-to-door beauty titan that launched the iconic "Ding Dong Avon Calling" advertising campaign, presenters Brian Sullivan and Jim Cramer were interrupted with the news that unusually large amounts of stocks were moving this morning with no explanation. RadioShack, which once sponsored Team RadioShack with cyclist Lance Armstrong as one of its members, was one of the many stocks mysteriously rising with double-digit gains. Cramer could only comment that there were always rumors in the market and investors needed to be careful out there.

9:58 A.M. The peak of craziness

The floor reached its climax at 9:58 A.M. when the volume was six times greater, followed by a sharp fall off. This was when Knight found and killed the piece of software that had been tormenting it for the whole morning; however, the damage was already done. It would still take another 10-15 minutes for the build-up of orders that had already been sent out to be completed.

Why Knight took 28 minutes to stop the order flow was not clear until much later. Knight could have shut down its market flow to the exchange entirely but that could have jeopardized other orders, opening Knight up to additional liability. Neither Sadoff nor Sohos wanted to take that responsibility. As for Joyce, he was not present in the office.

One of the questions the SEC would later ask was why there appeared to be a breakdown in controls. There was no one person at Knight to take responsibility for the problem when it occurred, leading to further confusion and extending the time it took to stop the flow.

Joyce, the high school and college star athlete, was to pay the price of his successes on the field. Despite countless years of biological craftiness, the human knee does eventually breakdown, as Joyce learned. For most people, this occurs over the age of 65; Joyce was only in his late 50s.

The cartilage and the chondrocytes that once smoothed over rough surfaces between the tibia and femur deteriorates over time and leaves the person hobbling and practically immobile. This was for people who lived relatively quiet lives.

The worst debilitation occurred in star athletes such as Joyce. For most of them, speed and quickness were essential to a winning season. An athlete must be agile and quickly change position running from one direction to the next. Moreover, football athletes go head to head and exert tremendous amounts of energy trying to push back, pull, or take down the opposing player.[9]

Unfortunately for Joyce, nonsurgical treatment, rehabilitation and therapy had not been successful in calming the pain he was feeling for years; doctors suggested that the only way to heal his knee problem was through surgery.

On July 31, 2013, one of many quiet summer days in Wall Street, Joyce underwent knee surgery; he was getting ready to spend the days after resting at home. What could go wrong with deploying a piece of software to participate in NYSE's RLP? An event like that was not even in his radar, as it was business as usual.

For Joyce, the need to undergo surgery was coming at the worst time of his career, something he would only know later.

9:59 A.M. Message in a bottle

Joyce received a call that would dramatically disrupt his plans to recover after surgery. Sohos informed him of the chaotic situation Knight had gone through and assured him that the bleeding had stopped; Joyce became aware of the gigantic position his firm had taken and became worried the company might not survive.

Around the same time, Knight Capital decided to get a message out to its clients; it was intended to alleviate the impact of the trading blunder; it actually created the opposite effect.

Due to a technology issue, Knight is experiencing a delay in processing orders of Listed securities. We ask that you seek an alternate destination for the execution of these securities until further notice. Order handling and execution of OTC securities is not affected. Stay tuned for further updates Knight.

As it was expected after communicating such an explicit "sell" order, Knight's shares began to fall quickly and put option volumes went ballistic in the pits. Jon Najarian, optionMONSTER's analyst, said that within 30 minutes he was telling his clients that there had been aggressive purchases on Knight puts, a sure bet the stock would tumble. Normally 138 puts trade a day; that Wednesday saw a whopping 93,977.

10:00 A.M. Drama live on CNBC

By this time, it was public knowledge that the equity markets had been experiencing a unique situation to say the least. Melissa Lee, the star anchor of *Squawk on the Street*, was prompted to bring trading expert extraordinaire Pisani to attempt to explain what was happening. A CNBC reporter since 1990, Pisani had reported on Wall Street and the stock market from the floor of the New York Stock Exchange for more than a decade.

Pisani was at a loss to explain what was happening other than to point to the dozens of stocks that were being affected. He had been on the NYSE floor on Wall Street 111 at 9:30 A.M. when a mind boggling influx of orders on a number of different stocks had hit the markets. What wasn't clear was the reason behind such influx and whether these were legitimate trades or the result of a trading problem. By then, some stocks had been halted already and exchange officials were considering reopening them. As examples of impacted stocks, Pisani pointed to Nu Skin Enterprises (NUS) and Ford (F).

The mood at the Knight Capital booth on the NYSE trading floor was somber, with worried traders taking numerous phone calls as well as answering questions from NYSE officials who were making inquiries on the floor. Everybody on the floor was aware that the problematic trades were coming from Knight.

At another spot on the floor, a group of Goldman Sachs traders huddled together and pondered on what would be the effect on trades made and what trades would be canceled. Goldman Sachs would later provide a lifeline to Knight at more than a hefty price.

10:13 A.M. Unusual trading, very whippy trading

The news was now all over town; on the screens on CNBC, Wall Streeters could read, "UNUSUAL SINGLE STOCK VOLATILITY ATTRIBUTED TO SPECULATION RE: ALGORITHMS." Lee reported "unusual trading, very whippy trading in a short list of stocks, about 20 stocks." Moreover, CNBC was informing they had heard from a number of people on the floor that this was a problem stemming from Knight Capital. That's why the stock was moving down, very quickly, they said.

By then, Knight, which closed the day prior at $10.33, was trading at $9.49, an 8.13 percent decline. Pisani, an experienced reporter who had seen more than his fair share of past flukes, pointed to the unusually high number of transacted shares at that time of the day, "On the floor of the New York Stock Exchange we should be doing now 100 million, not 364 million; something is a little strange here." He was already considering an aggressive algorithm or an error; something that Knight was sending to the market or somebody using Knight's pipes. Knight was already trading down by 11 percent; was the market already assuming Knight would eventually face some sort of liability? Knight was now in crisis management mode, informally contacting news outlets and informing them that their algorithms were working fine.

As losses mounted, staff promptly grew concerned they would lose their jobs. Some started speaking to friends working at competitors. Executives at Knight were already on guard for potential poaching from Citadel. At the Chicago firm, Nazarali and Matt Cushman, senior managing directors who had resigned from Knight in February 2011, were only too happy to take calls from former colleagues and plot their transition to the Chicago colossus under chief executive officer Ken Griffin.

10:15 A.M. Back to normal?

Traders temporarily enjoyed a bit of relief when volumes returned to normal levels after 45 minutes of zig zags. The exchange operator announced later that it would cancel trades on six securities: Wizzard Software Corp. (WZE), China Cord Blood Corp. (CO), Reaves Utility Income Fund (UTG), E-House (China) Holdings Ltd. (EJ), American Reprographics Co. (ARC) and Qicksilver Resources Inc. (KWK). The NYSE had determined to cancel all trades in these six symbols that were executed at 30 percent or more above or below the opening price today between 9:30 A.M. and 10:15 A.M.

Wizzard Software Corp. (WZE), a company that offered speech recognition and text to speech products for developers and integrators, was a unique case. They normally traded 100,000 to 125,000 shares per day. On the opening, the stock had gone from $3.60 to $14 in seconds; certainly, all trades executed at prices of $4.68 or above were to be canceled. By 11:30 A.M. the stock was essentially back to $4 after trading around 300,000 shares, almost three times normal volume.

American Reprographics Co. (ARC), a $203 million specialized document services company out of Walnut Creek, California, saw some 3.54 million shares changing hands, compared to the average of 86,007 shares per day moved in the previous 30 days. The price hit a high of $5.70, up 30 percent, and a low of $4.21, down nearly 4 percent; by the end of the day, the stock ended up gaining just two pennies. ARC remained concerned that Knight was still holding positions in ARC that it would later have to dump, of particularly concern for its investor relations officials given the looming earnings report the week after. The confirmation from Knight that it had exited these positions didn't help much in making them any less concerned.

After these forty five minutes of hell, winners and losers emerged. Knight wasn't one of the winners. Instead, many big investors cashed in on the market volatility. They saw what was happening when the surprisingly large trades began to register, and they quickly moved to profit from the disruptions.

The winners were spread among the many proprietary firms which used specialized computer algorithms to spot and profit from market aberrations, including DRW Trading Group. Hedge funds and other asset managers that trawl the market looking to profit from abnormal pricing also won big.

But while many of these institutional traders managed to profit from the fiasco, individual investors did not fare as well. They had no way to do so without sitting in front of a computer watching the market all day.

10:30 A.M. Exchanges summit

The industry's preeminent self-regulatory organization (SRO), the Financial Industry Regulatory Authority (FINRA), convened a call with all of the major exchanges that would last for the rest of the trading day and center on the stocks that had been hit and where the trades had been executed. The SEC was having separate calls with Knight and the New York Stock Exchange as well.

Early in the call, exchange officials discussed whether the Knight trades could be treated individually instead of as a group event for determining when transactions could be canceled and at what price. The threshold for voiding trades in an incident involving 20 or more securities is 30 percent.

Defining the errors as individual events may have spared Knight from greater losses because it meant more trades would've been eligible for cancellation. In most cases, trades that occurred 10 percent or more away from their previous price could be voided when the error involves a single security. Officials from NYSE Arca and NASDAQ argued against this.

NYSE and Knight officials and regulators would spend hours going back and forth over the rules governing the cancellation of trades. Robert Cook, director of the SEC's trading and markets division, manned the calls for the regulator. Officials from the Commodity Futures Trading Commission and the Depository Trust & Clearing Corp., which clears trades, were also consulted.

By then, Joyce had made a series of phone calls to his top managers involved with the blunder. He wanted to better understand what Knight's chances were to trade out of the position without getting too badly hurt. He called the New York Stock Exchange and learned they had already been talking with the team in Jersey City. NYSE officials said the guidelines were clear, and in the end said only trades involving stocks that swung 30 percent or more could be broken. That amounted to trades in six stocks.

Ironically, during the phone call NASDAQ employees demanded that Knight provide a full accounting of its own technological problems. In recent weeks, Knight had recently harshly criticized NASDAQ for the technology flaws that the exchange suffered during the Facebook initial public offering (IPO) in May.

11:03 A.M. A mini dark pool within the NYSE

Richard Repetto, Sandler O'Neill's principal in their equity research team, appeared on CNBC to confirm that the issues were coming from Knight Capital, which still had not issued any statement. Pisani was pointing out to the NYSE's RLP which was "designed to essentially create a bit of a mini dark pool within the NYSE and sort of draw some order flow away from the wholesalers like Knight," as another potential explanation. Was that the reason why the shares of NYX, the New York Stock Exchange, were also down by about 2.5 percent?

In a 2010 paper, former SEC officials Robert Colby and Erik Sirri had documented individual investors sending orders through discount brokerages could benefit from having their trades routed off exchanges to wholesalers like Knight and Citadel. Knight participated in the practice known as payment for order flow, in which it compensated retail brokerages for sending their requests to transact securities. For instance, retail powerhouse TD Ameritrade received payments from Knight for directing listed equity order flow to this venue; payment was variable based on the size and type of security at the time of order execution and averaged less than $0.003 per share for order flow executed in the first quarter of 2013.

11:35 A.M. More than a hundred stocks
By this time, CNBC's Lee was confirming that there were more than a hundred stocks being reviewed by the New York Stock Exchange. "When you take a look at today compared to the past 10 trading sessions; some of the volume spikes were 1,000 percent or more of the average volume that we've seen over the past 10 days." Host Simon Hobbs reported as well that the New York Stock Exchange was confirming this was definitely not a problem at their end and that the RLP was functioning as intended. Meanwhile, Knight's stock was already down by 16.25 percent.

11:37 A.M. Knight's downward spiral
Despite the unusual activity observed in the day, there hadn't been any significant impact in the broader averages. The Dow Jones Industrial Average (DJIA) was then at 13,042.28, +0.26% up, while the S&P 500 1,381.94, +0.19% up.

Knight, meanwhile, was continuing its downward spiral, now down 23 percent; a few minutes later, the Dow Jones news service would confirm that there was a software problem being investigated at Knight Capital.

Chapter Two

The Biggest Risk for Financial Markets

"It is clear that at the pace we all operate, I was mistaken, regulatory risk was not our biggest issue, operational risk was and we unfortunately proved it. There will be, I believe, some deep thinking going into the strategy and hopefully the net outcome will be a more optimized organization going forward."

Constant regulatory changes and technological evolution have transformed the investing landscape so profoundly since the advent of the first electronic networks in the early 1970s that we are now speaking of a new game in town. The increasing speed of change has created ever short-timed winners and losers. Among the winners are those who recognize lasting trends from fleeting fads, embrace or disregard them accordingly and prepare themselves. The losers have bombed, been acquired or merged or passed away on to the better life. Regulators around the world are now in a race to respond to the evolution of technology in financial markets and prevent its operational challenges from becoming the biggest risk for financial markets. In this regard, Joyce's quote is memorable; Knight Capital unfortunately proved what operational risk can do to the system.

The components of this new game in town are not easy to understand for either individual or institutional investors. Esoteric names like high-frequency trading (HFT), the practice of using algorithms to transact a significant number of instruments in short timeframes to capture ever-smaller price discrepancies, are currently splashed in newspaper headlines every time mini crashes happen.

For most Americans, this practice would have stayed under the radar forever; however, high-frequency trading fell under a pesky microscope after the mother of all crashes, the infamous Flash Crash that occurred on May 6, 2010, affected both the U.S. equities and futures markets. Although regulators ultimately determined that the crash was initiated by a human decision and the equities market rebounded almost as fast as it fell in just 20 minutes, many in the financial sector and in government were uncomfortable at the thought of algorithmic trading programs potentially vaporizing massive amounts of equity values from the markets in a matter of minutes.

Since that fateful day in May of 2010, circuit breakers (which later were replaced by limit up limit down bands) have been put in place to prevent more wild price swings like the one created by the Flash Crash. However, despite strong criticism by many government officials and members of the financial community, there have yet to be thoughtful monitoring and precise regulations placed on trading activity – regulations that consider the consequences of high-speed transactions. This is the challenge facing the main U.S. regulators, the Securities and Exchange Commission (SEC) and the Commodities Futures Trading Commission (CFTC).

The intensity of the ongoing debate over high-frequency trading was kicked up a notch when an advisory committee to the CFTC concluded that a broad definition of HFT be adopted when implementing regulatory standards. This broad definition would include not only hedge funds, HFT-only firms, and proprietary trading desks, but also mutual and pension funds using any form of algorithmic execution. Proponents of a broad definition argued that a wide interpretation of HFT was the surest way to protect all market participants from harm. They worried that to propose a narrow definition of HFT risked allowing too many opportunities for any regulation to be circumvented by loopholes or future innovations in algorithmic trading.

However, there were members of the financial community who advocated for a narrower interpretation of high-frequency trading in order to make better use of resources in policing market activity. It was possible that a broad definition of HFT would lead to regulators having too many firms and funds to effectively keep tabs on, and thus allow for violators to slip through the cracks. For instance, some pension and mutual funds utilized algorithmic execution in order to reduce transaction costs. These lower transaction costs resulted in the fund having lower expenses, and therefore more money flowed to the end user, retail investor or pensioner, as a result. A broad definition of HFT would include these types of transactions as well as the HFT-only firms and proprietary trading firms using multiple algorithms to execute trading strategy. Although they were both forms of HFT, these were not identical.

Others had claimed that the best way to regulate high-frequency trading was to spend less time debating its definition and more time focusing on ways to police market activity; that was where real-time monitoring came into place. HFT had gained a strong foothold in exchanges around the globe; the recent growth in the number of electronic exchanges would ensure that high-frequency trading was here to stay.

The evolution of trading has also brought new types of trading venues called dark pools. Whether or not investors knew what one is, its name was not likely to elicit warm and happy images. In fact, the term was more likely to evoke images straight out of a horror movie, with the protagonist investor peering over the edge of a dark pool of water enshrouded in fog, waiting for the inevitable encounter with the despicable monster that lives there. In the media, the term dark pool most definitely had a nefarious feel to it. Although members of the media and the public alike were justified in their criticism of fraudulent dark pools such as Pipeline Trading, the vast majority of dark pools operating in the United States went about their daily business without fanfare and, most importantly, without drama. Whether intended or not, the term dark pool had become synonymous with sinister dealings in our financial markets.

This perception had been a windfall for media outlets as it was a great way to sell newspapers, increase subscriptions and boost ratings. In reality, the dark pool mechanism was no more or less sinister than other mechanisms in our financial markets structure. Dark pools were misunderstood entities in our financial marketplace. They had been in existence for only a fraction of the time that the exchanges had been around, and were therefore not as familiar to investors. This fear of the unknown, combined with consistent negative press, led to dark pools being branded as a detriment to the financial markets structure.

What many in the media and general public ignored was the fact that dark pools had grown out of an old concept known as upstairs trading. Historically, it referred to a transaction for an exchange-listed stock that did not take place on the floor of an exchange. This was the earliest form of off-exchange trading and was born out of a need for institutional traders to successfully buy and sell large positions in stocks, a practice known as block trading, without experiencing a significant negative impact on price.

Off-exchange trading has thrived over the years as a result of institutional money managers. Managing the money of thousands of individuals requires these funds to hold very large positions of stocks. Moving in and out of these large positions on a traditional exchange posed many liabilities for institutional traders.

This upstairs trading allowed institutional traders less exposure to price fluctuations in order execution because the orders were not posted on the floor of the exchange. Had these large orders been posted on the exchange floor, both the identity of the party and the size of the position would have been public knowledge. This information would have allowed faster competing traders to engage in "front running", a practice by which unscrupulous traders could use advance knowledge of incoming orders to buy or sell stock before placing the client's mandate; that would create price distortions by inflating buying prices and depressing selling prices.

As a result of having their competition front running their trades, institutional traders were subject to inferior gains. In an attempt to combat their competition, large block traders would split the large order (known as a parent order) into smaller orders known as child orders. These child orders would make it harder for opposing traders to identify the institutional block movements and undermine price for their own gain. Although child orders aided institutions in moving into and out of large positions, the uptick in the amount of orders still had the unfortunate consequence of enlarging trading costs. Ultimately, this increased trading cost limited the amount of money that would flow out to the end user of the money in the fund, in many cases a pensioner or retiree.

When one examined the trading structure in the "lit markets" through the lens of an institutional manager, it was easy to see why large block traders preferred to conduct business in an off-exchange venue. The ability to transact trades without having to face exposure from publicly viewable orders saved wealth management institutions both time and money.

Were dark pools negative by definition? In the same way that we would ask if high-frequency trading was negative, the answer would be absolutely not. What must be acknowledged was that like many of its counterparts in the financial world, dark pools could be either positive or negative (or neutral, for that matter) for investors and global financial markets. What was important to remember was that wrong-doing in our markets had long existed, certainly much before the advent of high-frequency trading or dark pools and, unfortunately, it would occur in the future. Effective regulation of our financial markets required a concerted effort to monitor all practices that undermined the faith of investors.

When one considers the financial regulatory turmoil surrounding J.P. Morgan's poor risk management and the LIBOR scandal, in which a number of investment banks colluded to keep their own borrowing costs lower, one was compelled to question whether the level of noise in the media was appropriate in its criticism of the nature of dark pools. Champions of the personal investor had long derided dark pools for their negative impact on price discovery. Perhaps these same advocates for the personal investor should turn their attention towards banks that traded recklessly with FDIC-backed deposit money and investment banks who colluded to fix a borrowing rate that affected millions of personal investors every day.

Institutional wealth managers were not the only people who profited from upstairs trading. The exchanges reaped benefits from off-exchange business as well. One of the ways exchanges made money was by collecting a tiny transaction fee each time a stock was bought or sold. While the exchanges certainly collected their fees for block trading activity, they also had to ensure that block trading would not interfere with other trading business. Since block trades could adversely move the price of an equity instrument simply by virtue of the size of the position in the trade, it behooved exchanges to conduct these trades upstairs.

By matching block sellers with block buyers after the exchange was closed (and therefore using prices established at the close of the trading day), exchanges were able to assist institutional managers in conducting their business while also ensuring that exchange-listed equities would not be subject to volatile price swings which could hinder the trading volume of other market participants.

According to Rosenblatt Securities, trading separate from the U.S. exchanges had doubled since early 2008, excluding the largest electronic communications networks (ECNs). ECNs were lit automated trading systems and functioned exactly the same way as the exchanges did with respect to matching trades and executing orders.

Credit Suisse's Crossfinder, the world's largest dark pool, traded almost 132.5 million shares on average, daily in January 2013, or 1.9 percent of total U.S. volume. Credit Suisse was the bank that stopped voluntarily disclosing the amount of trading volume on its Crossfinder platform, as reported by agency brokerage Rosenblatt Securities and research and advisory firm Tabb Group in April 2013. Goldman Sachs's dark pool, Sigma X, was the next largest with 1.6 percent of U.S. equities volume in January; Knight Capital's Knight Link system had 1.4 percent, while Barclays and GETCO both had more than 1 percent each. Rosenblatt reported that 13.5 percent of equity volume was traded in dark pools during the same month.[1]

It was no secret then that the exchanges were lately opposed to the expansion of dark pools in financial markets. Whether it was a quote in an article, an op-ed piece, or a television interview, members of the executive teams of exchanges from around the world could be found discussing the pitfalls of dark pools in financial markets. However, it was not difficult to note the irony of the situation; it was the advent of upstairs trading at the exchanges that had allowed the dark pools of today to come into being. Furthermore, the NYSE Euronext's RLP that prompted Knight Capital to update their trading software was essentially a dark pool within the NYSE that focused on retail investors. While the exchanges were crying foul over the development of a concept that they created and were trying to leverage, their cries were falling on deaf ears, for institutional investors were shouting back: dark pools are here to stay.

Top exchange executives raised concerns about the proliferation of dark pool markets at a Senate hearing on December 18, 2012,[2] arguing that continued flow of trades to the opaque trading venues could be a disadvantage to the overall markets and retail investors. Exchange officials said they worried about the advantage that large financial institutions have when they route order flow to their own dark pool trading venues for a "first look" before routing to public markets. "Our main concern is about the overall market quality and we worry that if enough flow migrates away from public markets and it continues to degrade the quality of the public market. That is a disadvantage for the overall market which certainly retail is a big part of," Joseph Mecane, the NYSE's chief of equity, had argued.

On the other hand, Robert Gasser, CEO of Investment Technology Group, which owned a brokerage as well as operated a dark pool, argued that a broker routing customer orders through its own anonymous trading venue could produce a "very positive outcome" for its investors. "I can demonstrate that when I do internalize, it is a very positive outcome for our client and lower trading costs in a dark pool that is anonymous with no interaction with various participants in the lit market."

As more trading has moved from exchange floors to computers over the last decade, the speed of execution jumped along with the potential for cascading problems. Trading firms, market makers, brokers, investment banks, as well as exchanges and other trading venues were linked in a network of complex computer systems that competed to execute trades as fast as possible. That competition, combined with the never-ending array of new rules, forced market participants to constantly improve their systems. But the intricate network of players and systems created a much wider range of potential problems for trading systems, making testing costly and difficult.

Good testing required a firm to imagine everything that could possibly go wrong and how the system would interact with other systems. Predicting every plausible scenario was certainly not an easy feat, as Knight would later demonstrate.[3] For Knight's Joyce, though, the U.S. equity markets were still the most efficient in the world:

"The reason we know that is because we done something kind of crazy in this day and age: we looked at data. Let's think about who we heard from the last few hours, few days on this topic. We heard from some professional

institutional investors, who want to see all the flow in the world because it benefits yet they won't show you theirs. We heard from a high frequency trader who was quoted in an article, turned out to be some fail-type frequency trader who was looking for some kind of a possible whistleblower payout. There was a reporter who wrote an article in the Wall Street Journal who also happened to write a book on a topic impaling high-frequency trading. So, was that reporting or editorializing? All the data shows that the market has never been more efficient. There are some data points out there that indicate that they should be addressed and rules should be changed. Let's make some smart rules based on data."

For the NYSE's Larry Leibowitz, high-frequency trading was simply electronic trading by automated means, one where "a bit of a bubble" had arisen as the financial crisis created lots of the volatility and volume that such systems were built to feast on. Leibowitz suggested that clearer reporting on the activities of high-frequency traders was necessary to help counter some of the worry about the business and to rebuild investor confidence in the public equity markets.

Leibowitz believed that broad public suspicion of the vexingly complicated market mechanics, with more than a dozen exchanges and perhaps 50 dark-pool electronic markets, was based on "more fiction than fact." It was the job of the SEC and the industry to help "separate fact from fiction," he added, pointing to the futures markets' move to tag and report HFT order flow as a good start in tracking potential abuses.

There was no question that regulatory reform for our financial markets was a daunting process. The evolution of technology in trading had brought tools that could be positive or negative for investors and global financial markets. Analysis of real-time trading data would provide for effective regulation of high-frequency trading. This in turn would provide peace of mind for market participants that were currently weary of the extent by which electronic trading dominates the markets.

Technology was here to stay, said Leibowitz, and had been a huge windfall for end investors, whether retail or institutional through lower trading costs and faster systems. "The real question is: how do we regulate and surveil it in a way that gives people confidence that they have a chance?" While the SEC had "a full plate" in working to implement the massive Dodd-Frank Act's financial regulation law and undertaking several insider-trading cases, Leibowitz said the agency needed the industry's support in improving market transparency and efficiency. "We have to take a step back and look at the good and bad in all that has occurred in the last 15 years and figure out how to markedly improve it, without giving up a lot of the good," he said. "We do have an obligation to make people feel it's fair."

Some critics of the current market structure had said that bolder reform was needed. One change that had been contemplated was a financial transaction tax, which would force firms to pay a small levy on each trade. At the right level, this could pare back high-frequency trading without undermining other types, supporters said.

"It would benefit investors because there would be less volatility in the market," said Representative Peter DeFazio, a Democrat of Oregon. He introduced a bill containing a financial transaction tax in 2012. Opponents of such a levy claimed that it could hurt the markets and even make it more expensive for companies to raise capital. "I would be very concerned about unintended consequences," said Gus Sauter, the chief investment officer at Vanguard.[4] But Representative DeFazio, who favored a levy of three-hundredths of a percentage point on each trade, said he thought the benefits of high-frequency trading were overstated. "Some people say it was necessary for liquidity, but somehow we built the strongest industrial nation on earth without algorithmic trading," he said.

Others were content with the limited safeguards on trading which the SEC applied after the Flash Crash of 2010 sent the broader market plummeting in a matter of minutes. But big investors like T. Rowe Price, members of Congress and former regulators thought that the SEC and the industry had been too complacent and needed to do more to understand and control the supercharged market. Democratic U.S. Representative Maxine Waters of California said the "drumbeat" of errors in stock markets showed the need for stronger controls. "Things are happening far too regularly," said Ed Ditmire, an analyst at Macquarie Securities who focused on stock exchanges. "It's not nearly as solid a market as it should be, so there's plenty of room for improvement."

"You've got 13 exchanges, 50 dark pools, brokers that internalize client orders at their own desks and thousands of algorithms pumping orders in milliseconds," said Larry Tabb, founder of Tabb Group, a financial consulting firm. "The structure just may be too complicated to work."

Regulators made changes to the markets over the last two decades that had taken it out of the hands of a few New York institutions and allowed dozens of high-frequency trading firms from Chicago to Amsterdam and new trading venues to dominate the stock market. Some large institutional investors such as Vanguard had said that the increased volume of trading had made it easier to get in and out of stocks, lowering the ultimate costs for individuals who invested in popular vehicles like mutual funds. But even people who had previously defended the advances in trading technology said that too many problems may have been overlooked.

Prior to the implementation of decimalization early 2000s, the U.S. equity market had used fractions as pricing increments (a tradition that came with the Spanish), and had done so for hundreds of years. Traders had to be very good at adding and subtracting with fractions with different denominators, a feat in and of itself.

The SEC had started examining the prudence of the fraction pricing structure in the mid-1990s. At the time, the SEC concluded that 1/8th of a dollar tick sizes were causing artificially wide spreads and hindering quote competition, leading to excessive profits for market makers.

The SEC had also expressed concern that 1/8th fraction pricing put U.S. equity markets at a competitive disadvantage to foreign equity markets that had long used decimal pricing increments. Finally, in 2005, the SEC adopted Regulation NMS Rule 612. The one penny MPV (1/100 of a dollar as Minimum Price Variation) essentially applied to all listed stocks at all price levels, changing the tick size for most stocks from 1/16th and 1/32nd of a dollar to one penny.

Market-maker profits were related to transaction costs paid by investors, which in turn depended on the size of the spread and any profits a market maker might have made from price movements in the stock, plus well-known rebates from the exchanges. In theory, larger tick sizes encouraged dealers to make a market in a security because the tick represented the minimum round-trip profit to a dealer who could buy at a lower bid price and sell at a higher offer price. However, larger tick sizes also could increase transaction costs for investors because the tick size represented a floor on the quoted bid-ask spread. On the other hand, a reduction in tick sizes increased the number of possible price outcomes which might have increased trade time.

When investors decide to trade, they must also decide whether to submit a market order or a limit order. Because limit orders were an important supply of liquidity in the markets, the understanding of the tradeoff between market and limit orders allowed a better understanding of how decimalization affected the supply of liquidity. With a market order, investors were guaranteed an execution at the prevailing market price. With a limit order, investors had more control over the execution price and were likely to receive better prices, but they were not guaranteed an execution. Hence, investors traded off the price advantage of limit orders with the execution certainty advantage of market orders.

The tradeoff between market orders and limit orders after decimalization could have changed in several ways. Because effective spreads declined with decimalization, the price advantage of limit orders declined. Further, the execution certainty advantage of market orders might have been greater because others could more cheaply obtain price priority over limit orders resulting in less execution certainty for limit orders. Therefore, some investors might have chosen to submit market orders under a penny tick size while they would have submitted a limit order under a larger tick size regime.

In contrast to the United States, with its essentially flat, "one size fits all", tick size regime, many other countries had adopted tiered regimes that provided greater variability for tick sizes based on the price level of a stock. These included Hong Kong (11 price levels), Japan (11 price levels), Taiwan (6 price levels), South Korea (4 or more price levels), United Kingdom (4 or more price levels), Germany (4 price levels), Australia (3 price levels), and Singapore (3 price levels).

Such tiered tick size regimes allowed stocks to trade at percentage tick sizes that were believed to be more consistent across a whole range of price levels. In the United Kingdom, tick sizes were also tiered based on the type of stock. For example, stocks included in the FTSE 100 Index, the FTSE 250 Index, and those outside those indexes had different tick tables with progressively wider tick sizes as average capitalization and trading volume decreased.

The existence of considerable variation in tick sizes in markets in these other countries suggested that the U.S. market would probably benefit from a broad review of tick sizes, and such a review would be informed by the experience in these countries. What had to be further determined was whether changes in decimalization to raise the tick size might have led to transaction costs going up without discernible benefits for retail investors and small companies trying to raise capital.

High-frequency trading calls for high-frequency regulation. Following on Knight's trading failure, an owner and operator of a high-frequency trading operation pointed out that Knight had failed in their responsibility to create a 'fair and orderly' market as a market-maker firm. "This type of problems severely erodes the public's confidence in the markets to function smoothly even during times of actual catastrophe. Without confidence in the operation of the market, as we have seen during the financial crisis with credit markets, the entire financial industry can come very close to grinding to a halt. And this would have severe repercussions on every corner of the economy."

This owner went on to propose that exchanges and regulators have to keep "real-time" monitoring of the markets, and not be "notified by e-mail within minutes." He stated, "Think of the markets as a highly competitive hockey game, where the referees have to skate along with the players and catch every movement as it happens. Watching the game on a 5-10 minute tape delay would be useless. If you let a hockey fight go on for 5-10 minutes without referee intervention, there would be a full bench-clearing brawl when the referees rushed to ice after viewing the tape delay."

To meet the challenge of funding this type of real-time monitoring, the solution was that high-frequency trades would need to 'pay more' for their exchange fees. "I am very well aware of the irony, as a HFT operator myself, but rest assured: the smooth operation of the markets would ultimately benefit us in the long run. FDR was absolutely right when he picked Joe Kennedy as the first chairman of the SEC, stating, 'takes one [crook] to catch one.'"

This view from inside the markets built into the argument that if high-frequency trading was predicated on speed, its regulation must have also been built around the same requirement. The aim of financial markets regulation was to create an atmosphere of trust for market participants. If a non-HFT market participant believes that he or she couldn't enter into fair transactions, then that individual will not invest in that market. To create that atmosphere of trust and effectively regulate global financial markets, regulators must be armed with the capacity to analyze trading activity in real-time.

Analysis of market activity would provide regulators with access to live order information and transactions. Real-time information would allow regulators to see everything that was occurring in the markets, no matter how quickly the order information was being posted and transactions were occurring. This would require significant commitments to invest in both human capital and information technology; however, it was vital for regulators to level the playing field of high-frequency trading in order to best supervise it. Once regulators truly possessed the ability to analyze trading activity they would become empowered to identify potential wrong-doing and address it promptly.

Furthermore, real-time policing of the marketplace for potential malfeasance was the most efficient way to regulate high-frequency trading. Opponents of HFT often cited its ability to manipulate price as one of the most dangerous problems facing non-HFT investors. Price manipulation could take place either through the use of wash trades (a trade which involves a party buying its own contract) or from quote stuffing (layering). Rapid analysis of market data by regulators would help to curtail these practices by identifying them and taking immediate action.

Another way to potentially regulate high-frequency trading involved looking at the algorithms implemented by traders (appropriately protecting their intellectual property) in order to ensure that these had been properly tested for use in markets, and controls were in place to stop them if necessary. While this might have served to provide a stronger framework for algorithm development and testing, it would not allow regulators to effectively oversee markets via the transactions executed by these same algorithms, unless it was coupled with real-time monitoring. This type of regulation would expand on the market access rule the SEC attempted to use to penalize Knight.

However, when considering technology, mistakes were bound to happen. Trading firms were expected to have controls in place and invest in the technology to keep up to date. Most companies would realize the need of these controls and honestly attempt to implement them, but their IT departments would soon hit a wall, because of a lack a proper budget and other problems. Management constantly scrutinized technology budgets and didn't want to spend the money on safeguarding their systems. Circuit breakers, kill switches, fuse boxes or any type of failsafe mechanisms always got cut, as companies reasoned accidents would never happen. It was a fallacy, a lunacy, a heresy. It was not the lack of technical capability. Management cut these investments all the time. Certainly, these safeguards did cost money.

It was all about resources and funding to get it done; if a firm was not going to make a priority spending money to make sure that they were safeguarded and the SEC was not going to mandate it to a level of detail or technical specificity that made it impossible to duck it, then accidents were going to happen. Only in July 2013, FINRA would send letters to about 10 trading firms asking nine detailed questions about how they used and deployed algorithms; the SRO was asking the trading outfits to disclose whether they used kill switches to halt individual algorithms and under what conditions they would shut off trading.[5]

For trading firms, not having kill switches in place was tantamount to drivers lacking auto insurance. Do we really need auto insurance? If so, which coverage do we need? It is money out of the door. A lot of people risk their lives not having auto insurance because they just don't want to spend the money on it; but if something goes wrong, they will find themselves in trouble; so the government requires people to have auto insurance. If people get into an accident and don't have insurance, they get their license revoked.

The same analogy could be used in the trading arena. If you had a specified level of insurance around your capabilities, you would be welcome to trade. Firms needed to have standards in place that could be thoughtfully audited on a regular basis by the regulators, either the exchanges, SIFMA, the SEC or the CFTC. Unfortunately, there were very few real truthful audits that really went on, as people viewed it mostly as a huge pain in the ass. "Let's just get this done" was the battle cry.

Trading firms would have liked to minimize regulation overall because it was challenging and costly. Yet, in some ways, bad business decisions could be prevented by appropriate regulation. It was a constant push and pull.

The recently proposed Regulation Systems Compliance and Integrity (Reg SCI), which would require exchanges, dark pools, ECNs and clearing firms to comply with requirements regarding their automated systems that support the performance of their regulated activities, is a step in the right direction.

As explained by commissioner Luis Aguilar, the proposed rule would move beyond the current voluntary program and require the entities above to establish, maintain, and enforce written policies and procedures reasonably designed to ensure that its systems have adequate levels of capacity, integrity, resiliency, availability, and security to maintain the entity's operational capability and promote the maintenance of fair and orderly markets, mandate participation in scheduled testing of the operation of the entity's business continuity and disaster recovery plans, including backup systems, and coordinate such testing on an industry- or sector-wide basis with other entities, and finally make, keep, and preserve records relating to the matters covered by Reg SCI, and provide them to SEC representatives upon request.

Both before and after the Flash Crash, individual markets participants had experienced systems-related issues. CME accused Infinium Capital Management in October 2009 of "failing to diligently supervise its systems, employees or agents" and said that by "allowing a malfunctioning [automated trading system] to operate in a live trading environment, Infinium committed an act detrimental to the welfare of the exchange;" as a result, Infinium was slapped with $850,000 in total fines for computer malfunctions.[6] In February 2011, NASDAQ revealed that hackers had penetrated certain of its computer networks, though NASDAQ reported that at no point did this intrusion compromise its trading systems. In October 2011, the SEC sanctioned EDGX and EDGA, two national securities exchanges run by Direct Edge for violations of federal securities laws arising from systems incidents. In the Direct Edge order, the SEC noted that the "violations occurred against the backdrop of weaknesses in respondents' systems, processes, and controls." In March 2012, NASDAQ said Octeg, GETCO's trading unit, violated its rules during from May 2010 through December 2011; the examination, conducted by FINRA, concluded that "the firm failed to establish and maintain a reasonable supervisory system, including but not limited to its written supervisory procedures and supervisory and operational risk control systems related to the oversight of high-frequency trading and algorithmic trading."[7] More recently, in 2012, systems issues hampered the initial public offerings of BATS Global Markets and Facebook.

While these were illustrative high-profile examples, they were not the only instances of disruptions and other systems problems experienced by market participants. Furthermore, disruptions have originated not only at exchanges, dark pools, ECNs and clearing firms, but also in the heart of trading firms, which leads to the question why those were not covered by the proposed regulation. None other than GETCO wrote in a response to a public consultation about MiFID from an E.U. commission, "Authorized firms engaging in automated trading should have in place robust risk controls." Isn't it in high-frequency trading firms' best interest to provide the same operational assurances requested from exchanges, dark pools, ECNs and clearing firms? While the SEC has leveraged the market access rule to require participants with direct access to have suitable "risk management controls and supervisory procedures reasonably designed to manage the financial, regulatory, and other risks of this business activity," the additional system safeguards proposed by Reg SCI are even more relevant for trading firms.

As pointed out by John Rapa, Tellefsen and Company's chief executive officer, market impacting events cannot be easily foreseen nor adequately tested for; the next major headline event will not necessarily be the same as these.[8] That's why Bloomberg Tradebook's CEO Raymond Tierney's observation that there was currently no integrated end-to-end testing infrastructure in the equity markets took on additional relevance.[9]

"Both buy-side and sell-side participants cannot test end-to-end connectivity, execution, allocation, settlement and clearing unless they use live orders in the production environment. As a result of the absence of a testing infrastructure, market participants are forced to use live orders to test connectivity, FIX messaging, allocation, and straight-through processing systems. This practice not only increases, but also creates, the very type of operational risk in the national market system that the Commission is concerned about. The practice of testing system infrastructure in a live production environment should not be permitted in markets populated by retail investors."

Tierney argues that the best way to implement a testing infrastructure is for the SEC to set forth a set of principles for production testing for the entirety of the national market system and then to let the industry come up with a solution. The SEC needs to do more from the driver's seat to ensure these solutions satisfy minimum standards. "No amount of regulatory paperwork is going to do any better than that to make sure that firms do their absolute utmost best not to mess up Knight style," said James Angel, associate professor of finance at the McDonough School of Business, Georgetown University.[10]

Commissioner Aguilar made the observation that senior officers needed to take the most appropriate steps to ensure compliance at a time when the SEC was eager to restore trust in the markets. The commissioner's suggestion was that senior officers needed to certify, in writing, that entities had processes in place to establish, document, maintain, review, test, and modify controls reasonably designed to achieve compliance, and that the annual budget and staffing levels should have been adequate for the entity to comply with its obligations.

The Sarbanes-Oxley Act of 2002, section 302, "Corporate Responsibility for Financial Reports," required the CEO and CFO of publicly traded companies to certify the appropriateness of their financial statements and disclosures and to certify that they fairly present, in all material respects, the operations and financial condition of the company. That was not the first time, and won't be the last time either, that executive management had been asked to provide some form of assurance on the overall financial statements or the details and assertions that underlie the statements.

While it remains to be seen whether this type of certification statement, signed, notarized, and available for public view, would be the final and necessary measure to ensure the public that management would take full responsibility, and be held legally accountable, its mere existence would put the onus on CTOs and CIOs to go beyond rubber stamping their staff's decisions and declarations. It was not about having the most sophisticated kill switch in trading entities' infrastructure; it is about management defining and constantly monitoring the appropriate criteria by which these switches will be activated. Indeed, conventional wisdom suggests that when people know they can and will be held accountable for their actions, their behaviors change. Furthermore, these new rules should make it easier for government officials to make fraud cases against executives found to have intentionally filed false certifications under perjury charges.

While some might question the additional value of these certifications in the same way they questioned the Sarbanes-Oxley Act, enforcement of the laws is what is important, not the public relations value of a few more signatures on a certificate of integrity. Indeed, enforcement of these laws is what will bring out the added value of any statement. Enforcement actions against those who perpetrated fraud in these cases will go a long way toward restoring investor confidence and limiting the impact of the biggest risk for financial markets.[11]

Chapter Three

Flash Crash, Pipeline, BATS and...

With progress came unexpected challenges which demanded new solutions. While some blamed electronic trading for the trading incidents of the previous years, from the Flash Crash through the Pipeline Trading fiasco to the failed BATS Global Markets IPO, others instead called regulators to step up their game and work harder to guarantee fair and orderly markets.

On the morning of May 6, 2010, the U.S. stock market opened on a downwards trend as investors were concerned over Greece's debt crisis. At 2:42 P.M. the DJIA was down 300 points. However, the media hype surrounding the Flash Crash was ignited by the following event: shortly after the 300 point mark drop, the equity market began to nose dive, dropping an additional 600 points within five minutes. By 2:47 P.M. the DJIA suffered close to a 1,000 point drop, the largest one-day point decline in history. At 3:07 P.M. the market was able to recover from this 600 point drop. However, immediately following the event, regulators and investors became concerned over identifying the cause of the crash and developing measures to prevent a future occurrence.

This event came to be known as the Flash Crash of May 6, 2010. It was explored and discussed in great detail by the joint report filed by the SEC and the CFTC on September 30, 2010 concluding a five-month investigation led by Gregg Berman. The report, "Findings Regarding the Market Events of May 6, 2010" stated that the cause of the crash was due to an unidentified mutual fund selling 75,000 orders of future contracts, known as E-Minis, which resulted in a $4.1 billion sale. E-Minis were used by traders to bet on the future performance of stocks within the Standard's and Poor's (S&P) 500 Index.

The report focused upon liquidity and identified the cause of the crash to be due to two liquid crises, one at the broad index level with E-Minis and the other at the individual stock level, as a result of the mutual fund's selling of 75,000 E-Minis. The report concluded that the sell order was so large that it overwhelmed the market's available buyers which led to a depletion of liquidity in the market. This led to the sudden drop in prices of the stocks as there was not enough liquidity to allow for securities to be traded without changing their prices.

The first liquidity crisis which dealt with E-Minis centered on high-frequency traders quickly buying and reselling E-Mini contracts to one another leading to a "hot potato" effect. In a matter of 14 seconds, contracts were exchanged 27,000 times. This generated high trading volume but little net buying. Only 200 were actually bought and sold. The effect was that the depth of the buying market for the E-Minis plummeted to 1 percent of its level from that very morning.

The second liquidity crisis which dealt with individual stocks occurred when automated trading systems (ATS) used by market makers paused. The reason for the pause was that these systems were designed with such a pause when prices moved beyond the system's set parameters. The pause allowed for traders to assess the risk before resuming trading. Traders realized the increased risk. Some reacted by increasing the spreads between their buying and selling points, some used manual trading, and others withdrew completely. Market makers from over-the-counter markets began routing their trades to the exchanges, which led to a further increase in the rising volume. Orders were competing against one another as liquidity dwindled. According to the report, all of these combined factors culminated in the crash as liquidity dwindled.

The unidentified mutual fund had been identified by the media to be the Kansas-based Waddell & Reed. The algorithm that was used by the mutual fund was supplied by Barclays Capital. However, the parameters of the algorithm were left to the discretion of the firm. Waddell & Reed's 75,000 sell of E-Mini contracts was not unusual. In most instances, the sell occurred over a span of hours averaging five hours.

In this case, the sell occurred within a matter of 20 minutes, after the firm started its program at 2:32 P.M. The firm did not set its parameters with concern to time and price, which ultimately led to the crash. Rather, as high-frequency traders bought the contracts, the algorithm responded by increasing the amount of E-Mini sell orders in the market. What happened was that the high-frequency traders realized they bought an excessive amount of "long" positions and thus began to sell, causing Waddell & Reed's algorithm to accelerate its selling. It had been speculated that the algorithm's parameters were sensitive to volume. Waddell & Reed's execution rate was set to 9 percent of the trading volume calculated over the previous minute.

Following the increase in selling, the pressure was removed from the futures market and transferred to the stock market. This outlines the two liquidity crises discussed within the report, the shift from the future markets (E-Mini contracts) to the stock markets (individual stocks). The shift was caused by arbitrageurs who were investors that profit from price inefficiencies by making simultaneous trades that offset one another and profit by capturing 'risk-free profits.' The arbitrageurs bought cheap future contracts and sold cash shares on the stock markets.

The effect of this event was that there was an abrupt drop in prices of individual stocks (the shares of prominent companies such as Procter & Gamble and Accenture traded down for as low as a penny or as high as $100,000) and exchange-traded funds (ETFs). The market was only able to recover after a five second pause initiated by an automatic stabilizer in the futures exchange, specifically the Chicago Mercantile Exchange (CME) Stop Logic Functionality.

Nanex, the market-data firm, disagreed with the SEC-CTFC's joint report's findings. The firm stated that Waddell & Reed did not buy and sell without concern over price as suggested within the report. The founder, Eric Hunsader, reviewed the 6,483 trades made by Waddell & Reed as it sold its 75,000 contracts. Hunsader's finding was that the orders were made passively.

The meaning of his finding was that the firm sold at preset prices that appeared only when buyers for that price appeared in the market. Thus, the mutual fund was sensitive to price. It was not removing liquidity but rather providing it.

Hunsader identified the crisis as occurring between 2:41 P.M. and 2:44 P.M. During this three minute time period the market fell 5-6 percent. His analysis was that the drop was due to high-frequency traders. Usually speed traders provided liquidity as they were ready to buy and sell at certain price points. However, the market condition of May 6 caused for the high-frequency traders to dump their stocks, an accumulation of 2,000 E-Mini contracts, to avoid losses. Hunsader's analysis stated that the speed traders aggressive selling of stocks was what caused liquidity to dwindle, not Waddell & Reed's passive orders.

However, even accepting Nanex's conclusion, there was no reason to crucify them. The high-frequency traders aggressively sold stocks to avoid losses, a logical response that shouldn't be condemned.

The shock caused by the Flash Crash prompted the financial world to take a pause of its own as regulators were investigating the cause of the crash. The question on everyone's mind was, "how do we prevent a future occurrence?"

Pipeline Trading was founded as an alternative trading system (ATS) designed to protect institutional investors from the pitfalls of exchange trading. The concept for Pipeline was hatched in Boston, Massachusetts at Fidelity in the early 2000s. Fidelity aspired to design a new ATS for large block traders and partnered with Fred Federspiel, a physicist who had taken his talents to Wall Street, to help build their ATS platform.

Like Knight Match, Knight Link, and other dark pools, the foundation for Pipeline was built on the strength of anonymity. Institutional large block traders would be able to enter orders into the Pipeline system anonymously and be able to have these orders matched without suffering information leakage that would lead to inevitable front running and price risk. To this end, Pipeline claimed that its system offered "predator proofing" by not allowing high-frequency traders to enter the ATS and game trades.[1]

The Pipeline software that Federspiel designed worked by having the symbol of a stock light up in orange on a user's computer screen when an order for that stock was placed. In keeping with the standard operating practice of a dark pool, the user could not see if the order was to buy or sell and price and quantity information of the order was also not available. Lastly, platform users were unable to see any information about who placed the order.

Once completed, Pipeline leased the software from Fidelity and established an office in New York City. Federspiel was named president of Pipeline Trading and Alfred Berkeley III was named chairman. Berkeley, a former president and vice chairman of NASDAQ stock market, was believed to be a strong choice for chairman as he would be able to tap into his array of contacts to attract investors to use Pipeline's systems to trade.

Like all alternative trading systems, in order for Pipeline to be successful, it needed to have ample order flow to effectively match orders when its system conducted crosses. Crossing was when the software employed in an ATS looked at its orders to best match buyers and sellers. The greater the order flow for an ATS, the more able it would be to match participant orders. If Pipeline did not have robust order flow then participants in the pool risked having their orders go unfilled. This would cause client orders to linger on the system for prolonged periods of time and this occurrence would be very detrimental to Pipeline's business as users of the system and dark pools in general relied on speed of execution as a fundamental reason to utilize an ATS.

Pipeline was hoping that its order flow would be cemented by Fidelity using the ATS for a large portion of its trading. However, just prior to Pipeline's starting date in September 2004, it became apparent that Fidelity would only use Pipeline to execute a small fraction of its orders.

Faced with a problem of order flow volume, Pipeline opted to create a subsidiary trading operation to aid in filling customer orders. This undisclosed subsidiary was entirely owned and funded by Pipeline and was originally created with the sole intention of providing liquidity for the orders of customers trading in Pipeline's dark pool.

This subsidiary trading operation, known initially as Exchange Advantage, was later renamed Milstream Strategy Group. Pipeline anticipated using the subsidiary only until it gained enough volume to satisfy its order flow solely through the use of customer orders, a concept known as "natural liquidity."[2] Once it was determined that Pipeline had enough natural liquidity to fulfill customer orders without interruption, the subsidiary trading group would be dissolved.

However, Pipeline's order flow via its natural customers never reached a level where the firm could discontinue the use of its subsidiary trading outfit to fill orders. As a result, Milstream Strategy Group continued to operate in the Pipeline ATS and continued to be opposite positions of Pipeline's institutional clients.

It was this persistent operation of the subsidiary trading group which brought Pipeline into problematic circumstances. First, instead of seeking alternative clients or considering a partnership with other alternative trading systems, Pipeline invited trouble by not only continuing the operation of its subsidiary trading group but also adjusting its modus operandi. Because it was launched to help fill customer order flow, the trading outfit would often look to acquire shares on the open market in order to satisfy client demand. As a result, the trading outfit initially operated at a loss.

This changed in 2006 when Pipeline hired Gordon Henderson to run Milstream Strategy Group. Upon his hiring, Pipeline gave Henderson the authority to make adjustments to Milstream staff as well as other changes he deemed necessary to make Milstream's operation more profitable. As a result, Milstream quickly began making money off of client orders.

Milstream's profitability was aided by a high-frequency trading program developed by Milstream's first director, Henri Waelbroeck, who like Federspiel was also a physicist by training. In just a two-year span, Pipeline had gone from running a subsidiary trading group designed to help fill orders to running a subsidiary trading group that was making profit off of the institutional clients who utilized the ATS.

Pipeline advertised that it had "no proprietary trading desk gaming customer orders." Clearly, this was not the case with Milstream Strategy Group gaming customer order flow to make profitable trades. A series of Pipeline advertising and public statements also claimed that the trading opportunities within its ATS were natural. This was also not the case as Milstream was on the opposite side of a number of trades transacted within Pipeline's system. After all, if Pipeline had sufficient natural order flow to satisfy its customer demand, it would not have needed the Milstream operation in the first place.

Pipeline enabled the Milstream Strategy Group to violate the fundamental tenets of ATS operation. Through monitoring the Pipeline ATS system and comparing liquidity for equities in other pools, Milstream was able to discern if orders that flashed in the ATS were buy or sell orders. One way Milstream accomplished this was to monitor demand for stocks in other dark pools. Another method Milstream employed was known as "flashing". Flashing was when a trader placed a number of orders and then instantly canceled them. For some, order flashing was one of the hallmarks of high-frequency trading and was used to gauge the market depth of a security at a certain price.

Additionally, Pipeline would often relay information to Milstream about the identity of a customer. Pipeline would not divulge the actual identity of an individual client behind on order, but the ATS would inform Milstream as to the type of client making the order, such as if the client was a dealer. Through a combination of flashing, the monitoring of other dark pools, and communication with Pipeline during the trading day, Milstream was able to successfully identify whether an order posted in Pipeline was a buy order or a sell order.

Once Milstream had identified the nature of the order it could then front run the trade in order to create an arbitrage opportunity. This included buying shares from another market and selling them to a client on the ATS to fulfill the buy order. Also included in the Milstream practices was short selling after determining a customer had placed a sell order. By buying shares in the ATS from a customer, Milstream could conveniently cover its short positions without risking undue order exposure in the market and simultaneously ensure that the client's buy order was satisfied.

Pipeline, as a result of a recommendation from its legal counsel, did notify most of its clients that it was possible that unspecified Pipeline affiliates could trade on the ATS. However, they informed clients that any affiliate who was trading on the ATS would receive no preferential treatment regarding the order or trade data of other users of the ATS. In actuality, Pipeline occasionally informed Milstream of the order and trade data of other customers at the completion of a trade.

While these practices directly undermined the good faith agreement between the ATS and its customers, Pipeline went even further to ensure the success of Milstream in the form of policy construction. As an ATS, Pipeline was not subject to the strict regulatory rules of the exchanges and as a result could craft policy and make policy changes without any prior notice or explanation to customers. Milstream had input into designing the Pipeline rules that would prevent "predatory behavior." Milstream was also given insight into how Pipeline would police the ATS in order to monitor inappropriate trading behavior. None of Pipeline's other customers were given input regarding how the platform was to be run, nor were they given insight into how it would be policed.

While Milstream was engaging in these suspect trading practices daily, Pipeline claimed through its advertising and communication that it would not reveal the side of its client orders nor would it reveal the prices of those orders. It went on to further state that the ATS was not subject to leakage (information leakage) because it denied arbitrageurs and high-frequency traders the information necessary to front run trades posted on the system. Pipeline even went so far as to claim that its ATS was "predator proof" and "leak proof", and that investors would be protected from the market impact of predatory trading on their orders. In a 2005 statement made available to journalists and industry participants, Berkeley reiterated that "Pipeline's new technology reduces market impact by denying day traders, predatory dealers and other speculators the information they need to front run institutional investors' orders".

Of course, this statement was misleading as Milstream was the counterparty to a majority of the trades executed within Pipeline's ATS. By trading on the same side as many of Pipeline's client orders,

Milstream manufactured arbitrage opportunities and benefited from these same opportunities. The reckless creation of these arbitrage opportunities subjected Pipeline clients to the exact execution risks that users of the ATS sought to avoid, namely information leakage and price manipulation.

Ultimately, the deception couldn't last forever. Pipeline was forced to pay $1 million to resolve U.S. claims it failed to provide the confidentiality and liquidity it advertised to customers. Both Federspiel and Berkeley agreed to pay $100,000 to settle the claims.

After the settlement became public, the company tried to repair relationships with customers; however, mutual funds and other institutional investor clients and brokers wanted new ownership for the company. Ultimately, Portware bought the firm's Alpha Pro technology and Algorithm Switching Engine, tools to determine how to execute larger orders.

On Friday March 23, 2012, BATS Global Markets, the holding company for BATS Exchange and BATS Europe, was supposed to go public and demonstrate to the world how ready they were for all companies to skip the NYSE and the NASDAQ in the IPO game. Unfortunately, it turned out to be the epic failure of the worst IPO ever.[3]

BATS, which stood for Better Alternative Trading System, had been founded by Dave Cummings in June 2005 as an electronic communication network (ECN) in Kansas City, after many years running the incredibly profitable Tradebot Systems, a firm that practiced a particularly fast form of "algorithmic" or "black-box" trading in which computer programs decided when to buy and sell securities. Once in 2008, Cummings told students that his firm typically held stocks for 11 seconds and that they had not had a losing day in four years.[4]

BATS Global Markets was a leading operator of securities markets, and it was the third largest stock exchange operator behind competitors NYSE and NASDAQ in the United States. Unlike traditional market operators, BATS was a technology company at its core. BATS developed, owned and operated the BATS trading platform.[5] It operated two stock exchanges in the United States, the BZX exchange and the BYX exchange.

In October 2005, BATS received a minority investment from the even more incredibly profitable GETCO. Co-founders Stephen Schuler and Dan Tierney said that "given the opportunity in the rapidly consolidating ECN space, we believe BATS has the right combination of technology, people and vision to create new levels of innovation and efficiency. We have had a long relationship with Dave Cummings and have great respect for him. We believe that BATS is well positioned for success."[6]

In 2007, Cummings stepped down and returned to Tradebot. He was replaced as chief executive officer by Joe Ratterman, who had been associated with the company from the start. An accomplished water skier, rock climber, track and distance runner and professional photographer, Ratterman held a degree in mathematics and computer science from Central Missouri State University.[7]

BATS prided itself on its absolute performance and reliability of the system. "To some extent, reliability is kind of a price venture. You've got to be up. You've got to be functioning and running around the clock, around the market hours," Ratterman had said. Not all of their competitors were actually up all the time, he added, and they did have system failures. "We've been, so far, blessed with a system that has held up exceedingly well, better than our competitors. So the reliability thing is certainly winning favor, and whenever our competitors have major outages it certainly makes our customers wonder why they are sending their flow elsewhere."

After months of planning and anticipation, BATS Global Market finally attempted to launch a lucrative IPO on March 23, 2012 as the first listing on its own exchange, but it almost immediately found out that something went wrong with the company's computer system.

BATS' stock price, which was expected to debut at $16 a share, fell to as low as 4 cents a share. BATS withdrew its IPO the same day after the market closed.

The software problems not only led to BATS Global Markets canceling its own IPO, but also contributed to a glitch allowing shares of Apple (AAPL) to briefly plunge nearly 10 percent.[8] The plunge affected Apple's value on all exchanges, triggering a so-called circuit breaker which temporarily halted trading in the stock.[9] BATS halted stocks on its exchange that were affected by the glitch, including stocks with ticker symbols between A and BFZZZ. Later on the same day, the erroneous trades for Apple were canceled as if they had never happened. The problems triggered by a "software bug" were resolved and the affected market was reopened.

Trying to rationalize this horrific bug, Ratterman explained that despite the software being "rigorously tested" over a series of months, with trading firms and underwriters frequently testing it with real-world conditions (though with test symbols, not live securities), a "unique combination" of order types led to the problem moving from auction to trading. So much for absolute performance!

On the following Sunday, March 25, Cummings wrote a widely distributed e-mail that shocked the trading community by calling to withhold the bonuses for the company's executives.[10]

"Dear Trading Community,

In light of BATS botched IPO, several people are asking: What should BATS do now?

Understand this is Serious

First, I recommend suspending all bonus plans at BATS. In this business, mistakes cost money.

Fix the Bug

Ironically, the software bug itself is probably the easiest thing to correct. The fix should take less than a week. Given the importance, they need to test and retest the code for a couple weeks.

This was a freak one-time event. BATS has built great software over the past 6 or 7 years. The BATS matching engine has literally matched BILLIONS of orders without problems. However, the code to open an IPO is new. It has been tested in the lab, but until this week not in real-world production. These systems are very complicated. Bugs do occur. BATS just happened to discover a bug at the most embarrassing time possible.

Defend Electronic Trading

Before I got into trading, I worked at a healthcare software company, Cerner, ticker CERN. I called my broker for a quote, "24.00 bid 24.50 ask, what do you want to do?" I hung up. NYSE's website claimed they "filled the average market order in only 23 seconds!"

Over the past decade, electronic trading has brought huge savings to investors. The old middlemen lost their fat spreads, and some are now the most vocal critics of HFT. Some in the media love to overhype the occasional glitches. They envy people who make money. American Capitalism is sometimes messy, but it is what makes this country great.

When the public wants to invest, they can push a button and get a fair fill in less than a second. The markets will never be perfect, but the reality is that they work very well.

Sincerely,

Dave Cummings"

Following the failed IPO, Ratterman decided to give up his chairman position. "Splitting the two is the much favored approach," Charles Elson, director of the University of Delaware's John L. Weinberg Center for Corporate Governance, had said. "It gives the board more authority" he added. Ratterman received the "unanimous support" of the directors to keep the positions of CEO and president through.[11] In July 2012, BATS Global Market named a former SEC commissioner, Paul Atkins, to the role of non-executive chairman of its board of directors.[12]

Up until the IPO, BATS Global Markets had a great reputation and had been very reliable. BATS' difficult debut on that Friday led some traders to question whether the exchange was reliable enough to compete with its bigger rivals. "I think some companies might say 'if they cannot handle the IPO of their own stock, how can they handle the IPO of our stock?'" said Dennis Dick, a Detroit-based market structure consultant and trading member at Bright Trading. "There is going to be a confidence issue of listing on BATS."[13] "We feel absolutely terrible about letting our customers down," said Ratterman. "The fact that our own stock was out there to be traded for the first time and we showed system problems eroded customer confidence," he admitted.

Further analysis showed that, even before the glitches appeared, the offering was off to a rocky start. When trading in BATS shares opened at 10:45 A.M., they were down 75 cents, to $15.25. As a result of the first trade of $15.25, there were already some investors who bought the IPO and wanted to sell their entire position before the computer system issue happened.[14] Though BATS had identified the software problem related to its own stock within two-and-a-half hours, it ultimately chose not to reopen trading, with banks' underwriting syndicate desks informing them that many early investors were lining up to sell, and ultimately to withdraw the IPO. If the underwriters had attempted to reopen trading in the stock, "it was going to be a bloodbath," one trader said. One Wall Street analyst said the price might have fallen to $12 a share or even lower. Even worse, investors might have sued based on the argument that BATS did not adequately disclose the risks of its trading system not performing.

The company's trading volume that day fell several percentage points below its normal 11 percent participation, as customers rerouted trades to other platforms. Ratterman said that he viewed that drop in business to be temporary, though he offered no balm for irritated investors who had agreed to buy shares in the IPO.

"It is not widely unusual for exchanges to have system issues, but because they happen to go public today makes it more newsworthy," said Mike Shea, a managing partner at Direct Access Partners in New York.

Critics of BATS and other electronic exchanges said computer glitches could lead to a rapid cascade of errors that resulted in precipitous dives and market turmoil. "It was just another black eye for the fragmented equity structure," said Joe Saluzzi. Along with partner Sal Arnuk, Saluzzi was founder of Themis Trading, author of *Broken Markets: How High-Frequency Trading and Predatory Practices on Wall Street are Destroying Investor Confidence and Your Portfolio*, and a frequent critic of U.S. current equities market structure. "Every day we see things like Flash Crashes and now IPOs that cannot get off the ground."

One thing that the failure of the IPO did not change, according to Ratterman, was the continued path that modern stock markets had followed in the last decade. BATS had been founded on the principles that more trading platforms and increased computerization would be better for investors over all. The problems on Friday were not expected to change the growth of either.

Chapter Four

The Men Behind Knight

Behind a success story there is always a brilliant mind. Behind Knight Capital, there were two. The geniuses were Walter Francis Raquet and Kenneth David Pasternak, two of the original founders of the firm in 1995 along with Steven Steinman and Robert Lazarowitz. Although Raquet is the one who came up with the idea of Knight, Pasternak's more visible role earned him the Ernst & Young Emerging Entrepreneur of the Year award in 1996. The two partners performed very different roles in starting Knight. Raquet used his vision and charisma for the company to attract investors while Pasternak used their capital to make money trading. Both performed equally important roles, but Pasternak is credited with most of the success, due to the greater exposure he received.

Raquet had graduated from Andrew Jackson High School in Cambria Heights, New York, as the 1,100th in a class of 1,400. He had come from humble beginnings as the son of a fireman (someone who instilled in him the virtue of honor and integrity) and a part-time secretary. Continuing the Big Apple approach, Raquet enrolled in New York University and graduated in 1966 with a bachelor of science in accounting; he had also briefly studied computer science. After being offered a teaching fellowship at New York University's Graduate School, he joined Price Waterhouse to practice accounting.

Raquet's computer science background served him well as he continued his business career with Weeden & Co. He was hired in 1968 to help them organize their financials so that they could eliminate wasteful spending. In his first year there, he saved the company $2 million dollars while they were only making $10 million dollars a year. They doubled his salary and gave him a $10,000 bonus. At age 26, he was made the controller of the company. This was something that he was very proud of as Weeden & Co. was then the tenth largest company on Wall Street and he achieved this powerful position at such a young age.

He then went on to join Cantor Fitzgerald in 1977, a brokerage firm started by Bernie Cantor and John Fitzgerald. The company hired him as their chief financial officer. After a couple of years he became the executive vice president. Although he liked his time at Cantor Fitzgerald, he was soon looking for opportunities elsewhere.

Raquet would then enter into one of the more interesting times of his life. In 1980, he moved to Sentinel Financial Instruments (SFI), a firm that traded government securities with a tax emphasis for wealthy individuals. He was hired as the number two person and was to receive five percent of profits in the company. There were about 20 similar companies on Wall Street, but this business still made Raquet uneasy. Customers would be directed to Sentinel by tax-shelter finders and the firm would conduct internal government bond transactions "created solely to achieve beneficial tax results." Raquet would often hear other SFI employees refer to the nominal traders as "fantasy island traders."[1]

Raquet recalls going to the CEO of the firm after two weeks on the job and saying, "I believe what we are doing is illegal."

"Absolutely not!" was his reply. "Go to the partner at Peat Marwick. Go to the partner at our law firm. Talk to them, tell them everything." Raquet followed his advice and everyone said the business was legal.

Raquet then focused on what he knew best, to efficiently organize the company's financials. It took him about two months to get all the books and records balanced. He discovered something shocking. He discovered that the company had $40 million in capital as opposed to the $15 million that everyone else thought. When he brought this up to the CEO's attention, he ordered the traders to incur on a fictitious loss of $25 million and give it to the customers. All of the trades were paper only as no money changed hands.

After this discovery, he immediately began to look for another job. When he left the company the same year, he was still worried that he would be implicated if the company blew up and it became exposed. Raquet was working hard for his reputation and did not want to lose it so early in his career.

He consulted attorney Stanley S. Arkin while at his new job as the controller for Paine Webber. Arkin and Raquet discovered that there were billions of dollars of tax fraud involved with 20 companies on Wall Street that were similar to Sentinel. Raquet, acting on the advice of his lawyer, came forward voluntarily and provided the information to the United States Attorney's office; in order to avoid getting in trouble, Raquet trained government officials to show them what was actually going on and how to prevent this in the future.

On November 17, 1981, more than 100 boxes of business records were seized from the offices of the defendants, Suite 2105 at 100 Wall Street, with machine guns and army personnel. The seizure was based on a search warrant stemming from Raquet's information. He testified against the defendants, receiving many death threats along the way.

After this episode, Raquet was working as the corporate controller for Paine Webber. By then, the firm had 161 branch offices in 42 states and six offices in Asia and Europe. With the acquisition of Rotan Mosle Financial Corp. in 1983, Paine Webber had developed a national distribution network and with its active advertising campaign "Thank You Paine Webber" developed its brand throughout the 1980s. The company would later consolidate its two divisions, Paine Webber Jackson & Curtis and Blyth Eastman Paine Webber to form Paine Webber. Raquet was hired to salvage the financials and save the company from going under. Raquet used his many connections in the computer services industry as well as his own skills to save the company in 49 days.

Raquet recalls one of his first encounters with Paine Webber's chairman Donald Marron (who would later found private equity firm Lightyear Capital) and vice chairman Dugald Fletcher; he was in charge of systems and operations and wanted to close down a GNMA (Government National Mortgage Association or "Ginnie Mae") business that was dragging down 20 percent of Paine Webber's net profit.

Raquet told them, "I put the systems together for that when I was at Cantor Fitzgerald. The firm will do it as a service bureau for you."

Fletcher said, "Before you do that, I will have my systems people evaluate the Fitzgerald system."

At about 5 P.M., Raquet got a call from his boss and he went to Fletcher's office. He was smoking a pipe and sitting at his desk.

Fletcher said, "My people evaluated your systems at Cantor Fitzgerald and said you're full of shit."

In those days, that would have been called a "nuke". It took thirty seconds for Raquet to collect his thoughts.

He finally said, "Fletcher, tomorrow morning I will come in and I am going to put $50,000 on your desk and bet you and those assholes you work with that I will put in your system in eight weeks without you and any of those assholes' help."

All of a sudden, Fletcher looked at him and he didn't know what to do. He grabbed his desk drawer and was going through things and humming. Then Fletcher suggested the meeting was over.

They went to Marron's office, told him what happened and he asked, "You think you can do it?"

Raquet challenged him, "You want to bet $50,000? I will put the system in and save the business." Raquet went on to fix the issues that were choking the firm.

Raquet concluded that success on Wall Street was about being gutsy. "You have to take shots; there's a lot of dishonesty in business and people are trying to exert power over you. It's part of corporate strangling; not everything is based on integrity."

Raquet moved in 1982 as become a partner with Herzog, Heine & Geduld (HHG), a very dynamic wholesaler on Wall Street that had survived substantial challenges and changes through many decades, where he directed the firm's marketing efforts. HHG needed to increase its technological capabilities, so Raquet developed the Continuous On-Line Trading System (COLT), the first sophisticated equity inventory management system, of which he owned 30 percent. COLT allowed traders to monitor their on-line positions and automatically report NMS transactions to NASDAQ within 90 seconds and volume in other NASDAQ issues at the end of the day. This system allowed the firm to move from two percent of the NASDAQ to six percent. HHG later sold COLT to 21 of the top equity-trading firms including Goldman Sachs.

HHG wanted Raquet to stay, but the idea of a leadership role at another firm sounded too good to pass up. Raquet was offered jobs at many top trading firms. He ultimately decided to join Troster Singer in 1992 because of the opportunity to become its next president. Troster Singer, a subsidiary of Spear, Leeds & Kellogg (SLK) that made markets in a number of securities traded in the NASDAQ market, hired Raquet for his wide range of contacts and his skillset.

SLK had been founded as a partnership in 1931 by Harold Spear and Lawrence Leeds. In 1941 they took on a third partner, 26-year-old James Crane Kellogg III, who would be highly influential in the growth of the firm; in 1936 he was able to raise $125,000 to buy a seat on the New York Stock Exchange and at the age of 21 became the youngest seat holder. Nineteen years later, Kellogg became the managing partner and under his leadership the company was quick to buy out the books of stock owned by other specialists who were retiring. In many ways, Kellogg laid the foundation for today's firm, responsible for its diversification beyond market making into such areas as clearing.

Kellogg's son, Peter Rittenhouse Kellogg, although not the eldest of four sons, would be the one to carry on the Kellogg tradition on Wall Street and build upon what his father started. Because his father had instituted a rule at SLK that forbade the hiring of kin, Kellogg found a job on Wall Street in the early 1960s with Stern, Frank Meyer & Fox, initially working as a clerk on the New York Stock Exchange floor. It was here that he gained a practical education from the people who worked for his employer's agent, Dominick & Dominick. Like his father, he proved to be an adept trader, so much so that the partners at SLK petitioned the elder Kellogg to bend his rules and bring Peter into the firm. Thus, in 1967, Peter Kellogg became a partner at SLK at the age of 25.

Some of SLK's attempts at diversification in the 1960s did not prove as successful as the firm envisioned. However, clearing (settling trades for other firms for a fee) forced SLK to pay strict attention to costs and apply computer technology, preparing the firm for the large trading volumes that became routine as the decades progressed. SLK had started the 1970s with just 50 employees, but over the course of the next decade it would swallow up a number of longtime Wall Street specialist firms. Jimmy Kellogg retired in 1978, replaced as SLK's managing partner by his son. Another area SLK entered as a way to pick up some of the business moving away from the exchange floor was over-the-counter dealers. In 1977 SLK acquired dealer Troster Singer, making it a subsidiary.

Immediately, Raquet made an impact. In the first six weeks he landed a deal that generated $80,000 in extra salary for himself. It was the biggest deal they had ever achieved. Unfortunately, other members of the management team were bitter about this because Raquet was already making a million dollars and was too fast paced, even though they were all making in excess of $10 million.

Raquet goes on to say, "I brought in a lot more business but they decided not to pay me which led to many fights. It was weird. This guy, Ralph (Valentino), and I started head-butting. It was hard to have a realistic talk the bigger pictures."

He remembered once sitting in a trading room with 167 people; the firm had about 300 people. Valentino, who was the president of the firm, liked to use the microphone and make big announcements, and also some not so big.

At that time, America was following the story of Katie Beers who had been kidnapped in New York on December 28, 1992, at age 9. She had left a message on her godmother's answering machine saying, "I've been kidnapped by a man with a knife." On January 13, 1993, she was found alive in a bunker built by her assailant in Bay Shore, New York. How did the firm's employees know about her rescue? Valentino got on the microphone and said, "Hey. Doesn't everybody know they found Katie Beers and she's safe?"

This is what Valentine would do all the time. Anyone visiting the company would have known that the president of the company liked to have fun. Employees were still chuckling when fifteen minutes later Valentine gets on the microphone again and screams, "Someone stole my Caesar salad! I'm dying."

Valentine was about 300 pounds and went on, "I'm really serious about my diet. If I catch the person who stole my salad I am going to fire him."

Raquet, being the wisecracking jokester he was, just couldn't resist. He picked up the phone, pressed the intercom for the whole firm to listen, disguised his voice and said, "Ralph, they may have found Katie Beers but they will never find your Caesar salad."

Ralph got back on the microphone and exploded, "Who did that?" He still wonders about the prankster's identity.

"You just have to keep a little humor in your life. The key thing in life is laughter," said Raquet, remembering this anecdote.

For Pasternak, Raquet was an idea guy, a visionary. "Walter didn't get along with his recently hired manager Ralph Valentino, who was basically an incompetent. I didn't like Ralph myself either. I was already making $25 million dollars in my 30s; I used to complain to Ralph's head, Peter Kellogg, that I would leave the firm, because he made me report to Valentino. I was a partner; Walter was not a partner. He was more subordinate to Ralph, and Walter also held him in low regard. So Walter was looking to do something else."

John Hewitt, who would later become president of Knight Securities, agreed that Raquet was the ultimate entrepreneur. "Walter was the guy that had the sense that things were going to be done more by computer. Literally, he spent a year plus living in a sailboat docked somewhere near Jersey City. I admire people that take an idea and live it. He didn't understand the trading part. He was always like a back-office operations kind of guy at Paine Webber. He would know everything about Paine Webber operations and back-office. You know, I was with Phelan when he tells Marron that Paine Webber was out of control and the exchange was going to shut it down in 24 hours because they had just messed up all of their execution process. Walter didn't have a good background in terms of what he had done but he was an entrepreneur that figured out an idea that was that going to turn out to be a very significant idea."

"But he brought in Pasternak," added Hewitt with a different tone of voice. He recalled the dinner he had once with Raquet and his wife Nancy.

She said, "John, you have to understand. Ken is insane."

Hewitt was not sure what to believe. "It took me a while to get there; they were right, but having said that, Walter brought in Ken. So a lot of Knight Securities was Walter and Ken sniping, bitching and moaning about each other. Walter couldn't get a role, couldn't get a management role at Knight that made any sense, so he was kind of like doing marketing or sales. He had no organization that reported into him."

"The Knight Securities people were almost uniformly the laziest bunch of people you could ever meet in your life. They couldn't work an eight-hour day. They couldn't work. They were just lazy. When I had to go and do work and put together a big partnership in Europe, Raquet, to his credit, would work with me. And he would be shoulder-to-shoulder and flying all over and working from eight o'clock in the morning to ten o'clock at night, from breakfast to dinner. So, he really believed in Knight. He really worked hard at it."

Who was this "insane" Pasternak? He was born on February 21, 1954, in New York City, and raised in Fleischmanns, a village in Delaware County in New York. It was said that during mid-century the permanent population of the village was around 500; but by the Fourth of July, there would be 10,000 in town. Fleischmanns High School, founded in 1928, struggled to operate with such limited enrollment and had to be consolidated with Margaretville's school in the fall of 1969.

Pasternak was the guy who as a first grader sold candy to his classmates at a profit; on his lunch hour, he would go down to the local grocery store and buy penny candy which he sold for a nickel to the other school kids. By the age of 12, he developed a thriving business in used bicycles. As a college student at the State University of New York at New Paltz, while classmates were staging widely reported sit-ins against perceived discriminatory hiring practices, he was buying cars in Canada at bargain-basement prices and selling them in the United States for profitable markups. This was the guy who always spoke fondly of his father, Heinz, and the inspiration he provided.

Heinz was a first generation immigrant who came from Austria. He never made more than $15,000 a year in his life until Pasternak became wealthy. He had at least five to ten different entrepreneurial endeavors during his lifetime. His projects ranged from buying real estate to various enterprises associated with the automotive industry, including a gas station, a towing business, and selling used cars. It was the paternal enterprise which led Pasternak to the used car business while in college; he eventually became a car dealer, buying and selling mostly Volkswagens.[2]

"My father is an Austrian national, so he has a Germanic, mid-European mentality, which is the mentality that the father is a breadwinner and the mother does most of the childrearing. So if you wanted to interact with the father, it had to be through business. I actually came out as a nine-year or a ten-year-old boy, and I don't know anyone who did that. My other siblings felt like my father ignored them, which he did by today's standards."

Pasternak's father would take his son to do business with him. They would go to upstate New York and buy used cars. "It was a way to interact with him, to get his attention. I always asked my father questions. I would not tell him that he was a jerk."

Pasternak would ask him, "Dad, you are buying these cars, but you are not keeping records, how would you know if you are making any profit?

He would say, "I have it in my brain."

Pasternak would reply, "I don't think you even know what your cost basis is."

Over time, Pasternak learned he could make bigger profits in a half year versus three years by selling to wholesale markets.

"So I said, 'Why don't we sell them overseas, but just take the brakes off, or not even keep the brakes or the interior? Certain parts have low yields, and we could sell them overseas, where there is a higher demand. Why don't we take them and sell them to overseas wholesale markets?' So we had these discussions. After a while, I convinced him that it was a shitty business. He never kept any books. Instead, I liked sports trivia, so I used to memorize the batting average of every baseball player; I liked to play around with numbers."

The most exciting part for young Pasternak was when his father let him go to auctions and talk to used car dealers. "They thought it was cute that a fifty-year-old brought his twelve-year-old kid. I used to do all the negotiating. And the guys thought it was neat that I was bargaining. I had a pretty good database on cars, so my father let me buy and sell cars. I bought a few at 12, but it really started at 14, 15. I was probably buying many of his cars. I was a tall kid, probably at 15, I looked 18. He would always encourage me to be entrepreneurial, and he was proud of me that I could buy a car. I had a better insight on what kind of cars you can sell for and how much you can sell for. It was a small market; we sold no more than 50 cars a year. Later on I went to college, which was a bigger market, and then it was wholesale; the gist of it was a lot of thought process on price formation and about buying things and selling things."

While Pasternak was attending the State University of New York in New Paltz, his father cut a deal with a local new car dealer back home in the small upstate New York town of Fleischmanns. Pasternak's father would buy the dealer's entire inventory of used cars and therefore get a special price; he could then put a low price tag on the cars to move them out the door.

Pasternak earned his undergraduate degree from New Paltz in 1976. One day, when Pasternak was home from college, he asked how much his father wanted for a Volkswagen parked in the corner of the used car lot. His father said $800 and Pasternak said, "I want to take that car to college. I'll give you the $800 the next time I come home from school." Once on campus, Pasternak sold the car for $1,400 to a fellow student.

The Volkswagen story was just a beginning. Pasternak discovered Canada as a source of car bargains. With a partner, he began bringing in run-down cars from "The Great White North" where he bought them for very little and then fixed them up. Soon his partner, his brother and sister and his cousins were going with him to Canada to drive bargain-bought cars across the border straight to a repair shop. Once repaired, Pasternak sold the cars at dealer auctions for $2,000 or more for cars that cost less than $1,000, repairs included. He went even further; he used records to track past sales data so that he could produce a model for car prices. It worked very well and he was making six figures in his early 20s. Pasternak would later write his senior thesis on car trading, where he talked about market inefficiencies. He ended up learning about NASDAQ and the stock market.

Pasternak stated that his experience with car trading forced him to learn about the markets, even before he knew anything about finance. Pasternak was an education major, so his proficiency in mathematics may have helped his understanding. After one semester, however, he had realized that he was not cut out for the teaching profession, and continued working in the car trading business. His experience there piqued his interest in market making. Meanwhile, his father was getting bored in his late 70s, so he started a car service. "I learned from his mistakes and I learned from some of his successes," said Pasternak.

Pasternak liked to refer to himself as from upstate New York. But for Hewitt, who was from the real upstate (North Syracuse), that came across as snobbish. "He was just from the Catskills! When I met him, he impressed me as being kind of a hillbilly. He was uncouth. He was an intelligent hillbilly but he was loud. He was willing to state an opinion, it wasn't great information, but he could at least state a principle. Because he was an upstate New York guy, I kind of liked him. He was definitely that type of person that comes from there. He was kind of a sloppy guy."

Hewitt admits that Pasternak found himself at the right place at the right time; he is not sure if Pasternak realized that. "They weren't driving towards becoming an internet broker. It just happened. He had no idea what that meant. It just happened and it happened just like that. And Ken was bright enough to be able to ride that momentum. So, I guess to come to a concise description, I thought he had a good upstate New York persona. He was intelligent enough. He had some insecurity though. He would always tell you that he got into Harvard University but he didn't want to go there since his father thought he was going to Poughkeepsie or something. That struck me as making a bad judgment call in terms of one's education. But ultimately, when you are riding a powerful idea, you just focus on riding it and he was good at riding it."

Pasternak never got into Harvard University, of course; instead, he became a celebrity alumnus at his local university. In 2007, the Pasternak Family Foundation provided a $100,000 lead gift to the State University of New York at New Paltz' School of Business for the Kenneth D. Pasternak Trading Room. The School of Business, which opened 24 years after he graduated, dedicated the room in October 2007. His civic involvement was not limited to the School of Business, to where he returns periodically to speak with students and share the secrets to his success. Pasternak also joined the New Paltz Foundation Board in 2006.

For a young man who was a second generation immigrant and a graduate of an only somewhat selective state school, to join a firm that was a market maker was a significant challenge. "I wanted to learn about markets, so I started to keep logs. I wanted to learn why markets were inefficient. There were no computers back then. I would take whatever data I had, and then compile it, and analyze it using, not Excel, but performing some of the functions that you would do on Excel. It would be less scientific. I started to think about why markets were inefficient. I started to think about price formation and how inefficient that was. Then I started to think about NASDAQ stock markets. Then I said 'Holy cow, why am I bothering with these stupid cars when I could be in the stock markets?'"

After graduating college in 1977, Pasternak's first stop was not the classroom but selling for Dictaphone, where he was predictably successful but far from satisfied. After six months at Dictaphone,

Pasternak was looking for a change and moved to Jersey City. Through mutual contacts, Pasternak met Lenny Walker, who was a vice president at Troster Singer.

"I pestered the guy. I met him a few times, and he wouldn't hire me. And then I kept pestering him. As I was dating this girl who lived in Rego Park, Queens, I would visit her taking the E train from the World Trade Center. Once, I saw Lenny sitting in the subway; he was visiting his father once a month in Forest Hills. So I sat next to him. He was a Jewish man, and later I learned that he wouldn't hire anyone who was not Jewish. He thought I was an Irish man. I told him I was Jewish and about my background trading cars. He told me to come in the next day, and he gave me a job. It was like serendipity."

Pasternak promptly accepted the job that he was offered at Troster Singer as a librarian getting paid 175 dollars a month; back then, a studio apartment was $500 per month; Pasternak was also working as a bartender on weekends, making $400. So overall, Pasternak was already making around $25,000 per year, typical starting salary for MBAs.

"One of the jobs there was memorizing quotes. A lot of the senior guys were 'quote boys' or 'quote girls,' and I wasn't even that. So I would come out at lunch time, and there was this girl who would always forget her quotes, so I would memorize her quotes. Lenny gave me her job after a week. And then I started doing other stuff, because I liked numbers. Six months later, Lenny went to his house in Florida. He got laryngitis, and he couldn't come in for a month, so I was trading for him. And I made a lot of money. I was making $100,000 in profits per month, much better than anybody expected."

Pasternak's next step was to lobby for a transfer to the trading department. When the managing partner pointed out that there were people in the company who still hadn't been made traders after 10 years, Pasternak let the managing partner know that he had mastered the trading business and could easily get a job elsewhere. The managing partner got the message, and promptly put Pasternak to the test. His first trading assignment was the company "dogs", the stocks no one else wanted to struggle with. Pasternak finished in the money in his first year. By 1987, he was a special limited partner at SLK, a manager in the trading room, and creator of one of Wall Street's first training programs. By 1991, he was "running the room" as director of the firm's trading operations.

During this time, the NASDAQ market was growing fast due to new technology. Online dissemination of quotes allowed for trading to grow by almost ten times in the late 1980s. Pasternak knew there wasn't enough automation in the trading room. The system was dependent on humans and human market making. Pasternak, at the time, was just a low-end executive.

Still, he remembers those days with great fondness. "When you disagreed on something, you could get away saying to your CEO: 'Hey, you are a jerk!'". At that time, everybody on the trading floor was "someone's cousin Vinny", meaning somebody who most probably didn't graduate from college and lived in Staten Island, as opposed to bigger firms where connections were determinant to get through the door.

Pasternak was persuaded that with the right training program traders could become as successful as him, so he convinced his CEO to let him hire people who showed ambition and stamina no matter where they were coming from.

One of the things that Pasternak did at the firm was to develop an aptitude test. The test emphasized the trader's analytical skills and the ability to visualize difficult concepts, articulate opportunistic ideas, solve tough problems and make fast decisions that were logical based on available information.

"For example, an individual may be posed with a situation in which his aunt gave him three quarters and five nickels and was asked what to buy with that. So the question would ignore half of the information it gave them. In the same way, the market gives you a lot of irrelevant information. So the ability to separate the information from the noise was very predictive for a good trader," said Pasternak, who produced the program with a Princeton professor at a time when running trading education was still considered revolutionary. Two nights a week there would be lectures from outside teachers.

Pasternak ended up bringing in really good traders to the firm. By implementing his training program he began to understand how to build teams and build technology. Pasternak remarked that he was a top producer himself. He would not ask other traders to do something he wouldn't do himself. Out of the 10 people in his initial class, Pasternak is proud to say that five of them became worth more than a hundred million dollars.

Steven Starker was one of the first people Pasternak hired as institutional sales trader and market maker in 1987 that went into the training program. Starker would later be appointed to the firm's executive committee and co-CEO of the capital markets division. Following the 2000 acquisition of SLK by Goldman Sachs, Starker spent three years as a partner in the Equity Trading division before setting out to found Bass Trading, a predecessor of BTIG, the trading firm he co-founded later in 2003. Throughout the years, Starker has been rumored in 2012 to be partnering with Kenny Dichter, Marquis Jet founder, Doug Ellin, the creator of HBO's "Entourage" and Brian Perkins, a former Johnson & Johnson executive, in a group that intended to bid for the Mets and later for the Yankees, if the Steinbrenner family decided to put the Bombers for sale. With a net worth of three or four hundred million dollars, according to Pasternak, Starker was in position to afford those luxuries in life.

A proud moment for Pasternak would await him at SLK. His co-worker Raquet would come to him with an idea that would change their lives forever.

Chapter Five

The Ascendance of Knight

Although Pasternak never showed lack of ambition (he doesn't hide that he always wanted to be the CEO of a public company and not of a small partnership), Knight's idea loomed only as an outgrowth of happenstance. Raquet, who came in 1992 to SLK as head of marketing and technology, approached Pasternak on developing a five-to-ten-year business plan over the course of a month to create a next-generation market maker.

SLK had started to provide automated execution order management and an execution system in 1988. Pasternak started to see the behavior of somebody who was empowered in real-time information and real-time trading strategy. That was the precursor of the self-directed investor, he thought. At that time, people would be paying a fee to call in for information. Pasternak's brother, who was a mathematician and programmer with a PhD in computer science, told him that those fees would go away because "there is a thing called internet". Pasternak thought that if everyone could get real-time information free then self-directed investors, supported by discount brokers and online stock purchasing, would become dominant and transform the securities industry. By the early 1990s, Pasternak and Raquet believed that traditional market makers were losing touch with the times.

A book called "Where Good Ideas Come From" concluded that innovations usually occur when ideas from different people "bump against each other" and spawn a winning combination. That certainly explains the dynamics of the interaction between Pasternak and Raquet; they both had an Ah-Hah! moment. Raquet was knowledgeable about what was happening at the level of decision makers, so his Ah-Hah! moment was to realize that small brokerage firms were not big enough to be market makers, they did not know about making markets, and needed a capital market strategy; some of them had bought market makers themselves, and the firms without one were at a disadvantage. Pasternak, on the other hand, was very knowledgeable about what was happening at the point of sale and had become convinced that technology and the internet were game-changers. The pair recognized that their point of views were complementary.

Raquet clearly understood capital markets and Pasternak had the required trading proficiency. Raquet used his connections to put together the roundtable, and Pasternak built the business in the back. Robert Greifeld, who was then with Automated Securities Clearance and later the CEO of NASDAQ, advised Pasternak in the effort to build a trading system with tremendous volume capabilities.

Greifeld's expertise impressed Pasternak so much that years later, as NASDAQ board member, he would suggest his appointment as CEO to succeed Harvard Business School MBA Hardwick "Wick" Simmons by the end of 2003. Pasternak, who never hid his disdain for MBA-type executives, justified his recommendation, "Simmons was basically incompetent, so we were looking for a new CEO after he was removed. They had a list of normal Wall Street operational guys. I thought NASDAQ had to be looked at as a technology utility type of company. I said that Wall Street guys don't understand technology; they think it's like a corporate monopoly, a monopolistic type of premise, both for destinations and for listings." On May 12, 2003, the board of directors of NASDAQ appointed Greifeld president, chief executive officer and member of the board. Simultaneously, Greifeld was relinquishing his seat on the board of Knight, the largest NASDAQ market maker.

"Walter had technology insights, and I had a trading background. We had a symbiotic skillset. Walter and I understood what the internet would do for self-investors. We actually wrote a business plan together to serve the discounters; it was rejected by Spear, Leeds & Kellogg," said Pasternak.

In hindsight, it was clear that volume would make all the difference in the world. "In 1994, Spear, Leeds & Kellogg did 5,000 trades a day, and in 2000, Knight did 500,000 trades a day, 100 times more. Walter and I had the insight that the internet would liberate self-directed investors and volumes would explode; so our hypothesis was correct. We also knew that there would be automation and economies of scale, and Spear, Leeds & Kellogg didn't understand that. We really tried to sell Spear, Leeds & Kellogg the idea, but it was rejected. They basically said: 'Why would we want to kill the golden goose?' Well, we said, you could get ahead of the curve or react to it."

"What happened five years later? We had $400 million dollars in revenues and Spear, Leeds & Kellogg had $50 million; Knight had a $6 billion dollar market cap, so you can come to your own conclusion," said Pasternak in his typical know-it-all tone.

Both founders credit the idea to create Knight to Lawrence Waterhouse, then Chairman of Waterhouse Securities, the fifth largest discount firm in the United States. After receiving his bachelor's degree from Villanova in 1959, Waterhouse had pursued graduate studies at New York University and served in the U.S. Marine Corps, reaching the rank of captain. He later worked for Reynolds Securities and also Chemical Bank, where he was a vice president. In 1979, he founded Waterhouse Investor Services, which was acquired by Toronto Dominion Bank in 1996, taking the name TD Waterhouse. Subsequently it was merged with another large discount brokerage firm, Ameritrade. It was known currently as TD Ameritrade in the United States and TD Waterhouse in Canada.

In November of 1993, Raquet was having breakfast with Waterhouse, president of Waterhouse Securities. He had just heard the news that Mayer & Schweitzer, a market maker in OTC securities that operated its own automated execution system, had been bought by Charles Schwab. Waterhouse was concerned that Charles Schwab would be able to offer impeccable execution while running a very profitable operation. Waterhouse asked Raquet if he could find a better market maker to buy.

Raquet understood that Waterhouse worried he would be missing out on profit opportunities by not owning its own market maker. Yet, his firm didn't have enough order flow to support a dedicated market-making operation.

That night, Raquet woke up at 3 A.M. and had the idea that if he could put five Waterhouses together he could have a great firm. He spent the next three hours putting a business plan together and called Larry at 7:30 A.M. and made an appointment for 5:00 P.M. the same day. He walked out of his office at 5:45 P.M. with a commitment for $5 million.

The next step for Raquet was to see if Pasternak would be interested. Raquet was nervous because if Pasternak ever told his boss, they would have been less than a footnote in history. Raquet spoke to Pasternak and in five minutes he got his commitment.

Pasternak had plenty of time to reflect on Raquet's drive to start the firm. "He's the kind of guy who cuts to the chase and then he has a eureka moment. 'If Ameritrade, ETrade and Waterhouse aren't big enough alone to partner with, then a group of them are big enough. Let's get a group of them together.' He thought he could get seven of these firms to invest in a joint venture."

Raquet and Pasternak decided to test the idea by convincing brokers to take a stake in the venture and founded Roundtable Partners. The idea for the name (and later for Knight) came from King Arthur's famed roundtable around which he and his knights congregated. As the name suggested, it had no head, implying that everyone who sat there had equal status.

Pasternak and Raquet made a simple but effective pitch to convince their future partners to take a stake in the venture. By sending their orders to the new market maker for execution, they would be compensated directly for order flow and indirectly by their ownership of the firm. It was a win-win for everybody. Surprisingly for them, instead of lining up seven partners, they signed up twenty seven firms, some of which were of the new online variety. These online operators, in the words of Institutional Investor, were "the rocket fuel for Knight's business."

At the time Knight was founded though, no one quite understood the ease in which the Internet would enable individuals to execute their trades online, said chief financial officer Robert Turner. "Some innovative firms had platforms to allow individuals to electronically trade but when Knight first started the concept of using the Internet to trade was in its infancy. Knight's broker dealer owners were innovators in low cost on-line trading and Knight was a beneficiary of that order flow and the internet boom in online trading. You could say we were lucky but I would say we were in the right place at the right time, with a great management team with innovative technology and that we knew how to deploy the technology in a quick and cost effective manner with an obsessive attention to detail and control. Both Kenny and Walter understood that technology was key to Knight's success."

Raquet would go on to gather more companies for the roundtable. "We were able to get Southwest Securities, Grunthal Financial, Ameritrade and Scottsdale to commit $10 million in a series of meetings that took about thirty minutes each. Over the next couple of months we lined up to ten additional investors."

One of those additional investors was ETrade. Initially, they made a $1.3 million capital commitment, equal to the firm's capital, but later lowered it to $500,000, still wanting to be part of it. They then had enough money to start their venture. Ameritrade was quickly sold too; "Kenny is one of the brightest guys I've ever met," said Michael Anderson, a vice president there. Raymond James also hopped on board and made a $5 million commitment. From a total of $14 million in investments, they required a 5 percent deposit from their investors. By the time they closed the deal, it had not even been a year.

Although Raquet was able to recruit many outstanding partners, there were some which eluded him. There was this one company he really wanted to bring on board, yet they wanted a special deal and that became very hard. This firm wanted Raquet to give them a little more interest to get into the deal. Raquet didn't break the trust the other partners had deposited on him. This firm was already a Trimark customer and later became their customer too. Every month, Raquet would send the president a letter of how much in profits he had missed. "If you had been a partner I would be sending you a check for this much money," Raquet would write. Sometimes, the check could have been $300,000-$400,000 a month; back in the 1990s that was a lot of money. This president couldn't take it anymore and ended up calling one of Raquet's partners pleading, "Please. Please. Don't have Walter write me those letters. It upsets me for days." I wrote him a letter the next month and said, "Write me a check."

As the key pillars of the project, Raquet considered Pasternak and the Trimark group. Trimark was one of Raquet's customers, which he was then making $80,000 a month from. Soon, Roundtable was looking to find another party that had a strategic advantage to fill out its business. It formed subsidiary Knight Securities to make markets for stocks listed on NASDAQ and the OTC Bulletin Board, and in 1995 acquired Trimark Securities which then served as market maker for the New York Stock Exchange and American Stock Exchange equities and whose biggest competitor was a firm called Bernard L. Madoff Investment Securities, which at one point was the largest market maker at the NASDAQ. Madoff would later be convicted of running a Ponzi scheme and arrested in December of 2008.

Steven Steinman had founded Trimark in 1986 to execute block trades involving securities firms and institutional investors, such as investment companies and pension funds. Trimark was the second largest third-market firm at the time and was doing 25,000 to 30,000 trades daily. Their market share was between 4 to 6 percent of the NYSE volume. Steinman and chief operating officer Robert Lazarowitz had decided to sell their firm to Roundtable Partners for no money down and a small minority interest because they believed that the new combined entity would be far greater. "Yes, that's a great idea. What a great way to grow, as you know your customers are your partners," they had said.

The way the roundtable worked was that the strategic partners who provided the order flow owned 60 percent. Pasternak, Raquet, Steinman and Lazarowitz each owned 10 percent of the company. The four had decided to split their shares evenly so that they did not spend time arguing about capitalization. Although Steinman and Lazarowitz hadn't brought in as much capital, they provided an existing business to the startup that was substantial and the connectivity to all of their customers. "That is very hard to get. It probably takes a year to a year and half to build a computer that links all the order flows. They were taking a big risk and we are trying to make it work," said Pasternak.

"Trimark already had the capability to trade any symbol at the NYSE. Equally important, they had connectivity to our potential customers. We only had to write a master interphase that allowed us to run in twenty four hours, while it had taken Trimark seven to eight years to create that connectivity. They were an undermanaged company. We could correctly say we knew that, as we were projecting $25 million in year one, following Walter's strategy. Just to give you an idea, they made $4 million when we took them over, and $30, $40 million in the first year they were part of Knight."

Roundtable Partners was formed on March of 1995. The New York Stock Exchange learned of the Trimark acquisition and feared Roundtable Partners could become too powerful. There was a rule on the books that said no NYSE member could own 24.99 percent of "third-market-maker" firms like Trimark. None of the members owned more than 9 percent of the partnership. No one was violating the rule. However, Dick Grasso, the NYSE head, evaluated them as a group and found they owned 40 percent of the new entity. Therefore, as a group, they violated the rule. The NYSE was its regulator, which made them very nervous. The people at Raymond James panicked and said, "I'm not going to attack my regulator who is Dick Grasso." They dropped out. The new venture was in a dilemma because of the NYSE rule. What Raquet did was to take the remaining money from their deposits and sue the NYSE.

Raquet engaged Harvey Pitt, who would later become the 26th chairman of the SEC, to present his case. Pitt was the senior corporate partner at Fried, Frank, Harris, Shriver & Jacobson. Pitt impressed Raquet as incredibly brilliant and was told what the issue with NYSE was about.

Pitt concluded that this was the most ridiculous and absurd abuse of power. "The NYSE is a monopoly," he thought.

Raquet and Pitt had a 45-minute meeting with Grasso. What Pitt did was basically to tell Grasso that he was violating every single rule and that it was a monopoly. Pitt told him that his firm had all funds committed to take this case to the Supreme Court on a contingency basis and that he would take apart the NYSE's monopoly unless he lets Roundtable go into business.

Grasso could only put up his hands and said, "I surrender. Let the boys go into business."

Raquet and the Knight people would forever remain indebted with gratitude to Pitt.

Pasternak's trading know-how and Raquet's contacts and knowledge of brokerage companies had moved the project ahead to high-speed, high-volume operation. Furthermore, keeping costs in line was also of importance, hence the decision to set up shop in Jersey City, where rent was much lower than on Wall Street. Even years later, the stained carpets had not been replaced, paper cups were still the norm (Pasternak's assistant said that he wouldn't let her buy glasses), and the only art on display were the scribbles done by Pasternak's kids and cherished by their bighearted father; once he had escaped work to buy a doll-house kit at the store formerly called Doll House too, a castle-like structure that hugged the edge of state Route 28 in the town of Kingston, New York, and assembled it for his daughter Sara. He had driven past the store countless times in his youth and as a college student; many years later, Pasternak would buy the quirky structure with grand retail plans that didn't pan out.[1]

Hewitt, who brought his assistant when he came from Goldman, laughs remembering that she promptly wanted to know where the dining rooms were at Knight.

Roundtable was able to close the deal with $17 million. They were to occupy 106,000 square feet of the building on 525 Washington Boulevard in Jersey City. It was there where future CFO Turner first interviewed with Raquet and Pasternak. "Kenny and Walter were in the process of trying to obtain a broker/dealer license from the NASD and the two of them were working in a tiny office using folding card tables as desks. Walter took me to the floor in the building that would become the trading floor. It was raw space and the construction of the trading floor was going to begin shortly. I was instantaneously sold on joining the company by his enthusiasm and charm. Kenny was charismatic and very warm. I knew it would be an adventure and that I would enjoy working with Walter and Kenny."

Raquet said that the process of launching the startup was nerve-wracking. "No one is able to appreciate the entrepreneurial aspect of it. Whenever I hear President Barack Obama criticize business people, he has no idea, he's never been in business, he's never held a real job, he's never held a job in the private sector, which is real life. He has no appreciation for what business people go through to create business: the risks they take, the capital they put on the line, the money they can lose, the stress, and the sacrifice. He has no clue."

More challenges awaited the firm that was set to start on July 17 with 75 employees. Just six days earlier, on July 11, Raquet was sitting down to have lunch on his birthday when he got a call from the NASDAQ relaying a decision that had been taken at one of their subcommittees. They had decided that because the new firm was going to make markets in 2,000 stocks, a special restriction had been put on $10 million of their capital, turning them unable to meet the minimum capital requirements to start operations. For all practical purposes, the subcommittee was putting the firm out of business before it even started. Needless to say, the committee that made this decision was full of their competitors, Mayer & Schweitzer included. Raquet told Pasternak about the call. "Kenny was visible upset and went home," he said.

Out of five top NASDAQ individuals, Raquet knew four of them pretty well. Raquet got them on the phone and threatened each one of them saying, "I will use every dollar I have, I will call every reporter I know, I will sue everybody and make your life miserable for the rest of your life unless you change this. How can you let our competitors put us out of business? This is America. This is not a communist country. You are putting us out of business before we start." That was on a Tuesday night. On Thursday morning Raquet got a call saying, "You have no restrictions."

Raquet's aggressive nature had saved Knight once more. His connections helped him overcome most of these initial obstacles. The company's founders started priding themselves on being a morally good company.

"Over the last 25 years I have worked for a number of firms and have studied what elements made the company successful and what diversions were destructive and hindered a firm reaching its full potential.

"Backstabbing, office politics, inability to delegate responsibility, personal agendas, greed, hunger for power – these are the qualities that prevent a firm from reaching its potential and make going to work unpleasant.

"Ken and I want to set Knight apart from our competitors by creating the kind of environment which rewards teamwork, mentoring, honesty, integrity. And allows each individual to maximize his or her potential by openly learning, not being embarrassed to ask questions."

Raquet also made it clear that his employees would know the extent of his reach in the market-making world. Raquet said, "While I was a partner at HHG, I helped build the largest correspondent network in the industry. My vision is that we will all work together to create an even larger correspondent network." To add to this point, Raquet predicted Knight would rise above the rest, berating Knight's competitors by citing specific examples:

"One of them is managed by 2 individuals who have a contest to see who can take the most vacation time.

"Another is managed by an individual who thought it would be OK to go into competition with his customers.

"Another is managed by 2 individuals who are at the end of their careers and the new management is turning it into a corporate bureaucracy.

"Another is managed by a highly successful individual but he wants to make all the decisions himself and will not delegate responsibility."

Raquet also wanted to demonstrate to the new Knight employees that the company was investing in the future. He and Pasternak had spent an incredible amount of time selecting their trainees. An advertisement in The New York Times for its trainee program had resulted in more than 500 resumes. After interviewing 50, they selected 10 for the trainee program. "Our trainees have great potential but to develop that potential is going to require that the more experienced traders participate in developing their raw talent. There is over 500 years of experience in this room, let's make a commitment to use it. We want everyone in this room to be successful and feel good about themselves and coming to work every day. By treating each other with respect we will succeed in making Knight a one of a kind place to work," said Raquet to his employees the day the firm started operations.

Starting a company from scratch was very challenging and incredibly exciting, remembers Turner with fondness. "The management and the employees were highly motivated to make the business a success. Virtually all of the employees that joined Knight on day one came from well-established competitors of Knight and had high paying jobs. The employees were attracted to Knight because they were entrepreneurial self-starters and wanted a situation where their compensation was based on how much they produced without caps and the usual office politics."

Initial trading at Knight was more than challenging and less than auspicious indeed. The first opening hours were a nightmarish catastrophe and traders lost hundreds of thousands of dollars getting used to constant changes implemented on-the-fly by developers. Knight started with 2000 stocks and should have started with many less.

By the end of the year, Roundtable was only the 88th largest market maker of the NASDAQ, but it was growing very quickly. In eighteen months, they shot up to number one out of 550 market makers. Raquet credits their success, among other factors, to their automatic execution; when an order came in, it was automatically executed and there was no delay. During the dot-com boom, in 1996, 99.3 percent of Knight's orderings were executed in less than a second. Their turnaround speed and pricing were right on meeting market needs. People tended to equate fast executions with trade quality which was beneficial for the firm.

Knight was basically saying yes to everything. The invariable results were that clients were pleased with the immediate execution of their orders; brokers were pleased too, as they had somebody running a service that they could rely on so they could focus their resources on selling in the market. Of course, it was great for Knight too, because even under the smallest of the spreads, their trading was extremely profitable.

They also put stop losses on all NASDAQ stocks, something that nobody had ever done before. Pasternak said, "Why not? The NYSE does it, then we can too." All the big firms would send their stop losses orders. At Waterhouse they were advertising stop losses; they didn't want to execute them so Knight did. Knight had the most robust computer systems, backing up twenty firms: Merrill Lynch, Fidelity, Mayer & Schweitzer, and more, adding up to 25 percent of NASDAQ's trades.

The biggest complaint in the NASDAQ market was that in the NYSE the opening price was visible before it opened. Knight translated this to the NASDAQ by their supreme confidence in their ability to predict prices. They guaranteed the opening prices of the NASDAQ market, which was something no one else had done and have not since. They guaranteed it to 2200 shares, which was a big seller. Firms would send Knight all their opening orders, enabling them to out-service the rest of the marketplace.

Knight at some moment reached 40 percent or 50 percent of all U.S. retail flow. Traders were using the inventory left over from automatic executions. Again, this flow wasn't aggressive, meaning it wasn't coming from the sharks of the industry; it was virgin flow coming from the newly empowered class of retail investors. Knight was capturing the spread and the brokers (its investors) had all the benefits brought by automatic execution. Plus, traders in the market-making department were generating quite a lot of money.

This was paradise for Knight's management, employees and investors. However, everything was changing by the turn of the century. Sophisticated and day-trading flow started growing dramatically and markets started going down coinciding with the bust of the bubble. A flow that had been a really nice flow became a really tough flow. Some firms had learned how to game Knight as well and make money off of Knight.

The spreads went down dramatically with decimalization. Back then, traders were able to get a lot of money by capturing spreads. When they were making markets in stocks with a minimum unit of trade up or down of an eighth of a dollar, traders bought instruments for a price that was at least eighth of a dollar less than the price at which they sold those instruments. Market makers could buy on an eighth and sell on a quarter and make an eighth, even if it was only a penny share! With decimalization, the minimum spread became one hundredth of a dollar, a penny! Since market making made money primarily from the spread between quotes, this change in regulation significantly reduced the profitability of their trades.

Pennies made traders' lives easier from the arithmetic standpoint as they didn't have to think the arithmetic too much. However, spreads got tighter as there was only a penny to gain. It changed the way traders operated. It created more opportunities for risk takers. It became worth it to take risks since there was a lot less spread capture.

The market was going down too. One of the biggest sources of revenue was the IPO industry; that revenue source just went out the window; for a period of time, it was dead.

Knight reached a market capitalization of $725 million in 1998, impressive compared with the $17 million they started with in March of 1995. In February 1999 Knight's market cap was around $2 billion. In 1999 they would reach $8 billion. Knight also experienced an impressive growth in the number of shares traded. In 1996 they did 11 billion, then 18 billion, then 38 billion, then 81 billion. Then on a single day, February 24, they did 877,000 trades with 810 million shares changing hands.

In April 1998, the firm incorporated Knight/Trimark Group in Delaware, a preliminary step to making a public offering of stock. But even as the company began to pitch its offering, it came under a cloud when it was revealed that Pasternak faced disciplinary action from the SEC from his days at Troster Singer, the result of a SEC probe into the conduct of NASDAQ market makers. The firm had been charged with colluding to keep spreads artificially wide. All told, 24 firms, including SLK, had faced antitrust charges and reached a $1 billion settlement with the Justice Department in 1996. But the SEC was continuing to look into the matter.

Knight had not been a target of the Justice Department investigation; instead, it benefited from the situation. Although Pasternak now faced a possible civil penalty and suspension from trading for a failure to adequately supervise the activities of some Troster Singer traders, he was never charged with any violation. Moreover, the suspicion did little to hinder Knight's initial public offering, which was not met with much institutional excitement but still managed to sell. It went public in July 1998, raising $145 million when the firm had around $500 million in revenue. At that point, Roundtable Partners became a wholly owned subsidiary of Knight/Trimark Group.

Knight experienced some pressure to go public because a lot of the original partners wanted to have an exchange price and a trading instrument. They all had balance sheet issues and different attitudes toward the stock. Pasternak pointed out four reasons why they moved ahead with the IPO. First, they wanted to equitize their employees and they needed stock options to do that. Second, they held the belief that as a public company with a multibillion dollar capitalization they could get institutional business into their product platform. Third, they wanted to launch new products and they ended up doing the acquisition of Arbitrade, which was very successful. And fourth, they wanted to go to Europe and miserably failed.

Ultimately, Pasternak thought the firm needed to make itself a public company to make its employees stick around and have valuable stock options, particularly to compete with competitors. Going public and becoming visible added legitimacy to a company. "You are a private company and you have a two hundred million balance sheet; two years later, you are public and have a billion dollar balance sheet; if you want to be block trader for top institutions, it's a pretty compelling story," Pasternak said.

Knight went public in July 1998, raising $145 million when the firm had around $500 million in revenue, at which point Roundtable Partners became a wholly owned subsidiary of Knight/Trimark Group. Robertson Stephens was the lead banker; the firm had been among the most active investment banks in the technology sector at the height of the internet boom. Robertson Stephens was among the "Four Horsemen" firms devoted to technology deals in Silicon Valley along with Hambrecht & Quist, Montgomery Securities and Alex. Brown & Sons. At the time of its closing in 2002, Robertson Stephens was the only one of the Four Horsemen remaining as an independent, operating firm in the aftermath of the bursting of the dot-com bubble.

Pasternak actually rejected Bear Sterns and Merrill Lynch's propositions as lead bankers because they wanted to sell the firm as a mere financial institution with a price-earnings ratio of ten. Instead, Robertson Stephens' Chris Bulger, global head of technology and services investment banking, wanted to sell Knight as an innovative growth stock that was worth of a price-earnings ratio of forty; that would have ultimately led Knight into becoming in the same league as CISCO or Dell. Thrilled by the prospects, Pasternak picked the West Coast banker.

Aside from shrewd moves, Roundtable was the beneficiary of good timing. According to Business News New Jersey, "The company's start meshed neatly with changes in the way NASDAQ operated. The SEC all but shut down a long-time income source for NASDAQ brokers in 1997 when it blocked them from setting artificially wide spreads between the selling and purchase prices of stocks. When that changed, NASDAQ's wholesale business became less fragmented as market makers like Knight stepped into a void the new regulations created."

Raquet considered Pasternak as one of the best traders in the business, and Pasternak recognized Raquet as the visionary guy. However, tensions always existed. Pasternak focused on the P&L, the practical measure of success or failure of traders, while Raquet focused on profits. "There was a good tension between my conservatism and practicality and his thinking out of the box and vision. But we always had a collegiality between us."

Pasternak pointed out that Raquet was always thinking about making acquisitions. For him, Raquet was always a very aggressive guy in business. Sometimes, Raquet would want to spend a lot of money to make a lot of acquisitions or hire people with very big guarantees. Raquet was always thinking about game-changing type of events, and Pasternak was more conservative. "The firm had a 100 percent compound growth rate and quickly we were ranked in the top five. My incrementalism was still pretty aggressive. It's always good for an organization to have someone who is pushing the envelope like that. Even though Walter was a co-founder, and in many ways the birther of the idea, the entrepreneurship relates to the CEO," said Pasternak.

For him, Raquet was very social and a natural marketer but not articulated enough to take the top post at the firm. By contrast, Pasternak was easy to speak to for partners and investors and proved especially adept with the media; in short time, Pasternak became the face of the company.

Raquet had always considered Pasternak the ideal partner in this venture. He said he wouldn't have started Knight without him. "Besides being one of the best traders, he is by far the best mentor in the business. Ken cares more about how successful his associates are than his own success."

Ultimately, Raquet believed that their success was a decision not a circumstance. "Ken and I would never have left our jobs if we wanted to open an ordinary OTC traders firm. From the very beginning we were convinced that if we assembled a group of highly talented traders and assistants, a top notch support staff, a large order flow and managed the firm imaginatively, we would be the largest and the best firm in the OTC marketplace."

Pasternak felt Raquet expected a higher visibility from the moment they founded the company. "There are people in very big companies who are not necessarily the CEO, yet they are recognizable, such as Steve Wozniak and Paul Allen, but that's very rare. I mean, typically even if you are a co-founder of a company, the CEO is the public face of the company. Raquet was disappointed that it worked out that way. He never was CEO of anything. He was always CFO or whatever number two person. Walter, like certain people, wanted power or fame, notoriety."

In typical Pasternak fashion, he recounted the discussions the founders were having when coming up with ownership shares. "Some of them were trying to jockey who had more worth over each other. Although everyone mentioned that I had more value than any of the three, I gave them the soup example; a person can supply the water, another, the pot, another, the fire, and another person, the spices, and that makes the soup. One could say the pot was more valuable, or the fire; but if you collaborate in making a soup, you kind of have to use an inappropriate metric to say you are all equal because you couldn't do it without each other. I very much recognized that that was not good for us. We were going to create a multibillion dollar company, we were all going to have adequate wealth, let's try to pull together. Let's not be upset because I am the CEO and you are the vice president."

The tensions didn't finish with the establishment of the roundtable; these just had started. There was an existential disagreement about the place Knight would ultimately have in history. Pasternak was betting that the company would go up forever and anybody who sold one share of the stock was not loyal; therefore, he didn't sell any of his shares. Friends think he held on to his stake even when the market turned against them. He made a lot of money nonetheless, yet he could have made more investing the proceedings on something else.

On the other hand, Raquet understood better than anybody else that Knight had been at the right place at the right time. He understood that in some way Knight got lucky, caught a wave at the beginning and was to make a lot of money for some time. Furthermore, without having a formal title, he was losing power and growing increasingly concerned with Pasternak's management, or lack thereof. He was the only major shareholder who understood that this was not going to be everlasting. "He did best because he understood that he got lucky," said a former employee.

Raquet was able to protect his shares through a collar. He would buy an equal amount of call options and put options for his Knight Capital's stock. This action would ensure that there was a floor and a ceiling of how much a stock could rise and fall in any given period. If the stock rose above the agreed upon call option price then Raquet would forgo the addition capital gains. However, if the stock fell below the agreed upon put option price, then his capital losses were limited to the value of the put options. Needless to say, Pasternak, whose diversification efforts went nowhere near Raquet's sophistication, went ballistic when he learned of the structure Raquet had put in place.

Ultimately, Raquet wouldn't feel comfortable working for the company he had co-founded. Pasternak didn't intend to stay after his contract expired at the end of 2001, yet, Raquet understood he wasn't in the short list for the top post. Feeling marginalized, he decided to leave and start anew a few years later with WR Group.

Raquet seemed to fulfill his ambition for notoriety upon his departure from Knight. He would often appear in pictures at New York and Palm Beach society magazines such as New York Social Diary, Westchester Look, Fairfield County Look, Panache Privee, PatrickMcMullan.com, attending benefits and parties.

There were only so many weekends in the summer and so many benefits that Raquet could go to. Still, he managed to be described as "shallow publicity hound" by the blog Greenwich Roundup, which suggested that he – and other socialites – should "grow a spin and say I like reading about myself in the Greenwich Post Column that everyone in town can't stand to read."[2]

Raquet was married to glamorous wife Nancy Shaw Raquet. She had been an executive with AT&T and General Instrument and later had founded Shaw Communications in 1982 (which became Interact), a strategic public relations consulting business specializing in executive speech writing, annual reports and communications strategies in support of Fortune 100 corporate clients. She had retired from her business in 2000 to devote her professional skills to charitable organizations, being on the boards of Greenwich Hospital and the Schepens Eye Research Institute (a Harvard affiliate) in Boston. In 2012, she accepted a position on the board of Couture Council associated with The Museum at the Fashion Institute of Technology in Manhattan.

Not only were his social appearances interesting, but also Raquet's real estate moves. Palm Beach Daily News would report in 2011 that the Raquets had sold a lakefront home with total living space, inside and out, measuring 18,286 square feet, for $19.51 million; they had paid a recorded $9 million for the property in 2003.[3] The Raquets also had a home in Greenwich, Connecticut.

Knight was riding high early in 1999. Hewitt couldn't hide his amazement when he joined the firm. Knight had gone from being a little startup and doing a little bit of business to all of a sudden being in the middle of the internet explosion. Suddenly, there were hundreds of thousands of orders a day and most of those orders were going to Knight. The traders were able to take out huge spreads on these orders.

They were making a lot of money, admits Hewitt. On the institutional side, the same thing, he added. Knight was providing the liquidity in more stocks than anyone else so the institutions would turn to Knight and the firm would make a lot of money taking advantage of the lack of transparency that existed in the marketplace and marking up the executions. The firm had a big opportunity in looking like it was way ahead of everyone else. Indeed, Hewitt claimed doing the 'show business' part of making people believe that they were indomitable. "We made it seem that it would only be soon that we would dominate 20-30 percent of the market share in Europe," he added.

"Knight was one of the fastest growing companies to ever list on NASDAQ. It was hard to believe that an upstart firm had at a point in time a market cap greater than Bear Stearns," said Turner. The stock market continued surging and suitors like Morgan Stanley and Lehman Brothers were approaching Pasternak about selling the firm. Lehman Brothers wanted to take a 20 percent stake in Knight; Pasternak balked at the offer. Following up on Paulson's mandate, Goldman Sachs came in too saying it wanted to engage in business with Knight; Goldman ended up camping in Jersey City with 15 to 20 of their top people, including A-team stars like Steven Mnuchin and Peter Kraus.

Mnuchin had been born to wealth and privilege. His father, Robert had retired as a general partner at Goldman Sachs and owned C&M Arts, an art gallery in New York. His mother, Elaine Terner Cooper, was a trustee of the Whitney Museum of American Art in

New York. After graduating from Yale in 1985, Mnuchin worked at Goldman Sachs for 17 years, serving as executive vice president, chief information officer and member of the Management Committee. He would leave in 2002 to work for Yale roommate, Eddie Lampert's hedge fund.[4]

Kraus had been named a partner at Goldman in 1994 and managing director in 1996. During his more than two decades with Goldman Sachs, this formidable deal-maker served as member of the management committee as well as co-head of the financial institutions group. He was co-chair of the Friends of the Carnegie International, a member of the board of directors of Lincoln Center for the Performing Arts and the chairman of Lincoln Center's Art Committee. He would later become chief executive officer of AllianceBernstein. He had earned an MBA from New York University and a bachelor's degree from Trinity College.

Did Knight have a bench as solid and impressive as Goldman's? Not even close. Their conversations went from doing collective ventures in Europe to outright acquisition. Goldman kept telling Hewitt, "John, you need to want to sell the company. We cannot engage with you without certainty that you want to sell the company."

Pasternak decided it was a good deal but he would like the title of co-head at Goldman Sachs. Hewitt told Pasternak that it wouldn't be a good idea since they were on a whole different playing field. He suggested asking for the title of vice chairman, an honorable title. Furthermore, Pasternak would have probably ended up as global head of equities. Pasternak was closed, Goldman Sachs co-head with Paulson or no deal. Was he dreaming or trying to stop an obligatory due diligence prior to any deal? If the deal had occurred, that would have been a powerful market maker; it would have given Goldman the trading platform it was looking for.

Hewitt believed that Pasternak was convinced Knight would have never passed Goldman's in-depth due diligence. Was Pasternak afraid that Goldman would have realized and made public that the end of the good times was close? Or did he really think front running was the fuel behind the firm's money machine? That would have been a deal killer for any proposal.

Ultimately, Pasternak downplayed how advanced these conversations were. "We had four or five overtures. I would say Goldman had a really low overture. Goldman had a few lunches with us and that was about it. I think they were trying to pick our brain. They were scared that we had connectivity to the public and the public was in control, particularly with new issues. That somehow changed capital markets with the internet and players like us so they were trying to understand the space and trying to conserve their relevance."

Pasternak argued that Goldman was initially not ready to pay $4 or $5 billion; Herzog, Heine & Geduld was to be acquired in 2000 by Merrill Lynch, so Knight was one of few players left in the wholesale market. Merrill Lynch indeed shelled out $914 million for Herzog, Heine & Geduld in a transaction led by its top electronic trading executive and future Knight's chief executive officer, Thomas Joyce.

Goldman would end up shelling out $6 billion for Spear, Leeds & Kellogg, a deal that was called by Forbes a "billion-dollar blunder." Why? The acquired operations were to be hit by the collapse of trading revenue, compression of spreads and regulatory investigations into whether the industry had been wrongfully profiting from customer orders.[5] At that moment, to say that Goldman was not ready to pay those billions for Knight would have been the understatement of the century.

Some of the directors found out about these conversations and were not laughing, including Joe Ricketts, the entrepreneur who created Ameritrade. Ricketts immediately resigned saying it was unprofessional and unethical not bringing Goldman's initiative to the board. Raquet thought that none of these conversations had gone far enough to be put to the board's consideration.

David Shpilberg, who would later join as chief operating officer, reflected that the company missed huge opportunities that were making themselves available. Knight was a well-capitalized company with no debt, he said. The company could have expanded, acquired, and taken over a lot of other companies (what Raquet was pushing for) or could have merged with several investment banks that were very interested in making a deal (Goldman Sachs). He blames missing those opportunities on unrealistic visions by Pasternak, who would always insist on receiving a top post; invariably, the deals fell through.

"I doubt he made all these decisions by himself; he convinced the board to always rely on his judgment; 'you got to trust me.'" Soon later the company began to go south, and down south.

For a while, Pasternak could afford to be demanding, given Knight's strong growth. It was now the NASDAQ's top market maker, a meteoritic rise achieved in just five years. According to a Fortune magazine profile published in September 1999, Knight executed some 40 percent of all online trades and controlled almost one-fifth of the trading in NASDAQ/OTC stocks. That was more than Merrill Lynch, Morgan Stanley Dean Witter, Goldman Sachs, and Salomon Smith Barney combined, and almost twice as much as the number two firm, Charles Schwab. Ranked by volume in U.S. equities, Knight/Trimark was five and a half times bigger than the American Stock Exchange.[6] Unfortunately, that wouldn't last long.

Chapter Six

Knight in Free Fall

By May 1999, when Knight's stock made a 2-for-1 split, Pasternak's stake in the company was worth about $610 million. At that time, the market was going into a very bullish mode and there were stocks trading at $100 that would later collapse (with the exception of five or six that were on the path to prove their viability such as Amazon). Knight did a secondary offering at the height of 1999 with the stock at $43 and less than 3 months later the stock was trading at $161. That was probably the height of competitors ETrade and Ameritrade as well.

That fall, Pasternak was planning to take Knight out of the shadows with a $10 million national advertising campaign that aimed to convince ordinary investors of the value of doing business with Knight, sort of an "Intel Inside" model. The little known firm looked this way to upgrade its image: it hired Omnicom Group's specialist in financial advertising to put together the firm's campaign.

In addition, Pasternak wanted to beef up his executive talent pool to prepare for expansion. He decided to hire John Hewitt, a Goldman Sachs vice president in the electronic trading group, as president of the Knight Securities unit. Hewitt was expected to help the firm become involved in other kinds of securities, including options, as well as to spearhead international expansion.

Hewitt expected to leave a mark at Knight.[1] He recalls, "I had built businesses from scratch at Goldman Sachs; I knew everything from finding the building to hiring people. Building infrastructure and support was important. We had some great people there. When you wanted to build a business, you took a couple of athletes who were Goldman Sachs people and understood how Goldman Sachs worked. They would be terrific and capable of building the business. Knight did not have any of these people. They lacked these individuals and they also lacked anyone with international experience. The chief financial officer did not even have a passport!"

At the time, even by the inflated standards of high finance, Wall Street was overflowing with holiday cheer, setting aside $13 billion to pay bonuses 20 percent more than the prior year. Yet many Wall Streeters were leaving to join online startups, technology companies and venture capital firms, the pillars of the new economy, where they sometimes took home more than their old bosses from day one.

Hewitt, who had long expected to retire as a Goldman Sachs employee, was getting enticed to change paths. "All the Wall Street firms, Goldman Sachs included, have become so successful that they have a vested interest in the status quo," Hewitt said. "The more I thought about it, the more I felt I had to go somewhere that had a sense of speed and that wasn't afraid of the future."

Hewitt had dinner with Pasternak who told him Knight needed to hire someone from Morgan Stanley or Merrill Lynch because they got the business to a certain level but it was still really ragtag. Pasternak said they needed to add to the professionalism and creditability of the firm.

"Why don't you hire someone from Goldman Sachs?," asked Hewitt coyly.

"Would you come over?" replied Pasternak.

"I would love to do it," was Hewitt's response.

Pasternak promised to call the search off and gave him an offer on the spot.

By that time, Hewitt had some really dreadful stuff going on with his personal life. After a 30-year marriage, his wife had decided that she wanted a divorce. There was mental illness involved and also children. It was just the most challenging moment in his life. Even though he was doing fabulous at Goldman, Hewitt felt like he had to clear the deck and do something different since it was so painful for him. From the time he had the dinner with Pasternak, it would take him only a few weeks to accept.

Hewitt had been exposed before to working with startups. For him, startups were all interesting and "almost cute", yet he felt it would always be just a matter of time before Goldman Sachs would be able to disrupt any of their business models or figure all out. He knew the Goldman Sachs approach was so simple yet so powerful. You just get really smart people. You make them work in team formation. Ultimately, if you are patient and you think really big, you will get there. "So I was trying in a sense to build a Knight inside Goldman Sachs, in terms of the transformation of the trading model. It was more of should I stay at Goldman and try to build it or should I just go and take it forward, take that model forward at Knight. And, truth be known, it was because of personal reasons that I decided to go to Knight."

Hewitt was coming on board with a tremendous recommendation from Robert Rubin, the former Goldman Sachs' co-chairman and co-senior partner along with Stephen Friedman, and future Secretary of the Treasure. It couldn't have been any other way. When Hewitt became vice president and later senior vice president at the New York Stock Exchange, he was the youngest officer to achieve such rank while at the exchange.

Hewitt had been born in North Syracuse, upstate New York, as the oldest of six kids. "I was a pretty smart kid and then I was a good athlete". He got married early at 18 after receiving an undergraduate degree from the University of Rochester in Political Science. Being a basketball player, he did some work in the inner city, running the basketball program for mostly black and Spanish kids. He later obtained a JD from Boston University School of Law and a LLM degree in Corporate Law from New York University. While at school, Hewitt wrote a paper that suggested commodities would become popular financial instruments. That led him to a job at the New York Stock Exchange in 1978, as they were trying to build a futures exchange.

Hewitt quickly moved up to become an executive assistant to John Phelan, who was about to become president and then chairman of the stock exchange. "The only other person who rivaled me in terms of time spent with Phelan was Dick Grasso," said Hewitt. Phelan was the NYSE chairman who introduced computer technology to the Big Board in the 1980s and was widely praised for his calming response to the stock market crash of October 1987. In a message to Phelan several days after the crash, President Ronald Reagan praised the functioning of the exchange during the panic. Phelan read the message aloud to his staff from the podium overlooking the trading floor, "The calm, professional manner of dedicated men and women striving to meet unprecedented challenges undoubtedly helped assure investors of the soundness of the institution." Phelan passed away exactly three days after Knight's trading fiasco at age 81.[2]

Hewitt stayed at the exchange for eight years; one of the great benefits of working with Phelan was that he got to know everyone within the financial world. "That may sound like an exaggeration but it really wasn't," said Hewitt. One of the people that Hewitt worked with was Rubin; back then, he was chairman of the exchange's quality markets committee. With his endorsement, Hewitt moved to Goldman Sachs in 1986, where he became the administrative officer for the Equities Trading Division led by Robert Mnuchin and Rubin.

"I helped merge the two divisions, sales and trading. I had responsibilities for the financial stuff, technology stuff, people stuff, planning stuff. I was the chief of staff at the internationalization of Goldman Sachs's equities world. I did a variety of things. Almost everything I did had some element of technology associated with it, some element of global exposure, and there was always a big investment behind, which is the nature of Goldman Sachs, the big component."

At one meeting with his boss, Hewitt was asked:

"What would make the most money in the world?"

"I know the answer. It's Japan, and it is going to involve technology," he said.

"You know what, that sounds right. Go do it," his boss replied.

Hewitt said that was part of the glory of Goldman Sachs. "Within a month, we had 70 people on the way to Japan to build a trading platform and to do everything associated with baskets and futures trades. We ended up being able to do in 20 seconds what it took them over 30 minutes to do, which meant the Japanese firms couldn't compete. Up to that point in time, Goldman Sachs thought it would never make any money in Japan, it just seemed too hard. But we started making a lot of money after that."

In his 14 years spent at Goldman Sachs, Hewitt was involved in building businesses that included NASDAQ, derivatives, Japanese warrants, European warrants, a Swiss private bank and, more importantly, electronic trading. He was also given key roles in the international expansion of Goldman Sachs and the coordination of business development and infrastructure.

Hewitt ended up writing a business plan that said the firm had to change their business model. Goldman's equities world was founded on the principle that the firm would forever get six cents and a quarter a share in each trade. In fact, if the firm could have held the line at a penny, it should have signed immediately, but Hewitt knew they wouldn't have been able to hold the line at the penny. Instead of doing a few transactions with big volumes, Hewitt argued they need to do a lot of trades and build a business mode that was viable with small spreads. Goldman Sachs had to become way more proprietary. "After a lot of hooting and howling, it turned out that my bosses thought we ought to give that a go," remembers Hewitt proudly.

So he and his boss Duncan Niederauer, the future NYSE chief executive officer, were put into something called the electronic trading unit, which was just the two of them. "We built the unit at Goldman Sachs and as part of that we did a significant number of deals. I guess my thesis was instead of trying to figure it all out ourselves, we should jump in the pool and form partnerships and get involved with other people because we had so much to learn."

By 2000, Goldman's involvement in two dozen new electronic trading ventures was putting it at the center of a new financial world; the bank was on the way by year's end to have spent $5 billion in five years on technology, building an arsenal aimed at making money whichever direction the market went.[3]

That same year, Goldman would spend $1.6 billion on technology, more than the combined revenue of Yahoo, Ebay and E-Trade, the high-flyers of the time. Goldman staffers were plugged in to 20,300 PCs and workstations, backed by 80 trillion bytes (80 terabytes) of storage. Some 18,000 miles of cable and 30,000 phone lines snaked through its New York headquarters, linked to offices around the world by a fiber network that could zap data at 6.1 gigabits per second.

A derivatives trader in New York had up to 180 phone lines at his desk. He was able to access a world of information from four flat-panel screens, tracking stock and options prices, spreadsheets on implied volatilities, newsfeeds from Reuters, Bloomberg, Bridge and more. Trading tools provided a break down, in real time, of the positions of a single trader, his or her team and the entire firm.

Behind this momentous push was chairman and chief executive Hank Paulson himself. Driving this huge investment in hardware, software and communications links was his belief that technology would fundamentally change the way securities were traded and drastically increase the variety of what was traded. Electronic links between buyers and sellers would squeeze the last penny out of transaction costs. Prices would be visible to everyone, and millions of individuals would be able to trade almost any instrument, anywhere.

Trading accounted for 36 percent of Goldman's $13 billion in annual revenue, and that revenue wouldn't go away. Goldman's floor trading apparatus cost the firm almost $100 million a year, much of which could have been eliminated if the technology was good enough. In essence, Goldman Sachs was in a race to exploit the technology that otherwise might destroy it. The firm upgraded its Internet trading systems every month or so. It held stakes in six electronic trading upstarts, even though they were reviled by the stock exchanges themselves.

It was Hewitt who was leading these efforts. He became involved in innovations in the options markets, including the building of the International Securities Exchange. He was also very involved in market structure innovations at the NYSE and NASDAQ, including the creation of ECNs, in particular Archipelago. Hewitt was known as "Spock" within the Archipelago team, due to his mysterious resemblance to the brainy Vulcan on Star Trek.[4]

Hewitt and Jerry Putnam, the founder of Archipelago, met once, hit it off and became friends forever. Like Hewitt and only a few others, Putnam had spent the time to go through the three hundred pages of new regulatory sleep aid called Order Handling Rules, released by the SEC on 1997, which amended the Quote Rule and introduced the Limit Order Display Rule.

The SEC's Limit Order Display Rule required market makers to display customer limit orders that were priced better than a market maker's quote, or add to the size associated with a market maker's quote when the market maker was at the best price in the market. The rule gave investors the ability to directly advertise their trading interest to the marketplace, enabling them to trade inside the current bid-ask spread and thereby compete with market-maker quotations and narrow the size of the bid-ask spread.

The amended Quote Rule required market makers to display in its quote any better priced orders that it placed into an ECN. Alternatively, instead of updating its quote to reflect better priced orders entered into an ECN, a market maker may have complied with the display requirements of the ECN Rule through the ECN itself, provided the ECN ensured that the best priced orders entered by market makers into the ECN were included in the public quotation, and provided "equivalent" access to the ECN for brokers and dealers that didn't subscribe to the ECN, so that those brokers and dealers may have traded with orders entered into the ECN.

This legal mambo-jambo was anything but ridiculous. The rules set the stage for the future impressive growth of ECNs and the even more impressive interest taken by all financial players big and small.

Goldman Sachs was one of those players salivating for a way to buy a ticket for the party. Archipelago was set to become an innovator in the ECN space but, not surprisingly, it had no money. Somehow Goldman Sachs enjoyed access to limitless barrels of green paper, so it didn't take much for Hewitt to persuade the firm to invest $10 million. A deal was sealed in Chicago with a handshake.

The deal between two gentlemen was unbeknownst to Christos Cotsakos, ETrade's chief executive officer, who was already swarming through the ECN landscape and focusing on Archipelago; he had gone as far as to start bragging that a deal with his firm was just around the block; when he learned that Goldman Sachs had already made a move, he simply flipped out. He persuaded shareholder Bill Lupien, a former Pacific Stock Exchange specialist and Instinet CEO, to offer Putnam a check for $100 million for his company. Putnam politely declined. Putnam, the man who had hit dead end after dead end in his career for decades, had declined a $100 million deal because of the hand shake.

Hewitt was impressed and worried at the same time. He persuaded his team to up the ante and offered Putnam $25 million for a stake in his firm. Furthermore, he invited ETrade to invest $25 million as well. Under the agreement, Goldman Sachs and ETrade, as well as founding partners Putnam's Virago Enterprises and Townsend Analytics, would each own one-quarter of the voting interest in Archipelago.

The all-electronic financial marketplace would later merge with the NYSE under the name NYSE ARCA, and complete its initial public offering in 2006. When Archipelago went public, Paulson said investing in the firm had been the most important deal Goldman Sachs ever did because of what it meant to the U.S. capital markets.

Among the other things that Hewitt got involved in along the way was a deal with Merrill Lynch, Morgan Stanley, and Knight Securities to invest in ECN startup BRUT. That's where Hewitt met Pasternak, as both were always attending meetings to discuss strategy. "I knew the Knight model. And took advantage of being on the board of BRUT to get to know him better, to get to know more about Knight," said Hewitt.

Once at Knight, Hewitt held meetings with the most senior employees; he realized that traders were driving the business. Consequently, the firm displayed a wild, unorganized, cowboy culture, light-years different than the more structured Goldman Sachs. "They were woeful," he concluded. There was a well-respected consultant called Reid Whittle, who had been brought in to the exchange by Rubin from Goldman Sachs, and was very involved with organizational and people analysis. Whittle had set up the evaluation system there, reusing the system from Goldman Sachs.

Hewitt called him, "I need your help."

"How many people do you have in what you consider your team?' he replied.

"Let's say 15."

"Well, how many of them do you think need to be replaced?"

Hewitt said, "15."

Whittle just laughed. "Come on. That can't be."

Whittle took two months, interviewed everyone, and then came back to Hewitt.

"Holy smokes. You were right. This is a disaster."

Pasternak and Hewitt had agreed that Hewitt would drive the technology. "At that time, Knight was pretty much breaking down, almost daily; there would routinely be one or two breakdowns a week where they had to redirect customer order flow to someone else. It wasn't that the infrastructure was defective; it was that process discipline didn't exist. So, you would have people trying to put in new software in the middle of the day. It was that much of a drama."

Hewitt brought in 1999 another Goldman alumnus, Diego Baez, who had been responsible for developing the firm's proprietary trading software. Baez graduated from the University of Houston in 1988. He worked as a consultant for almost a decade for firms as diverse as Banco Bamerindus (Brasil), Lehman Brothers, Unix System Laboratories and IBM Speech Recognition Lab. He would later move to Goldman when he got to know about Knight. Why was he interested in Knight? "Goldman Sachs was doing about 50,000 trades a day. Whenever trades would go up to 60,000, everything would break, whereas Knight was already doing half a million trades a day."

Hewitt asked Baez to understand the models in the electronic market-making group and explain to him the unifying logic behind them.

Baez came back and said, "It doesn't exist. Everyone has their own way of doing things."

Upon further review, Baez concluded that Knight's technology was top-notch in some areas and not up to par in others. On the backend, which was basically trading and operations, it was just fine, he concluded.

Based on his experience at Goldman Sachs, Baez focused on how to make money out of the flow. He developed a number of algorithms that took advantage of the benign flow coming from retail investors. Baez would look at the P&L on a daily basis and load the information into a data warehouse; he would look at the data and figure out which clients were making money, which clients were losing money and which types of order flows were good or bad; he would then tweak the mechanisms that were used for executions so that the firm could make more and more money. In no time, Baez hired about 45 people at Knight. "I hired a fabulous team from everywhere. I think I had people from Goldman, Merrill Lynch, from hedge funds. It was a fast expansion as well."

Hewitt was determined to put some order in the technology organization. He discovered that people just didn't bother testing. "Shpilberg was the one that ultimately made the Knight technology platform work and I must say: if David and I had stayed, the Knight story would be vastly different. The firm would have never had a technology meltdown."

Shpilberg had joined the firm in April 2000. He had received a Civil Engineering degree from Peru's best university, Universidad Nacional de Ingeniería, and later went on to earn a master' degree in aeronautics and astronautics, and later another one in operations research. He finally obtained a PhD in Management Science at the Massachusetts Institute of Technology.

Hewitt had worked with Shpilberg at Goldman Sachs, where Shpilberg was the global CIO of equities and asset management. There, Shpilberg developed and implemented real-time equities and derivatives trading systems that operated on three continents and improved the productivity of the sales and trading teams, enabling more profitable strategies to be pursued systematically through algorithmic automation. After Goldman, he had gone on to become vice-chairman and global head of IT consulting services at Ernst &

Young, the highest-paid partner, where he drove the rapid growth of its multi-billion dollar information technology consulting, system integration and outsourcing capabilities worldwide, advising some of the largest clients of the firm on IT strategy and outsourcing.

Shpilberg had been doing some consulting for Knight while he was still at Goldman Sachs. He discovered Knight's technology had just outgrown its capacity and needed a lot of significant changes and improvements. "At times, we controlled almost a third of the trades on NASDAQ at any given time, so we increased the capacity tenfold. It was a very large operation already."

Shpilberg thought Knight was becoming a larger and larger enterprise and needed more structure and organization. "I was there for a bit less than a year and a half. I would say the first half was euphoria and growth and expansion." Unfortunately, the second half exhibited Knight already in a tightening mood, as the company was losing some of its mojo.

Shpilberg reasoned, at the time, that Pasternak was looking for and welcoming structure and increased technological capabilities. He thought the existing infrastructure had exceeded the capacity of what a business could do, and that they needed to add new talent to build the next-generation environments and help with their expansion in the nearest states and globally. "We first started utilizing what we had and started expanding in capacity, and then beginning to look at business opportunities from better uses of technology."

One of Shpilberg's priorities was to improve the productivity of the sales and trading teams by using more automation. The plan was to eventually go from a few hundred traders to tens of them, a reduction of 70 or 80 percent which would make the remaining traders more analytical and wiser. Shpilberg argued that this was the approach of the future; nobody would enter trades directly, as whatever information traders were seeing on the computer screen had already been entered somewhere else.

"So the computers have to be making the real-time decisions; you just have to set the right rules and right strategy for it and have the computers made the decisions," he added. His plans, going against the culture and the personal interest of some of the old-timers who were very close to Pasternak, were derailed.

Turner reflected on the backlash. "The speed of change along with the decrease in the company's profitability, which directly affected the pay of many trading and sales employees, was naturally difficult coming off of the success we had enjoyed. The addition of new managers with different ideas as to how best to transition the company was in stark contrast to a company that had had a paternalistic and entrepreneurial feel. The transition to a more corporate environment was not what many employees had signed up for."

Another area Pasternak asked Hewitt to focus on was international expansion, and by that Knight meant the old continent. As soon as his second day, Hewitt was requested by Pasternak to research the Easdaq Stock Market, a European version of the NASDAQ based in Belgium. It turned out that Easdaq (an acronym for European Association of Securities Dealers Automated Quotation) had been created with high-level sponsorship by venture capitalists who needed a platform so that they could take their startup companies public.

Pasternak wanted to take a majority stake in the European exchange or buy it completely and then use it as a platform to enable Knight Securities' trading business model throughout the continent. Given the whole construct of the European Union, if you could do business in one country, you could do business in all countries. This was because Europe was so splintered in terms of marketplaces like the London Exchange with the U.K. stocks, French exchanges and Spanish exchanges; the goal was to do all of this in one platform electronically at low-cost execution. Costs in Europe were wildly high especially for clearance and settlement. So that was just a huge opportunity, Hewitt agreed.

"So it took me the rest of the week and I pretty much bought an exchange in Europe. After that, I started going to Europe pretty much every week for over the next year; I would fly out on Sunday night and come back on Friday, just to spend the weekends with my children."

Pasternak had insinuated he would be eager to cooperate on building the trading business in Europe. Hewitt recalls, "We went over it a couple of times and it was simply that Ken was not a traveler. During international trips you do not sleep. Ken did not live up to it. It was a big mess. We also had a disagreement as to how to build a business. Ken's an idealist. We had a few guys already there engaged in small institutional orders. Ken wanted to put a small trading business together. It could be an automatic exchange. I told Ken what had worked once upon a time in Jersey City would not work again in Europe. The element of surprise was gone. Goldman Sachs, Merrill Lynch, everyone was trying to figure out the electronic trading business."

Pasternak became very critical of his newly appointed president. "Hewitt brought this detrimental behavior to Knight. I fired him later, two years later. He tried to destroy the firm. He spent his energy trying to create power structures and destroying enemies and no energy trying to build businesses. It was shocking but Bob gave him a tremendous reference. I met him because at the time there were a lot of JVs around at the exchanges, so the exchanges were losing market share and there were ECNs and various things. At Goldman, he was in charge of their electronic strategy, so he did, I don't know if you remember, but they actually bought into a company that tried to do capital market deals on the net. Eventually its founder and Hewitt became partners."

Pasternak was referring to Wit Capital, a firm founded by Andrew Klein, a former lawyer who had created a stir in 1995 by bringing Spring Street Brewing public over the Web. Their success raising almost $2 million led to the creation of closely held Wit, a company that originally tried to set up its own electronic trading system but met with initial resistance from securities regulators. Wit then began focusing on providing shares of initial public stock offerings underwritten by other investment banks to its small base of 17,500 brokerage customers.

It was then that Goldman decided to acquire a 22 percent stake of Wit for about $25 million. As Goldman was planning to go public in the next few weeks, firm officials wanted to use their online strategy buying Wit as a selling point to institutional investors interested in buying shares of Goldman.

Pasternak harbored dreams of convincing mutual funds, pension plans, and other large institutional investors to trade through Knight. Pasternak's grand plan was that people all over the world would soon know his firm because everyone, from the smallest of small investors to the biggest of big institutions, would trade every type of security imaginable through Knight.

But it wouldn't be easy, McLean concluded. "Some traders say that Knight is unwilling to commit the big sums of capital needed to trade with institutions. Unlike the Goldmans of the world, which will take a loss on trades to curry favor with big clients and win other business, Knight doesn't have any other businesses. And institutions need to do business with the big firms in order to get research and access to products like IPOs."

In some respects, however, Knight's ambition was borne out of necessity. Its core business was coming under pressure from new computerized trading technologies, in particular electronic communications networks, which had the potential to diminish the need for market makers. ECNs did not buy stocks, but merely coordinated buy and sell orders electronically for a fee. They were more matchmakers than market makers, but they were still very much a threat to Knight's business.

For McLean, the risk for Knight wasn't just that ECNs existed, but that its founders, the online brokers that made it so powerful, might switch their loyalties quickly. Like everyone else, online brokers were tripping over themselves to throw money at ECNs. Waterhouse had invested $25 million in Island ECN; ETrade surprised Knight by taking a 25 percent stake in another ECN, Archipelago. Since Knight's IPO, its original investors had cut their ownership from 43 percent in aggregate to around 30 percent. Upon its offering, Knight stopped sharing its profits with them, and in the year before, as spreads had collapsed, its payment for order flow had shrunk too.

All of this meant that Knight's original partners, on whom it still depended for some 40 percent of its volume, had less to gain from sending trades to Knight and more from sending trades to their ECNs. Most ECNs were still too small to execute all that volume. Yet, it didn't take a long time for ECNs, which initially catered to the most sophisticated traders, to realize that they needed to go after the retail investors too, those who traded through the Ameritrades of the world.

Matthew Andresen, one of the business development wizzes behind Island ECN, took this revelation to heart. Andresen had received his combat training at Duke University, where he was an All-American fencer. What drew him to New York in 1993 was a desire to further sharpen his edge, as top American fencers had done for decades, by training at the New York Athletic Club. Like many before him, Andresen, an Olympic alternate in 1996, turned to a trading job on Wall Street to keep him in food and foils. After stints serving coffee at Lehman Brothers and day trading, Andresen joined Island ECN in early 1998.[5] Andresen would later lead Citadel Execution Services (CES) and found Headlands Technologies, a market-making firm based in Chicago and San Francisco.

Andresen reached out to Christopher Nagy, head of trading for Ameritrade. Nagy had joined Ameritrade in 1999 as a trading manager responsible for day-to-day operations and would go on to spend 12 years at the firm. During his tenure, he became very vocal on equity market structure and regulatory issues, speaking on behalf of his retail investor client base. Prior to that, Nagy had been vice president of trading at U.S. Bancorp Piper Jaffray and served as an off-floor vice chairman of the Philadelphia Stock Exchange from August 1999 to August 2004. He would later create the consulting firm KOR Trading. KOR stood for "King of Retail", and seemed to make a reference to a Traders Magazine cover story in 2010, in which Nagy was called "The Retail King".[6]

Andresen wanted the firm to start routing some of its unsophisticated flow to Island. It was a hard sell. Ameritrade had a deal to send most of its orders to Knight, which in turn, paid Ameritrade for the orders, promising to provide good execution. As Island ECN didn't want to get into payment for order flow arrangements, there was nothing the small firm could offer to Ameritrade other than fast execution. For Nagy, that was not enough. But Knight, better than anyone, should have known that overnight the small can become big; Knight's value proposition could have decreased and the ECNs value proposition could have only grown over time.

In order to fend off any potential advances in this front, Knight invested in a small ECN called the BRASS Utility (BRUT), owned by Automated Securities Clearance. Pasternak believed that a consolidation of the ECNs would ultimately benefit investors seeking to execute limit orders by becoming complementary, not competitive, with Knight. Was this just wishful thinking? Only time would tell.

Knight clearly had benefited from a bull market, and as the stock market began to recede in 1999, investors questioned whether Knight could sustain revenues under normal trading conditions, since its business model was very much dependent on volume and volatility.

"The first quarter and the second quarter were so good, I think investors tended to extrapolate that and I think many of the analysts did as well in their earnings estimates and it just truly wasn't a sustainable environment. So, third quarter came crashing back to earth," commented Greg Smith, analyst at Hambrecht & Quist. Pasternak added, "We saw those rates moderate to again historic growth rates that we have always enjoyed which were 100 percent. So I think both the analysts and the management here again are quite pleased that we still are maintaining 100 percent year-over-year growth rates on volume." For Peter Ramsden, a portfolio manager at Loomis Sayles, "the story had changed a lot in the past six months."

As soon as the firm failed to maintain its growth rate, investors punished the stock. After reaching a high of $78 in May 1999, it dipped below $25 in October. "The marketplace underwent a fundamental shift in the third quarter of 1999 compared to the first six months of the year. During the past quarter, there were decreased trading volumes and volatility as a result of lower retail volume and greater than expected seasonality in the marketplace," said Pasternak. He still remained confident that Knight would "continue to experience year-over-year increases in volumes and earnings in excess of 30 percent as it diversifies its revenue stream and expands its market share."[7]

The writing was on the wall with the upcoming move by the NASDAQ to begin using a decimal pricing system, a change that would tighten the spreads between the price at which Knight bought and sold stocks resulting in smaller profits. Not many people at Knight foresaw the threat of decimalization; Pasternak certainly didn't. Raquet only did theoretically; he thought he could have slowed the impact. They should have known better.

Shpilberg became persuaded decimalization was the foremost reason for Knight's decline. In order to get better prepared, Shpilberg tried to automate all trading activities. He realized that when the spreads began to narrow a lot of different fast trading strategies became viable. It wasn't viable to buy and sell very fast when paying an eighth all the time. However, paying only a couple of pennies every time made trading a lot particularly worth it, especially when dealing with high-liquid stocks. He rationalized that there was no trader in the world who could trade fast enough to make sufficient markets for all instruments. "Only computers could do that," he concluded.

In addition to decimalization, Turner includes the SEC Order Handling Rules and the arrival of electronic trading systems (ECNs), all of which negatively impacted profitability at all market makers. "To survive and to continue to thrive required rethinking the business model. Kenny understood better than anyone that to continue to grow Knight we would have to add new lines of business and this is the rationale for the purchase of an options market maker and the Deephaven hedge fund. Also, we needed to look at expanding overseas which is why the company established a market making operation in London."

In 2000, Knight/Trimark Group changed its name to Knight Trading Group and recorded $1.4 billion in revenue. Just the year before, Pasternak had been named Emerging Entrepreneur of the Year by Ernst & Young. The firm took a number of steps in an attempt to diversify and secure its independent position, which was further jeopardized by a consolidation trend that saw a number of major Wall Street firms acquiring NASDAQ market makers and taking in house business that might have been directed to Knight.

Knight had begun diversifying its business by acquiring Arbitrade Holdings (later renamed Knight Financials), a little-known Minnesota firm that specialized in identifying trading opportunities using computers, for $393 million on November 18, 1999. Knight had been exploring for some time the acquisition of an options market maker that could generate anywhere between $250 and $500 million to top-line growth.

Arbitrade had been founded by Minnesota native Irv Kessler and Israeli Efi Gildor on the proposition that technology could improve profitability and reduce risk in the options market-making business. Kessler, a University of Minnesota graduate, traded as proprietary options market-maker, trained and financed over 75 other options market-makers, started a clearing firm for floor traders, and established a Chicago Board of Options Exchange (CBOE) post. Gildor was a fighter pilot who had begun his doctoral studies at the University of Chicago, and worked as an options trader for Kessler; he developed computer solutions for advanced options trading, worked for Goldman Sachs and other companies, before rejoining Kessler in 1995 to found Arbitrade with a third partner who specialized in computerized options trading.

Arbitrade actively made markets in options on individual equities, equity indices, fixed income instruments and certain commodities in the U.S. Through its U.K. brokerage subsidiary, Arbitrade made markets in options on individual equities and equity indices in Europe as well. Arbitrade also maintained an asset management business for institutional investors and high net worth individuals through its subsidiary Deephaven Capital Management, which had been founded by Kessler in 1994.

Peter Hajas, Arbitrade CEO, decided to stay at the helm of the newly renamed entity, Knight Financial Products, and business quickly surged, providing the parent company with a welcome source of revenue as NASDAQ trading volumes appeared to have crested. Knight also planned to diversify internationally by becoming a member of the London Stock Exchange, Deutsche Börse, and Euronext Paris, hoping to become a market maker in each. It also entered into an alliance with Japan's Nikko Securities.

Hewitt, however, had reservations about this deal, starting with the motivation. Knight was heralding a transformation in the options industry even more pronounced than the one experienced in the equities market earlier. "Once again, the variables at play are regulatory change, integration of technological advances and the rising importance of self-directed investors and resulting volume increases. We see a compelling need in the options market for the customer-driven focus, scale, technological prowess and reliance on human capital inherent in Knight's proven business model," Pasternak had said. He was off regarding the new compelling needs in the options market; instead, Pasternak was avoiding getting the stock killed by analysts who had been told over and over that Knight's market-making model in equities was transferable to other markets.

Hewitt's next concern was the motivation of Arbitrade's management to continue working hard for the business. He had trouble understanding how three really smart guys who created a profitable business could be motivated to stay after selling out. Each of them is getting more than a $100 million apiece.

Hewitt said to Ken, 'How am I going to make these guys to care? How am I going to make them pay attention?"

The idealist Pasternak replied, "No. No. No. They really believe in this."

Hewitt's concerns increased when Gildon bought a helicopter for $20 million. A few months later, Gildon was out. He claimed he wasn't realizing his potential there.

"Knight didn't accept my philosophy. I'm a great believer in computers and thought Knight didn't focus enough on computerized trading. Knight focused more on human capital, and since I didn't think that was my expertise to try to change and influence things from inside, I left the company to work independently." He had a non-competition agreement with Knight in certain fields, especially in technical matters for stock trading.[8]

The board and major shareholders were worried about the firm's performance and possible takeover due to its depressed stock price. The markets had turned into a vicious bear environment for Knight. Even "Money Honey" Maria Bartiromo was joining the emerging chorus on her CNBC show.

Bartiromo grilled Pasternak on April 14, 2000. After Bartiromo's taped interview with Pasternak, she went to a live session with Bear Stearns analyst Amy Butte, who dumped on Knight some more. Pasternak wasn't given a chance to respond. Some viewers were quick to point to CNBC's apparent conflict of interest, as it owned a minority stake in Archipelago, a ferocious competitor of Knight.[9]

From the tone of the interview, CFO Turner concluded that Bartiromo had an agenda. "She was trying to discredit Knight, a highly successful and innovative company that was challenging the existing pecking order of the firms on Wall Street. I believe that the major Wall Street firms were astounded by Knight's success and how quickly the firm became the number one market maker both in NASDAQ and in the third market (the trading of NYSE equities off the exchange). Perhaps CNBC was influenced by the established firms to believe that Knight must be doing something inappropriate to become so successful so quickly. Knight provided consistently high quality trade executions to the customers of broker dealers that sent their order flow to Knight and to the institutional customers that used Knight for large trades. Execution quality and technology were the reasons why Knight grew as quickly as it did, plain and simple."

Hewitt recalls, "It took zero time for the economics to fall off the cliff. The traders were unable to make money anymore. The whole compensation model fell. The market also kept going down. We were losing millions of dollars every single day."

"I can't deal with this dead market anymore!" Pasternak once screamed in front of Hewitt.

Pasternak was saying that he hated his job and that he wanted to quit. Hewitt was convinced his resignation would not be good for Knight; he preferred the firm to come up with a program that would show the markets that they were changing leadership in a formal way.

"However, with Ken every day was a different story. One day he would get a call from Michael Eisner who wanted him to run Disney; another day, the Democratic Party of New Jersey wanted him to run for the Senate; then Jack Welsh wanted him to run GE; then Yahoo decided they wanted him to run it. It was pretty scary."

Hewitt talked to the board of directors and told them he thought Ken was stressed and wanted to be elsewhere. However, the board was dragging its feet and did not want to talk about it. They told him to wait and see what happens.

"We're sitting there losing $3 million a day. Customers were calling me. We needed a fire pass to get him out. We had to figure out a way to move it in the direction we wanted to. They decided the problem was the technology; that was a distraction. Walter was blaming Shpilberg for technology. It was the traders losing money. It was only one day a month we were making money. Everyone wanted to quit. Ken told me at the end of the day he was going to quit. I did not understand."

Pasternak changed completely, agreed Shpilberg. "He took a much more random management approach and spent more time trading himself. That created a more demoralized environment as profits were coming down."

Hewitt recalls being called to Pasternak's office. He believes that someone might have told Pasternak that he was getting the executive committee to fire him (he was not) and he reacted. Pasternak said he had talked to the general counsel and said they needed to make management changes.

Hewitt felt slapped in the face when he was fired and replaced by Hajas. "I was trying to be a friend to help him out of a tough situation; he hated his job, the company he helped start was going to hell. They fired Shpilberg too." They did so in July 2001.

Among this turmoil, the independent directors began to ask Pasternak to step down. By the end of 2001, Pasternak decided to retire at age 47, giving up the chairmanship and CEO role, some six months before his contract was set to expire. There was no need to feel pity for him, though. He placed ninth on Forbes' financial services executive pay list for year 2001, and number 51 overall, with a total compensation package of $26,488,000; this included a base salary of $250,000 and a cash bonus, of $26,213,000. Because Pasternak owned founders' stock, he was compensated primarily in cash, and in terms of cash, he was the highest paid CEO in 2001.[10]

How could the odd, intelligent and challenging Pasternak end his tenure this way? Was it because of the supreme self-confidence brilliant minds display once they touch the sky? Did he ultimately become narrow-minded, as Shpilberg claims? It was probably a bit of all of the above.

Hewitt admits Pasternak's brilliance in the trading and strategic rooms. Throughout the years, he had met the legendary traders. He felt that all of the great traders had different brain configurations. They had either loose screws or no screws where other people had all screws. That enabled them to see opportunity differently and to forget when they made a mistake. For him, great traders didn't overthink when they had a bad trade. "Ken had a lot of screws missing. He was excellent at things that were strategic and opportunistic. He was really good in that macro view. He saw the importance of buying a control stake in Easdaq because of how the European Union was going to work which would have allowed the Knight model to work there. What a great insight."

Did he like Pasternak as a person? "I liked Ken because I understood where he came from. He could be charming but also a total asshole, boorish, and mean. But when things were going well, he was the good guy, the guy who could see opportunity and act fast."

Pasternak was one of those managers who would spend every day in the office. He was noted for his big presence on the trading floor in the Fortune profile prepared by Bethany McLean (of Enron fame). As CEO, he earned a salary of just $250,000, but he also collected 35 percent of the net pretax profits of his personal trading account. He spent about 10 percent of his time on the trading desk, and he was a very audible presence. "Come on, take care of it! Do you guys have any idea what you're doing? You have no friggin' idea! Just think for 30 seconds. You just lost $50,000 there. Total incompetence!" Pasternak said he earned $9 million in 1998 and that he had already topped that in the first three quarters of 1999. He chalked up Knight's success not just to its volume but also to proprietary trading methodologies that he said he had developed over his decades in the business. "I'm not trying to be obnoxious, but there are things that I know that would take you five years to understand."

Pasternak's huge ego was reflected indeed by his beginning a lot of sentences that way. "I'm not trying to be obnoxious, but..." McLean thought he often was exactly that, but she admitted so far his attitude had worked wonders. "He knows how to get what he wants and his ambitions are limitless. He thinks that soon the market will operate around the clock and around the world. And he plans to be ready. Knight is aggressively hiring both techies and traders."

Pasternak's wasn't the only ego that needed a check at the door. There were a lot of big personalities, especially in the early days. For many of his colleagues, Pasternak was still the most intellectually honest person. He wasn't the greatest businessman; however, he was honest when dealing with customers, a truly honest person, they said. Nobody would have been able to question his integrity.

For Turner, Pasternak was more than a great trader. "I believe he understood the market making business better than any of the top executives at Knight's competitors and this was an important factor in Knight's success. He was a trader's trader and had the respect and admiration of the market makers. Kenny was also a technologist and had a keen understanding of the BRASS trading system and the compliance related implications. Kenny had an open door policy and all employees had direct access to their CEO. Knight was initially a very entrepreneurial firm with a feeling that we were all in it together and that every employee could prosper at the firm. In summary, Kenny talked the talk and walked the walk and every employee admired and respected his trading and leadership abilities and his caring and warm nature. Kenny was a very unusual leader."

"Kenny didn't build a business, he built a family," an old-time employee said. "He built a family that everyone liked to be a part of even if sometimes you hated it, even if sometimes people couldn't stand it. The company changed dramatically different with Joyce."

One of the last instances where employees felt the strong camaraderie at Knight's trading floor cultivated by Pasternak was on September 11, 2011. "The worst day ever," traders coincided. They watched the first plane from across the river. Two days earlier a plane had landed at Liberty Island, home of the Statue of Liberty. They thought somebody wanted to parachute. However, on that fateful Tuesday, panic and desperation ensued as traders watched both planes hit each World Trade Center tower and started thinking about their relatives and friends. Pasternak was seen talking on somebody's cell phone, screaming. Many employees who lived in Brooklyn and Manhattan would be left stranded as bridges were closed to traffic.

How was Pasternak's departure received by the rank and file? "It felt like the beginning of the end, and everybody knew it." Pasternak had been a paternal figure for most. "If somebody needed two weeks off, he was very understanding. If somebody had troubles, or was going through a divorce, he was there to help. There were some crazy guys working on the trading floor, and when they got too far and when they needed to go away Kenny took care of them. Kenny was kind of buddy with everyone."

"I didn't like being the CEO of a big company," Pasternak would say. "I was already looking for an opportunity to retire. I always saw myself as a business builder. I had some health issues. I had diabetes and weighed 325 pounds."

While it may be true that Pasternak didn't like the complications of running a big company, the dream of working at an entrepreneurial company lived on for the legions of traders he had trained and mentored over the years. Unfortunately, Pasternak didn't have the appetite to start anew.

Pasternak would always remain attached to the firm he had co-founded; he hated the idea of the firm eventually being acquired by a competitor and losing the name he loved so much, Knight.

Charles Doherty, a veteran Knight board member, was assuming the role of non-executive chairman of the board, while director Anthony Sanfilippo, who had been responsible for Knight's operations in Europe and Japan as head of global equities, and for Knight's listed equities business as president and CEO of Knight Capital Markets, was being named interim CEO. The interesting detail was that the firm had already announced Hajas would serve as interim chief executive.[11] However, he had since departed the company.

Pasternak declined to comment on the change of plans, only to confirm that he would serve out his remaining term as a director, which expired at Knight's annual meeting in May 2002, and he would continue to act in a consulting capacity until his contract expiration on July 8.[12]

"There was a period when Peter was the president, and I was still the CEO. I already had fired Hewitt. Peter had a very big derivatives group at UBS. Even though the job paid $25 million, I don't think he thought it was the right compensation. He didn't manage his expectations on compensation; by the summer time he left. He started to understand the public obligations; he was kind of a good business chief, but not CEO. He didn't like the fact that there are a lot benchmarks. There were some people who were overcompensated based on some benchmarks. There were 8 or 9 heads of NASDAQ firms that were paid 5 percent of the P&L, which was standard and customary back in those days. If I wanted to be a trader, I got the same rate. The problem was I would have made $175 million, and superstar traders were making $25 million. Unfortunately, in some people's mind, I was making twice the rate I was supposed to so I offered not to trade. In fact, I was earning a lower rate than everyone else."

Hewitt had a different take on Hajas's resignation. "He might have been there only for a few months as president, when he finally said, 'Screw this. These guys are bad guys.'" Hewitt became convinced management lied to him about what they were going to do for him; ultimately, it didn't make any sense for him to stay anyway because Hajas couldn't run the equities market; he just didn't understand that part, said Hewitt.

During his initial interview rounds, Hewitt approached John Leighton, the head of Knight's institutional sales desk and one of four brothers employed by the firm. "Tell me what you do. Tell me how this works here at Knight," asked Hewitt to Leighton.

Leighton described what he did to the best of his ability.

Hewitt replied, "You know. I don't understand this. I didn't understand a word you said. Try it again."

Leighton was starting to feel the heat yet he described again what he did for five, ten minutes.

"I have no idea what you are saying. It makes no sense to me," replied an exasperated Hewitt. "How much money did you make last year?"

"$25, $30 million," Leighton replied.

"You know how much the best sales traders are paid? What is it that you are doing that makes you so valuable? There is got to be a reason, so what's the reason?"

"Well, we take risk," Leighton said confidently.

"You know, we did that at Goldman Sachs too. We took risks. We get 10 percent of the commissions taking risks. So, that can't be the right answer. I am going to think about this."

Hewitt went to Pasternak and expressed his puzzlement. Something is way wrong he said.

"You people are paying him so much money, $25 million, and he can't describe how he makes money. I think the only explanation that comes to my mind is that he is front running. That is the only thing that comes to mind," Hewitt said. Before jumping ship, Hewitt had been aware of rumors about front running at Knight. None other than John Mulheren had warned Hewitt to be careful.

Mulheren was a Wall Street legend that had earned hundreds of millions in the 1980s as a stock and option trader. The father of seven kids could have been seen wearing a Santa Claus costume in Christmas time driving around New Jersey and giving out presents to the poorest kids. A protégé of Ivan Boesky, Mulheren was implicated in the insider trading scandals of the late 1980s and was convicted on fraud and conspiracy charges in 1990. His involvement in the scandals and his relationship with Boesky were discussed with great detail in James Stewart's bestseller *Den of Thieves*.[13]

That Mulheren, who suffered from bipolar disorder and died of a heart attack in 2003, took the interest in warning Hewitt of the regulatory risk he was taking didn't seem to be reflected in the firm's leadership behavior.

Pasternak would explode with Hewitt's assertions, "No, no, no. You just don't understand our business model yet."

Hewitt replied, "You are damn right; I don't understand your business model. But I do understand how this business works and what I am being told is not credible."

Pasternak was confident there was nothing illegal going on, as well as Raquet. The chief legal counsel, Mike Dorsey, also agreed with Pasternak.

Hewitt added, "I remember telling the general counsel that if they didn't think it was illegal that they should call in the SEC and tell them what we're doing. He did not want to do that. If you're not willing to tell the regulators what we're doing then you expect it to be fine? It's unlikely."

Pasternak ultimately said to Hewitt, "If you want to hire someone else, go hire someone else." This is the point when Hewitt hired Robert Stellato, who had been the leader of the NASDAQ sales team at Goldman; he had indicated a desire to join Hewitt at Knight, but he was not able to join for a long time, many months. It turns out that he was laying the groundwork to sue Goldman Sachs for age discrimination. He was ultimately hired as head of global institutional sales at Knight. A few months later, Hewitt was sitting in London on the balcony floor of the London Stock Exchange and received a phone call. It was Stellato.

"So, what is going on, Bobby?"

Stellato said, "I got them. I know what they are doing. I got the tickets. I got the transactions. They're front running. They're stealing."

Hewitt called up Pasternak and told him, "We have a problem. Let's fire these guys immediately.'"

Pasternak details the series of events with Stellato saying, "I hired John Hewitt and Robert Stellato from Goldman Sachs in 1999, just two very disappointing and inept executives. I fired them right away in 2000. They had good credentials but were very bad. Stellato tried to blackmail me for a $25 million severance. This was in 2001; I refused to pay him blackmail and then he leaked the story to The Wall Street Journal where he accused me of things, which he recanted later on. He fabricated a lot of stories, which his lawyer told him to say to get some leverage on me but he would not testify because he would've perjured himself. The SEC built its case on the premise that we made too much money. Actually, the customers set the commission rate on the trades on behalf of outstanding performance. So the SEC thought they could extort a settlement but I could spend $6 million on my legal defense. I could sue them in court for reputational damage, etc. That happened between 2004 and the court date which was in June 2008."

Pasternak irately commented, "One of the trades was Cisco, where Intel was the seller of a large position of Cisco. They went to Goldman who wanted to charge a commission which was too high. They went up to us and we charged a fraction of what they charged. If I tell you that Joseph Leighton made $3.5 million in 15 minutes, would you say that he did something wrong? What if I tell you that it was a $50, $60 million trade and the customer set the commission rate? Would you still say they did something wrong? As a supervisor, when I saw that information, I didn't think anything was wrong. The customer set the rate, and he provided a great service."

"I actually defended the Leightons; I wasn't even on his chain of command. They actually tried to charge me even though I wasn't even his supervisor. I certainly can tell you Joseph didn't do anything wrong. The customers testified that he didn't do anything wrong and that they didn't feel they were being ripped off; instead, the accuser refused to testify. The SEC had a theory based on money. What if I told you that there were people at Goldman Sachs, Morgan Stanley or Credit Suisse who made more money? Joseph was not even in the list of the top ten most paid. Some people thought it was immoral to make $25 million."

Both Raquet and Pasternak have commented on the SEC, stating that there could have been some element of jealousy driving the accusations.

Pasternak said, "One of the reasons why they suspected me is that I was making more than $100 million from trades. They are probably thinking that if a person makes so much money, then he must be making it illegally, he must be breaking the law."

Raquet further explored this idea. "Knight, because it was so big and so profitable, became like a poster child. You get jealousy, some people say, 'how is Knight making all this money?'"

In addition to troubles with the SEC, on March 7, 2005, NASD (National Association Of Securities Dealers, which was succeeded by FINRA) charged Pasternak and John Leighton, who headed Knight's institutional sales desk, with supervisory violations in connection with seemingly fraudulent sales to institutional customers in 1999 and 2000. Joseph Leighton, John's brother and another one of the brothers that had made Knight their home, had agreed the same year to pay more than $4 million to settle civil charges brought by the SEC and NASD.

NASD, of which Mary L. Schapiro was then vice chairman, charged Pasternak and Leighton for failing to supervise Joseph and failing to establish and enforce a system designed to ensure compliance with federal securities laws and NASD rules. According to their release, from January 1999 to September 2000, Joseph was responsible for generating nearly $135 million in trading profits for Knight, or approximately 30 percent of the trading profits of Knight's entire institutional sales desk. NASD's complaint called the magnitude of the profits generated by him, both in absolute terms and in profit per share, "extraordinary." Schapiro was quoted condemning the supposed fraud.

"In this case, it is inconceivable that fraudulent trading of this magnitude could go on for so long and generate such an exorbitant amount of excess profits and escape detection by the firm's supervisory systems and the supervisors themselves. Supervisors are obligated to take appropriate steps to ensure that persons acting under their supervision comply with securities law and regulations, and we will not hesitate to take action against supervisors who fail to fulfill that responsibility,"

A couple of years later on April 11, 2007, a NASD hearing panel issued $100,000 fines against Pasternak and Leighton. In addition, Pasternak was suspended of all supervisory capacities for two years, while Leighton was barred in all supervisory capacities. In a 2-1 ruling, the panel found that Pasternak and Leighton had failed to supervise Joseph Leighton's trading activities.

"For all intents and purposes, Joseph Leighton ran the Institutional Sales Department as he saw fit. Pasternak, John Leighton, and Joseph Leighton each concluded that as long as the customers did not learn of the extraordinary profits Knight earned on their orders, there was no limit to the amount the firm could make on an institutional order."

In fighting both cases, Pasternak displayed the intensity he was well-known for in business. "I didn't care how many millions of dollars the legal bills would be; I just didn't want my children to read that their dad was a bad guy. One of the things the SEC tried to accuse me for is that I was failing as a supervisor. I had these what-if statements that actually produced reports on what happened. They thought I was going to pretend that I didn't know." Indeed, SEC attorneys had written in their trial brief that Pasternak and Leighton throughout this litigation had tried to portray themselves as "aloof, remote managers who could not have known of the long-running, large-scale fraud." The opposite was true.

Pasternak's defense was that he knew what his employees were doing because he had these what-if statements. "So not only was I supervising them, I was doing a superb job. So the judge ruled me innocent." "Mr. Pasternak is innocent," his attorney, Howard Schiffman, had anticipated, adding there wasn't a single piece of evidence that Pasternak did anything wrong. Similarly, John Leighton's attorney, Joel Davidson, had said, "We think he fulfilled all his duties and responsibilities and we think the SEC charges are totally unfounded."

It wasn't until June 2008, when in courtroom one at the federal courthouse in Trenton, N.J., Pasternak and Leighton won a big victory against the SEC. U.S. District Court Judge Joel Pisano's ruling brought a partial closure to a legal drama surrounding allegations of fraud at Knight that had dragged on for years, cost Knight $79 million, and ended the securities industry careers of three former Knight executives. Pasternak finally felt vindicated. "The SEC knew that they didn't have a case so they thought they could extort a settlement on me. But it's unfortunate it takes five years and millions of dollars in legal bills to deal with the strong-arm tactics of the SEC."

In the NASD case too, ultimately Pasternak and Leighton had the last laugh, not without investing significant resources in their defense. On March 4, 2010, the National Adjudicatory Council (NAC) of FINRA issued a ruling dismissing charges that Pasternak and Leighton were responsible for supervisory failures in connection with alleged fraudulent sales to institutional customers. This ruling completely reversed the earlier hearing panel decision that found Pasternak and Leighton had violated FINRA's supervision rule. All sanctions against are Pasternak and Leighton were vacated by the NAC's ruling. Pasternak, chairman of KABR Real Estate Investment Partners, a real estate investment firm, could finally claim complete victory.

Raquet expressed similar sentiments saying, "The company, unfortunately, paid 80 million dollars to settle. I never saw any evidence that we did anything wrong. And we looked through the stuff really hard, I never saw any evidence that we did anything wrong. Every example we saw, we were able to find out why it was misinterpreted. And you do realize that we are dealing with sophisticated institutions. Can you imagine giving an institution a bad price? We did it with professionals on the other side to ensure they are getting the best price, it's not as if you are giving it to a retail client that doesn't know anything about the market. Bob Stellato cost Knight a zillion dollars, not only in market value, but also in wasted time and everything. And that's what ended an unfortunate chapter. It caused Kenny an incredible amount of grief."

Knight had been struggling with plunging trading volume amid the stock market's 2-year-old slide. While the firm was dealing with changes in management, its trading rivals had been making job cuts, as it was clear there was overcapacity in the industry.[14]

Sanfilippo had been given the OK to do anything to return the company to profitability. That management wanted this to happen "sooner rather than later" which was demonstrated by Knight's decision to cut 8 percent of its staff in March 2002. Furthermore, after Knight released its earnings in April, Sanfilippo had said the company's goal was to cut at least an additional $30 million from its costs. It had shut down its options-trading businesses in London and Australia, and had already made limited layoffs at separate business units, Deephaven Capital Management and Knight Capital Markets.

Chapter Seven

New CEO on Board

"While high-frequency trading firms can ably defend themselves, Knight Capital Group's view as a leading market maker is that high-frequency trading didn't cause the Flash Crash, the withdrawn BATS Global Markets IPO, the mishandled Facebook IPO or our August 1 technology issue. Further, any balanced discussion regarding the market impact of HFT must acknowledge that firms provide essential liquidity to all market participants.

The article fails to note that retail investors today benefit from the lowest trading costs and the highest execution quality in history. Under measures established by the SEC, independent data show near-continual improvement in terms of speeds, spreads and price improvement since inception. Likewise, independent data bear out the dramatic declines in the costs of online and broker-assisted trades since the mid-1990s.

Knight is far from "hobbled", as the article asserts. Knight's core activity is providing trade executions to retail investors and institutional investors, including mutual funds and pension funds. Despite the firm's modest size, we currently rank first among leading market makers in retail U.S. equity volume and second among all securities firms in overall U.S. equity volume of exchange-listed stocks and exchange-traded funds.

While superb, the U.S. equity markets don't function perfectly. The article fails to note that in congressional testimony I put forward specific recommendations intended to improve the markets, including eliminating "maker/taker", requiring quotes to have a minimum duration and widening spreads for illiquid stocks, unlikely to draw support from HFT firms.

Tom Joyce
Chairman and CEO, Knight Capital Group"[1]

Soft-spoken yet determined. Humble yet intelligent. Aggressive yet reserved. Calm yet forceful. Those are some of the adjectives that describe Joyce, a man known for the great lengths he took to defend his company against competitors and its own mistakes. The letter above published in The Wall Street Journal, in response to an article that critiqued high-frequency trading's efforts to sway regulation, painted Joyce in his full armor.

Thomas Michael Joyce started from humble beginnings in a small town just outside of Boston. He was raised as the oldest of five children in a Catholic family in South Weymouth, where an important component of the Naval Air Reserve Training Command was located; the Naval Air Station South Weymouth hosted a diverse and changing variety of Navy and Marine Corps reserve aircraft squadrons and other types of reserve units throughout the years until its closing in 1997.

Joyce's father was a lineman for Boston Edison (a regulated public utility that provides electricity to the Boston area) and his mother was a homemaker. All the Joyce children attended Catholic schools, even though the family could barely afford it.

When asked to describe himself, he demurs, "My mother always said self-praise is no praise." However, friends characterize Joyce as a normal boy who was quiet and kept to himself and yet he was very confident, loyal and smart.

At Boston College High School, Joyce competed successfully in several sports. He swam, ran track, as well as played baseball and football. Furthermore, as a senior, Joyce was Massachusetts' touchdown champion; in other words, he was the best in the entire state. "He could play almost any sport. A real gifted athlete," friends say.

His successes in football and baseball helped enormously in his acceptance to his choice college, Harvard. He rejected full ride athletic scholarships to Duke, Boston College and Villanova, even though he had to pay with loans and grants to attend Harvard.

Joyce enrolled in Harvard College in Cambridge, Massachusetts, which was a mere 20 miles from his childhood home. Before entering the classroom at Harvard, Joyce knew he would contribute more than just his grades to the school. Before classes started in September, Joyce was training hard at preseason, preparing for the upcoming Ivy League season and their big rivalry game against Yale. Football was not the only sport Joyce played; later in the spring he knew he would be on the baseball team as well.

On housing day during his freshman spring, he waited to see where he would be living for the next three years. The knock at the door came and it was revealed he was destined to live in Kirkland house, where decades later Mark Zuckerberg would come up with the Facebook concept out of dorm room H-33. Because of its close proximity to both the athletic facilities and classrooms, Joyce had ideal living conditions. Luckily for him, the far off-campus housing known as the quad (formerly Radcliffe College, a women's liberal arts college) was not incorporated into the housing system until he graduated in 1977. This saved him from the long mile and a half trek to practice every day.

Over the next couple of years, Joyce became a very distinguished athlete in both sports. This was the man who would put his best steady efforts day in and day out. Practices could be very inconsistent for some athletes, but not for Joyce. He became a three-year varsity letter winner on the baseball and football teams and was highly regarded by both coaches.

During his sophomore year, baseball coach Loyal Park (who was also the freshman football coach) complimented his right fielder saying, "Power hitter sophomore Tom Joyce...added depth to the team."[2]

During his senior spring, Joyce was elected the team's only senior captain, giving him an enormous amount of leadership responsibility. The Harvard baseball team posted a 22-7 record under Joyce as the captain in 1977, improving immensely from the disastrous 17-18 record they had the year before. The Harvard baseball machine had different parts that year but was operated by the same man, coach Park.

He had not begun his 1977 season with the proverbial clean slate, "Let's forget about last year" feeling that coaches are usually allowed after a sub-par season. Park was going into his ninth year with the team closely watched by critics who deemed it necessary to malign him when his team failed to garner any post-season honors for the first time since he had succeeded Norm Shepard in 1968.[3]

Stories and letters were printed accusing Park of racism, immaturity, back-stabbing and favoritism. Insinuations that Park should be fired, if he didn't resign first, abounded. All because of a 17-18 season. Park looked at it all very philosophically.

"If I had started thinking about what had been written all the time I would never have been able to do my job. My job is to coach Harvard baseball and do it in the best way I know how. As long as I am doing what I feel in my heart is right, I can live with anything that is said or written about me," Park said.

There was a time in early April when Park, a towering figure at 6' 2", was not able to bring all his players to spring training in Sanford, Florida. The National Collegiate Athletic Association (NCAA) only allowed a certain amount of players flying. Park wanted to take more players, so he lent his car to the half dozen teammates, who drove all the way from Boston to Sanford. After the week of training, they drove all the way back up.

Everything indicated that the season's 22-7 record would be the beginning of a successful run. While Joyce would be missing the next year, coach Park was finding himself with an overabundance of substitutes there. "Our two years of experimenting are gone," Park would summarize; "We'll leave nothing to chance now. We know exactly where we're headed."

During his junior fall, the Harvard Crimson wrote about their football star, "One of the two line backing spots is set with Tom Joyce, whom Restic terms as 'outstanding' Joyce, who is also captain of next spring's baseball team, was particularly outstanding in last fall's demolition of Brown, when he was selected the ABC-TV Defensive Player of the Game." The article was referring to Joe Restic, the coach who devised a complex offense known as the multiflex while coaching in Canada and later brought it to Harvard, becoming its longest-serving football coach, from 1971 to 1993.[4]

Not surprisingly, the Harvard football team gave Joyce access to other future leaders, such as Steve Ballmer, the current CEO of Microsoft. Ballmer was the manager of the team; he would plan the road trips, he would bring down all the equipment, he would take care of the logistics and he would perform all the duties needed to travel the 60-person football team plus coaches. As expected from a future Microsoft leader, he was very dedicated to the success of the team; that might have left a strong impression on roommate Bill Gates, the Microsoft founder, for he pleaded Ballmer years later to join his startup.

There were approximately 160 to 170 players starting in the football team; they were the best and the brightest kids coming from all over the country. Throughout the months, the number would decrease dramatically. The football team had 11 players for offense and 11 for defense, for a total of 22 players. The team revolved around the first and second groups; the starters and the backups; those 44 people were the stars.

Some would go on to become Rhodes Scholars (the world's most prestigious scholarship), doctors, lawyers, executives and self-made millionaires (or billionaires such as Ballmer). Some just focused on sports; in fact, a couple of Joyce's classmates were quite successful in the NFL. They were a diverse group, comprised of blue collar, middle, upper-middle and upper class kids. These were teammates that worked hard together, communicated well and experienced quite a bit of success; they went on to be Ivy Co-Champs in 1974 and Ivy Champs in 1975.

"Be quick, but don't hurry." That was one of the maxims that famous basketball coach John Wooden popularized. He was the "Wizard of Westwood" who won 10 NCAA national championships in a 12-year period, seven in a row, as head coach at UCLA. For Joyce's friends, that maxim applied to him like none other. "He was very friendly, steady, a very quiet friend. He would be almost a stoic presence."

After baseball, football or basketball, Joyce would hang out with his PiEta Speakers Club fellows. For all his successes at Harvard, Joyce earned his induction into the school's athletic hall of fame as one of the stars of the decade. Joyce was also a founding lifetime member of the Harvard Varsity Club, a community of over 20,000 current and former Harvard athletes and the ideal platform to expand his professional connections. Joyce would soon learn that valuable life lessons did not always come the easy way.

On the evening of Monday, November 15, 1976, the Harvard College football team "broke training" with a dinner at the Harvard Club on Commonwealth Avenue in Boston. At around midnight, about fifty football players went to the "Naked I", a bar on Washington Street in Boston's "Combat Zone". It was nothing unusual to come to this part of town; in fact, it was a tradition. At closing time, around 2AM, the football players left the bar in various groups to share transportation back to Cambridge.[5] Joyce's group decided to grab some pizza before heading back to the rooms.

Chester Stone, the equipment manager of the football team, had offered to drive six team members back to Harvard College in the team's equipment van. Another teammate had arranged to provide transportation for four others; his car was parked on Boylston Street.

As Stone and the accompanying students headed toward the van, they talked to two black prostitutes on Boylston Street, who joined them at the van. When they left, one of the players found that his wallet was missing. Suspecting that the women had taken it, he and his teammates jumped from the van and pursued them. At the entrance of Bumstead Court, an alley off Boylston Street and adjacent to the Carnival Lounge, their path was blocked by a black man, the bouncer at the Carnival Lounge. The football players returned to their van, got in and pulled up to Boylston Street.

As the van proceeded east on Boylston Street, one of the football players inside the van saw one of the black women walking west on Boylston Street.

He shouted, "There she goes."

One of the players jumped out of the van to pursue her. The van pulled into an alleyway next to the Silver Slipper Bar, and the rest of the football players jumped out to chase her. The woman was stopped by three other football players who were standing on Boylston Street. She screamed and ran toward the Tremont Street intersection. The football players from the van and those standing on Boylston Street began running after her.

The black woman reached the intersection of Tremont and Boylston Streets as Saxon caught up to and grabbed her. She fell to the pavement. Saxon pulled her to her feet. When she regained her footing she ran away, southward, down Tremont Street toward LaGrange Street. Suddenly, a black man interceded and knocked one of the players down. The football players then advanced toward the black man. From the corner diagonally opposite, another man shouted, "You came to the Zone, you got burned. Now clear out of here. Get the hell out of here." Two more showed up and what ensued was a fight that resulted in Thomas Lincoln and Andrew Puopolo being stabbed multiple times in the chest. Deprived of oxygen as a result of his injuries, Puopolo suffered extensive brain damage. He remained in a coma at the New England Medical Center for 31 days before suffering a fatal heart attack on December 17, 1976. He died while still attached to the respirator that had been keeping him alive. Ironically, he had been planning to attend medical school.

Because of their acceptance into such a difficult university to get into, Harvard students tend to have a sense of invulnerability, as they have likely succeeded in almost everything they have attempted. This can be harmful and dangerous as it becomes difficult to evaluate limitations and to properly adjust risk. While Joyce was not in the group that got into a fight, he was close enough to see the scandal and the police as they cordoned the area. The death of his classmate and teammate gave Joyce a sense of humility as it provided a real world example of the susceptibility to danger for someone who was just like him.

With a solid resume, Joyce had advantages that many people could only dream of. Graduating from Harvard with a bachelor's degree in economics as well as his leadership roles on two sports teams gave Joyce the potential to do great things. The humility from his Catholic upbringing combined well with his real world experience; anything other than greatness would have almost been a disappointment.

One of Joyce's close friends, John G. Taft, chief executive officer of RBC Wealth Management, thought that Joyce's character was the reason why Knight was saved so quickly after its trading malfunction on August 1, 2012, whereas other companies with similar issues were not spared because of the bad character of their CEOs. He said he knew many people who considered Knight to be one of the few honest companies left on Wall Street. For Taft, Joyce had changed the reputation of the company completely.

After college, Joyce's interest in finance led to his desire to pursue securities trading. He began studying for his series 7 exam, which he passed in 1978. His first job was to manage his wife's parents' money; he was living then in a small West Quincy apartment. Later, as a Smith Barney stockbroker on the West Coast, Joyce acted also as a salesman, attempting to lure investors to allow him to trade their stocks. He did not like this much because he admitted being "a lousy salesman."[6] He then moved to manage a small hedge fund, unsuccessfully. These failures ultimately led him to try a different type of trading, block trading. He passed the series 3 exam in 1985, which enabled him to sell futures and commodities.

Joyce's first big break came in 1987 when he was offered a job at Merrill Lynch, one of the biggest financial services firms. He started as a block trader, primarily concerned with equities. He juggled huge chunks of stocks and this gave him the gratification he was looking for. As he performed successfully in his new role, he moved up the ladder at Merrill Lynch, passing many exams to qualify for higher positions. Four years after his entrance to the company, he became the head of the block-trading floor. A year later, Joyce became the head of the firm's U.S. equities unit. At this leadership position, Joyce doubled the unit's revenue and garnered attention from the executives above him. Three years later he attained the head of global equity ecommerce position at Merrill Lynch.

At Merrill Lynch, Joyce sought Ivy League athletes as traders because of the ideal working conditions. He said the work favored "people who are bright, can multitask and can take criticism on a regular basis, much like being coached." Donna Rosato, a news editor and writer for The New York Times and later at Money Magazine, profiled Joyce by the end of the year of his hiring at Knight. She said that he exemplified a leader in a similar way to being a captain on a sports team. She said that he was an aggressive kind of guy and scrapped his way to the top. She also said that he wasn't a particularly nice guy in that he was not trying to appease everybody. She said, "He had an agenda and he was going to do everything in his power to carry that out." For Joyce, if it meant pissing someone off, then that was something he had to live with. Rosato went on to say that he did all of this in a humble manner, never bragging about himself or forgetting his humble roots outside of Boston.

This captain-like mentality apparently did not mean he was a harsh man that garnered disfavor with some of his "players." The former chairman of the New York Stock Exchange, Dick Grasso, had known Joyce since he was a trader at Merrill Lynch. Grasso commented on Joyce saying, "When even your most bloodthirsty competitors speak highly of you, that says a lot."

Joyce picked up the name T.J. at Harvard; he continued using it at Merrill Lynch when his supervisor said there were too many Thomases on the trading floor. At Merrill Lynch, colleagues described Joyce as an even-tempered leader who praised in public and chastised in private. Later at Knight, Joyce had said, "I've yelled at work twice in my life, and I regretted it both times." However, Knight co-workers claim to occasionally hear Joyce's irate voice from outside his office.

Most fellow workers thought of him as very thorough, knowledgeable, and well respected; he was definitely seen as a down to earth guy. He wouldn't display knee-jerk reactions in front of colleagues.

Joyce's passion for the business was evident. He didn't come across as a snobby individual in front of his employees; he would sit down next to traders at their desk and go about their business, and ask questions like any normal colleague would.

Former colleagues said his mild manner should have been misinterpreted. "He doesn't have an ego, but he's very determined and gets things done," said James P. Smyth, a colleague at Merrill Lynch who joined Knight as a senior vice president after Joyce was chosen to lead Knight. "There are a lot of people who are very disappointed he is no longer at Merrill Lynch, but I knew he had an ambition to run something."

A leadership change at Merrill Lynch enabled the ascension of E. Stanley O'Neal as future chief executive. This made Joyce realize he could not climb the ladder any further. Joyce said it was "obvious that some of the senior jobs I was positioned for weren't coming my way." If he could not lead at Merrill Lynch, he would do so somewhere else.

That ambition was clear when Joyce accepted in 2001 an offer to join Sanford C. Bernstein & Company, a smaller firm specializing in sell-side research. Joyce was the Global Head of Trading for the branch of AllianceBernstein L.P. with ambitions to climb the ladder there as well.

He worked closely with Sallie L. Krawcheck, then its chief executive and later chief of Citigroup's global research and brokerage group and Bank of America's global wealth & investment management division. Krawcheck commented on his tendency to hire athletes, saying, "You get very competitive, intelligent people that way." She also called Joyce "a bright individual with absolutely impeccable ethics" and "that rarity on Wall Street, an expert manager." This relationship was short-lived and only after a year Knight Capital had an open CEO spot and Joyce felt this opportunity was too great to pass up.

The main criticism Joyce has faced in regards to the event on August 1 is how his team handled (or mishandled) the incident; for some, a lack of action is always reflective of the CEO's leadership. Joyce didn't arrive at work until around noon that fatal day. The time period for the ongoing error was fairly long, yet no one realized or knew what to do. Could this be a sign the company was unable to act without its leader present? Or did it reflect bad leadership because Joyce did not have a system in place to safeguard against such calamities? Raquet, a co-founder of Knight, argued for the latter.

Raquet considered it a gross negligence and incompetence of the CEO to not have a circuit breaker safeguard system for situations such as these. "Management screwed up. The CEO screwed up and he should be fired. Do you have an action from the stockholders against the management for being grossly incompetent? How could you lose that type of money? How could you expose the company to that type of liability? It's all management. It's not technology. It's management. It's accountability taking."

Joyce and Raquet never seemed to have a good relationship after all and the following might fuel a negative opinion of Joyce, but Raquet does bring up an interesting point about controls.

"My initial reaction was how the hell could something like that happen? I mean we had more controls on risk so the automated executions could be shut down. It was probably 15 people that could just take things down, you could override things and lock things down. It was beyond my comprehension how something could run and not be shut off. It couldn't have happened under Kenny's and my watch, we had so many controls that something like that could not have happened. And I don't know how... it's beyond me. Trading is risk, you have to be able press the button and stop things. You can't have something in a little black box take over and ruin your life. The company was not being run by hands-on management like when Kenny and I were involved."

This theme of not being a "hands-on" manager has been brought up before with Joyce. People had criticized him for being on the golf course more than at his Knight office. "He was always out with clients. He worked from home; he worked from the office; he was often out," traders said.

This has been brought up by shareholders as well because they felt management was not doing their best to monitor their investments. Joyce had responded, saying that golf is a therapeutic activity that allows him an outlet to free his mind of the stresses of work so that he can put much more into work when he is there.

Similar criticisms have been made of President Obama and former President Bill Clinton. Like Joyce, Clinton responded in an interview with Golf Digest Magazine, saying, "I never feel bad when I see a president on a golf course. Presidents need to rest their minds, not just their bodies. They need the exercise, the fresh air. And they need to do something that, literally, takes them away from what they're doing."

After the August 1 event, the board apparently had not lost favor with their CEO, as shown in a 10-K filing. It read, "For example, in order to retain such key personnel, on December 19, 2012, we extended the employment contract with Thomas Joyce, our chief executive officer and Chairman, to continue his service for the Company." The memo went on to state that the extended contract was initially active until December 31, 2014.

Two years after his college graduation, Joyce married long-time girlfriend, Elizabeth (Lisa) Reid, in 1979. Lisa was raised in Hingham, Massachusetts, just 8 miles north of South Weymouth. She went to high-school at Notre Dame Academy, a private, all-girls Roman Catholic high school in her town. The Notre Dame Academy cheerleaders had been very successful in the past few years in competitions; since Notre Dame Academy was the sister school to Boston College High School, which Joyce attended, the girls would often come to cheer for the Eagles football team in home games.

Lisa graduated from Simmons College and became a trader at Alliance Capital. She was a very successful athlete as well; she was a figure skater and played tennis and golf.

The Joyces were very similar because of their professional background and love of sports. Joyce was involved with his three children's athletic development as well as coaching them in football, basketball and baseball in his spare time.

Shortly after Joyce was hired at Merrill Lynch, the couple's first child, Kelly, was born in 1988. Until very recently, Kelly had been an account executive with Joele Frank, Wilkinson Brimmer Katcher, where she developed and edited communications materials and strategic positioning and messaging for clients across a variety of industries; she had interned there in the spring of the year which she took off between high-school and college. She graduated in 2011 with a bachelor of arts in history and literature from Harvard, her father's alma mater. She finished high school in 2006 at the Convent of the Sacred Heart, where her mother had held several volunteer roles from 2003 to 2008. After her freshman year at Harvard, she interned at Sandler O'Neill, Knight's primary banker throughout most of its recent history.

In 1990, the Joyces' second child was born, Nancy, named after Lisa's mother. She graduated in 2012 with a degree in art history and environmental sciences from the University of San Diego, and in 2008 from the Convent of the Sacred Heart. She was an ad sales coordinator with DIRECTV after working as an educator with Lululemon Athletica. She previously interned at IXTLAN Production where she assisted Oliver Stone (who directed *Wall Street 2: Money Never Sleeps* at Knight's trading floor) and his staff in the production of a movie, *Savages*, released in the summer of 2012. She spent an exchange semester at St. Clare's College, Oxford University, and most recently visited East Java, Indonesia, where she hiked Mt. Bromo.

Their third child, named Ryan, was born in 1995; he had graduated from his senior year of high school in 2013 at the Salisbury School, an all-boys, private college-preparatory boarding school founded in 1901 and located in Salisbury, Connecticut. Like his father, he pursued athletics and was named most valuable player of the Junior Varsity lacrosse team in 2011 and was a two-year varsity letterman. He played club lacrosse for the New England Storm, a prominent lacrosse program in Connecticut; that year, he had suffered a bad accident from which he had recovered completely. He was also the manager of the varsity soccer team and the managing editor of the school poetry publication, the Quill. Ryan would enroll in the University of Richmond in the fall of 2013. Showing her commitment to her loved ones, Lisa had been part of the Salisbury School Parents Association as the Spring Athletic Chair.

The family's permanent residence was in the wealthy town of Darien in Connecticut. Joyce founded and served as a Director of the Darien Rowayton Bank, and participated with The Community Fund of Darien. The Joyces had another property called Beaver Pond in Lackawanna County, Pennsylvania. The couple enjoyed sports together and could be frequently seen playing golf on the Liberty National Golf Course in Jersey City, very close to Knight Capital's headquarters. Reimbursement of Joyce's annual dues for membership there was one of the most appreciated perks as CEO of Knight in addition to company-paid gym membership plus a car and driver for his daily commute between his home and the office.

Joyce used his love of golf for benefits though as he had hosted and donated to various charities through the sport. Joyce used to host 18 holes of golf and lunch at Liberty National Golf Course where proceeds going to a number of charities. Joyce also participated at his son's school charity events at the Apawamis Club in Rye, New York, to play in the first annual Fall Classic Golf Tournament. The proceeds supported the Freedom Fund, the Peter A. Fitzgerald 1993 Scholarship and general scholarships at Salisbury School. Joyce also made Knight Capital one of their Fall Classic Sponsors & Auction Donors.

Joyce served on the board of directors of Special Olympics of Connecticut and the Alfred E. Smith Memorial Foundation. Joyce also joined the Ronald McDonald House New York board of directors in October 2010. He also contributed to The Home for Little Wanderers in 2009. In addition, the Joyces served as the gala chairs for the Inner-City Scholarship Fund on Tuesday, May 15, 2012. The Friends of Inner-City Scholarship Fund raised over $800,000 at their 36th Annual Gala; funds raised at this event supported scholarships and enrichment programs benefiting inner-city students attending ICSF supported schools.

Joyce didn't hide his sympathy for Republican candidates. He had contributed $5,000 to Knight's PAC, Good Government Fund in

November 2012. In the year before, Joyce backed Republican candidates Steve Obsitnik for Congress (he lost), Christopher Shays for the Senate (he lost), Mitt Romney for President (should I say it?) and Justin Bernier for Congress (he lost). The only Democratic candidate he supported was Robert Menendez, who was running for reelection for a full second term to the Senate in 2012 and won. Sticking with golf (or Democratic candidates) was the way to go for Joyce.

Lisa had also consistently contributed to various Republican political campaigns and endorsed political figures such as Nevada Senate candidate, Sharron Angle. In a glowing profile in The Darien Daily Voice,[7] Lisa was praised for her active participation at the Community Fund of Darien's Advisory Board, the Allocations Executive Committee (during five years) and the Youth Community Fund, as an adult advisor since its inception; previously, she had been selected as the 2011 YWCA Woman of Distinction in Darien. The Norwalk Citizen praised Joyce for her passion for helping children, which is exemplified by her advocacy and volunteerism for eight years in the Shepherds Program, a nonprofit organization committed to assisting at-risk inner city Connecticut youths. "Joyce facilitated the Shepherd's Literacy program and also served as a sponsor and mentor for several years to two at-risk students who are now pursuing college educations."[8]

Not all has been good for the Joyce family though. In 2003, one of their friends, Clementine Burtha, filed a lawsuit against the Joyces because she sustained an injury while on the Joyce's 150-acre Beaver Pond property. The Joyces allowed their friend and others to use their residence during a weekend for free. Burtha was using the Joyces' property to snow-tube when she sustained injury from crashing into some trees. The court ultimately ruled that RULWA, a law that frees property owners from being liable for injury of others on property that has massive amount of undeveloped land, freed the Joyces' from responsibility. In May of 2004, there was an appeal to this ruling by Burtha's lawyers, stating that the Joyces' should pay for damages because RULWA should not have applied in this case. A private settlement was ultimately agreed upon between the two parties.

Lisa's mother, a teacher named Nancy, passed away at her Hingham home after a period of failing health on May 25, 2011. She had lived in Weymouth before moving to Hingham in 1964. She retired after many years as a teacher at Plymouth River School in Hingham. Nancy was a treasurer for St. Vincent DePaul Society at the Church of the Resurrection and was a member of the Hingham Historical Society and Hingham Garden Club.

More recently, Joyce's personal electronic address and credit card information was in a database of Stratfor's clients that was hacked by Anonymous, the loosely associated network of hacktivists, on December 25, 2011. Strategic Forecasting, more commonly known as Stratfor, was a private intelligence agency based in Austin, Texas, that published a daily intelligence briefing since its inception in 1996; Barron's once referred to it as "the Shadow CIA". The attack began with the release of Stratfor's client list posted online, followed by the release of accounts in batches believed to belong to its customers. The release announced included emails, passwords, home/office addresses and credit card information (full 16-digit number, expiry date and CVV number). The list of the leaked accounts was made available online for users to check if they were affected.[9]

Chapter Eight

Stabilizing the Ship

Following up on the plan devised by consultants brought in by Joyce, Knight decided to focus on the needs of institutional clients and enhancing its offerings. Knight determined it was more efficient to buy soft dollar and commission recapture capabilities than to continue building them from the ground up.

Joyce interviewed for Knight with the backing of former CEO Pasternak. "I personally nominated Tom to be on the short list of people who could succeed me," said Pasternak. "I think Tom is a good guy. Tom is more of a traditional, Harvard-educated, what I call a non-practicing executive." Before making him an offer, the board asked Turner to meet with him as well. "At my meeting with Joyce, I gave him a candid assessment of the company's strengths and weaknesses, and my recommendations as the initial steps that should be taken." Turner in turn recommended the board to hire Joyce.

Joyce was drawn to Knight because he had admired its original forward-looking positioning since Pasternak and Raquet founded the company. Pasternak had said, "Joyce saw that Knight's market strategies were ahead of its time and would adapt well with the changing markets. As the markets became more reliant on technology, Joyce admired how Knight could not only keep up, but also stay ahead of the competition."

Joyce was also attracted to Knight because he wanted to improve the company's reputation to a level above that of its competitors. He perceived that a lot of institutional clients felt that Knight had mistreated them during the internet bubble.

Armed with more than a decade of experience at Merrill Lynch, having traveled extensively and having done pretty well monetarily speaking, Joyce would try to make Knight more of a corporate, mini-Merrill Lynch culture. Ultimately, he was committed to make the firm more respected on the Street.

Former colleagues and industry friends say they were not surprised that Joyce was chosen to lead Knight, partly because of his clean reputation. "It was extremely important to us to have someone with an unblemished record because some of Knight's business practices had been called into question," said Doherty, the director responsible for hiring Joyce along with the headhunting company Heidrick & Struggles International. From 1986 to 1992, Doherty had been president and chief operating officer of the Chicago Stock Exchange, and had then become managing director of Madison Advisory Group, an investment advisory firm.

Joyce came into Knight wanting to establish a pristine reputation in the industry; this meant firing people who did not fit his mold. The widespread rumors of Knight's employees practicing illegal trading gave Joyce enough ammunition to send packing those who were even tangentially associated. This included the majority of the existing management, regardless of their qualifications. In this regard, the testimony of CFO Turner is very telling.

"Tom came from Merrill Lynch, a big firm with a corporate environment that was very different from Knight. I believe that Tom took a measured approach when he initially became CEO and tried to gain a full understanding of the company and its people before making any changes to the business. I did get the feeling that Tom may have believed to some extent the big firm Wall Street chatter that Knight personnel may have had a culture, in the past, of bending the regulatory rules and had somehow engaged in inappropriate conduct. This may have colored his thinking."

Joyce's move has been questioned by a number of people, including co-founder Raquet. He states that Joyce wrongly fired experienced personnel that had proved invaluable to the firm. He points to chief financial officer Turner as a victim of this witch hunt. Raquet states, "Turner was the CFO who was there from the inception, who had so much knowledge and, in my opinion, was so capable of an individual." Raquet goes on to say how this was not good business practice on the part of Joyce as "the CFO and all his relationships are so valuable and I don't know if he was insecure and wanted his own people, but if I know he is the CFO from the inception, is very capable and has relationships... that made no sense whatsoever... you have to have some continuity."

Turner himself remembers feeling marginalized from the get go. "I tendered my resignation in February 2003, about eight months after Joyce's arrival. I had the distinct impression that Joyce wanted to wipe the slate clean of the original management group. While I certainly respect a new CEO's desire to choose his own management team, I felt there was a lot I could contribute given my deep knowledge of the company, my relationship with the board and the company's employees, and the research analysts following the company."

Joyce started his new job on May 30, 2002. Days later, on June 3, a software glitch caused Knight's computers to dump almost one million of its own shares, trades the NASDAQ later canceled at the firm's request. The sell orders sent Knight's shares plunging more than 50 percent in before-the-bell trading. The stock later recouped most of the loss, ending at $5.92, off 43 cents, or seven percent, for the day.

Joyce explained that a trading workstation that hadn't been updated sent out "phantom orders" to sell Knight stock below the market price; most of these orders were sent to Island ECN.

"Two or three things you could never imagine came together," said Joyce. "The stars misaligned."

Knight had successfully appealed to NASDAQ regulators that the 1,000 trades should be canceled. "It's our contention they are erroneous, as there was never a real order," said Joyce. NASDAQ halted trading in the stock about three-quarters of an hour before the 9:30 A.M. EDT opening bell, pending news. Ultimately, trading resumed at midday.[1]

On the trading floor, one could hear Joyce address his employee for the first time when he said, "I'm Tom Joyce and, yes, I know that our stock is trading at 14 cents."

This was not the best start to the new image of the company that Joyce was striving for. In fact, it was the worst start. The following day, June 4, an article in The Wall Street Journal included the front running allegations made by Stellato. The shares went down more than 30 percent; later, Knight's shares bounced off their lows after the company issued a statement saying it would prevail in what it deemed "a private arbitration matter made public."[2]

Knight would later disclose that the SEC was formally investigating these accusations. A class-action lawsuit on behalf of Knight investors followed in June. Joyce said he was always confident that the front running accusation was false, and he was eager to remove the regulatory cloud over Knight. "Depending on what the SEC puts in front of us, we hope to hasten the process of putting this behind us," he had said.

A few months after becoming CEO, Joyce engaged consulting shop Bain and Company to help him devise his strategy for successfully going forward. As part of the strategy, Bain came up with a detailed plan of acquisitions, strategic planning and technology evolution away from traders and towards computers. One of the components of this new approach included changing the payoff for traders. Base salaries and bonuses (the meat of the pay) were out; commission-based payments were in. What was already a risky career path was becoming an even riskier proposition; traders could potentially earn just zero. Joyce had promised the staff they would make more or less the same amount of money. Instead, traders were incensed by the change. They saw this change as a creative way to start funneling compensation from the traders to the executives.

All of sudden, traders found themselves without a consistent salary. That was worrisome for those who had families. People thought about quitting en masse. However, there were not many opportunities out there; most of the competing firms were smaller. Traders realized that if they went somewhere else, they still wouldn't be able to make as much money, as only Knight afforded them with profitable opportunities. "As a trader, I agree that anybody who sits at a seat in the trading room is going to make a certain amount of money; I could make $3.5 million for the firm, so my salary would be 20 percent. However, management didn't see things that way."

Traders were becoming enraged with the influence exercised by big shot consulting firms over Joyce. They complained about seeing their total compensation reduced while spending millions on consulting teams which were camping at their headquarters.

There were sales consultants, strategy consultants, brand consultants, you name it. Traders just didn't know what they were trying to do. "We were not in a position to dictate direction. There were a lot of things being done and we didn't understand why they were doing them." Employees groused about seemingly knowing what needed to be done to advance the business and that they didn't need consultants to tell them that.

"So much for the C.E.O. honeymoon period," Joyce said. "It was insane. Those first few weeks were like the 1987 market crash all over again. Everywhere I looked, there was awful news."

Joyce just couldn't catch a break. However, his unpopular decisions helped to turn the company in a positive direction. After the negative return of $43.2 million in 2002 on revenues of $527.4 million, in 2003 he raised the revenue to $670 million, posting a net income of $38.5 million. He generally gave the company a more focused direction, forcing traders to become more involved with client service rather than pure sales. Joyce expanded Knight's institutional trading business because it was becoming more profitable than trading for individual investors. In the process he hired many veteran-trading executives from companies like J.P. Morgan, Goldman Sachs, and UBS PaineWebber.

In January 2002, the NASD fined Knight $700,000 and ordered it to pay $800,000 to clients because of a number of market making and trading violations. Knight faced further investigations into its conduct initiated by a whistleblower, the former head of Knight's institutional trading desk, Stellato. He accused Knight of engaging in front running, meaning, Knight and its employees had been profiting in advance from customer orders they knew would push the stock of a company up or down. What was behind Stellato's allegation of the existence of an elaborate system of trading-rule violations at the company that cost investors millions of dollars? Was it only a nefarious appetite for litigation and millions?

In a written response to the NASD, the company disputed Stellato's allegations, asserting there was no illegal trading at Knight. In fact, the company would say Stellato drummed up the front running stories in order to mask his own failings as a manager, which ultimately led to his termination. While Knight acknowledged it asked the Leighton brothers, two senior traders whom Stellato accused of front running, to resign, the company claimed those departures weren't the result of unlawful activity, but rather personality clashes between the traders and Stellato.

The Wall Street Journal offered an example based on Stellato's sealed arbitration complaint, "If an investor wanted to buy, say, 1,000 shares of Intel Corp., that person would call their stockbroker, who would arrange to have Knight place the order. But before doing that, Knight's trader allegedly would at times buy Intel stock for his own Knight account, presumably getting in at a cheaper level than what the price would be when the customer order was finally filled. In some cases, the trader's buying could even drive up the stock price, making it yet more expensive for the customer who placed the order in the first place."[3]

Joyce counterattacked by hiring the "best law firms"; on October 2002, he categorically announced that a review of trades showed that "no front-running or trading ahead occurred." Despite Joyce's assurances, on November 12, 2002, Knight announced that the SEC had begun a formal investigation into the allegations of improper trading practices. Knight disclosed in a quarterly report that the SEC had issued a "formal order" for investigation, meaning its informal inquiry had been upgraded and investigators now had the authority to subpoena testimony as well as telephone and bank records.

"We want to be as transparent as possible," Joyce said. The regulators "got the last bit of information from us two weeks ago. They haven't asked for anything more in the last few weeks. Everything they've asked for they have."[4]

In 2004, Knight began to come out from under the cloud of litigation when it reached a settlement with the SEC and NASD, agreeing to pay $79 million in penalties, interests, and trading profits. The whistleblower suit was also settled in 2004 when a NASD-overseen arbitration panel ruled against Stellato, who had maintained that he had been wrongfully fired because he exposed Knight's trading practice. Stellato had started this lawsuit when the old management was at Knight, giving the founders Raquet and

Pasternak an extreme amount of grief for no valid reason. The firm's counterclaims were also dismissed. With the legal issues then behind the firm, Joyce could fully concentrate on growing Knight, which continued to face challenges in a highly competitive and changing marketplace.

Joyce's perceived honesty would allow him to call out institutions that were not on par with modern trading methods. This valuation on technology was clear when we saw how Joyce berated other institutions for lagging behind. Specifically, Joyce criticized NASDAQ for their technological error during the Facebook IPO in May of 2012. Knight, as well as many other companies, lost millions of dollars because NASDAQ suffered a computer malfunction during the first few hours of the IPO, leading to millions of trades to be wrongly placed.

To reorganize the firm, Joyce added to Knight's ability to serve institutional customers by acquiring Donaldson & Co., on October 14, 2003, in a cash transaction estimated at approximately 6 million dollars.

Donaldson & Co., based in Atlanta, Georgia, was a leader in providing soft dollar and commission recapture programs to the institutional investment community. For Knight, it was adding an established business that immediately positioned them as one of the top soft dollar and commission recaptures providers in the U.S. During the third quarter of the following year, Knight announced a charge of $4.4 million write-down of goodwill. There was a good reason to believe that it was primarily related to the write-down of goodwill within Donaldson & Co acquisition. Sandler O'Neill & Partners advised Knight on this deal.

Knight had made significant improvements to the derivatives business it acquired through Arbitrade in 2000. The firm had adapted to the dynamic options market by increasing efficiencies and introducing new products and transforming the business into the attractive asset for any major financial conglomerate. In summary, the acquisition of the derivatives business had been widely successful. However, profits declined with the new management, which somehow concluded that Knight's strongest growth opportunities remained in its equity markets and asset management business through Deephaven Capital Management. In August 9, 2004, Knight sold its Derivatives Markets business to Citigroup for approximately $225 million in cash.

Fast forward to 2008 and a new top management at Citigroup would be dealing with massive credit-related losses; Citigroup's business units had numerous question marks[5]. Chief executive officer Vikram Pandit would state that each business line would be scrutinized with an eye toward selling assets to shore up the capital base. However, one strategic component, systematic trading, the result of Citigroup fusing well-thought-out acquisitions (including ATD) with legacy systems to form a global trading powerhouse, was heading in the opposite direction.

Citigroup's acquisition of the Knight's unit had added scale to its U.S. equities business and enhanced its growing derivatives business' top-tier order-routing and market-making capabilities. Prior to that, "Citigroup was involved in more traditional equities trading, using technology mainly for risk and pricing systems," said Bret Engelkemier, head of global systematic trading. "Now, technology is crucial to the actual trading process, with hundreds of thousands of trades going through per day."

How could Joyce justify handing Citigroup out a golden goose? "The proceeds from the transaction will allow Knight to drive enhanced returns for shareholders by creating a ready pool of cash for a variety of corporate purposes, including share repurchases, reinvestments in our core businesses and acquisitions." This justification for the sale falls flat on the ultimate successful deployment of the platform by a competitor. Furthermore, Knight attempted its return to the business with its acquisition of Penson Futures in 2012.

In May 2005, Knight acquired the Attain electronic communications network from Domestic Securities, continuing the assimilation of ECNs by markets and broker-dealers.[6] Attain, created in 1998 by Harvey Houtkin, was an alternative trading system (ATS) that operated an electronic communications network for the trading of NASDAQ securities. Attain allowed people who wanted to trade stocks to place orders that were matched with others seeking to trade.

With the acquisition of an ECN, Knight was trying to broaden its suite of products to serve the execution needs of broker-dealers and institutions. The goal for the new ECN was to provide a stable, fast, competitively priced and anonymous execution platform for trading of NASDAQ, exchange-listed and OTC Bulletin Board securities.

However, Attain's technology needed a complete revamp, according to Sadoff. The electronic communications network evolved into Direct Edge, soon the world's fourth-largest equity exchange, with Knight having a 20 percent stake.

Direct Edge would become an important component of New Jersey's burgeoning financial ecosystem. More recently, Direct Edge trailed NYSE and NASDAQ in size and vied with BATS Global Markets the title of third largest stock market in the United States. In addition to Knight, the list of shareholders included a powerful roster of financial players: International Securities Exchange, Goldman Sachs, Citadel Securities and JPMorgan, among others. At the helm was William O'Brien, a former lawyer for Goldman Sachs, who grew accustomed to a reverse commute every day from his Manhattan apartment.

Direct market access was at the time one of the fastest growing parts of the institutional trading business. On June 16, 2005, Knight acquired Direct Trading Institutional, firm that been founded in 1997 to provide institutional investors better trade executions and lower trading costs. The firm offered a full-service trading desk as well as "soft dollar" programs to improve returns and lower operating costs.

While upon the close of the transaction Knight made a $40 million initial cash payment, the transaction also contained a two-year contingency from the date of closing for the payment of additional consideration based on the profitability of the business. For this concept, in the third quarters of 2007 and 2006, Knight paid $10.4 million and $12.7 million, respectively.

From this acquisition, Knight expected to follow the changes of the market and become the leader of the institutional trading business. Direct Trading enhanced Knight's ability to achieve its goal. After the acquisition, Knight utilized Direct Trading as the foundation for its Electronic Services offering.

2005 turned out to bring two good deals for Knight. Its goodwill increased $28.5 million. After the acquisition, these two companies brought Knight over $15 million annual revenue.

It was on January 24, 2006, when Knight acquired Hotspot FX in an all-cash deal for approximately $77.5 million. Hotspot FX was a privately held firm founded in January 2000 by a team of senior foreign exchange managers from major international banks. Joyce had assured shareholders that electronic foreign exchange trading would continue to rise dramatically, especially as more institutions embraced FX as a source of alpha, and not simply a currency hedge.

Hotspot FX offered institutions and dealers access to electronic spot foreign exchange trading through Hotspot FXi, an e-financial marketplace where buyers and sellers worldwide could trade directly and anonymously with each other, obtain price improvement for their trades and lower their overall trading costs. Hotspot FX's platform had experienced remarkable monthly growth since its inception at the beginning of the decade.

The acquisition of Hotspot FX proved very successful; it was widely considered the firm's best business. Although part of a bigger firm, Hotspot FX had been able to maintain its unique culture; it had always been run as a separate unit with a culture based on providing institutional FX trading, rather than simply being the Forex division of Knight.

Knight Hotspot FX earned a number of accolades throughout the years. It had been recognized for Most Improved Market Share among multi-bank and independent platforms in Euromoney's annual benchmark survey of the global FX industry. Knight Hotspot FX's market share among spot FX reporting venues rose to approximately 9.55 percent in 2012 from 8.71 percent in 2011. By April 2013, Knight Hotspot FX's $30 billion per day in trading on its network accounted for a record 10.26 percent market share.

Demand for institutional Forex products remained strong, as seen by the acquisition of FXAll for $625 million by Thompson Reuters and a smaller deal of FXCM buying Lucid Markets for $176 million. While only a third of the size of FXAll in terms of daily FX volumes, it was understood a Hotspot FX potential sale after the acquisition by GETCO could have gone for north of $300 million.

Knight acquired Atlanta-based ValuBond in October 2006 for $18.2 million in cash.[7] A couple of years later, and signaling the completion of a series of technology upgrades, product enhancements and staffing increases, the company introduced Knight BondPoint, fully integrated with its direct-market access (DMA) and trade execution services.

"As a result of the technology integration, we have not only added scale to our solutions, but also offer new and cost-efficient ways to access Knight BondPoint by leveraging Knight Capital Group's extensive connectivity infrastructure," had said Marshall Nicholson, head of Knight BondPoint. The relaunch represented an opening up of the platform, or a "decoupling of liquidity from the application," with which brokers would be able to connect to BondPoint more directly via FIX and third-party applications.

Wirehouses such as Citigroup and Merrill Lynch could just take their Application Programming Interface (API), much the way the equity world worked.

The former ValuBond operated a centralized, electronic interdealer, cross-matching bond trading system that acted as a distributor of liquidity to retail clients through broker reps. Knight bolstered several elements of the platform's compliance functionality with improvements such as exception reporting, trade execution documentation and archiving.

Fixed income was a vast and growing asset class still largely untouched by automation within the broker-dealer space. Multi-asset class diversification and technology trends were fueling demands by investors for the same fast, efficient trade execution in fixed income that they had come to expect in the equities market. Knight believed that both American and European clients would increasingly want to provide electronic access to fixed income, from the same platform that they can access other asset classes like equities and foreign exchange.

It was with the mission to grow BondPoint and Hotspot FX in the U.K., continental Europe and Asia that Knight would later hire Albert Maasland as senior managing director, head of international. Maasland was joining Knight from Saxo Capital Markets where he served as Chairman of U.K. and South Africa with a responsibility for strategic growth initiatives in the U.K., Sub-Saharan Africa, India and Canada. Prior to that, he had been global head of business development for Standard Chartered Bank where he led the strategy for expanding the bank's footprint through e-commerce across Asia, the Middle East and Africa.

More importantly for Knight, Maasland had spent 11 years at Chase Manhattan Bank where he had a number of Sales Management roles in Transaction Banking before taking over as Head of FX Sales from 1989-94, a period during which Chase rose to become the number two FX bank in the industry (from number fourteen). Maasland had more than 25 years' experience in the global capital markets including earlier positions at Cognotec, Deutsche Bank and HSBC. In addition, he served on the board of governors at the Universal Business School of Mumbai, India. He had a bachelor of arts in commerce and economics from the University of Toronto in Ontario, Canada.[8]

As algorithmic trading increased in a fragmented market environment, Knight was looking for an acquisition that could have enhanced its trade execution services and provided them with a significant advantage as demand continued to grow for sophisticated, next-generation algorithms.

In 2007, Knight Direct purchased EdgeTrade, an independent, agency-only broker-dealer and software developer, for around $59.5 million in cash and stocks. Joyce said he focused on EdgeTrade because of the client base they had, and they were developing some very clever technology products that were getting rapid adoption.

Beyond the immediate opportunity to cross-sell EdgeTrade's algorithms to clients through Knight Direct, Knight's multi-asset class execution management system, Knight anticipated demand for new algorithms that would cover international equities as well as additional asset classes such as foreign exchange and options.

EdgeTrade's acquisition proved transformational for Knight's cash sales traders. From basically marketing Knight's wholesale and institutional order flow to hedge funds, sales traders were now expected to cross sell them to their clients, which changed their previous role of strictly being cash sales traders. The trend became more popular every time Knight acquired a new company. Cash and sales traders of course had seen the writing on the wall. With electronic trading, they were going down the path of irrelevance; there was not much they could have done. Had it not been for Gregory Voetsch, who had been with Knight since September 2002 and was the head of the company's institutional client group until January 2010, the cash sales trading business would have been history, as it hadn't made any money in the past 2-3 years. Voetsch had been previously a NASDAQ sales trader at Salomon Smith Barney and an equities sales trader at Jefferies, and had demonstrated a lot of respect for the sales traders.

Joseph Wald, the former EdgeTrade's chief executive officer, became managing director and head of its institutional electronic trade execution services. One of the new algorithms he introduced at Knight in 2009 was Oasis, a smart order execution algorithm that was tailored specifically to source small and mid-cap liquidity. Oasis was designed to optimally handle the trading obstacles typically associated with thin and difficult-to-trade names (less than 2 million shares traded per day) for which Knight's market share of 38.9 percent in stocks was crucial. For Wald, Oasis was a next-generation algorithmic strategy that recognized there were increased overall costs and risks associated with trading small- and mid-cap stocks, such as higher volatility, less liquidity and wider spreads.

Knight introduced later in 2010 algorithmic pairs trading capabilities for institutions designed to increase fulfillment rates through improved liquidity sourcing. Traders used pairs trading strategies to capture the spread between two or more related securities, keeping risk low by remaining market neutral. After the turmoil of the last several years, Knight believed investors were more interested than ever in managing risk by taking a market neutral approach while residual uncertainty remains. At the same time, merger and acquisition activity was expected to continue to rise due to a reinvigorated investment banking market, while robust issuance of preferred stocks had created more opportunities to pair preferred instruments with their common stock counterparts. Wald was confident Knight had the algorithmic pair trading technology to help institutional traders make the most of these opportunities.

One of Knight's latest offerings developed by Wald's team was the enhanced Sumo algorithm which looked to execute blocks with immediacy through focused size discovery. Sumo, which had an "amusing name" according to CNN's Paul La Monica ("Aren't most sumo wrestlers too big to be fast?," he had quipped), used real-time and historical liquidity measures to complete an order as fast as possible. Knight redeveloped the Sumo algorithm to account for the increasing use of shorter-term trading strategies and their impact on liquidity. Sumo aimed to target liquidity provided by effective counter-parties to institutional traders, including passive or neutral electronic traders. Sumo allowed clients to interact with market participants using shorter-term strategies in a benign way through size discovery and trading signals to determine the appropriate speed, interaction rate and order size for effective execution, while camouflaging their trading activity.

"Certain high-frequency strategies have adapted to glean more and more information from the slice and spray approach of many of today's buy-side algorithms, making these traditional 'cost-biased' smart order routers less effective over time. Sumo counters with a 'size-biased' routing strategy to find larger blocks of liquidity at fewer venues, moving orders through the marketplace in such a way as to reduce information leakage."

Knight's algorithmic suite was made accessible to clients through Knight Direct as well as through a number of third-party execution and order management systems via Knight Direct's FIX capabilities. The algorithms were powered by FAN, a smart order execution algorithm which sourced liquidity from multiple destinations simultaneously, while adapting to market conditions in real-time and re-circulating orders to where executions were occurring.

With the goal of including institutional fixed income capabilities to offer their clients, on July 11, 2008 Knight acquired Libertas Holdings, for $50 million in cash and $25 million of unregistered Knight stock.[9]

Libertas provided trade execution services and investment research across a broad range of fixed income securities, including high yield and high grade corporate bonds, distressed debt, asset-backed and mortgage-backed securities, convertible bonds and syndicated loans. The firm also provided capital markets services to growing companies in need of financing to support expansion.

On January 21, 2009, Knight promoted senior managing directors Gary Katcher, head of global fixed income, to executive vice president. Katcher had been the founder of Libertas Holdings.

"Gary is building a terrific business at Knight Libertas, which has allowed Knight to immediately expand our offering across asset classes with institutional fixed income. Since Knight acquired Libertas in July of 2008, we have been exceptionally pleased with its growth momentum and its contribution to our company. Gary has quickly established himself as a leader at Knight. I am pleased to acknowledge Gary's and Knight Libertas' achievement today with his promotion."

It was during the following year that the acquisition of Libertas started to show its value. In 2009, Knight Libertas achieved its first year performance target which entitled the sellers to receive $33.3 million of the aforementioned earn-out in 1.6 million shares of unregistered Knight common stock. 50 percent of such shares would be issued in July 2010 and the remaining 50 percent would be issued in July 2011. Knight Libertas was a riskless principal fixed income broker-dealer specializing in a variety of fixed income products.

Back in 2004, Knight's management had considered asset management business vital to the growth of the company. On January 27, 2009, Knight Capital's Deephaven Capital Management agreed to sell the assets of its largest fund to Stark & Roth (which managed about $10 billion in assets) for $7.3 million.[10]

Many hedge funds and asset managers had struggled with redemptions since the global credit crisis ballooned in the second half of 2008, as investors fled for the safety of cash and government bonds. This triggered forced sales of many assets, depressing markets worldwide. Deephaven, the asset management arm of Knight Capital which had posted a pretax quarterly loss of $5.7 million for the fourth quarter of 2008, managed about $4 billion at the start of that year. That slid to $2.7 billion at the beginning of October, when the firm halted investor withdrawals after clients asked to redeem more than 30 percent of their capital. The fund was managing about $1.2 billion by the time of the sale.

Knight owned 51 percent of Deephaven, with the rest in the hands of three senior partners, Matthew Nunn, Colin Smith and Shailesh Vasundhra[11]. The senior partners had bought back a 49 percent stake in Deephaven from Knight in January 2008. Provisions of that deal called for Knight to receive virtually all of the proceeds from the sale to Stark.

On July 1, 2010, Knight announced the completion of the acquisition of Urban Financial Group, an independent mortgage company and a leading originator of home equity conversion mortgages (HECM), or reverse mortgages, insured by the Federal Housing Administration.

Urban Financial was an originator of direct and brokered residential mortgage loans and an originator of FHA-insured HECMs. Based in Tulsa, Oklahoma, Urban Financial had 109 employees and branch offices in 10 states. The company offered or purchased residential mortgage loans in more than 30 states.

In connection with the close of the acquisition, Urban Financial founder and chief executive officer Bryan Hendershot was appointed managing director, head of mortgage origination. He would report to Ronak Khichadia, managing director, global head of ABS/MBS.

On October 4, 2010, Knight completed the acquisition of Astor Asset Management, a money management firm specializing in macro-economic strategy and ETF portfolio construction, for approximately $18 million. Pursuant to the purchase agreement, 40 percent of the purchase price would be paid in the form of restricted shares of Knight. In connection with the close of the acquisition, Astor founder Robert N. Stein was named senior managing director, Head of Global Asset Management and signed a four-year employment contract that included incentives based on future performance.

Astor's approach to investing, which involved modeling economic data and utilizing low-cost ETFs to capitalize on cyclical changes, resonated with advisors. Knight believed it could accelerate the growth in assets under management by providing introductions to Knight's clients among the leading wirehouses and broker-dealers.

On October 28, 2010, Knight acquired Kellogg Capital Markets' designated and lead market-maker businesses, which made markets in approximately 800 NYSE and NYSE Amex listed securities and 322 NYSE Arca exchange traded funds (ETFs). Knight anticipated that it would assume Kellogg's responsibilities across its entire portfolio of NYSE, NYSE Arca and NYSE Amex-listed securities as well as Kellogg's participation in the NYSE Amex Universal Trading Platform (UTP) program.

The acquisition would build upon Knight's electronic market making business by adding another venue in which to make markets. It would also leverage Knight's strengths in trading technology to efficiently provide liquidity for its new listing companies. Kellogg's Designated Market Maker (DMM) business would complement Knight's own current liquidity providing activities as a Supplemental Liquidity Provider (SLP) on NYSE and a NYSE Amex UTP DMM. It was very important for Knight to generate additional revenue, as volumes had been declining.

Amid the bleak trading environment, Joyce had decided earlier in October 2010 that he would fire approximately 8 percent of his staff. That was the beginning of a series of layoffs that impacted Knight every four or five months. Layoffs were always traumatic; people would leave the firm and wonder who was next. "Folks looked over their shoulders a lot," said a trader. "They would send out a general broadcast. They would have a press release, which was the same as the internal e-mail; I don't think there was anything generally different to it. The people who were typically laid off were salesmen, sales traders, market makers, vice presidents, and managing directors."

After an acquisition hiatus of almost a couple of years, on May 29, 2012, the firm acquired Penson Futures, a top 30 FCM (Futures Commission Merchant) in the U.S. that was a member of the Chicago Board of Trade, the Chicago Mercantile Exchange, the Kansas City Board of Trade, NYSE Euronext LIFEE, the Minneapolis Grain Exchange, NYMEX, COMEX, ICE Futures US, ICE Clear Europe, NYSE LIFFE, One Chicago and LCH.Clearnet.[12]

Penson Futures provided futures execution, clearing and custody services to facilitate transactions among brokers, institutions and non-clearing FCMs on major U.S. and European futures and options exchanges. Penson Futures also offered risk management and consultation services and operated an electronic futures trading platform for professional traders and individual investors.

Upon the close of the acquisition, the FCM would operate as a division of Knight Capital Americas (KCA), formerly known as Knight Execution & Clearing Services, which provided institutional sales and trading services and investment research across a range of equity and fixed income securities, including high-yield and high-grade corporate bonds, distressed debt, ABS and MBS, convertible bonds and syndicated loans.

In hindsight, many of Knight's acquisitions and sales under Joyce at the helm didn't turn out as well as expected. Co-founder Pasternak has commented on Joyce's business decisions, saying, "Tom has done some things that have helped to keep the company going. He has made a lot of acquisitions that have yet to pay off. He sold some assets that later doubled and tripled its value and bought some stuff that doesn't even exist anymore. He bought a lot of businesses. One of my complaints is that he tries a lot of things in a big operating business."

Pasternak believed that Joyce probably destroyed a billion dollars of assets by selling things at low prices and buying things that were not worth anything. That was too much to stomach for the former car dealer used to always buying low and selling high.

Chapter Nine

Unfriending Facebook

If there was ever an IPO everybody wanted to get in on, it was certainly Facebook's. Yet, despite a reputation as home to the most successful tech IPOs, NASDAQ failed to deliver a smooth ride for all involved in this mammoth transaction. Knight's Joyce became infuriated with NASDAQ and the alternatives it offered for participants to recover their losses.

The social networking company Facebook held its initial public offering on May 18, 2012. This was one of the biggest IPOs in technology, and the biggest in Internet history, with a peak market capitalization of over $104 billion.

Facebook's founder and chief executive Mark Zuckerberg had for years been unwilling to take the company public and had resisted a number of buyout offers after Facebook's founding. Of all the suitors courting Zuckerberg in the fall of 2005, the most enterprising was Michael Wolf, then president of Viacom's MTV Networks and former McKinsey & Company director; he had heard college students in MTV's focus groups talking incessantly about the new site, and he was determined to snag it for his parent company.

"Friending" Zuckerberg proved to be a formidable challenge to overcome.[1] The company did, however, accept private investments from companies and venture funds.

When the number of shareholders crossed the 500 threshold, Facebook had to take the company public. Zuckerberg retained control over the company, despite its being a public entity.

Facebook's long-anticipated initial public offering was ultimately plagued by a series of problems: (1) NASDAQ suffered a computer malfunction during the first hours of the IPO, leading to tens of millions of dollars in trades being wrongly placed and incensing brokers like Knight; 2) Its underwriter, Morgan Stanley, claimed that the initial price was too high with too many shares; 3) Some Facebook executives were accused of alerting industry insiders to Facebook's earnings before they were public. Facebook, Morgan Stanley, and NASDAQ were facing litigation over the matters. The stock price decreased to less than half its IPO value in three months.

Robert Greifeld, the NASDAQ chief executive officer, had fought tooth and nail to win the coveted Facebook IPO from the Big Board's hands. Trading was supposed to begin at 11 A.M. of May 18, 2012. However, it was delayed around half an hour due to technical problems with the NASDAQ exchange. For nearly two and a half hours, NASDAQ wasn't sending out trade confirmations, making it impossible for firms like Knight to tell their clients what they had bought or sold.

At 12:01 P.M., Joyce sent an email to Greifeld urging him to halt trading in Facebook shares. There was no answer. The stock struggled to stay above the IPO price for most of the day, forcing underwriters to buy back shares to support the price. Only the aforementioned technical glitches and underwriter support prevented the stock price from falling below the IPO price on the first day of trading.

About three hours later, Joyce called Richard Ketchum, FINRA's head, and told him the industry was "getting crushed." FINRA was the largest independent regulator for all securities firms doing business in the United States. Created through the consolidation of NASD and the member regulation, enforcement and arbitration operations of the New York Stock Exchange, FINRA's mission was to protect American investors by making sure the securities industry operated fairly and honestly. All told, FINRA oversaw about 4,400 brokerage firms, about 162,930 branch offices and approximately 630,020 registered securities representatives, operating out of Washington D.C., New York, and 20 regional offices around the country.

At the closing bell, shares were valued at $38.23, only $0.23 above the IPO price and down $3.82 from the opening bell value. The opening was widely described by the financial press as a disappointment.

Joyce sent another email to Greifeld at 5:07 P.M. describing the IPO as a "disaster". No answer. The Wall Street Journal would later report that Greifeld had been on a plane coming from Silicon Valley and had just landed at Newark at exactly the same time of Joyce's email. That's why not even Schapiro was able to reach him at 4:03 P.M., as Greifeld's armrest phone didn't work and there was no Internet access on the flight.

About 10 minutes later, Joyce called Schapiro, who put him on speakerphone with Cook. Joyce told them the Facebook's glitch-ridden IPO would cost investors tens of millions of dollars. The SEC officials said they were already looking into it. It was only around 6 P.M. that Greifeld was able to return Schapiro's call, summarizing the problems and the actions his team had taken as best he could.

Schapiro had been appointed by President Obama to serve as the 29th chairman of the U.S. SEC. During her tenure, the agency had improved its enforcement program, creating new structures, procedures, and programs to better address the modern financial markets. Schapiro led the agency through one of its most active rulemaking periods, and enacted many other investor protection measures. However, the agency had also struggled to enact rules for implementing the financial-regulation overhaul mandated by the Dodd-Frank Act, to keep pace with real-time monitoring of high-speed trading, and to win legal settlements that passed muster with a public seeking to place blame for the financial crisis.

Former SEC commissioner Annette Nazareth, later a partner in the Washington D.C. office of Davis Polk & Wardwell, and former SEC general counsel and senior policy director David Becker, now a partner at the Cleary Gottlieb Steen & Hamilton law firm in Washington D.C., exchanged emails obtained through a Freedom of Information Act request filed by Bloomberg News that discussed Schapiro as the leader of the top financial regulator. In October 2009, Nazareth wrote that the chairman appeared "really exhausted and downbeat" when she spoke to a New York conference sponsored by SIFMA. "It must be very difficult," Nazareth said in the e-mail.

Becker responded that it was "an impossible job" to be SEC chairman. "The demands from various quarters are strident and irreconcilable, and the agency, as you well know, is a huge management challenge".[2] Not surprisingly, after four years at the helm, Schapiro announced her resignation effective December 2012. Later in April 2013, Schapiro joined Promontory Financial Group as a managing director and chairman of its governance and markets practice.

On Sunday May 20, Greifeld called Joyce at his home in Connecticut, to defend NASDAQ's performance. Once Facebook shares started trading, Greifeld said, the market was working smoothly. "What are you talking about?" Joyce responded, saying the lack of trade confirmations had caused mass confusion. The call lasted a few minutes. The two men hadn't spoken since.

"Yes, I have spoken to him. And I expressed our views. He expressed his views. Obviously we agree to disagree and we had a very professional conversation a few days after, over the weekend of the IPO."

The following day on CNBC's *Squawk on the Street*, Joyce spoke with Cramer and pummeled NASDAQ calling Facebook the worst performance by an exchange on an IPO ever.

"First of all, I want to point out that, this wasn't in anyway shape or form, an industry failure. This is not a systemic issue. All of the financial services firms that were out there handling client flow handled it perfectly. This is not the first IPO that's ever come down the pipe. They understand the process and handled it perfectly. The failure was NASDAQ's. It was NASDAQ's failure. As you heard me say, in the not too distant past, this was arguably the worst performance by an exchange on an IPO ever. And I say exchange."

Joyce was not talking about the fundamentals of Facebook. He was not saying anything about how the underwriters handled the deal. He was speaking about operational issues of an IPO.

"So, at 11:05, we are going to do something. Nothing happens. They kind of go radio silent. Maybe a couple of brief updates until 11:30. Then, there was a trade on the table. Going into that trade, they knew. They knew they had technical issues. They knew they had systemic issues. And they proceeded to continue. Now, we made fun of BATS a couple of weeks ago. They had a problem, they pulled back. NASDAQ went at it full board. Problem. Big problem. That created the second problem. For 2 1/2 hours, we didn't hear a thing. We were trading blind for 2 1/2 hours."

Joyce complained that the information flow was completely squeegee and it turned out that Knight owed institutions reports because they were trying to sell, for example, at 41.5.

They opened at 42. You do a report. We ended up when the reports came in around 1:50, 2:00, we found out we were not net short; we were net long. So, it was just series of events I had not seen before and so that's why operationally it was a failure. You can't stop communicating. So, they fundamentally had an approach going into it that was maybe a little predetermined. Were they stubborn? I don't know. When you know you have a technical problem, of the size that they had, I think you have to take a step back and either delay the opening later in the day or perhaps. They were kind of lucky it was over a weekend. They could have easily over the weekend gone after software issues they discovered and opened it this morning."

NASDAQ held a conference call on Sunday and indicated that they had tested their systems over and over and thought they were ready to go. Obviously they weren't ready to go.

"Apparently, they didn't test the cancel part enough. That's what it was. As you indicated a different price, you had a limit, you canceled the order and put in a new limit. The communication and technology that was taking place on that just continued to fail. Systems can handle the flow. That's one of the best things the exchanges have done in the last five years is ramp up for the data they process and the trades they process. The system can handle the flow. This particular software issue couldn't and we should have stepped back."

Knight wouldn't have been the only firm impacted. Was NASDAQ willing to admit the issues and make brokers whole?

"I think that they understand how important this is. Because dozens of financial service firms were affected here. I am sure that Mr. Greifeld understands the gravity of the situation and will go out of his way to make people whole to the extent they can. I would think that the NYSE feels their position right now is pretty competitive. They will have to make the case to the issuers that it was an anomaly. I wish them well."

The May 18 tension and Joyce's outspoken media appearances on the subject eroded a relationship that went back to the 1990s, when Joyce, then at Merrill Lynch, was a customer of Greifeld's technology company called Automated Securities Clearance, developers of BRASS (a technology platform which later would become the industry standard trade order management system for NASDAQ stocks); this firm was later purchased by SunGard in early 1999.

BRASS (Brokerage Real-Time Application Support System) provided the NASDAQ trader everything he or she needed to operate electronically. BRASS served indeed over 3000 desktop terminals in roughly 200 brokerage firms representing over 50 percent of NASDAQ volume. Automated Securities Clearance was also the majority owner of BRUT, officially called the BRASS Utility, an electronic communications network. Minority equity partners included Goldman Sachs, Knight, Merrill Lynch and Morgan Stanley Dean Witter.

In February 2000, BRUT completed a merger of equals with Strike Technologies; the new entity was, at the time, the third largest ECN in terms of volume. Early 2004, NASDAQ's Greifeld decided to buy BRUT for $190 million in cash; at the time, the exchange said the acquisition would position it for forthcoming market structure changes being contemplated by regulators by providing NASDAQ with the ability to route orders via an internal broker-dealer to multiple liquidity pools; nevertheless, NASDAQ and SunGard planned to enter into multiyear processing agreements.

Greifeld was a director on Knight's board when the company hired Joyce as chief executive in 2002. Similarly, Joyce joined NASDAQ's board in 2003 at the same time Greifeld was appointed president and CEO. Both stepped down years ago from each other's boards.

Knight was also listed on NASDAQ for 12 years with the symbol NITE, until 2010, when Joyce moved the listing to NASDAQ rival NYSE Euronext with the symbol KCG, saying Knight belonged on the NYSE alongside financial giants like Goldman Sachs. Behind the scenes, Joyce had been irked about Greifeld's efforts to rein in off-exchange trading pools like the ones Knight ran, including Knight Direct, Knight Link and Knight Match, which were managed by managing directors Meaghan Mullins, Erica Attonito and Tara Muller.

Mullins had been the executive selected to ring the opening bell on February 25, 2010, when Knight officially started trading at the NYSE. She was the only female at the widely-admired NYSE balcony, joined for the occasion by Mike Strashnov, Cushman, Bill Cronin,

Mike Corrao and Joyce. With almost a decade with the firm by then, Mullins had played an important role in guaranteeing access to Knight's products from buy- and sell-side Order Entry Management Systems (OEMS). A few months later in May, Knight would be established as a destination on the Secure Financial Transaction Infrastructure (SFTI) network by NYSE Technologies, providing access to its electronic market making, Knight Link access to equity liquidity, Knight Direct multi-asset class EMS and agency-only algorithms, the Knight Match dark pool, the Hotspot FX ECN and Knight BondPoint's fixed income ECN.

"Knight is pleased to open our products to the wide breadth of NYSE Technologies clients over the reliable and resilient SFTI network. We are committed to providing as many points as possible for market participants to access Knight's liquidity, and our establishment as a destination on the SFTI network furthers our goal," Mullins had said.

She would celebrate her 35th birthday on September 1, 2012, six days in advance at City Bistro Restaurant Lounge Bar in Hoboken; she used to hang out on the roof, her favorite spot. A baking aficionado (once referred as June Cleaver's reincarnation by fellow managing director Tonya Basso-Walker), Mullins would "torture co-workers" with chocolate cookies she prepared specially during holidays; she would confess that she had more "specialty" pans than she knew what to do with. Torture in the family would be endured mostly by her father Tim and younger brother Danny (including a one eyed smiley face wearing a graduation cap). Friends would call her Martha Stewart and jokingly nag her to open a bakery.

Erica Attonito, who happened to be pregnant the month of the incident, was recruited by Loyola College for her excellent tennis ability and more than stellar lacrosse skills. Originally from Madison, New Jersey, Attonito had been instrumental in Loyola's team clinching the CAA regular-season championship with a 6-0 record. "She wasn't the best lacrosse player at Madison High School, but what I liked about her was her drive, that inner instinct to be the best. She was spunky," said Loyola coach Diane Aikens. "We could count on her to come off the bench and score the big goals."[3]

Attonito's drive served her well at first BT Radianz first and later at Knight. One of her colleagues highlights her knowing how to treat people and delivers results. "She is intelligent, savvy and puts the customer first with integrity." Another one pointed out her going above and beyond the call of duty. "Erica is very responsive to any type of business matter that comes her way. Erica is on her game day after day. Due to her hard work and dedication, she overachieved year after year."

Tara Muller was responsible for the Knight Link business across asset classes. Before decamping at Knight, Muller had spent ten years as sales specialist at Reuters America. She was a proud co-founder of Knight's Women's Professional Network, an entity that attempted to serve as a vehicle for women to network and develop opportunities with both their peers and senior management to help foster professional and personal growth. It was the ideal forum for women at Knight to unite, thrive and succeed, according to its website. She was also active in the Securities Traders Association of New York and Chicago.

Joyce soon emerged as the most outspoken critic of Greifeld's leadership. "This is just business," Joyce had said in a recent interview. "Bob Greifeld is a nice man, but I think their organization failed on several fronts."

Joyce became one of the first major brokerage-firm executives to blame NASDAQ's glitches for their losses, which Knight had estimated at $35 million just for the firm. Since then, he had lambasted the exchange group's plan to compensate for loss claims related to the IPO. NASDAQ had said in June 11 that it would seek SEC approval to pay out $40 million, a fraction of the $500 million or so in total losses estimated by Wall Street firms.

"NASDAQ created this problem. NASDAQ needs to come up with the solution to the problem. And they are not even in the ballpark with what they are proposing. From what I can gather and I am no expert on what they presented, I don't know the details, I know it was $40 million, $13 million of which is cash, which looks like they are giving money back they made on their short and not a whole lot else. So, I just think that they need to understand what their clients went through, be a little client focused, and come up with an appropriate solution. The solution they put forward is frankly anemic."

For Joyce, the key issue was how NASDAQ could have allowed a market to operate for two and a half hours without the street knowing what positions it had.

"Were clients taken care of? Were their tickets matched up? Where was the information? You can't trade blind, no more than you can drive blind on the LIE. You can't trade blind in the markets of today. So, the issue is the mistake, the bad decisions, the situation they created and it isn't a binary thing. It isn't a simple solution to it. The knock on effect for what they did affected everything, from mismatched orders to lost orders and, yeah, we do have some clients that we felt an obligation to. It would be nice if NASDAQ felt like they had an obligation to their clients."

Joyce said that he didn't want Knight being a poster child for the Facebook/NASDAQ situation. He was just stating the facts and it was the industry that had an issue with NASDAQ.

"I was talking about the industry issues well beyond any individual references I made to Knight Capital Group and I will continue to do so. This is an industry issue. We got punched in the nose as I said on the panel that day. We definitely got punched in the nose and a lot of us did, but NASDAQ's failure wasn't limited to what we were doing on our desk. The failure radiated across Wall Street."

NASDAQ had announced a plan to discount trading fees as part of a make-nice offering to clients who lost money.

"My view is that paying the street back with rebates on order flow is, if you will, too cute by a half. I don't understand why they think they should

get more business because of their behavior on the Facebook IPO. If I were a competing exchange, like the New York Stock Exchange, I assume, I believe they stated something. Certainly Bill just said something."

DirectEdge CEO Bill O'Brien blasted the proposal too, saying he didn't think it was even legal.

"Any exchange pricing proposal has to be filed with the SEC and there is a process depending on the way it is filed to be handled. I don't think this is legal. I don't think it will get approved by the SEC. I think we'll be talking about this for a very long time."

Niederauer, already irked at Greifeld because of his failed attempt to take over the Big Board, was none too pleased either. Niederauer blasted Greifeld's discounting dictum as a cheap way to try to leverage its mistake into increased trading volumes.

"This is tantamount to forcing the industry to subsidize NASDAQ's missteps and would establish a harmful precedent that could have far-reaching implications for the markets, investors and the public interest."

Tabb Group's Larry Tabb summarized the situation, "This situation [between NASDAQ and other institutional traders] is going to get ugly. When you admit to an error and you seek to compensate people partially they are going to get upset."

On June 20, Joyce testified before a House Financial Services subcommittee, arguing that their business democratized a stock market once dominated by a handful of Wall Street firms. Joyce took swipes at the exchanges, but more surprisingly, also at high-frequency trading firms. Even though Knight is also part of that business, Joyce had said regulators should experiment with slowing them down, leveling the playing field for small investors.

He suggested requiring buy and sell quotes to last at least one second, an eternity for speed traders used to canceling orders in fractions of a second. Across town, at a Commodity Futures Trading

Commission hearing, his comments had popped up on the smartphones of other high-frequency trading executives.

Some scoffed, saying the idea, previously rejected by regulators, would force them to retool their businesses. "Ask T.J. if he would go first and tell us all how it feels," Chris Concannon, a partner at high-frequency trading firm Virtu Financial, later told another attendee. Concannon had the background to step up his rhetoric; prior to joining Virtu in 2009, he had worked at the SEC in the mid-1990s and later held several positions at Island ECN and Instinet before joining NASDAQ in 2003 when it bought a business owned by Instinet. He spent six years as executive vice president and CEO of NASDAQ's European arm. He would meet on April 10 with the SEC's new chairman Mary Jo White about overseeing the agency's trading and markets division; it had been chairman White's first day on the job. Concannon had said he planned to say in Viola's team.

In another of life's ironies, destiny would be having Virtu later attempting twice to make a deal with Knight, in early August and late November.

At first, Greifeld had offered just a $40 million voluntary payout to the firms that suffered losses in Facebook's public debut. Greifeld had described the $62 million sweetened offer as the "definitive" plan that would satisfy the majority of traders. Ultimately, Knight Capital decided to back NASDAQ's $62-million plan, despite resistance from Citigroup and UBS, as described in a letter to the SEC on August 29.

Knight, along with Citigroup and the Securities Industry and Financial Markets Association (SIFMA), had recommended a broader discussion of the limitation of liability that exchanges enjoy for financial losses resulting from their own technical mishaps. NASDAQ's reimbursement plan was voluntary since the exchange's cap on specific losses it causes is $3 million. SIFMA was the leading securities industry trade group bringing together the shared interests of more than 650 securities firms, banks, and asset managers; it had been formed on November 1, 2006, from the merger of The Bond Market Association and the Securities Industry Association.

"As exchanges have evolved over the years, with greater and greater emphasis on profits and business expansion, the time is right for a more fulsome discussion on this issue," Knight said in a letter.

Knight said it supported the plan proposed by NASDAQ to boost the pool for payments to $62 million from $40 million and to reimburse brokers in cash instead of a combination of cash and credit. However, Knight did urge the SEC to reject a portion of NASDAQ's plan requiring firms that sign on to waive their right to sue the exchange, likely before they knew how much they would be reimbursed. Knight had said that would set "a harmful precedent".

"Setting forth those types of requirements in the context of a rule filing inappropriately mixes commercial issues with regulatory requirements," Knight said in the three-page letter also addressed to SEC's Schapiro.

It said if the SEC disagreed and determined that some form of release was appropriate, it should only be sought after NASDAQ members were notified of the amount NASDAQ was willing to pay under the terms of the accommodation plan.

UBS was joined in ripping Greifeld's sweetened offer by Citigroup. Both companies urged the SEC to block the NASDAQ plan. Moreover, UBS was threatening to sue the exchange. "The proposed accommodation policy unfairly sets a monetary cap that is vastly disproportionate to reported trading losses resulting from the Facebook IPO," wrote UBS general counsel Mark Shelton in a comment letter to the SEC on August 22. "UBS alone suffered losses in excess of $350 million, the vast majority of which resulted directly from NASDAQ's unprecedented failure to deliver execution reports for tens of thousands of trade."

One thing going for Greifeld was that after August 1 at least some of the heat had been taken off NASDAQ when one of its toughest critics, Knight Capital's Joyce, suffered a technical glitch that put his trading firm on the brink of collapse.

On October 26, 2012, the SEC issued an order instituting proceedings to determine whether to approve or to disapprove the NASDAQ's proposal. On December 7, NASDAQ submitted a new letter to respond to additional comments filed in connection with the above-referenced proposal to amend NASDAQ Rule 4626 ((Limitation of Liability) to establish a one-time, voluntary accommodation pool of up to $62 million to compensate NASDAQ members and their customers for objectively measured losses directly arising from system difficulties NASDAQ experienced during the initial public offering of Facebook.

Finally, on March 25, 2013, the SEC approved NASDAQ's compensation plan for firms that lost money in Facebook's market debut, in what amounted to a victory for the exchange operator that also set the stage for potential lawsuits from firms seeking more. $62 million was a far cry from the $500 million in estimated losses from Facebook's initial public offering. However, if NASDAQ would have been mandated to make whole all the brokers that lost money in the IPO, that might have bankrupted the exchange and significantly disrupted the delicate U.S. market structure.[4]

Chapter Ten

What Made Knight Tick and Profit

It was in early July of 2012 when NYSE received approval from the SEC to establish the RLP, which would direct trades from retail investors on to a special dark pool where trading firms could bid to offer them the best price. Trading would not be visible to the public. The program was a direct challenge to the current industry practice that had seen most trades from retail investors directed to a few Wall Street firms that bought or sold the shares before the trades could reach one of the nation's regulated exchanges.

The SEC had approved the RLP on a pilot basis after months of deliberation, despite the opposition it faced from many corners of the industry. Critics of the program, Knight among them, had said it could lead to an increase in trading away from the exchanges and accelerate the fragmentation of the nation's stock markets. The proposal had also been controversial because it would allow the exchange to execute stock trades in increments of less than a penny. This had been possible in off-exchange venues but until then it had been illegal for the exchanges.

This program was intended to complement existing marketplace offerings for retail investors and for use by retail brokerage firms directly and market intermediaries that serviced retail order flow providers. Under this program, trades from retail investors were to be shifted to a special platform where trading houses competed to offer them the best price. The NYSE expected to activate the RLP on August 1, 2012.

Joseph Mecane, executive vice president at NYSE, had trumpeted the program as a way to provide price improvement for retail orders within an exchange environment, bringing individual investors new economic incentives and ensuring greater transparency, liquidity and competition. What he didn't expect was that the implementation of this program would later indirectly cause a leading participant in the market to suffer the most embarrassing glitch and endure five days of hell.

In a November 28, 2011 letter to the SEC commenting on NYSE's proposal to establish the RLP, Knight's General Counsel, Leonard Amoruso had pointed out certain components of the proposal that had the potential to cause significant changes to U.S. equity market structure, which at the moment was providing retail investors with better than even "equity execution quality and access to the marketplace."

"The 'positive experience' enjoyed by retail investors today is the culmination of years of rigorous competition and sensible, well-vetted regulation. As such, this 'positive experience' must remain sacrosanct when considering any change to equity market structure, especially some of the more profound changes contemplated by the current tiling. Again, we support the NYSE`s efforts to establish a program that will provide greater price competition for retail orders. When market centers compete on a level playing field, it inures to the benefit of investors."

Ultimately, in a bid to keep a grip on customers, Knight Capital pushed to accommodate its systems to incorporate NYSE's RLP on August 1. Unlike rivals that took a more measured approach, Knight Capital's presence on the day of the launch of the program would only continue the aggressive style championed by its chief executive officer of taking advantage of any opportunity to increase revenues and profits.

While the SEC only approved the RLP in June, the exchange had made sure that specifications of the changes had been available to market participants since early December; a testing platform had been available for six months. Over the several months before August 1, companies had tweaked their computer code to push itself on to the new platform; despite this extensive testing, the real test would come on launch day, when real trading had to be supported.

Hesitation from some competitors to participate in any new system-wide implementation from day one was common practice for any IT organization, despite the pressure from their business side. There was an increased chance of malfunction, as the sponsor's systems might not behave as expected, creating complications for all participants, even if their systems behaved properly.

For some firms, a few weeks of testing would not have been compelling enough to accelerate their participation in the RLP; the pressure to stay competitive meant that the time between developing new trading software and putting it in production became shorter and shorter and shorter. For Knight Capital, however, it was an opportunity not to be missed. You could only have expected thousands of eyes monitoring this deployment.

In the recent years, Knight had become a global financial services firm that provided access to the capital markets across multiple asset classes to a broad network of clients, including buy- and sell-side firms and corporate issuers.

The firm engaged in market making and trading across global equities, fixed income, foreign exchange, options and futures. Knight was the leading source of liquidity in U.S. equities among all securities firms across NYSE- and NASDAQ-listed stocks, ETFs and Over-the-Counter Bulletin Board (OTCBB) securities. The firm had three main operating segments: Market Making, Institutional Sales and Trading and Electronic Execution Services.

Market Making included all global market making across regions and asset classes. In addition to the electronic market making in U.S. equities, the segment included cash market making, DMM services at the NYSE, market making in European equities and U.S. options, and non-client quantitative trading, a euphemism to represent high-frequency trading.

On the other hand, Institutional Sales and Trading covered a range of activities including full service sales and trading across global equities, fixed income, ETFs and options, research, equity and debt capital markets, reverse mortgage origination and HMBS securitization, and asset management.

Finally, Electronic Execution Services consisted of electronic trading products that provided clients with market access, speed and trading efficiency. The offering included Knight Direct, Knight Hotspot FX and Knight BondPoint, each focused on different asset classes, equities, foreign exchange and fixed income, respectively.

Knight's trading technology was central to providing their clients access to multiple market destinations and trade execution services with deep liquidity and actionable market intelligence.

Knight prided itself in its robust technology infrastructure and flexible architecture which provided customers instant access across multiple asset classes to liquidity both within and outside of Knight. Their sophisticated execution platform and quantitative models allowed them to tailor their trading and routing technology according to client-driven parameters while adhering to the extensive regulatory framework.

Knight had built a gateway to the global markets with connectivity to multiple external market centers including ECNs, dark pools, exchanges and other destinations.

In addition, Knight constantly strived to develop new and more efficient ways to improve service to their clients. They had a large, experienced team of sales traders to ensure their clients were met with best-in-class service. Their high-caliber and experienced team of quantitative strategists and developers built and refined new models to help their clients achieve their trading objectives. Their motto was "The Science of Trading, The Standard of Trust."

Knight was not afraid to pay top dollar for the best talent money could buy. A top developer working at Electronic Execution Services' Knight Direct would have made $250K in annual total compensation and have seen it grow at 15 percent to 20 percent every year. Even a junior developer out of school could have expected a base salary of $100K and a bonus at the end of the year that varied from $5K for mediocre performers to $25K for top performers. Two or three years later they would be comfortably hitting $200K, enough to guarantee nice digs close to the office, which was a must given the long hours projects demanded in peak times.

Knight ran one of Wall Street's most successful and innovative automated electronic trading units at their Market-making group, ETG, which specialized in automated market making and principal trading. The group prided itself in their cutting edge quantitative models and trading technology so much as to make Citadel's Griffin salivate with anticipation of enormous profits by poaching former leaders Nazarali and Cushman and trying to replicate them. Knight's quantitative strategists developed statistical models of asset prices using data from the exchanges, company filings and other sources. These models detected and traded on market inefficiencies. The technologists in the group provided high-performance trading platforms with low latency with salaries that easily would have been double those in Knight Direct; $400K wasn't unusual in total annual compensation for top performers. Of course, they had to exhibit masters or PhD degrees from top schools, and be great at modeling complicated financial scenarios or finding statistical anomalies to exploit in high-frequency trading.

Furthermore, they had to persuade Unson Allen, ETG's head of recruitment, that they had the chops to succeed. Allen oversaw global recruiting efforts for ETG, group where she had worked since its inception, after receiving her bachelor of arts from the University of California at Santa Barbara; she had attended Lynbrook High School in San Jose, known as one of the top high schools in the Bay Area. She was based in the firm's Santa Clara office, which was conveniently located for her on-campus recruiting efforts near the University of California at Berkeley and Stanford University. Though recruiters tended to target the big name schools, Allen kept a close eye on schools such as the University of Illinois at Urbana Champaign, the University of Maryland at College Park and S.U.N.Y. Stony Brook on Long Island, all of which were well known for their computer science departments.

Allen had established Knight's campus recruitment effort which included the top domestic and international universities, as well as ETG's mentoring program; an application to join the Stanford Computer Forum, a collaboration effort between the Computer Science and the Electrical Engineering Departments at Stanford and global companies, described Knight as a firm at the forefront of electronic trading with people at the center of their business. "We are passionate about what we do, whether it is building sophisticated models and systems to improve trade profitability, execution quality and reliability, or putting minds together to help buy- and sell-side firms make smart trading decisions. Knight is a young and vibrant company founded with an entrepreneurial spirit that is woven into our culture and engenders innovation at every turn."

"We are definitely concentrating more time and effort in going out to the campuses," Allen had commented to Advanced Trading's Ivy Schmerken. "We want to be on the cutting edge of technology and quant strategies, and we want students to know that Knight is there." As Knight electronic trading business was growing, it had expanded across asset classes and geographies, adding strategies for foreign exchange, fixed income, options and international equities, according to Allen, and a number of the firm's new quantitative hires were to support that expansion. "In order to be successful, we need to hire more quants and add more strategies," asserted Allen, who noted that for the past two years Knight had looked to hire anywhere between 15 to 20 quantitative strategists.

Knight's ETG was competing for on-campus and experienced talent not only with similar groups at the large banks as well as hedge funds focused on automated trading, but also with Silicon Valley's startups and technology giants. Only recently it had become known to the press that a developer from Goldman Sachs was being charged for the theft of proprietary computer code used for conducting high frequency trades; Sergey Aleynikov had departed Goldman in 2009 to pursue a new opportunity with Teza Technologies, where he was going to show off his programming skills. He had excelled at programming while at Goldman making $400K but he had been tempted with an even catchier compensation: $300K salary and $700K bonus, which would allow him to be a bigger player in a smaller firm, doing the same job. On July 3, 2009, Alynikov, who had started with Teza in Chicago on the previous day, was arrested after Goldman tipped off the Feds about the computer code that he had stolen.

It wasn't unusual for recent graduates to be extremely picky. "I've had people in interviews ask me point-blank what the social value is that we're adding; it's very hard to compete with the well-known startups here in California," said Pang Chau, the Santa Clara-based managing director of in charge of ETG recruiting on the West Coast. As a computer-science graduate student at Stanford University in 2001, Chau was himself at first hesitant about taking a job in finance as well. He said he dropped off his résumé at a Knight Capital career-fair booth only because he felt guilty accepting the free T-shirt recruiters were giving away. "Once they're in the door, rarely do we lose them to tech companies."[1]

Canadian-born Nazarali had been a senior managing director responsible for ETG. He was the best regarded electronic trading executive at Knight, where he had spent 10 years, enjoying

Pasternak's full confidence. Prior to Knight, Nazarali was employed with management consulting firms Ernst & Young and Bain & Company. He had graduated from the University of Chicago's Booth School of Business with an MBA in 1994 and the University of Western Ontario with a bachelor of arts with honors in business administration in 1989. Nazarali served on the board of directors of Direct Edge and Easdaq N.V., owner of the pan European retail trading platform Equiduct. He was also a member of the New York Stock Exchange's Electronic Trading Advisory Committee.

Nazarali's transition to Citadel didn't hinder his enthusiasm to participate in the JPMorgan Chase Corporate Challenge; while at Knight he was able to finish the race in 25:45 (2005), his debut in the Citadel team was disappointing, 27:14 (2012); adding insult to injury, his colleague Cushman bested him in the race, finishing in 25:19.

In November 2010, just a few months prior to his departure from the firm, Nazarali was the only Knight executive (other than Joyce) to be featured in the book *Current Perspectives on Modern Equity Markets*, a collection of articles by financial industry experts. Other experts featured there included Professor Angel, Arthur Levitt (the twenty-fifth and longest-serving chairman of the SEC, 1993-2001, consultant to GETCO and Goldman Sachs, and director of Bloomberg LP), TD Ameritrade's Fred Tomczyk, Daniel Mathisson (managing director, head of Advanced Execution Services, AES, Credit Suisse) and NYSE's Niederauer, among others.

As expected, the book said that thanks to computerized trading, stock investors obtained "better service at a lower cost", because of a narrowed gap between the prices buyers bid and sellers ask. It urged regulators to "be sensitive to the 'unintended consequences' of poorly considered responses to concerns now being raised about recent changes in the trading environment, many of which are not universally understood." Needless to say, a lobbyist for Knight, David Franasiak of Williams & Jensen, showed the paper to regulators and congressional staffers, who in turn later repeated conclusions from it in hearings and meetings.[2]

In his essay *Overview of the U.S. Equity Markets Today*, Nazarali reflected on the U.S. equity markets being the envy of the world and the basis for Americans' wealth creation and innovation over the last 100 years. "Liquidity is unparalleled, and the fairness, efficiency, and cost unmatched." His take was that recent events like the Flash Crash had to be put in context; certainly, changes to the marketplace over the last ten years, primarily technology driven, needed to be reviewed and addressed, but carefully. Not in a vacuum, not as a knee-jerk reaction, he advised, but as a thoughtful, data-driven effort to protect this treasure.

Interviewed by Trades Magazine, Nazarali suggested new incentives for firms to be in the market more and provide liquidity, which had all but disappeared on May 6, 2010. Incentives could be in rebate form, or relief around short sales. He gave the example of NYSE's DMM and SLP programs, where it had been said, "We'll provide economic incentives to be at the inside. And if you are a supplemental liquidity provider and come on our platform at the inside at 'x' percentage of the time, we'll give you an enhanced rebate." Lots of people came on their platform, he said, and they started adding a lot of liquidity, which resulted in an increase in NYSE market share. "If you provide those types of incentives, people will respond to them and the market will be better off."

On September 24, 2010, Nazarali disclosed that Knight and the other four largest market makers (UBS, Citadel, Citigroup and ETrade) had discussed with federal securities regulators manipulative behaviors in U.S. stocks that happened the day before. These behaviors impacted shares worth less than $1 and were manifested by taking both sides of trades in order to earn big rebates. Nazarali said that this was happening for hundreds of millions of shares per day, adding that this type of market manipulation was hard to prove, although it was costing Knight tens of thousands of dollars per day on some days.

At issue was whether an individual trader was using separate brokerage accounts to trade against himself, something known as a wash trade. Exchanges charged fees to those that executed against standing buy and sell orders, something called a take fee, and paid rebates to those that provided standing orders that were executed against. This was known as "maker-taker" pricing. While stocks were normally priced in penny increments, rules allowed exchanges to price sub-dollar stocks in one-hundredth of a cent. The fees and rebates, however, were based on penny increments for all stocks, including sub-dollar stocks, which created a possible loophole through which traders could earn out-sized rebates. A trader could, for example, send a "limit order" bid through one brokerage account, and a corresponding "market order" to sell that same stock in another account. After trading with himself, the trader earned the bid's rebate and paid the smaller selling fee, which was usually fixed at retail brokers like ETrade, and walked away with the difference. In this scenario, market makers such as Knight would foot much of the bill.

For a short period in early 2010, large exchanges paid outsized fees and rebates in sub-$1 stocks, but, William Karsh, chief operating officer at exchange operator Direct Edge, said they did away with it in the spring after protests from market makers. Eric Hess, general counsel, explained Direct Edge's rationale better than anybody else in an April 28 letter to the SEC commenting on their Concept Release on Equity Market Structure.

"Certain recent rebate structure for sub-dollar stocks is an example of how liquidity incentives can bear an unreasonable relationship to the liquidity they are purporting to support. For example, until recently, NASDAQ BX offered a liquidity provision rebate of 0.25 percent of total value traded for sub-dollar stocks. This amounted to up to $0.25 per hundred shares for securities trading just below one dollar. Since the trading

increment for such securities is hundredths of a penny, an intermediary or investor acting through an intermediary could target liquid sub-dollar securities trading close to $1.00 within the NBBO's minimum price variation and only take on an economic risk of $0.01 per hundred shares (the difference between the bid and offer prices) and collect $0.24 per hundred shares in profit before factoring out nominal fixed costs. This is driven by an MPV (Minimum Price Variation) that is reduced by a factor of one hundred when a security begins trading below $1 per share, while maximum access fees (and rebates) are reduced only pro-rata. As this threshold is crossed, market structure drives the creation of new rebate trading strategies, as opposed to being a factor in other, stand-along trading strategies or business models.

"For this reason, Direct Edge announced our decision last month to effectively peg the rebate offered on sub-dollar stocks to the ratio of the Regulation NMS access fee limitation of 0.30 percent to the minimum price variation for stocks below one dollar. Using the above example, this means that the rebate can be no more than $0.00003 per hundred shares for taking an economic risk of $0.0001. As trading in sub-dollar securities has become an increasing component of overall trading volume, providing rebates to incentivize the provision of liquidity while confining such rebates to 30 percent of the MPV strikes the appropriate balance between competition and preservation of market quality. Most importantly, it discourages the provision of liquidity that is not driven by latent security demand, but rather by the receipt of an oversized rebate."

Nazarali's activism for the industry didn't stop when he moved to Chicago. He participated in the market technology roundtable put together by the SEC at their Washington D.C.'s headquarters; the panel was to discuss "the relationship between the operational stability and integrity of the securities markets and the ways that market participants design, implement, and manage complex and interconnected trading technologies", and Nazarali was to expand on the written statement already provided to the SEC. Few at Citadel were surprised to know that chief information officer Tom Miglis's habits included combing not only his carefully trimmed moustache but also every detail of the firm's letters to regulators.[3]

In his presentation, Nazarali was critical of his former firm's risk management processes. "So if you look at what happened at Knight Capital on August 1, the first five minutes of that trading was really a software problem. The next 35 minutes where the software was not shut off was really a risk management and control and management processes problem. And I think it's important for all of us as we make our systems more robust and improve how we implement the software, that we also put in place the right management and risk protocols so that if something like that happens we can pick up the phone and call the New York Stock Exchange and say, 'Shut off all trading. Kill all open orders.' If that had been done five minutes after on August 1 at Knight Capital, we probably wouldn't be here right now."

He contrasted this with Citadel's own "circuit breakers", which were no other than the controls Pasternak would have devised himself at Knight.

"For example, at Citadel, we have developed this fuse box technology over the last ten years, and it's a system that sits outside of your trading software, and it listens to all the trades and executions that happen, and under certain conditions much like your fuse at home will trip, if the ADV (Average Daily Volume) that you're trading is much higher than a set parameter, if your risk limits are much higher, if your P&L goes out of bounds, it will trip and then a human will then have to turn it back on. We fine-tune it every time we have a mistake. It has limits built in – whether exceeding average daily volumes, or risk parameters on a position in any single name, aggregate book or a market exposure gets too large. It's gone off a number of times, certainly. But that's why we're not in the news."

In response to a question from SEC commissioner Troy Paredes about how managers would know whether or not there's been enough testing, "So from a business perspective, how do you know; how do you think about enough is enough; now it's time to go ahead and roll it out?" Nazarali pointed out that nobody can really know if the testing was enough, and it was really just a business judgment in which you looked at the cost benefit of the potential error.

"So, for example, at Citadel Execution Services, whenever we do a rollout, there is a decision made where: okay, should we wait; should we do more, as you said, more testing, or do we implement this? And it's a cost benefit where you say: okay. There is a one percent chance of this creating a problem. How big a problem will it create? How many customers will it impact? And, you know, what's the magnitude of that? Okay. That's unacceptable. And you never know that percentage exactly because you may think it's one percent, but it could be three percent or half a percent, but it's really that kind of cost benefit where you try to anticipate the potential cost of something going wrong."

Schapiro immediately asked how do managers then think about the cost not just to customers, but to the broader marketplace, investor confidence, and the customers of other firms that may be impacted. Taken by surprise, Nazarali commended Schapiro for the question.

"Because we are such a large player in the market, we do consider all of those things on the market-making side. You know, we have roughly 25 percent market share in retail equity markets. So we realize that if there is an impairment of investor confidence, it's going to affect our business."

Before jumping ship, Cushman was a managing director at Knight, which he had joined in 2002. Cushman, who held a PhD in mathematics from the University of Chicago and a master's also in mathematics from Carnegie Mellon University, had taught a course in high frequency finance and stochastic control at Rutgers University and worked at Kromos Technology, a technology startup.

Cushman had been quoted for Knight's Annual Report 2007, "Quantitative models and automated trading strategies have revolutionized the financial markets over the past decade. At Knight, we take pride in bringing benefits of these innovations to every client, from an online broker to the largest institutional investor."

Just a month before leaving Knight, on January18, Cushman had participated in an SEC-sponsored meeting with market makers in equity markets regarding the Dodd-Frank Act. Participants there had discussed equity market making and the anticipated effect of the study's real-time short position disclosure and the pilot transaction marking regime on equity marking making and the markets.

Two months after their coordinated departure from Knight, on February 28, 2011, it was announced that Nazarali and Cushman would join Citadel in September. They were to work with groups across the firm including equities, currencies and high-frequency trading.

Hiring two of the most celebrated ETG executives from Knight at once didn't make Joyce very happy. If there was ever a single firm Knight thought of as its nastiest rival, it would have been Citadel. For Knight employees, it was a mix of hate, dislike, admiration and envy that was easy to go over with an interesting number of zeros in their paycheck. Citadel had tremendous resources and hired extremely talented people. There was an instance when a top technologist had just joined the firm; a talented guy with absolute ignorance of the industry. In barely two months, he became an expert, a feat unreachable for most mortals before 10 years. That was Citadel: full of people who really understood complex concepts quickly, people with the best chances of success. Of course, there was always the possibility that a new hire didn't perform according to expectations, but Citadel didn't have a problem getting rid of an employee and hiring a new person.

That was Griffin's competitive streak. He presided over one of the world's most successful and influential hedge funds with $11 billion in assets and 1,400 employees. Citadel had dramatically rebounded from the lows of the financial crisis. September 2008, he wrote in a letter to investors, was the "single worst month, by far, in the history of Citadel; our performance reflected extraordinary market conditions that I did not fully anticipate, combined with regulatory changes driven more by populism than policy." For 2006 and 2007, its main funds, Kensington and Wellington, had returned about 30 percent annually. However, in 2008, both funds were down 50 percent. Ultimately, the Kensington and Wellington funds capped off two years of solid returns in 2009 and 2010 by crossing their high water marks with gains of more than 20 percent, outperforming the industry average of five percent losses.

Nazarali eventually took over Citadel's CES in June 2012. CES was the unit responsible for funneling orders from retail brokerage firms to exchanges and private trading platforms. He was also overseeing Citadel's algorithmic trading business and Apogee, Citadel Securities' alternative trading system. CES had been led before by former Knight managing director Andrew Kolinsky, hired all the back in 2000 to manage U.S. broker-dealer sales and new business development; Raquet considered Kolinsky one of the top marketing talents in the securities industry.

CES, like other so-called wholesale market makers, had been hit by the glitches that struck Facebook's initial public offering on NASDAQ.

Michael Durbin, author of *All About High-Frequency Trading*, was one of the original CES developers and provided an impressive look at this monumental development.

"The Citadel system would not only calculate hundreds of thousands of option prices simultaneously, an impressive feet in its own right, but also inject streams of bids and offers into the markets at literally superhuman speed. The custom-built quoting engines would tirelessly inject many millions of quotes into the markets every day, each of them a binding commitment to buy or sell a listed option contract at some specified price, each one the result of a software program running on a computer. And while the quoters were busy doing that, 'electronic eyes' would scan everyone

else's quotations and orders, hundreds of millions per day, all in real-time. It would be like standing at the end of an open fire house and examining each drop of water before it hit the ground. When the electronic eye (or EE) found someone offering to buy an option for more than it was worth, or to sell it for less, it would immediately submit an order to take the other side of the trade for a tiny profit."

CES had become the number one market maker in retail order flow and the leading options market maker for retail broker-dealers, achievements that made Griffin very proud. CES was part of Citadel Securities, which executed over 21 percent of daily U.S. listed equity option volume and 13 percent of U.S. equity volume. "I am proud of the role that CES Retail has played in making markets more efficient and in delivering high quality execution for our clients," commented Nazarali. Chinese walls separate CES, based in New York, from the asset management side, confirmed Nazarali.

Putting Nazarali on top was just the first step to turbo charge CES's attack on Knight's territory. Nazarali saw tremendous opportunity to further expand their platform by making a push into the over-the-counter market, following their success as a wholesaler and market maker in NMS securities and listed options.

Citadel had started operations in October 2011 and had quietly become one of the top 25 market makers in OTC securities, ranked by the number of shares traded per day, making markets in around 6,300 OTC names and joining the upper echelons of OTC market makers, along with Knight Equity Markets, Citi/ATD, UBS Securities and ETrade Capital Markets.

However, the market maker could have a tough time out there getting business. Traders Magazine had talked to two buy-side managers, and both said they would not do business with Citadel despite the increased staff and focus. "I would not send them an indication or anything, as they are out there looking to get information and trade against it," one East Coast-based buy-sider said. "I don't like their business model, and on top of that they operate a hedge fund."

One large retail-oriented firm had said that while it wasn't its policy to comment on individual companies, the growth in Citadel's desk didn't hurt its chances of being a destination for order flow.

Citadel proactively reached out to Knight employees with the promises of hefty paychecks. "Citadel doesn't like it when it happens to them, but they don't seem to have a problem going after other people's employees," Dan Teed, who helped oversee about $100 million as president of Wedgewood Investors in Erie, Pennsylvania, had pointed out. "Citadel and Knight are direct competitors. It's not the main issue, but I guarantee that's part of the situation."

One of the first to follow Nazarali and Cushman in November 2011 was Matthew Taback, who was coming directly to the OTC trading desk. He had been a managing director at Knight, which he had joined in 2000. Taback attended Ithaca College between 1995 and 1999 and Lawrence High School in Cedarhurst, New York, graduating in the class of 1995. He had been a generous contributor to The American Foundation for Suicide Prevention.

In May 2012, Noel Dalzell, previously a director in broker-dealer sales, jumped ship. Prior to Knight he had spent 12-years at ETrade as vice president of trading. He would focus on inbound and outbound off-exchange trading and liquidity in his new role as head of strategy and new product development. The trend was to accelerate after August 1, when Knight employees were calling to their former colleagues as they were learning of the trading malfunction; just the following month, CES hired three more Knight veterans.

Mark Stehli, a 12-year veteran and snowboarding, sailing and kayaking fanatic, was to come on board as cash trader. At Knight, he was a director of cash trading for its market-making business specializing in Asia and Europe. He had received a bachelor's degree from the University of Vermont and was a member of the Manhattan

Sailing Club and the Amateur Comedy Club, and was also a member of the board of directors for the Georgiana Institute, a non-profit organization run by his mother Annabel. The institute had been founded to promote Auditory Integration Training as a non-drug alternative to cure autism; his step-sister Georgiana had recovered from autism, ADHD and dyslexia through the use of this therapy in 1977.

John Kane, a veteran with 13 years of experience, was enlisted as a sales trader on Citadel's cash desk. Kane spent his whole trading career at Knight, where he was a director of cash trading; he focused on proprietary NASDAQ Trading and market making to include both domestic and international equities. Prior to Knight, he had been a captain in the Navy. He had received an MBA in finance and operations from William & Mary Mason School of Business and a bachelor's degree in Environmental Sciences from the United States Military Academy at West Point.

Michael Donofrio, an eight-year professional, would come on board as a sales trader on the cash desk; he had spent his whole career at Knight, where he served as a cash sales trader for the last six years in the firm's market-making business. Donofrio graduated from the Wharton School of the University of Pennsylvania with an MBA in finance (2006) and Yale University with a bachelor of arts in political science and government. He was a generous contributor to New York Theatre Workshop.

Stehli, Kane and Donofrio would all report to Christopher Amato, a 19-year professional coming on board as head trader from ETrade to lead Citadel's OTC desk trading domestic and international equities. Citadel owned 9.6 percent of ETrade and Griffin was on the board; even with that, nothing could stop Nazarali from raiding a partner.

Amato was on a mission to build an NMS equities trading desk. These hires were part of the plan to grow the OTC business and broaden the firm's highly automated trading approach. "We're adding more team members as we build out a hybrid model that includes both automated and high-touch, person-to-person offerings. This positions us well to serve clients across the spectrum, from listed securities and OTC to less-liquid stocks and orders that require special care," said Amato, who reported to Nazarali.

The same month, Kristen Benza was named a vice president at CES. She had been a vice president at Knight's electronic trading division after joining the firm in October 2008 where she was responsible for creating and maintaining buy- and sell-side institutional relationships for algorithmic trading strategies utilizing next-generation smart order execution algorithms, and she specialized in small/mid cap stocks with average daily volumes of three million or less. Elected senior class president during high school at The Ursuline School, she had gone on to focus on business, entrepreneurial studies and golf at the University of Hartford. She became such a competitive golfer that she participated at the Dartmouth Invitational, September 18-19, 1998, scoring 111-94-205 and won the Eastern College Athletic Conference championship as member of the University of Hartford women's golf team. While at Knight, she was frequently seen attending industry Georgia Securities Association's 34th Annual Convention and Fall Outing and Security Traders Association of New York's 85th Annual Conference and Dinner.

So there was no doubt distrust hindered Griffin's proposal to rescue Knight over the storied first August weekend.

Public companies are mandated to divulge their risk factors for the continued existence of their businesses. Knight revealed a deep understanding of the number of things that could go wrong and bring the company belly up. How they prioritized their attention was a different thing.

Knight admitted not only the existence of a number of risks that may adversely affect their business, financial condition and operating results but also additional risks and uncertainties not currently known to them or that they currently deemed to be immaterial. The first risk for Knight was the conditions in the financial services industry and the securities markets, which may adversely affect their trading volumes and market liquidity.

Knight's business was primarily transaction-based, and declines in trading volumes, volatility, prices, commission rates or market liquidity could have adversely affected their revenues and profits. Lower price levels of securities and other instruments and tightening spreads could have resulted in reduced revenue capture, and thereby have reduced revenues from trade executions. Declines in market values of securities or other instruments could have resulted in illiquid markets, losses on securities or other instruments held in inventory, the failure of buyers and sellers to fulfill their obligations and settle their trades, and increases in claims and litigation.

It was only in the eleventh bullet that Knight considered capacity constraints, systems failures and delays as risks that could harm their business. Their systems and operations were vulnerable to damage or interruption from human error, natural disasters, power loss, computer viruses, intentional acts of vandalism, terrorism and other similar events. Extraordinary trading volumes or other events could have caused their computer systems to operate at an unacceptably low speed or even fail. While it wouldn't take an act of vandalism to cripple the firm, a human error would later be identified as the main culprit.

Knight had admitted that from time to time they reimbursed their clients for losses incurred in connection with systems failures and delays. Even after the August 1 glitch, Knight would have come to say that no client was negatively impacted by their mistake, a false point of pride among the almost absolute dilution for their original shareholders.

Over the years, Knight Capital had invested a significant amount of resources in order to expand their execution capacity and upgrade their trading systems and infrastructure. Knight's ability to identify and deploy emerging technologies that facilitated the execution of trades was key to the successful execution of their business model. Not only had technology enhanced their capacity and ability to handle order flow faster, it had also been an important component of their strategy to comply with government regulations, achieve competitive execution standards, increase trading automation and provide superior client service. In order to improve their efficiency and lower costs, Knight had automated their execution services through their internally developed quantitative models.

Knight used proprietary technology and technology licensed from third parties to execute trades, monitor the performance of traders, assess inventory positions, manage risk effectively and provide ongoing information to clients. Knight was electronically linked to institutions and broker-dealers, to provide immediate access to their trading operations and to facilitate the handling of client orders. In addition, their business-to-business portal provided clients with an array of web-based tools to interact with their Equity Markets' trading systems. Broker-dealers, both foreign and domestic, used this portal to send them order flow, access reports and use the other tools it offers to facilitate their business.

Within Equity Markets, Knight used a customized version of the BRASS trading system originally built by SunGard Trading Systems for OTC equities. "What a great system. With Brass, no one could beat us," traders said. Brass was as smart as any system could ever be; it had connections to all the different marketplaces and dark pools where you could have gotten an execution from.

For listed equities, they used a customized version of the Appletree trading system originally built by TCAM Systems. They also used an internally developed integrated institutional sales technology platform, which consisted of an order management system for the entry, management and routing of institutional orders, a system for the simultaneous distribution of indications of interest and trade advertisements to various sources, and a rules-based trade allocation matching engine to receive allocation instructions from clients and automate post-trade processing.

In the early 2000s, Charles Kennedy, Knight's director of trading technologies, led a consulting team defining the firm's new IT architecture and authored the business requirements for the firm's Smart Market Access Routing System, which would later become SMARS. Smart order routing systems function as an integral component of exponential trading techniques, working quite fast to compare rates throughout nearly fifty lit and unlit trading venues, guaranteeing that they will suit within any amount of various tactics that may be in play at identical times and then execute.

Each component of the trading system was very quick and synchronized. Trading formulas were rendered quickly. Similarly located databases in the trading venues were reliant and extremely fast, not to mention intuitive and flexible.

Surmising speed, traders were also in need of transparency. Traders wanted to be able to know how their merchants and brokers were utilizing the routing systems where their precepts were sent to, which dark pools were being targeted, and the amount of data regarding their placement that was getting divulged in the process.

The teams behind BRASS and SMARS would later become the protagonists of the August 1 incident.

Days before August 1, the team behind BRASS deployed a change that was essentially a flip of the meaning of a specific flag. SMARS followed suit by making the change in its end. However, in the evening of Tuesday, July 31, the BRASS team noticed there was an issue with their initial update and intended to roll it back. They directed the SMARS team to roll the change back too; unfortunately, SMARS missed one of its eight servers. The change both teams were trying to implement referred to the Power Peg software that handled peg orders.

Thanks to the type of development life cycle in a fast-paced company such as Knight, it was entirely plausible that nobody outside of the manager at the VP or Director levels (the person managing teams of four or five people) was even made aware that seemingly simple changes were being made in systems that supported Knight's global, multi-asset class platform. Neither the managing director nor the CTO for sure would have known about this change; what happened in a company of this size was that developers had free rein regarding small-scale improvements to the system that could be identified by individual contributors and implemented during regular updates.

The RLP certainly didn't qualify as small-scale improvement; testing had taken months and was coordinated externally with the New York Stock Exchange. However, the implementation of major systems like the RLP was always accompanied by small updates that were developed and tested by small teams; the particular nuances of those changes were not known to anybody other than their direct managers.

Developers at firms like Knight were always on the lookout for performance enhancements; in fact, a lot of their time was spent in making modifications to the systems, cleaning them up, and making sure they ran faster and faster. Once changes were done in a development environment, the change was tested in a completely sandbox environment, where testing could be conducted isolated from the production environment or repository.

Beta servers allowed for testing while trading in the market either with a limited symbol range or a limited set of volume. These servers were closely monitored as there were expected issues that could have the systems quickly shut off or fixed on the fly; thorough testing would guarantee situations like this wouldn't appear during real deployments.

The pace at Knight was so extremely fast that it was accepted that only the direct manager's sign off was required to approve production updates. Managing directors would only be informed after the fact or, heaven forbid, if a change failed.

To be fair, these application development dynamics were not unique to Knight Capital. The industry had accepted that things needed to move as fast as the fastest market participants. One trend that was clearly noticeable, though, was the increasing size of the penalties financial firms suffered when errors happened.

BATS Global Markets had to suffer the very public and expensive ignominy of not being able to launch its stock in its own platform. NASDAQ's technical failures during the Facebook IPO cost UBS $356 million and Knight itself and Citadel roughly $35 million each. In 2011, AXA Rosenberg shelled out $217 million to cover investor losses from what it called a "significant error" in the computer code for one of its investment models; it paid an extra $25 million penalty to regulators after it was caught trying to hide the mistake.

More recently, on Monday November 12, 2012, the NYSE had stopped trading in 216 securities and canceled their closing auctions because of an outage in a computer that matched buy and sell orders and process transactions. The affected stocks, which included Travelers and U.S. Steel, continued to trade on other exchanges such as NYSE Arca platform and NASDAQ. The NYSE was in the process of shifting companies to its UTP matching engines from its Super Display Book system and supporting database; on Friday, it had moved 109 corporations to UTP and added another 107 on Monday; those 107 would temporarily revert to their prior configuration.[4]

"Computers do what they're told," said Lawrence Pingree, an analyst at Gartner. "If they're told to do the wrong thing, they're going to do it and they're going to do it really, really well. The growing complexity is a huge contributor; you really can't have proper risk management until you have visibility." Financial firms and stock exchanges tested new software, but in trading, "the risk universe could change so dramatically within minutes that it's not humanly possible" to plan for every eventuality, he said.

Knight Capital had had its fair share of system failures which never received public attention due to the relatively small size, from thousands to a few millions of dollars. How to explain this worrisome trend? As technology was increasingly more complex, the set of tools developers had under their disposal was more powerful, making a single developer hour much more user-impactful than it was five years before. Essentially, individual contributors were being given additional functionality and increased responsibility.

Therefore, there was no need of a systemic error to cause multimillion dollar losses; a single line of code could cause millions and millions of dollars in losses. How absentminded management at Knight was about this trend could be illustrated by Joyce's response to a question by employees in a town hall meeting on the biggest risk that he saw. His answer: a rogue trader, never technology.

Société Générale was one of the firms that did have a leviathan loss due to a rogue trader. Jérôme Kerviel was a French trader who was convicted in January 2008 for breach of trust, forgery and unauthorized use of the bank's computers, resulting in losses valued at €4.9 billion. Société Générale characterized Kerviel as a rogue trader and claimed Kerviel worked these trades alone and without its authorization. Kerviel had told investigators that his trading behavior was widespread at the company and that getting a profit made the hierarchy turn a blind eye.

For investors, Knight acknowledged the seriousness of potential technology risks in its 2011 annual report, referring to "capacity constraints, systems failures and delays" as risks that could ultimately result in "transactions not being processed as quickly as our clients desire, decreased levels of client service and client satisfaction, and harm to our reputation." If any of these events were to occur, Knight could suffer substantial financial losses, a loss of clients, or a reduction in the growth of their client base, increased operating expenses, litigation or other client claimed regulatory sanctions or additional regulatory burdens.

However, oversight of technology risk was not commonly specified as a board responsibility in financial services firms. "If you go back 10 years ago there was no risk committee on these boards. Now all of a sudden everybody has a board-level risk committee. As things happen, what you are going to see is maybe we should be looking at these other issues too," said Bernard Donefer, a financial technology expert and associate director of the Subotnick Financial Services Center at Baruch College in New York.

Boards were generally concerned with credit and market risk, said Baruch's Donefer, and it would be unusual for a board to have a risk management process that specifically dealt with technology. "When they look at technology it becomes a lot harder to try to figure out exactly what is the risks that you are looking for; going forward, technology may be part of the risk management responsibilities of financial company boards."

Knight's 2012 proxy statement mentioned that the company's board and its committees met regularly to consider "significant risks" facing the company, but it did not specifically cite technology as a risk in that context. The primary responsibility for managing operational risk lied with operating segments, Knight said in its annual report. "As new products and business activities are developed, we endeavor to identify operational risks and design controls to seek to mitigate the identified risks," it said.

Top company executives responsible for risk management, according to the proxy statement, included chief financial officer Steven Bisgay (who was charged with the "enhancement of the company's overall risk management infrastructure") and Sohos.

Bisgay had been CFO since August 2007, a fast progression for somebody who had started as director of internal audit in June 2001. Bisgay had been employed as consultant with Price Waterhouse for almost 11 years. Bisgay received a bachelor's degree in accounting from Binghamton University in 1989 and an MBA from Columbia Business School in 2000.

ETG's Sohos had joined Knight in 2000 and had been a member of the senior management team since 2005. Among his responsibilities were the U.S. and European client trading books which included market making for retail order flow, Knight Link, and market making on the NYSE, NYSE Amex and NYSE Arca. Prior to joining Knight, he worked as a software engineer at IBM and as a senior scientist at Enviro Engineering. Sohos had a PhD in applied mathematics from the University of Arizona and a bachelor of science in mathematics from Panepistimion Patron in Greece.

Others with risk management responsibility included technology honcho Sadoff, who had been listed in 2006 as one of the top three highest paid chief information officers. During that year, Timothy Shack of PNC Financial Services was compensated $5.94 million, followed by Gregor Bailar of Capital One at $4.5 million and Sadoff at $1.99 million. On January 21, 2009, Knight promoted Sadoff to executive vice president.

"Steve has distinguished himself in leading Knight's technology team as it built one of the most robust trading platforms on Wall Street. Knight's technology is critical to our success, allowing us to support an outstanding voice operation and expanding [the] electronic side of our hybrid market model. A significant, near-term focus for Steve is to now support Knight's trading technology infrastructure internationally. Steve's guidance and keen business instincts over nearly seven years have made him a key contributor to the organization."

Hardworking, yes, yet no visionary, people close to him would add. "A really smart guy, really quick; he was always good at finding pluses and minuses to the situation," a trader would say. Sadoff was the well-structured guy Joyce thought he could trust.

He was also the ultimate family man too; Sadoff had been married to Alyssa Karp since July 4, 1987 and had two children,

Annabelle and Elliot. Alyssa had been a corporate art consultant for Greenberg-Nussbaum, a St. Louis organization that selected art for major corporations, and graduated from Washington University. She was a devoted mother who volunteered to work on events at the school and provided virtual care to Annabelle's Webkinz and a handful of Tamagotchi pets while she was away at camp in Pennsylvania.[5] Her encyclopedic knowledge and can-do attitude eventually led her to start a business, Momcierge, a concierge service for families in New York City, in 2006.[6]

Sadoff, whose father Armin was an orthopedic surgeon and mother Barbara taught a kindergarten class in Beverly Hills, was always the overachiever in the family. His sister Laura Sadoff Gramling would refer to him as her "studly award winning brother", she was referring to the number of awards Sadoff had collected (and been a judge to) throughout the years. Sadoff had been named one of the 10 most influential CIOs by Securities Technology Monitor in 2010 and received the American Financial Technology Award in 2010 for Best Global Deployment. In 2011, Knight had ranked 14th on the InformationWeek 500 for the second year in a row and was the leading company in the Banking & Financial Services industry.

Just one week before the trading incident, Sadoff had been ranked 43th in Institutional Investors' The 2012 Tech 50. In a boasting profile, Sadoff suggested that technology-driven organizations often frowned on anything "not invented here"; Knight Capital, by contrast, was "not afraid to fix up stuff; we prefer not to have to do that, but we have a good record on that front." The profile went on to describe the transformation of Direct Trading Institutional, a direct-market-access provider acquired by Knight in 2005, and relaunched later with Knight's smart-order router, data and graphical user interface as Knight Direct. "When I joined Knight [in 2002], market making was extremely manual," said Sadoff. "Now more than 95 percent of the order flow is handled by computer."

The head of operations, service and technology, and senior managing director Al Lhota had also risk management responsibilities. Earlier, Lhota headed junk-bond teams at RBS Greenwich Capital Markets. Prior to that, Lhota had worked at UBS in high yield sales in the U.S. and U.K. where he led the high yield team in London and worked to integrate the bond and loan teams. Following an earlier period at UBS in high yield sales, he and a group of partners formed Libra Investments, which was eventually sold to US Bancorp. He began his career at Scotiabank in sales of investment grade and high yield bonds.

In addition to Joyce, six independent directors sat on the board. Among them was James Lewis, a former Morgan Stanley executive who had served as head of Morgan Stanley's risk management committee. Board member James Milde, a former top technology executive with Sony Electronics and Pepsi Bottling, had "significant knowledge and understanding of matters related to information technology, an important area for the Company and its businesses," the proxy statement said.

"In performance of risk oversight, the board and its committees receive reports and regularly meet with the company's chief executive officer and other senior managers on significant risks facing the company, including enterprise, financial, operational, legal, regulatory and strategic risks. The independent board members also discuss the company's significant risks when they meet in the executive session without management."

Knight didn't list a risk committee by name. However, among the duties of the finance and audit committee were oversight of "risks relating to the financial statements and financial reporting processes, as well as key credit risks, liquidity risks, market risks, compliance risks and risks arising from related person transactions, and the guidelines, policies and processes for monitoring and managing those risks."

Risks should have been monitored indeed. Technology failures were already slowly eating Knight shareholders' lunch; they would become shirtless after August 1. Throughout the years, there had been many occasions where losses of $50K, $100K or more weren't even considered a serious issue; just small errors that were part of the course of business. There was a time when managers made a big deal out of these errors because these directly impacted their bonuses. Over time, that was no longer the case, which directly influenced an increased tolerance.

Just on July 31, the day before the big glitch, a Knight (KCG) trader on the floor of the New York Stock Exchange had flubbed an order for the stock Ensco PLC that cost Knight nearly $1 million.[7] The problem for Knight began when traders sought to profit on shares of Ensco, an offshore drilling company due to rebalancing of one of the Standard & Poor's indexes. Rebalancing usually leads to an initial spike in the price of stocks, and then a decline in their value. Shares had begun to rise on Monday August 30 to $56.22 but then fell nearly four percent the next day. The problem for Knight involved what floor traders were calling a "miscommunication" with another trading shop over how much Ensco Knight thought it had purchased. When the firm realized it was still holding shares of Ensco on Tuesday, the shares had fallen by $2.11. Knight had to split its loss with another firm, taking an $800,000 hit.

On November 3, 2010, the SEC adopted rule 15c3-5 ("Risk Management Controls for Brokers or Dealers with Market Access"), better known as the "market access rule". It required broker-dealers to establish, document and maintain a system of risk management controls and supervisory procedures that were reasonably designed to systematically limit the financial exposure of the broker-dealer that could arise as a result of market access and ensure compliance with all regulatory requirements that were applicable in connection with market access.

The rule focused on a practice in which broker-dealers handed their customers a special pass to access the markets called a "market participant identifier". The customer then gained direct access to the applicable exchange or alternative trading system (ATS), also known as "sponsored access". The rule prohibited broker-dealers from providing customers with "unfiltered" or "naked" access to an exchange or ATS.

Among other provisions, the rule required that brokers or dealers providing market access establish financial risk management controls and supervisory procedures that were reasonably designed to, among other things, "prevent the entry of orders that exceed appropriate pre-set credit or capital thresholds in the aggregate for each customer and the broker or dealer, by rejecting orders if such orders would exceed the applicable credit or capital thresholds, or that appear to be erroneous."

The regulatory risk management controls and supervisory procedures had to be reasonably designed to prevent the entry of orders unless there has been compliance with all regulatory requirements that must be satisfied on a pre-order entry basis, prevent the entry of orders that the broker or dealer or customer is restricted from trading, restrict market access technology and systems to authorized persons, and assure appropriate surveillance personnel receive immediate post-trade execution reports.

The financial and regulatory risk management controls and supervisory procedures required by rule 15c3-5 had to be under the direct and exclusive control of the broker or dealer with market access, with limited exceptions specified in the rule that permit reasonable allocation of certain controls and procedures to another registered broker or dealer that, based on its position in the transaction and relationship with the ultimate customer, can more effectively implement them. In addition, a broker or dealer with market access would be required to establish, document, and maintain a system for regularly reviewing the effectiveness of the risk management controls and supervisory procedures and for promptly addressing any issues.

Among other things, the broker or dealer would be required to review, no less frequently than annually, the business activity of the broker or dealer in connection with market access to assure the overall effectiveness of such risk management controls and supervisory procedures and document that review. The review would be required to be conducted in accordance with written procedures and fully documented.

From the exchanges standpoint, each equity-trading permit holder had been assigned a base credit limit. Credit limits were applied based on historical usage and may be modified from time to time if such modifications were deemed appropriate under the risk management controls. As orders were entered, the amount of available credit decreased; as orders were filled or canceled, the amount of available credit for incoming orders increased. Should a credit limit be breached, new orders would be rejected. The trade desk may reinstate or modify the credit limits after consultation with the participant.

Set to become effective on November 30, 2011, rule 15c3-5 attempted to prevent the mayhem of incorrect large-volume trades by requiring strict, well-documented controls from any firm with market access. With rule 15c3-5, the SEC was shifting focus toward preventing the wrong trades from happening in the first place. Ultimately, any firm with market access needed end-to-end compliance. However, was the SEC prescriptive enough to guarantee compliance with its rulings? Were its rulings crystal clear for trading firms? Did the SEC have the capability to verify that firms had functioning kill switches, circuit breakers or fuse boxes?

An important part of disaster recovery was maintaining a backup data center. How far away should the second data center be? The question arose after the 9/11 terrorist incident when significant areas of Manhattan were shut down. Shortly thereafter, the question on appropriate distance was raised by the Security and Exchange Commission, the Federal Reserve and the Office of the Comptroller of the Currency. In August 2002, they produced a white paper, Interagency Paper on Sound Practices to Strengthen the Resilience of the U.S. Financial System, which seemed to suggest that 200 miles would be appropriate between the primary and secondary sites. Among other sound practices, the paper declared:

"Have the agencies sufficiently described expectations regarding out-of-region back-up resources? Should some minimum distance from primary sites be specified for back-up facilities for core clearing and settlement organizations and firms that play significant roles in critical markets (e.g., 200 - 300 miles between primary and back-up sites)? What factors should be used to identify such a minimum distance?"[8]

This suggestion immediately came under question. Providing what is called synchronous replication of trading data and maintaining databases had a physical limitation of 100 miles. Beyond that, it was simply impossible to properly maintain the systems because firms couldn't back it up quickly enough to trade effectively. If something went down, firms would basically lose all their orders in the flight and minutes of data prior to that, so their recovery point was capped short. Didn't the authors of the white paper at the Security and Exchange Commission, the Federal Reserve and the Office of the Comptroller of the Currency understand the technical limitations of their suggestion or did they just arbitrarily come up with the 200 - 300 mile distance? "A backup data center hundreds of miles away can't effectively mirror data in real-time, so the risk of lost data between the last backup and the event is increased," explained Bill Ashland, founder of Disaster Game, a game that helped organizations prepare for disasters by creating highly detailed event scenarios.[9] Eventually, the final version of their white paper didn't include specific recommendations on miles between sites.

"The agencies do not believe it is necessary or appropriate to prescribe specific mileage requirements for geographically dispersed back-up sites. It is important for firms to retain flexibility in considering various approaches to establishing back-up arrangements that could be effective given a firm's

particular risk profile. However, long-standing principles of business continuity planning suggest that back-up arrangements should be as far away from the primary site as necessary to avoid being subject to the same set of risks as the primary location. Back-up sites should not rely on the same infrastructure components (e.g., transportation, telecommunications, water supply, and electric power) used by the primary site. Moreover, the operation of such sites should not be impaired by a wide-scale evacuation at or the inaccessibility of staff that service the primary site. The effectiveness of back-up arrangements in recovering from a wide-scale disruption should be confirmed through testing."[10]

The chief executive officer (or equivalent officer) of the broker-dealer was required, on an annual basis, to certify that the risk management controls and supervisory procedures complied with rule 15c3-5, and that the regular review had been conducted. The CEO certification was designed to hold executives accountable. But regulatory and brokerage lawyers agreed that the requirement's vague language made it difficult to pursue enforcement actions against individual executives.

Joyce was the CEO of Knight Capital Americas, the unit that included the market-making group where the August 1 error would later occur. Joyce assumed the subsidiary CEO role in July. The unit's former CEO, Joseph Mazzella, had certified Knight's compliance with the market-access rule before July. Mazzella, currently senior managing director, head of institutional equities, had joined Knight in October 2003 as managing director of listed trading after spending more than a decade at Merrill Lynch. He had started there in 1993 as an assistant in listed equities. From 1990 to 1993, Mazzella worked at Lehman Brothers, where he managed small and mid-sized institutional client accounts, and Drexel Burnham Lambert. Mazzella began his career in 1985 at the New York Stock Exchange specialist firm Carl H. Pforzheimer & Co.

By the time Knight was battling the trading incident on August 1, the SEC was in the middle of an examination of the firm's risk-management systems.[11] The SEC had already begun to look at Knight's risk management procedures. The examination involved Knight's compliance with the SEC's market access rule. SEC officials were conducting what was known as a "sweep" that had begun in the spring of the year to determine if firms like Knight were in compliance with the rule. The fact that regulators believed through their review that Knight's full compliance with the regulation could have prevented the trading glitch speaks volumes about their lack of knowledge how new developments were implemented at Knight.

Chapter Eleven

The Fight for the Firm's Survival

The irony of the day's issues impacting Knight's stock was not lost to CNBC host Simon Hobb, who pointed to Joyce's aggressiveness in his criticism of NASDAQ over its handling of Facebook's nefarious IPO. In fact, Joyce had never been afraid of publicly condemning exchanges in the past, or breaking with the party line regarding high-frequency trading. He would later point out, rightly so, that these two incidents had two completely different outcomes in terms of taking responsibility, "Knight Capital Group screwed up and Knight Capital Group paid the price. NASDAQ screwed up on that Friday and the industry paid the price. So, I think it's different."

12:00 P.M. Joyce finally in the office
In the morning of August 1, Joyce stayed home alone as Lisa had gone out for routine errands and appointments. After a first round of calls to his team and NYSE, Joyce was helped by his wife pick up his belongings and get on his chauffeured vehicle for the 52-minute ride from Darien to the firm's headquarters in Jersey City. It wasn't until midday when he made his entrance to the trading floor hobbled on crutches; he only stayed there for about 15 minutes, assuring people that everything would be fine. Trying to show no emotion, Sadoff and Sohos got ready to summarize the situation as best as they could.

12:11 P.M. Communicating a technology issue
It wasn't until around noon that Knight confirmed that a technology issue had occurred in the company's market-making unit. Why

Knight Capital sent an alert earlier only to insiders instead of all market participants (as it was required from all public companies) became the question making rounds throughout the morning.

"An initial review by Knight indicates that a technology issue occurred in the company's market-making unit related to the routing of shares of approximately 150 stocks to the NYSE," Fitzsimmons wrote in an e-mail. "The company's OTC securities and trading in its other businesses are not affected. The company continues to review internally."

12:15 P.M. Buying Knight puts

Najarian confirmed on CNBC's *Fast Money Halftime Report* that as soon as people heard there was a software glitch, they went right for Knight and bought puts. "The price of those options exploded of course, as the stock got hammered as the news got out." Put options, generally considered bearish bets, give the holder the right to sell shares at a specific price by a certain date.

According to optionMONSTER, about 3.8 million options traded in the first hour of trading, with NYSE volume trading at 150 percent of its normal volume. Options activity on Knight was more than three times the overall open interest of 10,969 contracts, with most action in put options, confirmed Interactive Brokers Group options analyst Caitlin Duffy. "Traders scrambled to get long downside puts as the stock spiraled lower this morning, with notable fresh interest building across all available expirations."

12:30 P.M. On the race for survival

Unbeknownst to the market, the race for survival had started for Knight with a single phone call. Niederauer broke the news to Joyce that most of the trades would stand. Joyce would try SEC chairman Mary Schapiro in the hope that she would show flexibility and overrule Niederauer's team.

Joyce phoned Schapiro. He interrupted her vacation in Maine pressing her to authorize canceling the erroneous and duplicate trades, sparing his firm from likely ruin.

There was no way that would happen, Schapiro told him. The trades would stand as the rules say they should. Her willingness to stand firm on a decision that would imperil a large firm was partly a reflection of the changes in place since the market collapse on May 6, 2010, known as the Flash Crash.

Exchanges canceled hundreds of trades afterward, angering market participants who said the decision was arbitrary and hurt market integrity. Under SEC pressure, rules formalizing the treatment of erroneous trades were adopted amid criticism by investors after exchanges and FINRA voided transactions totaling 5.6 million shares on May 6, 2010. The regulator added guidelines governing when sales or purchases of stock could be canceled after market makers claimed confusion about which trades would stand prevented them from acting during the rout. Schapiro said she would only stand by those guidelines.

That morning, executives at the New York Stock Exchange canceled transactions that were 30 percent or more away from their price at the start of trading, a decision which applied to six securities out of 140 that were reviewed. Unwanted transactions occurred for companies on the Big Board, Knight and in ETFs listed on NYSE Arca.

Obviously Joyce disagreed with Schapiro and later indicated he had hoped for more flexibility in how she responded to the error; at the end, he "respected" the decision. "We need to remember that the SEC's job, and this is hard for me to say, the regulator's job is not to save Knight Capital Group; the SEC's job is to make sure there is no systemic risk to the industry."

"I'll confirm we were in discussions with the SEC. I did speak with chairman Schapiro. We had a frank discussion. And she did what she thought was right for the industry. And I have to applaud her for her decision. I'm kind of biased. I wish she had made a different decision but I think she made the right..." Here Joyce corrected himself, "She thinks she made the right decision for the industry and I have to support her in that. She did what she thought was right for the industry, and I have to applaud her for the decision."[1]

Meanwhile, traders hadn't touched the humongous position Knight accumulated in the morning because they thought the SEC would authorize canceling the erroneous traders. A frank discussion with Schapiro could only have happened with the CEO of the firm; however, Joyce didn't speak with Schapiro until his arrival to the office.

Was Schapiro right? She was already facing an uphill battle trying to rebuild the SEC's credibility after the Flash Crash. The SEC was run by lawyers who strictly followed rules. Would they have agreed to change the rules every time there was a crisis? Knight's demise wouldn't have been the end of the world. Would she have taken a different approach if a "too big to fail" firm's existence was on the line? Most likely yes. However, Knight was small enough and had to survive by securing private funding.

Conversely, Joyce also did the right thing in asking Schapiro for a "Hail Mary" pass; chief executive officers had a fiduciary responsibility with their shareholders; unfortunately, only a few days later, shareholders would be subjected to a massive dilution as the price to pay for the firm's survival.

Schapiro didn't win brownie points with Knight's traders that morning. They argued the problem could have been fixed at a cost that wouldn't have taken anybody out of business. "Somebody along the way either doesn't understand the marketplace or doesn't have any intent of understanding. When people like that make a decision, they're stubborn and don't change it." For the traders who had to work to get out of these positions, it was clearly the wrong decision.

12:36 P.M. *Adding insult to injury*
Ratings agency Egan-Jones was lowering Knight Capital's rating
from B-plus to B, citing operating issues at the company. This
happened about half an hour after Knight acknowledged that a
"technology issue" in its market-making unit had impacted the
routing of shares of around 150 stocks to the New York Stock
Exchange, where abnormal volatility roiled the markets in early
trading.

12:41 P.M. *The NYSE finally speaks up*
"The NYSE and NYSE MKT are currently reviewing irregular trading
identified by our people and systems in 148 (140 NYSE/8 MKT)
symbols between 09:30:00 A.M. and 10:15:00 A.M. ET today. The
NYSE and NYSE MKT will provide updates with respect to these
reviews. At this time, we believe NYSE systems and circuit breakers
operated normally during this period, and we are working with all
market participants on the issue."

1:00 P.M. *Capital Punishment*
Malfunctions on Wednesday led the firm's computers to rapidly buy
and sell millions of shares in over 148 stocks for about 45 minutes
after markets opened. Those trades pushed the value of many stocks
up, and the company's losses occurred when it had to sell the
overvalued shares back into the market at a lower price. Knight's
decline continued with the stock down by 22 percent.

Knight's failure to respond sooner was particularly mystifying to
other market participants. As any IT manager worth his weight in
gold would recommend, introducing new software (not only trading
software) was sufficient reason for programmers and analysts to be
on high alert about unexpected consequences.

Many traders said it would have made sense if the firm's
employees had not caught the problems for the first minute or so,

given the speed at which Knight's program was firing orders. After that, though, the problems were visible for all to see.

Sophisticated trading firms were expected to embed warning signals into their computerized trading systems, so when all else fails, there was always a "circuit breaker" or "kill switch" that could immediately stop trading. That was the type of protection many high-frequency trading firms used when they noticed that the Flash Crash was underway in 2010; nobody wanted to be left holding instruments that were to lose value. Surprisingly this time, Knight didn't have this protection.

For Pasternak, the facts were clear: there was no circuit breaker in place. Furthermore, he said that during his time as CEO, he would sit down and look for certain behaviors from both a regulatory point of view and an operational point of view and do exactly what most firms do. He said he often performed this analysis as part of his job as CEO; not only Pasternak but also Raquet. "They were very hands on in the development of new code and very much involved with the roll out of new programs and insuring that the code included compliance rules of the business," said Turner.

"It is very easy to take a stereotypical approach to corporate events like we do to people. I don't think many people understand what happened and, to be honest, I wouldn't claim that I know anything internally. I only know what decision management made afterwards," Pasternak added.

Pasternak claimed they used to be able to clearly identify rogue trading behaviors. They would use technology to monitor trades and create what they called circuit breakers. So, in essence, he said, a piece of code acted as a rogue trade. When developing code, circuit breakers could be used to stop trading activity. They used to look across many variables: capital, P&L, and others. They could have a circuit breaker for any conditions impacting these variables. They could write a what-if statement to protect the firm against any extreme circumstances. For example, they could say they never wanted to risk more than 20 percent of their capital. If this would have been the case, they would have never lost more than that. "So the point I'm trying to make is that if you have any observable sense you would make what-if statements. Nobody at Knight in 2012 was thinking about putting circuit breakers in code. There was no circuit breaker in place."

Pasternak didn't want to be disparaging to Joyce. "I was a producing manager and I understood all the risks that could possibly impact the firm. I would write these circuit breakers myself and give them to the coders. So if I were there, this would never have happened because the what-if statements would have shut down the trade." Did Joyce have any of these concerns when he was wearing the CEO hat? Was he so enamored in working on his golf handicap that he failed to spend a minute thinking about the existence of circuit breakers? The facts don't speak, they scream by themselves.

George Hessler, executive at Lime Brokerage, suggested that a software glitch could have made the firm not aware of their own unwanted positions. However, good application programming discipline also meant there should be last-ditch backstop mechanisms to shut down trading when too many orders were going out or orders weren't getting updated the way they should have been.

Several market insiders said that they were bewildered with the events because in a market where trading losses can pile up in seconds managers typically had a simple command that could immediately halt trading.

"It's kind of mind-boggling that it got so out of control. Even just a minute or two would have been surprising to me. On these time scales, that is an eternity," said David Lauer, a trader at a high-speed firm until the previous year. "To have something going on for 30 minutes is shocking."

Howard Tai, an expert in high-speed trading at the Aite Group, said that at all the firms where he had worked, there were several warning signals built into every computerized trading system. When all else failed, there was always the "automatic kill switch" that could immediately stop trading.

Knight appeared to repeatedly send orders "where they were buying at the offer and selling at the bid, and some were on stocks with wide bid-ask spreads," Manoj Narang, CEO of Tradeworx, the high-frequency firm and technology provider based in Red Bank, New Jersey, added. Tradeworx had been referred by Raquet as "one of the most original approaches to quant investing we've seen – definitely one of the few elite quant funds out there."

"It was a slow, painful, 15-cents-at-a-time death by small cuts, only it was happening every fraction of a second because computers are fast," he said.

Narang's automated trading firm experienced a similar mishap in early 2012 in a broker's dark pool, or private venue. Firms supplying liquidity generally do so at the bid and offer prices. While Tradeworx's issue occurred because of system changes the firm didn't know about, the strategy was programmed to shut off after it lost $5,000, which took less than a minute, Narang said.

"What is confusing virtually everybody, including me, is why Knight didn't have an automated stop loss in their strategies," he said. "It was the first day of NYSE's RLP program so there should have been multiple layers of risk controls. In addition to having automated stop losses there should have been humans watching the strategy like a hawk."

"This is like a nuclear reactor or aircraft," said Roy Niederhoffer, whose R.G. Niederhoffer Capital Management uses Knight. "There has to be some way of seeing the state of the whole system." He claimed that there was "no excuse" for Knight failing to act sooner.[2] "Things can get out of hand very quickly and there is nobody who can immediately do anything about it," said Nanex's Hunsader.

Did Knight's failure indicate that the market was fundamentally flawed? Many of these fears originated from within the industry. Thomas Peterffy, founder of Interactive Brokers Group and a legend in the world of electronic trading, was persuaded regulators had created a situation that was beyond our ability to control. These problems would continue if they didn't slow things down, he had warned. "It may have a broader impact on Main Street, who looks at Wall Street and says it's just another illustration that the markets are broken and the little guy doesn't stand a chance," said Matt Samelson, founder of Woodbine Associates, a capital markets consulting firm.

"The machines have taken over, right?" asked a sarcastic Patrick Healy, the chief executive of the Issuer Advisory Group, a capital markets consulting firm. "When events like this happen they just reaffirm that these aren't investors, these are traders." Joe Anastasio, a founding partner of financial services consulting firm Capco, lamented the loss of human control in the markets. "We've been so focused on automated throughput of orders and high-volume execution with no human intervention that we have lost the human logic factor when things go wrong." One of the problems, he said, was that millions of orders stacked up overnight for automatic execution at the opening of trading, with a single error potentially creating an abundance of bad trades.

Conversely, Maureen O'Hara, a finance professor at Cornell University who sat on an advisory panel that explored reforms after the U.S. stock market collapsed inexplicably in a few minutes in the 2010 Flash Crash, was worried people would take a look and say there was something fundamentally wrong with the market. "There isn't," she emphatically said.

For Bruce Weber, dean of the Lerner College of Business and Economics, who co-wrote *The Equity Trader Course* with Robert Schwartz and Deutsche Börse's CEO Reto Francioni, this was clearly an issue with Knight's reliance on software to execute trades that didn't have the testing and quality-assurance function perfected yet. "As we've seen, the consequences of weak testing and bugs that slip through are enormous."

"When they put these things out in the world they are really being tried for the first time in a real-life test," said David Leinweber, the head of the Center for Innovative Financial Technology at the Lawrence Berkeley National Laboratory. "For other complex systems we do offline simulation testing." Leinweber had suggested to the SEC that it could do this simulation work with the help of the supercomputing facilities at his center.

Tim Hartzell, chief investment officer at Houston, Texas-based Sequent Asset Management, which oversees about $350 million, said, "You can see how that one black swan event can literally take this company out. Maybe this is the new chapter for program trading and algorithm trading. We'll have to go back and re-evaluate."[3] Larry Tabb, founder of Tabb Group, which researches computer trading, agreed on the need to go back to the drawing board. "If this happens to one of the most sophisticated players in the market, we really need to rethink our overall market structure, how fragmented and disconnected it is and how we control technology." Henry Hu, a former official at the SEC and a professor at the University of Texas in Austin, worried that the costs in terms of these random shocks to the system were occurring in ways that people never anticipated.

Scott O'Malia, a Republican commissioner for the Commodity Futures Trading Commission, had launched earlier in the year a group to look into the impact of high-frequency trading on futures markets. "Knight provides an opportunity to find out what the holes in the market are," O'Malia said. "What happened? What failed? What else could go wrong?"

The error ultimately caused Knight to place unauthorized offers to buy and sell shares of large American companies, in turn driving up the volume of trading as well as the price of their shares. Could this large number of orders be the result of make believe transactions created when the RLP was being tested? Didn't this test data somehow remain active once the system updates were installed and become actual orders once the market opened? Those were some of the ideas experienced programmers floated as the details were not apparent yet.

Sooner or later, Knight had to sell the stocks that it accidentally bought, most likely at a loss, which could have drained the firm's capital cushion and cause "liquidity pressures." The race for survival was on for Knight Capital.

2:00 P.M. Fire sale time

Schapiro's rejection of Joyce's entreaties set in motion the firm's scramble. Knight Capital was holding about $7 billion of stocks. In a scene reminiscent of the film *Margin Call's* "fire sale" sequence, traders worked frantically during the day to sell shares while trying to minimize losses, ultimately paring the total position to about $4.6 billion by the end of the trading day. But that was not enough. The firm needed to get a permanent solution to its problems. That's where Sandler O'Neill entered into the picture.

Sandler O'Neill had worked with Knight in countless transactions before, providing corporate finance and financial advisory services. Sandler O'Neill enjoyed a reputation as a trusted advisor by forming long-lasting relationships with clients, one of which was Knight.

Throughout the previous decade, Joyce had grown close to Brian Sterling, co-head of the investment banking group. Sterling had arrived to Sandler O'Neill from Merrill Lynch, where he was managing director in the financial institutions group. Before that, he was managing director at Wertheim Schroder & Co. Sterling had begun his career at Skadden, Arps, Slate, Meagher & Flom in the mergers and acquisition group. He held a JD from Yale Law School and a bachelor's degree from the Wharton School of the University of Pennsylvania.

Besides managing the relationship with Knight, Sterling donated to some of the same charities Joyce was interested; both had been recognized by the Dana-Farber Cancer Institute in their 2011 Honor

Roll of Donors, along with their wives, Lisa and Linda, respectively; the Dana-Farber Cancer Institute had been recognized for providing expert care to children and adults, and for groundbreaking cancer discoveries since its founding in 1948.

Knowing the magnitude of the gigantic task ahead, Sterling called Jimmy Dunne, Sandler O'Neill's senior managing principal and head of the executive committee. "I think I need you to be around. I would like to have you in on all these Knight calls."

Dunne earned a bachelor of arts in economics from the University of Notre Dame and was now leading a firm with more than 300 professionals in New York, Atlanta, Boston, Chicago, San Francisco and Memphis. Dunne was a Wall Street gold legend for a couple of reasons. First, he was the man who shot a 63 at Shinnecock Hills Golf Course, according to a Vault profile. This was a record, of course, for Long Island, which had served as the site of the USGA's U.S. Open Championship four times. More importantly, he was the man who was able to rebuild Sandler O'Neill after 65 of its employees were killed in the September 11 terrorist attacks on the World Trade Center; he was not in the office that morning.

What was Dunne doing out of the office on a workday? Dunne was on the sixth hole of the Bedford Golf and Tennis Club in Westchester, New York, trying to qualify for the U.S. Mid-Amateur Championship golf tournament. In a Fortune profile, Dunne recalled that a tournament official rolled up to the tee in a golf cart and told him he should call his office; Dunne was irritated. The guy followed him down the fairway. "A plane hit the World Trade Center," the guy finally said. "Did it break a window?" Dunne asked.

Dunne called the office from the bag room. No answer. He called home and reached his wife, but she was unable to speak. She handed the phone to a friend, who told Dunne, "You have to come to terms with the fact that most of the people in your firm are dead." He spent the frantic next few hours on the phone, and then boarded a train that was beginning to make its way back to New York City.

Dunne got into Grand Central Station a little after 5 P.M. and ran the six blocks to 48th Street, where Sandler O'Neill had a small office. He thought, "I can't run in there all crazed. I needed to arrive with a sense of calmness. I knew people were going to look to me." Later, Sandler O'Neill employees would remember Dunne declaring from the start that the firm would be rebuilt; his conviction gave them strength. "He made us feel like, 'I'll show you the path through the trees.'"

4:00 P.M. Not enough

The $4.6 billion remaining position would have prevented Knight from opening for business the next day. The brokerage firm would have lacked the capital required by regulators to offset risks from holding these stocks. Knight was reluctant to ultimately sell off those positions on the open market, so the firm's executives decided to find a partner in the next 24 hours who would buy them out.

Did Wall Street vultures already smell blood on the Street? This expression has become popular in financial circles when a firm experiences big trouble. It is time to put it to a good rest. It has been proven that vultures are attracted not by the smell of blood but of dead flesh; there is a sort of gas produced by the beginnings of decay. A piping company was once trying to find a leak in their lines; they pumped this gas through them and found where it was leaking out by looking were turkey vultures began to congregate. If vultures can't smell blood, how could Wall Street vultures?

If anything, Wall Street vultures were quick to acknowledge that Knight had very attractive businesses that were fully isolated from the trading blunder and therefore remained healthy; the proposals wouldn't take long to start arriving.

6:30 P.M. Let the bidding start

Wall Street equities trading desks saw this incident as an opportunity to make a quick buck. There was no way any of them would have accepted paying face value for a portfolio that was already being targeted by hedge funds. UBS, the first party to discuss with Knight Capital, wanted an 8 percent to 9 percent discount on the position.

UBS's equities trading desk was headed by Mike Stewart. Both Stewart and Joyce had long tenures at Merrill Lynch, though not at the same time. Unfortunately, the talks with UBS fell apart later that night; the terms sought by UBS reflected how dire Knight's situation had become.

Goldman Sachs then came into the picture. Just a few months before, the brokerage and asset management units of the firm (along with Vanguard Group and Dimensional Fund Advisors LP, among others) had increased their stakes in Knight Capital by 73 percent to 2.39 million shares, valued at $28.5 million at the end of June. Would they be interested in providing a lifeline to Knight?

9:00 P.M. Seeking emergency funding

Around the same time, Joyce called his longtime acquaintance Carlos Hernandez, J.P. Morgan's global head of equities at the time, to seek emergency funding to plug the losses from those errant trades in the morning. Hernandez had served as head of North American markets, capital origination and distribution of J.P. Morgan since November 2004 and served as its head of investment banking. He had joined J.P. Morgan in 1986 as part of the Investment Bank's training program, working later on a wide array of advisory and financing transactions for both corporations and governments, across various product groups and geographic regions. Previously, Hernandez had managed the Institutional Equities business for the Americas. Before joining the Equities Division, Hernandez had served as JPMorgan's regional executive for Latin America. Hernandez was a member of JPMorgan's Global Investment Banking Management Committee and served on the boards of Marketaxess, Music for Tomorrow, Calvary Fund and The Brunswick School in Greenwich, Connecticut. Hernandez held a bachelor degree in business from the State

University of New York, and an MBA from Columbia Business School.

Just a month later, Hernandez would change positions to become head of investor services, a business that combined the New York-based firm's prime brokerage, financing and securities-services units. The bank held more than $17 trillion in custodial assets for clients, and many experts in the industry saw these businesses as growth areas as new regulations were expected to require vastly more collateral for swaps and other derivatives trades. Hernandez's old place was to be taken by Tim Throsby; in the same restructuring, Blythe Masters, the long-time head of J.P. Morgan's commodities division, was adding regulatory affairs for the corporate and investment bank to her plate.

"We've had these issues," the Knight chief told his longtime acquaintance; Hernandez had been the person Joyce called most frequently when he had questions for J.P. Morgan. "We're looking for help."

Hernandez, who was just returning from business meetings in Mexico, knew that Joyce's inquiry meshed well with the type of roles J.P. Morgan had been asked to play in the past. During the financial crisis, the firm had snapped up Bear Stearns and Washington Mutual's banking assets at cut-rate prices. Its dealings with Lehman Brothers led to legal battles over collateral demands the bank made before the securities firm's demise.

J.P. Morgan was also a big creditor to MF Global Holdings, which had sent hundreds of millions of dollars in customer funds to the bank in collateral as it fought for its survival. Bank officials had said J.P. Morgan never intentionally accepted or held on to money that belonged in segregated customer accounts at MF Global. The bank would later return roughly $600 million that was trapped at the bank when MF Global collapsed in October 2011. J.P. Morgan even considered buying MF Global, but then backed away amid questions about money transfers that came up three days before the securities firm filed for bankruptcy.

J.P. Morgan's regular appearances in the most despairing chapters of so many companies' lives underlined the bank's everyday presence in today's financial markets, and the conservative hunger for risk that helped the bank come out of the 2008 financial crisis on better footing than most of its competitors. J.P. Morgan had suffered an embarrassing $5.8 billion trading loss in positions in credit derivatives made by employees in London who worked in the bank's chief investment office in early 2012; yet, the firm emerged from these episodes with a reputation for being a steely and often uncompromising creditor that drew a hard line in negotiations with those customers or rivals even as they gasped for air.

In his conversation with Hernandez, Joyce explained that a torrent of accidental trades that day had left Knight holding billions of dollars in stock positions, the result of unintended buying at the offer and selling at the bid, and Knight was trying to sell the positions in order to open the next day.

Hernandez asked Joyce whether J.P. Morgan could look at the securities with the aim of buying some or all of them. Joyce quickly said no; he went on to explain that Knight had been speaking to UBS, and when those discussions collapsed, the firm entered exclusive negotiations with Goldman Sachs. Joyce expected to need more cash and wanted to get J.P. Morgan to provide financing.

12:00 P.M. The sooner you can unwind that trade...
Smooth Hernandez had said he would need to talk to other J.P. Morgan executives. "The sooner you can unwind that trade, the better," he had told Joyce. "We'll get back to you." Top executives dreaded the fact that Knight itself was not able yet to calculate its total losses or know whether its deal with Goldman would close. Was this going to be another Bear Sterns? Only a minimal amount of due

diligence had been done on the assets of Bear Sterns prior to the acquisition.

J.P. Morgan had access to the careful due diligence they had conducted the year before when they considered acquiring Knight. While J.P. Morgan demonstrated again an interest in the firm's capabilities, its executives ultimately decided they had had enough bad press surrounding their own trading losses. The last thing management wanted, from a perception standpoint, was for J.P. Morgan to get involved with another firm that had experienced trading losses as well. J.P. Morgan ultimately balked at providing short-term financing as well, as it felt it was too risky.

J.P. Morgan's trading loss certainly dwarfed Knight's losses and threatened to tarnish CEO Jamie Dimon's reputation as the smart hand that successfully handled the bank during the financial crisis. Dimon, who until very recently was widely seen as President Obama's favorite Wall Street CEO, ultimately bore responsibility for the banks' loss of more than $6.2 billion in the first nine months of 2012 on bets by U.K. trader Bruno Iksil, nicknamed the London Whale. Iksil operated under Chief investment officer Ina Drew. For starters, Dimon's pay was cut in half to $11.5 million for 2012, compared with $23 million a year earlier.

The Chief Investment Office (CIO) was chartered with managing excess cash while minimizing risk using credit derivatives as part of a hedging strategy. Instead, their trades became so large that the bank couldn't easily unwind them. At the bottom of this miscalculation were blunders in the development, testing and approval of a new VaR model to measure the risk of their Synthetic Credit Portfolio.

VaR (Value at Risk) is a metric that attempts to estimate the risk of loss on a portfolio of assets. A portfolio's VaR represents an estimate of the maximum expected mark-to-market loss over a specified time period, generally one day, at a stated confidence level, assuming historical market conditions. Through January 2012, according to the 129-page report from a task force led by Michael

Cavanagh, co-head of the firm's corporate and investment bank, the VaR for the Synthetic Credit Portfolio was calculated using a "linear sensitivity model", also known within the Firm as the "Basel I model", because it was used for purposes of Basel I capital calculations and for external reporting purposes. The Basel I model captured the major risk facing the Synthetic Credit Portfolio at the time, which was the potential for loss attributable to movements in credit spreads.

However, the model was flawed in the manner in which it estimated correlation risk: that is, the risk that defaults of the components within the index would correlate. As the value of the tranche positions in the Synthetic Credit Portfolio increased, this flaw became more significant: the value of these positions was driven in large part by the extent to which the positions in the index were correlated to each other. The main risk with the tranche positions was that regardless of credit risk in general, defaults might be more or less correlated.

This limitation meant that the Basel I model likely would not comply with the requirements of Basel II.5, which had originally been expected to be formally adopted in the United States at the end of 2011. One of the traders responsible for the Synthetic Credit Portfolio therefore instructed an expert in quantitative finance within the Quantitative Research team for the CIO to develop a new VaR model for the Synthetic Credit Portfolio that would comply with the requirements of Basel II.5. They believed that the Basel I model was too conservative, that it was producing a higher VaR than was appropriate.

Early in the development process, the CIO considered and rejected a proposal to adopt the VaR model used by the Investment Bank's credit hybrids business for the Synthetic Credit Portfolio. Because the Investment Bank traded many customized and illiquid CDSs, its VaR model mapped individual instruments to a combination of indices and single name proxies, which CIO Market

Risk viewed as less accurate for CIO's purposes than mapping to the index as a whole. He believed that, because the Synthetic Credit Portfolio, unlike the Investment Bank, traded indices and index tranches, the Investment Bank's approach was not appropriate for CIO. The Model Review Group agreed and, in an early draft of its approval of the model, described CIO's model as "superior" to that used by the Investment Bank.

The Model Review Group, charged with the formal approval of the model, performed only limited back-testing. The group compared the VaR under the new model computed using historical data to the daily profit-and-loss over a subset of trading days during a two-month period, not even close to a typically required period of 264 previous trading days a year. In addition, they were pressured by the CIO to accelerate its review, overlooking operational flaws apparent during the approval process. For instance, it was found later that the model operated through a series of Excel spreadsheets, which had to be completed manually by a process of copying and pasting data from one spreadsheet to another. The Model Review Group discovered that, for purposes of a pricing step used in the VaR calculation, CIO was using something called the "West End" analytic suite rather than Numerix, an approved vendor model. CIO assured the Model Review Group that both valuations were in "good agreement".

On January 30, the Model Review Group finally authorized CIO Market Risk to use the new VaR model which would utilize the Gaussian Copula model, a commonly accepted model used to map the approximate correlation between two variables, to calculate hazard rates and correlations. A hazard rate is the probability of failure per unit of time of items in operation, which was sometimes estimated as a ratio of the number of failures to the accumulated operating time for the items. For purposes of the model, the hazard rate estimated the probability of default for a unit of time for each of the underlying names in the portfolio.

Once in operation, a spreadsheet error caused the VaR for April 10 to fail to reflect the day's $400 million loss in the Synthetic Credit Portfolio. This error was noticed, first by personnel in the Investment Bank, and by the modeler and CIO Market Risk, and was corrected promptly. Because it was viewed as a one-off error, it did not trigger further inquiry. Later in May, in response to further losses in the Synthetic Credit Portfolio, a review of the West End calculation led to discover that it was using the Uniform Rate model rather than the Gaussian Copula model, contrary to the Model Review Group's approval.

Although this error did not have a significant effect on the VaR, an operational error was found in the calculation of the relative changes in hazard rates and correlation estimates. Specifically, after subtracting the old rate from the new rate, the spreadsheet divided the result by the sum instead of the average, as the modeler had intended. This error had the effect of muting volatility by a factor of two and of lowering the VaR, minimizing the estimate of the potential loss in the Synthetic Credit Portfolio, which ultimately metastasized to more than $6.2 billion. Despite this humongous loss, J.P. Morgan disclosed a full-year 2012 record net income of $21.3 billion on revenue of $99.9 billion.

Instead of the financing Knight was desperately looking for, J.P. Morgan paid Knight $100 million for a basket of other securities, including U.S. stocks and less-liquid Canadian securities. J.P. Morgan had also agreed not to raise capital requirements on Knight's broker-dealer in London, ahead of the start of trading there.

2:00 A.M. A deal is reached

At this time, Knight was still working a deal with Goldman Sachs. The bank, a Knight shareholder, agreed to purchase those unwanted positions as part of one huge basket sale. Goldman Sachs ultimately negotiated buying the portfolio at a 5 percent discount, or about $230 million less than the value of the stocks. Knight had already lost about $200 million trading out of a portion of the $7 billion of accidentally purchased shares.

According to market insiders, 5 percent was an absolutely massive risk commission, "by an order of magnitude, almost"[4]. This could be explained by the fact that the entire Street knew about these positions; that was the main reason why the big broker-dealers bidding on this risk program wanted such large margin of safety: everyone was gunning against them already and the affected names could have been easily obtained. Which is why the information that Goldman Sachs acquired the portfolio didn't come out until Friday afternoon – they had probably traded it pretty aggressively by then to reduce risk.

Under trade-settlement regulations, the Knight-Goldman block transaction would have needed to settle three business days after the initial agreement, which meant the seller must have come up with the estimated $440 million in cash by Monday, which was more than its entire revenue in the second quarter of that year, when it brought in only $289 million.

As of June 30, Knight had about $365 million in cash, raising important questions about whether the brokerage firm could generate the additional money by the following week. Knight was still alive; would it be able to make it to the next week? Even more pressing, would Knight be able to survive one more day?

There's always a glimmer of hope in the darkest darkness, thawing out the horrible inertia of helplessness. This time, hope was ushered in by an email sent earlier that day from Jefferies' chief executive officer Richard Handler, who was vacationing in France, "I see what's going on. Give me a call. I have some ideas about how we can help."

The two executives spoke later that night, and Handler told Joyce his investment bank was in a good position to help Knight. Handler cited Jefferies's own experience navigating market turmoil, something it had faced just nine months earlier as investors speculated the firm might sink due to its exposure to debt issued by weaker European governments.

This shouldn't have been surprising: Handler had consistently been opportunistic when the right deal or potential partner emerged. Urban legend had it that when Handler learned of the resignation of a well-known and highly profitable investment banker from a major firm, he showed up in the banker's driveway the very next day to lure him to Jefferies. The bank's assistance to Knight had been fueled at least in part by the professional relationship between Handler and Joyce, who had known each other since Joyce became chief executive of Knight in May 2002.

Ultimately, Handler and Brian Friedman, chairman of the executive committee, would structure and lead Knight's rescue, with Jefferies committing $125 million of the $400 million investment and becoming Knight's largest shareholder. Friedman would become a constant presence at Knight's Jersey City office, from the moment he set up shop in an office two doors down from Joyce until the following weekend was over, spending at least 10 hours a day at the firm.

Chapter Twelve

Surviving One More Day

Knight was able to unload its unwanted positions before dawn on Thursday. That was just the first battle, but the war was not over. Charlie Gasparino, a senior finance correspondent described by MarketWatch as FOX Business Network's "Rocky Balboa", had quoted a Knight executive, "It's a warzone here; bullets are flying. I'm just trying to survive."

The firm was desperately trying to survive too, and only had a few days of breathing room to complete a deal, stabilize itself with a capital injection or go bankrupt.

Wednesday's flow of erroneous trades wouldn't settle until the next Monday, meaning that Knight wouldn't realize the estimated $440 million trading loss until then. Securities-industry law required stock trades to settle up to three days after the date of the transaction.

"They can survive a couple of days of harmed revenues," said Patrick O'Shaughnessy, analyst with Raymond James. "What they can't survive is capital calls or illiquidity." Citadel was well aware of the sword hanging over Knight's neck; a proposal of $0.50 - $0.61 per share had been disclosed, an offer that was ridiculously depressing and insulting to Knight.

Joyce had also seen his considerable stake in his firm almost wiped out in a matter of hours. As of April 2, Joyce owned more than 1.2 million shares of Knight Capital, with a market value of nearly $16 million; by then, his stake was worth less than $3 million. Joyce had tried to catch some sleep on the couch in his office Wednesday night. About 15 other employees, including General Counsel

Amoruso, had also stayed all night at the office. Amoruso was the treasurer of Knight's PAC, Good Government Fund.

On Thursday, food from McDonald's and pizzas from Domino's would be brought in to feed the employees.

Wall Street was becoming sympathetic with Knight's plight. "Tom's a really solid guy, a good leader," Paul Roy, the founding partner of London-based investment firm NewSmith Capital Partners, had said about Knight's CEO after the trading malfunction. Joyce had worked at Merrill Lynch through 2001 with Roy, who was then the head of the global equity markets division. "They reacted speedily and they've diagnosed the issue and quantified the problem. Whatever he's now putting into place, I'm sure it's not going to happen again."

Just the month before, some outside traders indicated they had experienced problems when routing trades through Knight Capital. Craig Warner, head of trading at Capstone Investments, a research boutique firm, said that a few weeks ago an order he placed with Knight went wrong. The trade was supposed to be spread throughout the entire day, but a half-hour before the market close, the remainder of the trade was executed all at once.

"It was alarming because if the stock had been really moving, it could have been a big problem," Warner said. "After having the issue I had last week and with the issue yesterday, I lost a lot of confidence in them," he said, adding that he was no longer using Knight to clear trades.

7:24 A.M. Knight provides update regarding August 1 disruption
"As previously disclosed, Knight experienced a technology issue at the open of trading at the NYSE yesterday, August 1. This issue was related to Knight's installation of trading software and resulted in Knight sending numerous erroneous orders in NYSE-listed securities into the market. This software has been removed from the company's systems.

"Clients were not negatively affected by the erroneous orders, and the software issue was limited to the routing of certain listed stocks to NYSE.

"Knight has traded out of its entire erroneous trade position, which has resulted in a realized pre-tax loss of approximately $440 million. Although the company's capital base has been severely impacted, the company's broker/dealer subsidiaries are in full compliance with their net capital requirements. Knight will continue its trading and market-making activities at the commencement of trading today. The company is actively pursuing its strategic and financing alternatives to strengthen its capital base."

Releasing an update that early in the morning of August 2 was just the first step on Knight's fight for survival. To say that their capital base had been just "severely impacted" was an understatement. When pressed later by Bloomberg Television's Erik Schatzker on the type of investor they were looking for, equity or debt, Joyce made clear they were keeping an "open mind" to any type of structure. Beggars can't be choosers.

Many of the company's biggest customers, including TD Ameritrade, the number one U.S. retail brokerage by trading volume (which usually routed about 4.5 percent of its orders through Knight), Vanguard (which typically routed about a quarter of its NYSE and NASDAQ trades through Knight), Fidelity Investments, Scottrade, ETrade, Pershing, a subsidiary of BNY Mellon and Invesco, had stopped routing orders through Knight. One of the biggest fears was that the company would collapse, landing trading partners with losses. TD Ameritrade's chief derivatives strategist Joe Kinahan had said that as long as Knight remained in good standing with the exchanges, his firm would send orders through it.

Knight itself was requesting customers to stop sending trades. That was because Knight was required to set aside more capital against each trade, so the more business it did, the more capital it needed. After the confirmation of the loss, the firm was determined to keep its capital demands to a minimum. Among those dialing back trading were Citigroup and J.P. Morgan, whose stock-trading desks handled big transactions for institutional investors.

There were also questions about how the firm's possible failure could affect the network of 800 smaller brokerages relying on it to process orders. Longview Capital Management, a Wilmington, Delaware-based registered investment adviser with $200 million in assets under management, was holding off from trading with Knight until "it gets its act together and tell us where they stand," had said Christian Wagner, chief executive and chief investment officer of the firm.

Exchange-traded fund issuers, for which Knight was the leading market maker, had been calling competitors to make sure they could step in if Knight did not execute trades in their funds. AdvisorShares, a Bethesda, Maryland-based exchange-traded fund provider with $670 million in assets that uses Knight as its lead market maker, had confirmed that the brokerage had contacted them on Thursday morning and addressed their concerns about some of AdvisorShares' ETFs that were trading at wider spreads than they would normally. That could have happened because market makers were not fulfilling trades.

According to an analysis by IndexUniverse, a San Francisco-based ETF research provider, retail investors and traders who wanted to buy and sell small, illiquid exchange-traded funds may have also been unwittingly losing money because of wider spreads in the bid and ask price of the ETFs at Knight since the incident.

10:00 A.M. Making friends with Ruhle and Schatzker
Many tough questions awaited Joyce as an assistant set up the microphone on his lapel for a Bloomberg Television's *Market Makers* interview with Stephanie Ruhle and Erik Schatzker. Canadian-born Schatzker pointed to the tremendous cost, initially estimated at $440 million, to exit the erroneous trades of the day before. "You have a big hole in your balance sheet. Your stock is under tremendous

pressure. You are trading at less than $4 a share. People want to know Tom and so I have to ask you, what's the chance that Knight Capital doesn't make it?"

"We know in days like yesterday and today, we have a lot of work to do. We got to make sure that we work with our counterparties, our clients to get the answers they want. And we are pursuing that as we speak. We are also exploring other alternatives such as strategic investments or investors and other financing alternatives. So, we have work to do and we are doing it right now."

Joyce was coy about what he meant when he referred to exploring strategic alternatives. He just pointed out that he was speaking to a lot of people, "people who are in touch with situations like this." That was a signal for Jefferies; the very same morning a team from the bank had set up shop at Knight's headquarters and wouldn't leave until a deal would be reached.

Even twenty four hours after the trading malfunction, Joyce was at a loss to explain what really happened to Ruhle. "We put in a new bit of software the night before, because we were getting ready to trade the New York Stock Exchange RLP program. Now, mind you, this had nothing to do with the New York Stock Exchange, it had to do with our readiness to trade it. And unfortunately, the software had a fairly major bug in it. It sent into the market a ton of orders, all erroneous. So, we ended up with a very large error position which we had to sort through during the balance of the day. It was a software bug. Except, it happened to be a very large software bug. As soon as we realized what we had, we got out of the code and it is gone now."

Trying to explain the forty five minute delay to stop the flow of orders, Joyce said that they were busy talking to their clients right away. "We alerted our clients immediately that we had an issue and they got out of the way, which is great because nobody else except for us was wounded by this activity. So, we don't think we actually acted in a slow fashion at all because our primary focus was on alerting our clients as the situation and keeping them out of harm's way."

Joyce acknowledged that human error played a role. "You can't immunize people against making mistakes. You can't keep people from doing stupid things, whether it is writing some imperfect code or buying the wrong stock at the wrong time." While some people would later criticize Knight for employing inexperienced technicians, this couldn't have been farther from the truth; even the most experienced people in technology make mistakes, as Knight had found out the day before.

Everyone in the financial circles wondered who would be held responsible for the trading mistake. When asked about it, Joyce didn't want to personalize things, at least for the world to see. "Somebody made an error. A human being made an error. Now, if you want to scapegoat somebody, if you want to get the effigies out, fine. Our firm was really healthy on July 31. We made a mistake."

10:44 A.M. "We don't think we acted in a slow fashion"
Pisani, "with all due respect," slams CNBC's Joyce for saying, "We don't think we acted in a slow fashion." Pisani's reply was that everybody in the industry would think forty five minutes was a long time. Meanwhile, after a sudden decline in the first minutes of the trading day, Knight shares were changing hands at 3.28, down 52.74 percent.

Right after Pisani's intervention, CNBC's Lee speaks with Justin Shack, managing director of Rosenblatt Securities. "Obviously a lot of people out there are saying this screams for more regulation. There needs to be somebody who's watching over the computerized trading." Lee then asked about Shack's point of view whether or not this could have been regulated out as a risk.

"I don't know if it could have been regulated out as a risk. There is a brand-new rule that the SEC put in place relatively recently called the market access rule that's supposed to provide for more risk controls for these sorts of orders in the market. What's interesting is each of the episodes we talked about, three of the four we talked about excluding the Flash Crash. [If] you look at the BATS IPO, Facebook and Knight yesterday, [these] were related to new code being put into place, related to the RLP program here. For Facebook, NASDAQ rewrote its software for the IPO cross and BATS attempted to become a listing market for the first time. In each case the code failed and it wasn't tested enough. I think it speaks to the need for better testing in advance of these things."

12:30 P.M. Speaking with Virtu
Knight was in discussions with trading firm Virtu Financial about a potential merger or infusion of capital that would make the two firms partners.[1] Like Knight, New York-based Virtu was a big player in high-speed trading and also a so-called designated market maker on the New York Stock Exchange, meaning it stood in to buy and sell NYSE-listed stocks at quoted prices.

Virtu was backed by private-equity firm Silver Lake Partners, which was also involved in the talks with Knight. Silver Lake was a U.S.-based private equity firm focused on leveraged buyout and growth capital investments in technology, technology-enabled and related industries; founded in 1999 by Glenn Hutchins, Dave Roux and Jim Davidson, the firm's portfolio included Avaya, Instinet, Sabre Holdings, Seagate Technology, Skype and UGS Corp. Previous investments in financial technology had included Ameritrade, Interactive Data Corporation, Island ECN, Mercury Payment Systems, SunGard and NASDAQ.

These discussions would ultimately turn out short-lived. Joyce was adamantly opposed to the idea of partnering with a competitor. By 1:01 P.M., Gasparino disclosed that Virtu was out as potential bidder. While this door was closing for Joyce, other doors would open. Meanwhile, Knight shares were trading at 3.18, down 54.18 percent for the day.

1:29 P.M. *Speaking with TD Ameritrade*

Joyce was also talking with the leaders of TD Ameritrade, chairman Joe Moglia, and chief executive officer Fred Tomczyk. Joyce had close ties to Moglia, as both were long-time Merrill Lynch executives.[2] After being a football coach for 16 years, Moglia had decided to start a second career on Wall Street; he joined a training class at Merrill Lynch with twenty-four MBA graduates and 17 years later was a member of the executive committees for both the institutional business and the private client business. He took the role of chief executive officer of the firm in 2001 and stayed at the helm for seven years before he became chairman. In that role, he was succeeding founder Ricketts and was succeeded himself by Tomczyk in October 2008.

Tomczyk had called Joyce to say he wanted to see Knight remain viable. "What do you need?" he asked. Tomczyk was by then a more than 25-year veteran of the financial services industry, and his strategy for the company relied heavily on maintaining a leadership position in the trading business.

Tomczyk had been chief executive officer of London Life; in fiscal 2009, in the midst of the crisis, TD Ameritrade produced record amounts of client trades per day, record net new assets and record new accounts, all while maintaining a clean balance sheet with a strong overall financial position.

Consulted a year before by Steve Forbes on lessons learned after the Flash Crash, Tomczyk was confident that the SEC had done a very good job of studying the Flash Crash and analyzing it, but that they were not finished with the job. "But I do think the number of the changes they've proposed and the number of changes they continue to look at, I'm not sure you'll ever guarantee it'll never happen. But I think that's just life. The reality is, I do think they're doing a lot of the right things and are on the right track."

So for him, the Flash Crash was just life: face it and move on. That was his message for Joyce too; although the two men weren't personally close, TD Ameritrade had been an important client of Knight's for many years. The brokerage wanted to see Knight survive to preserve competition among firms that make markets for retail customers' trades.[3]

That was not the only friendly cheer up hug received by Joyce. Co-founder Pasternak was speaking with Reuters about his confidence that Knight would rebound. "Whenever you have a company that lost roughly half of its tangible book value in five minutes, everything is on the table. All [Joyce] has to do is to pick up the phone."[4]

Ronald Kruszewski, chairman and chief executive of Stifel Financial, a long-term Knight client, picked up the phone and called Joyce to offer his help too. His firm, based in St. Louis, Missouri, had been formed as a financial services holding company in July 1983. It offered securities-related financial services in the United States and Europe through several wholly owned subsidiaries. Its clients were served through Stifel Nicolaus in the U.S., a full-service retail and institutional brokerage and investment banking firm. Kruszewski had been chief executive officer of Stifel Financial since September 1997, and was a board member of SIFMA, where Joyce also served.

Later in November 2012, the company would acquire Keefe, Bruyette & Woods (KBW), an investment banking firm headquartered in New York City that specialized exclusively in the financial services sector. The combination signaled the beginning of a period of consolidation in the financial services industry, as factors that included increased regulatory burdens, pressure on commissions, and persistently low interest rates had combined to severely crimp profitability. Investment bank Stephens rendered the fairness opinion to the board of directors of Stifel Financial on its KBW acquisition.

2:15 P.M. Frankenstein market

Saluzzi and Arnuk, the founders of Themis Trading, had emerged as leading critics of high-frequency trading and the very market in which they worked; Saluzzi wished Wall Street could go back to a calmer, simpler time, all the way back to, say, 2004, before the old exchange system splintered and murky private markets sprang up and computers could send the Dow into 1,000-point spasms. There was no scarcity of critics for the ultimate critic; Georgetown University's Professor Angel said Saluzzi was stoking irrational fears of a market that is providing good returns to investors, comparing him to people "who gripe that their cellphone is too complicated, ignoring the fact that 20 years ago they didn't even have a cellphone."[5]

So it wasn't a surprise to see Saluzzi on CNBC. Just after traders noticed something was amiss, Saluzzi was already pointing his barbs toward Knight's trading malfunction. "August 1 will echo May, 6 2010 in market structure failure. Can't wait for the postmortem to be issued in 5 months," he tweeted at 10:04 A.M. At 11:03 A.M., he ventured into unknown financial territory, "Market structure needs to be changed; until it does, this will happen again." Right after midday, at 12:14 P.M., he was already calling for action, "Every IR executive at these 140 companies should be picking up the phone and demanding answers as to what happened in their stock today." The list could go on and on with these gems; another tweet after the market closed, at 7:17 P.M., said, "Knight algo mayhem vindicates what Themis Trading and others have been saying forever. Market structure is BROKEN." One of Saluzzi's own followers answered, "How does one firm having an issue and footing the entire bill suggest market structure is broken?"

That was the key point. This was a company that had a technology installation issue, something that could have happened to any company, which ultimately exhibited a very high price tag. "We are concerned about the long-term health of the equity market; there is systemic risk built into this equity market," he told Brian Sullivan and Amanda Drury, co-anchors of CNBC's *Street Signs*.

"The decimalization and the demutualization of the stock servers set the stage for what we have in the Frankenstein market. There's years of regulations that kind of created this, but there's one thing, really one thing that really needs to be actually taken away right now, the make or take model where there're rebates."

Saluzzi stopped for one moment for a deep breath and went on. "Exchanges will pay you to add to their liquidity and then you pay to take away. This creates a distortion to the price discovery process. This creates a distortion of the smart order routers. This creates the dark pools for coming in. Why are there so many? It is because these are cheaper destinations and ping for order flow. It's this entire artificial game that's been created."

Everybody including anchors Sullivan and Drury could have been left wondering if removing rebates and eliminating dark pools would have stopped this technology installation issue at Knight Capital.

2:45 P.M. Bonds down

Knight's $375 million of 3.5 percent convertible bonds due in March 2015 were down 8.625 cents to 74.5 cents on the dollar and yielding 15.8 percent in New York, according to Trace, the bond-price reporting system of the Financial Industry Regulatory Authority. The debt was trading as low as 40 cents earlier.

Bloomberg reported that the bonds were convertible to stock at $20.87 a share. Investors who owned the note, including Goldman Sachs, Oaktree Capital Management, Invesco, and Citadel Advisors, could demand repayment upon a "fundamental change" in the company including a sale for cash or if a person or group disclosed a more than 50 percent ownership stake in Knight, according to a February regulatory 10-K filing.

4:00 P.M. The stock is down 80 percent in two days

As Knight was forced to seek new funding, employees watched in disbelief as its shares closed Thursday down as much as 80 percent from Wednesday at 9:30 A.M.

Trading partners were backing away from doing business with Knight too, with one major exception: Jefferies, one of the firms that continued to provide funding to Knight in the securities-lending market.

6:00 P.M. Mad Cramer

If there's a business show that expects not only to inform (or misinform, according to some critics) but also to entertain, it would be Cramer's *Mad Money.* Can you think of somebody else who promotes his holdings by leaving stock picks on his answering machine? Cramer did more than that; once, he described how he could push stocks higher or lower with as little as $5 million in capital when he was running his hedge fund.

Cramer had a Hallelujah moment for his followers that would have resonated even with Joyce (they had been classmates at Harvard College). Did we know that a company such as Knight could have been completely brought to its knees because of a software issue?

"We may have not been able to predict that a brokerage with a huge share of the stock trading could experience a 70 percent decline in its market capitalization. Even if it's run by one of the savviest business people I know, Tommy Joyce. I have known him for 35 years, I used to trade with him at my hedge fund and he was in my college class; he is a really good guy. We can use this new risk to recalibrate what makes for safer investment. Let's go from what we can learn from the Knight Capital Group implosion so we know what kind of stock we need to avoid in this in one of the toughest markets I have ever seen."

He was not only referring to Knight's trading debacle. "Just a couple of months ago, we saw Knight lose $30 million trying to place orders for Facebook. In other words, what I am detailing is that

Knight Capital is deeply in a business where a software glitch or a wrong keystroke can wipe out the company. So let's stand the Knight Capital story on its head, if Knight represents a company that could be destroyed overnight by a software glitch then we clearly want the opposite of Knight."

6:33 P.M. The regulators are looking over

Reuters reported that the U.S. Securities and Exchange Commission was considering whether new measures might be necessary to safeguard markets. "We continue to closely review the events surrounding yesterday's trading and discuss those events with other regulators as well as Knight Capital Group. We are also considering what, if any, additional steps may be necessary, beyond the post-Flash Crash measures that limited the impact of yesterday's trading," said SEC spokesman John Nester.[6]

6:44 P.M. Penson's assets under scrutiny[7]

Reuters revealed that the CFTC had dispatched a team to monitor Knight's futures brokerage unit. Knight had bought Penson's FCM, which had $411 million in client funds, in May 2012. Therefore, futures regulators were concerned about the customer funds that were part of Knight's purchase in May.

Confidence in the futures industry's ability to protect customer funds had been shaken dramatically after the failure of futures brokerages MF Global and PFGBest in the past year which was followed by accusations that the firms improperly raided customer accounts.[8]

CME Group, the future's brokerage's first-line regulator, was also monitoring the damaged trading firm. Jill Sommers, a Republican commissioner at the CFTC, had said she did not see any parallels between MF Global, Peregrine and the situation at Knight. "It isn't like we found out that Knight was stealing money. This isn't a ratings downgrade, this isn't a liquidity crisis. This was just a trading loss."

Sommers also noted that the CFTC had access to an electronic system with futures brokers' customer segregation and capital information, which allowed the agency to keep tabs on firms like Knight.

On the other hand, James Koutoulas, the lead lawyer for Commodity Customer Coalition, an advocacy group for former customers of MF Global and Peregrine Financial, expressed concern. "Those at Penson should be a little worried. We would hope at the very least that the customer funds would be intact. If we saw a shortfall, it would be very damaging to the industry." Finally, in a letter to clients, Knight Futures Division confirmed that customer's funds for commodity futures trading accounts were segregated and kept separate from the funds of Knight required by regulators.

The clock was ticking for Knight. Among the many callers who were reaching out to the firm was Howard Lutnick, Cantor Fitzgerald's chief executive officer. The firm's corporate headquarters on the 101st-105th floors of One World Trade Center had been destroyed during the September 11, 2001 attacks. This was the firm that had lost over two-thirds of its workforce. Lutnick, whose brother was among those killed, vowed to keep the company alive, and the company was able to bring its trading systems back online within a week.

Cantor Fitzgerald was among the first firms to notice the ongoing trading disaster at Knight. A message came over the speaker that something was wrong with Knight, so everybody was immediately prohibited from trading with them. Lutnick made an evening call that ultimately went nowhere. "Sure, we called and we said we would be happy to go and make an investment. Frankly, the guys at Knight wanted to split up the investment so no one strong would be a part of it, that's why six guys came in and recapped the company. With some private equity guys, we offered to go and take a look at the company." "Thanks, but no thanks, we have enough people," was the reply.

Chapter Thirteen

90 Interested Parties

August 3 started with a statement coming from chairman Schapiro, with which she was prodding her staff to come up with a rule to require exchanges and other market centers to have specific programs in place which would ensure the capacity and integrity of their systems. Her agency had already dispatched officials to the firm's Jersey City offices. In the agency's Washington D.C. headquarters, senior officials had worked through the night in offices without air-conditioning to monitor the firm's liquidity position; the office's air-conditioning had been programmed to shut off before midnight as an energy-saving measure.

"The apparent trading error by Knight Capital Group on Wednesday reflects the type of event that can raise concerns for investors about our nation's equity markets – markets that I believe are the most resilient, efficient, and robust in the world.

"Reliance on computers is a fact of life not only in markets everywhere, but in virtually every facet of business. That doesn't mean we should not endeavor to reduce the likelihood of technology errors and limit their impact when they occur.

"While Wednesday's event was unacceptable, I would note that several of the measures we instituted following the Flash Crash helped to limit its impact. Recently-adopted circuit breakers halted trading on individual stocks that experienced significant price fluctuations, and clearly defined rules guided the exchanges in determining which trades could be broken giving the marketplace certainty.

"In addition, existing rules make it clear that when broker-dealers with access to our markets use computers to trade, trade fast, or trade frequently, they must check those systems to ensure they are operating properly. And, naturally, we will consider whether such compliance measures were followed in this case.

"As with every significant incident of volatility that occurs in our markets, we will continue to review what happened and determine if any, additional measures are needed. That process has already begun.

"In particular, I have asked the staff to accelerate ongoing efforts to propose a rule to require exchanges and other market centers to have specific programs in place to ensure the capacity and integrity of their systems. And I have directed the staff to convene a roundtable in the coming weeks to discuss further steps that can be taken to address these critical issues."

By considering whether compliance measures had been followed in Knight's case, Schapiro was referring to their relatively new rule designed to protect the markets from rogue algorithmic computer trading programs, the market access rule. The SEC was already examining how the algorithmic error had been unleashed on the markets and whether the software used by Knight had been properly tested before it was put into use on Wednesday.

Michael Bachner, an attorney who had earlier represented a defendant in the SEC's first-ever market access case, said he suspected Knight would probably face regulatory troubles down the road. "With the magnitude of the problem that occurred, it seems to me there is a likelihood that there was some problem in their risk controls."[1] No other than Jefferies had agreed to pay $20,000 to settle allegations that it violated the market-access rule in trading of NASDAQ securities.

9:10 A.M. Making it to the weekend?

CNBC's Kayla Tausche was wondering live from Knight's headquarters if the firm would be able to make it through the weekend. "There is certainly a lot of interest in potentially doing a deal." Dunne was less optimistic about Knight's outlook, "I didn't think we'd make it through Friday. I really didn't."

However, the stock had been rising pre-market. Traders were saying that Knight was a safe bet at above the key $2 level as long as key capital levels were sound; the regulators camped out at Knight's headquarters were making sure that was still the case.

9:30 A.M. A very precarious situation

As the opening approached, Knight executives were working feverishly lining up short-term financing to get through the week. Knight and J.P. Morgan had discussed the availability of a $200-million revolver, the term for a credit line that could be drawn and repaid as long as the borrower met certain conditions; at the helm was J.P. Morgan along with half a dozen other banks.

Knight was relying on short-term funding, with circumstances changing too quickly to focus on accessing the facility before the weekend. "We need to get through Friday in order to get to the weekend," Joyce thought.

In a stream of calls to Hernandez and Michael Cavanagh, co-chief executive of J.P. Morgan's corporate and investment bank, other prospective lenders gained comfort. Cavanagh had led the investigation into the bank's own massive trading losses. J.P. Morgan executives made it known they considered Knight's assets valuable enough to offset banks' losses even if the firm folded.

Sandler O'Neill had been talking with Knight's rivals and private equity shops about either buying divisions of the firm or investing in the business. Knight had set up a data room for potential bidders to comb through its books.

Some large private equity firms were weighing whether to look at the company. Some that were particularly active in the financial services sector had been approached by Knight's advisers, yet, they were unsure about pursuing a deal with the firm.

"To go in fast and take a lot of risk, usually you do that when the terms and the price are safe," confided a senior private equity executive. His firm was approached but decided not to pursue Knight. One difficulty for bidders was estimating the size of potential legal liability that the company could face in any shareholder lawsuits or enforcement action by regulators. With little time to investigate the reasons for the trading problems, it could have been hard to assess the risks before making a deal.

Sandler O'Neill's Dunne and his team were busy fielding a lot of calls. "Most people wanted to buy certain businesses with very few calls about doing the whole deal; a lot of people wanted to come and look just to see what was around. The majority of people thought this would fail."

Among the businesses that Knight had discussed selling was its futures brokerage unit, Penson Futures. Potential buyers for the business include R. J. O'Brien, which was based in Chicago and was one of the oldest futures clearing firms in the country.

Others that had expressed interest in potential investments or deals included rivals to Knight such as Citadel Investment Group, Virtu Financial, Peak6 Investments, Cantor Fitzgerald, and Two Sigma Securities. Financial conglomerates such as Bank of America Merrill Lynch expressed an interest as well as private equity firms like Kohlberg Kravis Roberts (KKR), the multinational New York-based colossus specialized in leveraged buyouts (featured in The New York Times bestseller *Barbarians at the Gate*), and TPG Capital, one of the largest private equity investment firms globally, headquartered in Fort Worth, Texas.

A source at TA Associates, a private equity firm based in Boston, had confirmed that the company had signed a non-disclosure agreement. According to private equity investors, Knight would need to be broken up, "Knight has many more businesses than just the equity market-making business. Some are good and some are not. I'm not sure who would want them all."

12:35 P.M. Scottrade is back

Scottrade started sending orders to Knight after having pulled their business from the firm on Thursday. Knight executives were busy calling other trading shops, assuring them that it had locked up financing to operate throughout the day and asking them to resume routing client orders.

1:10 P.M. "Get a life!"

"I want you to know that Knight is a great firm and will find a solution to its problems. Get a life!" One female employee who was visibly upset yelled at CNBC's Mary Thompson, who was reporting from Knight's headquarters. No other employees would talk to the press. Meanwhile, Knight is trading at 3.27, up 0.69 (26.74 percent).

1:12 P.M. Pasternak back on CNBC

After a brief 20-minute ride from his office up the I-95 North, Pasternak was sitting on the set of CNBC's *Power Lunch*, ready to speak with Tyler Mathisen. The interview was widely followed on the NYSE floor and presented a bullish assessment of the company's future.

Pasternak told Mathisen that Knight could "definitely survive, even without the help of a financial savior." "If Knight should go under, you'd have a hole in the marketplace. Knight needs to restore the confidence of the community at large, but it's a very important player and frankly, was a very profitable player until three days ago."[2]

Pasternak also disclosed that he had been investing in Knight himself, to the tune of holding "a significant six-figure portion" of the company's shares. Asked about the ideal partner for the firm, he suggested a private equity firm that could understand "the DNA of the company" and preserve its independence.

Pasternak was also asked about Joyce's performance and whether he bore any responsibility for what had happened. "I think his crisis management so far has been exemplary; I'd certainly be a supporter." For a few seconds, Pasternak was forgetting what he really thought of Joyce's tenure at the top of the firm he co-founded.

1:40 P.M. TD Ameritrade is back too

Knight was also enticing its customers to resume sending client stock trades. After Scottrade, TD Ameritrade was now announcing they had begun sending client orders to Knight.

"After considerable review and discussion, we are resuming our order routing relationship with Knight," said CEO Tomczyk. "Our priority has always been the interests of our clients, their trades and their assets. Knight is one of many order routing destinations for us and has long been a good and trusted partner."

Others such as ETrade, Vanguard Group and Fidelity Investments were still routing trades away from Knight, evaluating the situation on a day-to-day basis.

4:00 P.M. Stock up

Shares of Knight leapt 57 percent on Friday, closing at $4.05. But they still remained down more than 60 percent for the week. Toward the end of the trading day Friday, employees in the Jersey City offices gathered around TV screens and cheered at this bit of good news.

4:30 P.M. Drawing the line of credit

On Friday afternoon, Knight officials contacted J.P. Morgan and said the brokerage intended to draw down the entire $200 million available through a revolving line of credit. Knight climbed off the mat, securing emergency financing that allowed it to continue operating for the day. Earlier that day, the firm had been confident enough to reject Citadel's offer of a loan as interim financing. On

Monday morning, an exhausted Joyce would call Hernandez to express his gratitude for the support.

5:31 P.M. Dour mood

By the end of the working day, the mood outside Knight's offices was dour, as security warned reporters not to harass employees coming in and out. One staffer, toting a set of golf clubs despite the catastrophe unfolding around him, said to Reuters, "I don't want to care," when asked how things were going. Another called the atmosphere at work "quiet, very quiet."

One trader said staff had received no announcements from management as yet but described the atmosphere as "definitely better than yesterday," with people trying to carry on as usual. But he noted the company's future remained in doubt. "I am grateful that at this point I still have my job. I thought by this morning we might have heard something. I think a lot of this stuff might get done over the weekend, maybe Monday the latest."[3]

6:00 P.M. Walking through the Citadel

Life at Knight's headquarters in Jersey City had proved especially tumultuous in the prior days. According to employees, who were not authorized to speak publicly, after the firm began telling customers about its emergency financing on Friday, its traders were clustering around television screens, searching for any scrap of good news. Staff members took heart later in the day after spotting executives from Citadel going through security at 545 Washington Blvd, the 25-story glass tower wedged between Newport Centre mall and the Newport PATH train station.

43-year-old Griffin, accompanied by a team of nine advisers that included Nazarali, had flown from Chicago in his private jet with a plan to bail out Knight for good, and wanted to bring it to Joyce personally.

Joyce and Griffin, who had both majored in Economics at Harvard University, didn't know each other well and had only briefly spoken on the phone. They had a 10-minute meeting, and the Citadel team was shocked to hear Joyce was going home to Darien. Joyce told Griffin his people were exhausted and the sides met just for about an hour.

By Friday night, Knight was aligning with Jefferies and accelerating negotiations into the weekend. Now the firm faced a desperate weekend of maneuvering to find a more permanent solution for its woes. Knight's short-term financing was meant to keep it alive until Monday, when its executives and advisers hoped to have deals completed to remove any doubt about the firm's future.

Joyce had three choices left: accept a $500 million bailout from his biggest competitor, take an offer from a group of clients and others that would dilute owners, or go bankrupt.

Shareholders had already faced reality; any alternative would dramatically wipe out their participations. Now it was more than the price of their shares. How could Knight's strengths be highlighted and its risks minimized in the eyes of potential investors? Which option would guarantee the minimum disruption to the company?

In the end, Joyce was advised by Sandler O'Neill to go for a consortium of firms led by Jefferies, the bank that was with him from the moment the disruption happened.

8:00 A.M. Back to talks

After dispersing to Jersey City hotels, the Citadel team returned to Knight's headquarters in the morning, meeting two hours later with their finance team. The session ended at 11 A.M. when the Knight group left for another meeting. That was the last the Citadel officials would see of them.

By deliberately not engaging with Griffin, Joyce temporarily circumvented the fate of Mitchell Caplan, the CEO of ETrade who gave up his post after Citadel invested $2.55 billion in the New York-based brokerage in November 2007. The offer from Citadel was silent on the permanence of Knight's management team.

Knight executives were dismissive about Citadel's offer, having talked to 90 different suitors, some offering loans as well, including KKR and Fortress Investment Group. "There would have been several redundancies had a deal with Citadel happened, and in the best of environments, which is a far cry from what we have today, significant job loss would have been likely," said Mike Shea, a managing partner at Direct Access Partners who worked at Knight from 1995 to 2002. "Clearly, Knight decided this was an unacceptable alternative."

2:45 P.M. "We're not getting anywhere"
Griffin and his team were still waiting in Knight's offices Saturday afternoon when Griffin went out to find his counterpart. Then Griffin told Joyce, "We're not getting anywhere," and threatened to leave. As he departed, Griffin voiced concern that rival investors were in the building and his group was being denied access, contention Joyce disputed, "He was getting the same amount of attention as everyone else."

Citadel found Knight's reluctance to consider its offer difficult to understand. On the other side, Joyce's team blamed the suitor for a lack of specifics over their debt proposal and was concerned Citadel was trying to pick up parts of the business inexpensively. Citadel didn't provide a specific term sheet or discuss details with Joyce before flying back to Chicago.

Griffin was right about the opposing group. The Jefferies team was also reviewing the trading firm's books. Separately, lawyers from Kirkland & Ellis were preparing a bankruptcy filing, in the event a deal could not be reached. Kirkland & Ellis' restructuring group had long earned a distinguished national and international reputation for providing effective legal advice and judgment in distressed situations such as Knight's.

After Citadel left, negotiations with the Jefferies team intensified because Joyce knew his options were narrowing. Since Friday, Jefferies had begun circulating a preliminary term sheet to potential investors based on the same deal format that would later be announced on Monday. Jefferies was backing the deal by making a principal investment itself. Jefferies, which signed an engagement document outlining the terms of the deal on Saturday night, had little trouble recruiting other investors among Knight's competitors, over Joyce's preference to reach out to investors who had a stake in seeing Knight survive.

Jefferies had brought GETCO in from the beginning over Joyce's objection. He had known GETCO's co-founders Schuler and Tierney for a long time. Furthermore, Joyce had met General Atlantic's chief executive officer Bill Ford in 2006, a year before they invested in GETCO. Ford and Joyce had explored a deal to acquire Automated Trading Desk (ATD); ultimately, Citigroup shelled out $680 million to acquire ATD in 2007.

He had been very adamant about not getting any competitor involved in the mix, a point he made clear to Jefferies. For him, a competitor like GETCO would only be interested in taking business away from Knight. GETCO raised the possibility of a merger; Joyce was opposed. Ultimately, Joyce would run out of time and be unable to find a suitable replacement to close the financing.

TD Ameritrade, the online brokerage house, stepped up its interest on Saturday as well after concluding the terms of the deal were reasonable; they had been brought on board by Joyce, as they had been a long-term client of the firm. Retail brokers like TD Ameritrade had a "vested interest" in Knight's survival to ensure that the amount of payment for order flow they received from wholesalers wouldn't decrease, Patrick O'Shaughnessy, a Chicago-based analyst at Raymond James, wrote in a note to clients dated August 6.

"What you don't want to see is losing one of the major participants in the market," Mark Freeman, who oversaw about $13 billion as chief investment officer at Westwood Holdings Group in Dallas, Texas, said. "Someone may say, 'Hey, these orders just get routed to someone else,' but it still matters how many participants you have. We see this in the bond market in terms of primary dealers. The fewer you get, liquidity becomes more of an issue."

Furthermore, TD Ameritrade exclusively cleared its clients' futures and Forex trades through Knight's Penson Futures. The Omaha, Nebraska-based brokerage's entire bond platform was also with Knight.

While there may have been some negotiations by others on terms, from the beginning Stephens, another long-term Knight client brought in by Joyce, was fine with the term sheet as it was presented. Stephens was a full-service, privately owned investment bank and private-equity firm founded by Witt Stephens in 1933 and later run by his brother Jackson. In 1970, Stephens had participated in Wal-Mart's IPO. Led since 1986 by Warren, Jackson' son, the firm had used its powerful balance sheet to expand when the financial crisis had hit.

Stephens was headquartered in Little Rock, Arkansas, in a 25-story building downtown that was opportunistically purchased brand new in a distressed sale in 1991 for $7 per square foot. Stephens' chief operating officer, Curt Bradbury, a SIFMA board member, would spend most of this tempestuous weekend holed in a hotel room with his chief financial officer and an investment banker from his firm, staying in touch with his firm's CEO by phone, as they monitored the progress of the negotiations.

The last to join was Blackstone, though it was well aware of Knight's business. Blackstone's chief financial officer, Laurence Tosi, who had joined the firm in 2008, knew Joyce from their days together at Merrill Lynch. Tosi had held a number of senior positions at Merrill Lynch where he was a managing partner including chief operating officer for the global markets and investment banking and finance director. As a young man, he had put himself through undergraduate, law and business school at Georgetown University. After what he calls a financial "struggle", he became one of the school's best donors. "I made the decision then that if I was ever in a position to afford future students the opportunity to go to Georgetown, I would do everything I could to make their dream a reality." Tosi and his wife, Alexandra, fulfilled that decision by becoming one of the first major donors to Georgetown University's 1789 Scholarship Imperative and endowing a perpetual scholarship named for his father.[4]

Unlike many private equity firms that had snubbed an approach by Knight, Blackstone took an active interest as it had been prepared to pay $1.2 billion to take Knight private just before the trading glitch. That price tag was four times Knight's market cap of $301.5 million at the close of Friday trading. Blackstone had conducted around six months of due diligence on Knight and was on the verge of completing the deal. Jefferies had ended up using Blackstone's "extensive" due diligence on Knight in the bailout, earning a $20 million fee in the process.[5]

This time Blackstone was told to either join the investor group or walk away.

9:00 A.M. Legacy still in doubt

Firm employees called and texted one another throughout the weekend hoping to expand upon what little information management had offered. When Joyce arrived at Knight's Jersey City offices on Sunday morning after barely four hours of sleep, the fate of his company and the legacy of his long Wall Street career were still in doubt.

Hobbling because of knee surgery and haggard from several sleepless nights, Joyce had been checking with Kirkland & Ellis about a potential bankruptcy filing, a real possibility if Knight failed to get financing by Monday. Knight's loss was bigger than the $365 million cash balance it reported as of June 30 and exceeded its market value of $398 million as of August 3. Securing additional capital to fund businesses such as market making was viewed as necessary to keep Knight afloat.

People trickled in and out of Knight's Jersey City headquarters that morning, with polo shirts and khakis outnumbering business suits. None of them would comment on the record to any of the journalists stationed outside. Around noon, platters of sandwiches and salads from Vito's Italian Deli in Hoboken were delivered.

12:00 P.M. An eclectic group of investors
The company's last hope was nervously resting by then on an eclectic group of investors split into various locations. Some investors, including TD Ameritrade, remained with Joyce in Jersey City pouring over Knight's documents. Others huddled at the Manhattan offices of White & Case, the law firm representing Jefferies in the deal.

4:00 P.M. Citadel's last-ditch attempt
Citadel came back with an emailed term sheet from Chicago offering a $500 million rescue loan with an interest rate of LIBOR (London interbank offered rate) plus 8.5 percent, which would have given Citadel a minority stake in Knight and a majority interest in its Hotspot FX unit.

While this offer was still subject to a potentially time-consuming due diligence, shareholder dilution would have been between 10 percent and 20 percent, as opposed to the 70 percent to 75 percent dilution embedded in the rival convertible stock offering being championed by Jefferies CEO Handler. By then, however, Joyce was far along with the latter and rejected Citadel for the third time.

In the evening hours, a deal looked promising. Knight employees were already buzzing about reports that an investor consortium had formed, prepared to inject new capital into their firm. While firms typically needed a shareholder vote to bless such a deal, the exchange had allowed Knight to proceed because the firm's survival was at stake. The SEC was monitoring Knight's compliance with capital rules. Cook had spent his birthday on Sunday tracking the final stages of the deal.

9:00 P.M. Crisis contained

When Joyce departed for home that night, lawyers had already reached a deal over a meal of Chinese food. The crisis had been largely contained. Knight had just survived the most harrowing week in its 17-year history and had staved off Griffin, whose overtures to Knight were never able to penetrate the distrust between the two firms.

"It's no secret that in the wholesale market-making space, firms are extremely competitive with one another," said Nagy, then president of broker consultant KOR Trading in Omaha, Nebraska. "It's no different between Ken and Tom."[6]

Chapter Fourteen

Enjoying the Light of a New Day

At 4 A.M. on Monday August 6, restructuring lawyers at Kirkland & Ellis stopped working on the potential Chapter 11 filing for Knight; the deal was done and the rescue payments totaling $400 million started coming in waves overnight.

These had been the most grueling days for the Sandler O'Neill team. Dunne, Sterling, managing principal Bob Kleinert (the former Princeton basketball player who had retired from the debt and equity syndicate desk at Salomon Brothers in 1997 and had agreed after September 11 only to help the firm until the end of that year), associate director Tom Gallagher (the former associate at Deutsche Bank who had also graduated from Dunne's alma mater, University of Notre Dame), associate Rory Shaw (the recently married Fordham University grad in the ultimate finance-meets-fashion East Hampton wedding to wife Kathryn, a Vogue associate), and analyst Tim Bemer (the lacrosse and football athlete at Malvern Preparatory School and captain of the lacrosse team during his senior year at University of Notre Dame), had barely slept since Wednesday. "I gained eight pounds on Thursday, Friday, Saturday, Sunday," remembered Dunne.

The misery (and later the celebration) was shared with the team from Wachtell, Lipton, Rosen & Katz. "Knight Capital had good lawyers," said Dunne. He was referring to partners Edward Herlihy (co-chairman of the law firm's executive committee who had advised Randy Lerner on his sale of the Cleveland Browns professional football team for more than $1 billion happening just days before),

David Silk (Michael Jordan's advisor on his acquisition of a controlling stake in the Charlotte Bobcats), Nicholas Demmo (member of the Order of the Coif, the prestigious honor society for United States law school graduates), Benjamin Roth ("rising star" in the area of mergers and acquisitions who had advised Walgreen Co. on its $6.6 billion purchase of a 45 percent stake in pharmacy chain and distributor Alliance Boots), Joshua Feltman (who had met Oprah Winfrey twenty one years before at an Academy of Achievement summit; Winfrey had written in his yearbook "Joshua, I will never forget the wonderful weekend we had together"), Philip Mindlin (board member of The New York City Partnership Foundation, a public charity affiliated with the Partnership for New York City Fund), Jeannemarie O'Brien (a recently named partner specialized in executive compensation and benefits), and Joshua Holmes (tax expert and competitive JPMorgan Chase Corporate Challenge runner with better and better times, 26:55 in 2010, 25:57 in 2011 and 23:37 in 2012).

In addition to Sandler O'Neill and Wachtell, Lipton, Rosen & Katz advising Knight on the transaction, there was a battalion of advisors working with the investors. Financial advisors included Joel Fleck, managing director of Barclays Capital, working with TD Ameritrade, and Morgan Stanley working with Blackstone. Legal advisors included Ronald Brody, Colin Diamond and Jill Falor of White & Case, working with Jefferies, Simpson Thacher & Bartlett working with Blackstone and Patrick Daugherty of Foley & Lardner working with TD Ameritrade.

"On Sunday, it was a couple hours, but that was a terrible couple of hours because, you know, it was just not a matter of announcing something. The regulators who were on site wanted the money in before the opening," Dunne said. That indeed happened, with the last few dollars from investors rolling in just 15 minutes before the trading opened on Monday morning.

It was time later in the day for a relieved Joyce to go on a conference call to announce to investors that Knight was still alive, thanks to a group of firms that included one of their fiercest competitors, GETCO.

Nervous about seeing the deal derailed at the last minute, however, the New York Stock Exchange was "temporarily" reassigning the firm's market-making responsibilities for approximately 524 New York Stock Exchange (NYSE) and 156 NYSE MKT listed securities to GETCO, the trading firm that was investing in Knight.

Upon Knight's completion and approval of a recapitalization plan, all temporarily reassigned NYSE and NYSE MKT securities as well as DMM staff, operations and systems oversight would be returned to Knight. NYSE's Larry Leibowitz would later explain to Bloomberg that they "did it because there was question about whether Knight would reach a deal; we didn't want to walk into Monday and have there be any doubts."

Leibowitz had been appointed chief operating officer in 2010 and was responsible for operations management, global cash execution and global listings. He had previously served as group executive vice president and head of U.S. execution and global technology from 2007 until 2009. He had joined NYSE Euronext in 2007, having served as managing director and chief operating officer of Americas equities at UBS Investment Bank. Prior to joining UBS in 2004, Leibowitz had held the position of executive vice president, co-head at Schwab Capital Markets, the trading and execution arm of Schwab. Leibowitz grew up in Lawrenceville, New Jersey, where he attended Lawrence High School; he later graduated from Princeton University with an A.B. in Economics in 1982.

There probably wouldn't have been anything else to add about Leibowitz if not for the blistering and funny coverage on May 10, 2010, of the Flash Crash incident on *The Daily Show*, the satirical news program that aired on Comedy Central since 1999. Jon Stewart, its host, was Leibowitz's baby brother. Most probably, Stewart consulted him about the story, as Leibowitz was "a person at the very heart of the mysterious Flash Crash that shook markets Thursday".[1] However, he wasn't mentioned in the show at all.

The NYSE had taken heat after the Flash Crash for delays as long as five minutes in quotes being reported on the Consolidated Quotation System (CQS) with time stamps indicating that the quotes were current. The only reference in Stewart's reporting to the NYSE was in Stewart's introduction to the segment, "As you know I am a bit of a stock market watcher. I like to follow the big board, where I often attempt to buy low and sell high." The day after, New York Magazine alerted readers in real time that Jon Stewart's unfunny brother was testifying about the Flash Crash; it pointed to Leibowitz's presentation in a House Financial Services Committee hearing on the need for regulators to request better circuit breakers to monitor high-frequency trading in order to avoid a Flash Crash repeat.[2]

Was Leibowitz informed of Stewart's report on the May 6 incident? He had said two months before that his brother hadn't been running to him to ask for advice, even when *The Daily Show* did tackle topics of his areas of expertise, among them high-frequency trading. But he admitted that being an older sibling, "I give it to him anyway sometimes." Would he ever go on *The Daily Show* as a guest? The answer would be no. "I probably wouldn't make a very good guest. I have tried to fly under the radar."[3]

Leibowitz had stated that it was hard to imagine two brothers who had chosen more different careers. At this point, they even had different last names. Jon had begun using the stage name "Jon Stewart" by dropping his last name and changing the spelling of his middle name "Stuart" to "Stewart"; he had implied that the name change was actually due to a strained relationship with his father, with whom Jon no longer had any contact. Leibowitz confided that their mother Marian, an educational consultant and teacher, "was pretty happy with both."

Under the terms of the plan (which had been already disclosed by CNBC's Kelly Evans around 6 A.M.), the new investors, which included the trading firm Jefferies, Blackstone, TD Ameritrade, GETCO, Stephens and Stifel Financial, would receive preferred securities, which would give them the right to buy new shares of Knight at a price of roughly $1.50 each. The week before the trading blunder, the firm's shares had closed over $10.

The owners of the preferred shares had the right to convert all or a portion of the preferred shares into Knight Class A Common Stock. Knight had committed to expand its board of directors by adding three new members, including an individual selected by Blackstone, an individual selected by General Atlantic (which was the only outside investor in GETCO), and an individual proposed by the board and acceptable to Jefferies.

"We are grateful for the support of these leading Wall Street firms that came together to invest in Knight. The array of participants in this capital infusion underscores Knight's critical role in the capital markets. With our financial position strengthened and liquidity restored, we will continue to provide clients with trading in a broad range of securities, high-quality execution and outstanding client service. Knight's financial position and capital base have been restored to a level that more than offsets the loss incurred last week. We thank our clients, employees and partners for their steadfastness during a brief yet difficult period and we are getting back to business as usual."

The rescue package arranged by Jefferies was worth about $400 million. Jefferies would invest $125 million, Blackstone and GETCO would spend $87.5 million each, TD Ameritrade contributed $40 million, and Stephens and Stifel Financial, $30 million each. This investment would significantly dilute the holdings of existing shareholders, with the new investors owning roughly 70 percent of the firm. But it would leave Knight alive and independent, averting a potentially messy bankruptcy.

Speaking on CNBC's *Squawk on the Street* with Bob Pisani at 9:35 A.M. and looking over Knight's trading floor, Joyce, looking tired and with hair thinning at both sides of the part, reflected on the number of phone calls he had received over the course of the weekend. People interested in the firm ran the whole spectrum, from private equity investors to distressed investors to clients. Strategic investors who saw some assets that they thought might be interesting also inquired about them.

"You know, the flattering thing is how the industry responded to us. The wildly flattering thing was how our clients responded to us." He and the board felt very confident that by signing on such a dilutive deal they had made the right choice for the firm.

In what could be considered the perfect "made-for-TV" euphemistic talk, Joyce said that he took a lot of pride in how Knight treated their clients. Was he saying that he was proud to have made a $440 million donation to clients without them asking for anything?

Tom Konrad, a Forbes contributor, was one of such fortunate clients. He was very surprised in the morning of August 2 when he got a confirmation from his broker that an old good-til-canceled limit order to buy MasTec, American multinational infrastructure engineering and construction company based in Coral Gables, Florida, at $14 had been executed the day before, although the stock was trading around $16 lately. MasTec was expected to post earnings later in the evening, and if recent earnings from competitors like Quanta Services and cable manufacturer General Cable were any guide, they would beat analyst expectations and possibly raise guidance, as they all had done in the first quarter.

Konrad's first suspicion had been that someone thought bad news was about to come out and had dumped the stock. But the news that morning cleared that up. MasTec was one of the 150 stocks, the NYSE had revealed, affected by the trading malfunction at Knight, and fortunately for him his purchase price was within the 30 percent band of the opening price which kept the trade from being canceled by the exchange. Like him, clients big and small around the country had benefited from Knight shareholders' largesse.

High-power executives love to be flattered and Joyce was no exception; Pisani might have spent hours preparing to deliver the most flattering business interview ever, even by CNBC standards, "You're one of the most respected men on Wall Street. I've known you almost 15 years and everybody; everybody has something positive to say about you." Joyce nodded nervously. "How do you feel personally about your reputation and what, if anything, beyond what you're doing now are you going to do to make sure that brand name Tommy Joyce (here Joyce smiled broadly) is still the top quality name that people always associate with it."

Joyce just couldn't believe it. CEOs all over would love to lose $440 million if such flattery was guaranteed to come afterwards. "You're very flattering by the way. Very nice things you just said. So, I guess the actions we have taken and actions we will take in the future will determine whether people have a high or low opinion of me." Just looking at the actions management had taken to protect shareholder value in the previous days didn't augur well for high opinions of Joyce.

Pisani didn't miss the chance to ask about Joyce's knee. "This man had knee surgery the day before (August 1), came in here on crutches. I have to say you are bending the knees alright. How are you feeling?" Joyce replied that the knee bent but it didn't bend freely. "We're still working on it. My doctor is irritated with me." No doubt shareholders were even more irritated with him; Joyce ultimately had responsibility for Knight's risk management practices.

"Was the company bought for a song?" That was a question for Dunne from Andrew Ross Sorkin, one of the most influential journalists in the finance world, multitasking at The New York Times and CNBC's *Squawk Box*. He had been the author of the bestselling book *Too Big to Fail* and had co-produced a movie adaptation of the book for HBO.

Dunne took issue with the question. "Bought it for a song? I think the stock is trading basically at tangible book value which is where Knight historically traded. What's interesting is that when you go to the brink on something, it is an energizing experience for a firm and I can speak a little to that." He was referring to Sandler O'Neill's own near-death experience right after the September 11 attacks.

"Knight was a superb firm before this unfortunate glitch. It will be an incredible firm after it. Certainly, the investors that came into this are going to do well. I think they'll do very well because the company will be better and stronger than ever."[4]

Most of the losses due to the dilution brought by the deal were to be borne by mutual funds that owned 54 percent of Knight's outstanding shares before the trading errors, according to data from Morningstar. Fidelity and its mutual funds were the largest owners of Knight shares, holding 15 percent of the company.

"What first needs to happen is a real good postmortem. Not about why there was a coding error. No one expects the CEO to look at lines of code and figure that out, but we do need to know about risk controls, why it took as long as it took to turn things off, and how much got done before things stopped. I think risk control is the first thing we need to hear about. As much as I don't like it, the shareholders took a beating, which is what we're supposed to do," Jay Kaplan, a fund manager at Royce & Associates, which owned 11 percent of Knight's stock and was its second-biggest holder as of June 30, said in a Bloomberg Television interview on August 7.

"Do we like what happened? No. Is it a reasonable outcome given what transpired? I suppose it is," he concluded.

Normally the dilutive share sale would have required shareholder approval, according to NYSE's Shareholder Approval Policy. However, Knight said its audit committee had determined that "the delay necessary in securing stockholder approval prior to the issuance of the preferred stock would seriously jeopardize the financial viability of Knight."

Because of that determination, the Audit Committee approved Knight's reliance on an exception provided for such a situation and Knight's omission to seek the stockholder approval. The NYSE didn't object to Knight's use of the exception and expected to approve Knight's listing application in relation to the proposed transaction on that basis.

Joyce would later explain that the only reason there was a lack of an opportunity to give shareholders a voice was because the company was under great stress and the NYSE had rules that dealt exactly with the situation of companies being under great stress. "So, we recapitalized the company in a moment of stress and that's why we didn't have a chance to communicate as well as we would have like to our current shareholders." Underscoring the heavily dilutive nature of the rescue, by the end of the day, shares of Knight had fallen more than 24 percent.

Did somebody think this massive dilution was fair for shareholders? For Stephens' Bradbury, it was business as usual. "Yeah, I understand that. What I'd say is that if you look at the situation, and there will be plenty of time to look at this, but it was either for the shareholders, the existing shareholders as of last week, you know, it was either this deal or nothing. In effect, that investment would have gone to zero. So, in this deal, they retained 25 percent or 30 percent of the company. So, to me, that looks like a fair transaction."

While original shareholders of Knight's stock saw the value of their stake diminish after a 61 percent plunge the week before, the firms behind the infusion were already sitting on potential gains. The shares represented by the convertible stock were potentially worth $843.7 million at August 7 closing prices.[5]

"Investors in Knight are getting a stake in a company with several very attractive assets at what might turn out to be a very attractive price," Patrick O'Shaughnessy, an analyst at Raymond James & Associates, had written in a message for clients. "Knight plays an important role in U.S. equities market structure and retail brokers have a vested interest in making sure competition for their order flow remains robust."

TD Ameritrade, one of the nation's biggest retail brokers, had long been one of Knight's most reliable clients. It was one of several firms that helped create the company that became Knight, and at the time of the trading firm's initial public offering in 1998, it owned a 9.25 percent stake. Since Knight's troubles began, TD Ameritrade had been one of the firm's most vocal supporters.

Blackstone had considered investing in Knight for some time. GETCO was one of the most successful high-speed trading firms that had yet to break into Knight's trademark business of executing orders from retail brokers.

On Monday afternoon, 20 minutes after trading had ended, Jefferies' Handler sent a memo to his staff noting the role the company had played in saving Knight. "A highly valued provider of stock market liquidity will be given the chance to thrive once again – great news for the health of the global financial markets," he wrote. "We are not doing G-d's work, but collectively we are making a difference." This valued provider was to resume its duties as a designated market maker on the New York Stock Exchange the week after, Leibowitz had confirmed, while praising both Knight and GETCO for their teamwork and collaboration to ensure smooth, efficient and seamless transitions.

Kim Hillyer, a spokeswoman at TD Ameritrade, said that they saw the Knight opportunity as a good strategic investment for their company. "If the single most important retail order flow provider in the country is on board with them, that's a huge vote of confidence," said Justin Hughes, a portfolio manager with San Francisco hedge fund firm Philadelphia Financial.

Stifel Financial bought its stake because it was an "attractive" financial investment, had said CEO Kruszewski. Regarding current shareholders not being consulted about the deal, he said to CNBC's Scott Wapner that when you had liquidity events the deal had to be done with speed.

Regarding Joyce, Kruszewski was in favor of keeping him as chief executive. "Absolutely. Tom Joyce is a first class CEO. What happened here was a black swan event. I'm certainly not condoning it. It did impact investor confidence. But recognize that what happened here was not the main trading system. It was an ancillary system. It cost a lot of money. That company stepped up, it settled their loss today. There was a $400 million loss that was settled today. Tom Joyce is an excellent manager. He has my full support."[6]

Stephens' Bradbury, in an interview with CNBC's *Fast Money Halftime Report*, had said he was long-time friends with Joyce and his firm customer of Knight for many years; he said that his firm indeed had approached Knight in that vein on Friday.[7]

For him, you didn't "have to get very deeply into it to figure out that it was basically a lightning strike, a unique event that was easily fixable. And that they had fixed it. But that because of the loss, and because they stood in front of the orders and took the loss there was going to be a recap needed."

He added, "All we could do was listen to management's explanation of what happened and their viewpoint about the mess. In the final analysis, we took their representation that it was a lightning strike and didn't compromise Knight's basic algorithms, trading systems and core competencies," Bradbury said.

About Joyce, he thought he had done a great job over the years building Knight into the trading powerhouse it was. He initially thought he should remain. "A good management team will take an event like this as an opportunity to reevaluate certain lines of a business and I think they'll do that; we have a lot of confidence in Tom Joyce and his team. But you know, Tom knows he's got a lot of work to do and he's all about that. I think he's a good guy and I think that he is a good manager and a good CEO and I think that's generally the way that the group feels." A few days later, though, he sounded a bit less enthusiastic while saying that Joyce was going to have to take his share of the blame. "Everybody that invested is gonna have to make their own judgment on whether Tom stays as CEO," he added.[8]

The most articulated response came from Daniel Coleman, chief executive officer of GETCO. Though his firm and Knight competed intensely in the trading of stocks and other securities, Coleman said buying into the stricken company represented a sound financial investment for GETCO and its own shareholders.

He likened it to Microsoft's move to invest $150 million in one-time and future nemesis Apple in 1997, another pairing of unlikely partners that breathed new life into the struggling Silicon Alley icon. GETCO was getting a strategic advantage via the deal as well, an inside peek at a bigger rival that had some lines of business GETCO did not.

For Coleman, "a world without Knight is a worse world as far as GETCO is concerned; it would be more expensive for everyone to trade." "In some places we bump heads, but we're all better off if Knight is a viable competitor." He said Knight's presence in U.S. markets was particularly critical for small and mid-cap securities, an area of expertise for the New Jersey firm.

"In some ways Knight's a competitor, in some ways they're a client, in some ways we're their client. But at the end of the day the liquidity they provide and I think the liquidity we provide probably makes both of us better. This is in our strategic interest to make sure Knight stays viable."[9]

"As a financial investment, Knight is a very valuable firm, but it needed liquidity and if it didn't have liquidity, a lot of that value was going to go away," Coleman said. GETCO thought it was a pretty good bet that by providing liquidity to Knight they could preserve its value and perhaps increase it. Increasing its value became GETCO's battle cry. In a 13D filing on August 16, GETCO disclosed an important 37.4 percent stake in the company (schedule 13D was filed by entities that acquire more than 5 percent of a voting class of a company's equity securities). The firm did not hold shares at the end of the latest quarter ending June 30.

Two weeks later, persuaded by Joyce himself on the day the deal was announced, all six investors would be selling part of their preferred stock in the firm to retail online broker Scottrade, one of Knight's biggest customers.[10] Scottrade was receiving a far smaller stake in the firm than the other investors, around $10 million, compared to anywhere between $30 million and $100 million for the other players. Still, why this last-minute inclusion of Scottrade into the deal?

Scottrade was a major customer of Knight, sending order flow to Knight's market-making business. Including Scottrade in the deal was seen as a thankful payback to a firm that both gave business to Knight and quickly redirected flow back to the firm on Friday morning when most other clients were still reluctant to do so. Scottrade was also GETCO's customer, so they would not have been bothered by this last minute inclusion.

Despite having lost money as a result of Knight's rescue, Pasternak told Reuters that he had no regrets about accumulating hundreds of thousands of shares in the company since August 1.

For Jeffrey Meyerson, market maker and senior managing director at Sunrise Securities, Knight's investors were making too much money from the transaction to be considering deals at the moment. "I'd be surprised if they have a concentrated strategy to break the firm up. The investors made a very shrewd deal and got some very cheap equity. They'll want to grow the company to sell their stock."

The rescue was probably more of a "buy low opportunity" than a plan to eventually split up the company, Larry Tabb, chief executive officer of research firm Tabb Group in New York, said. "There's a high likelihood they're not breaking up, given the investors that they have," Tabb said. "If it had been bought by one or two private equity guys, I would say it would get broken up. But you've got a whole consortium of different people," he said. "They would have a really hard time splitting up all the Knight assets."

"This is one of our largest and best-run market making outfits," said Professor Angel, who served on the board of exchange operator Direct Edge. "It definitely shows signs of confidence in Knight and its management that people are willing to step forward with this kind of a cash infusion."

"As long as they are alive, that is better than being dead, right?" Said Alan "Ace" Greenberg, the former chairman of Bear Stearns, which was taken over by J.P. Morgan, as it battled for survival in March 2008. "Where there is life, there is hope."

Knight hadn't done any new strategic planning as of August 6, Joyce said in an interview. Budgets and strategies would be set over the normal schedule toward the end of the year. The "footprint" of the company would "remain intact for a while," he said.

Joyce's line about the errant trading on August 1 was that it actually had nothing to do with the electronic trading group, or the algorithmic trading methods they employed, but rather with the firm's technology group or its network. While he was unwilling to say who was ultimately responsible for the glitch or why it took half an hour to stop the flow of mistaken trades, he stressed that the company was conducting an internal investigation into the matter and changes would be made once the investigation was complete.[11]

There was no need for Joyce to try to cover the sun with one finger. Sang's team had been told to go home for the day for one reason: they were the team directly responsible for the glitch. The first executive change after the trading malfunction would later be the removal of Sadoff from his role overseeing operations and technology and exile to Knight's Siberia developing the clearing, prime brokerage and futures businesses; Sadoff had neglected to stop the mistaken orders when that was his responsibility in the absence of the CEO.

In all fairness, Knight did harbor dreams of becoming a clearing powerhouse. It was in the spring of 2010 that Knight officials had told Clearing Quarterly & Directory, a supplement of Traders Magazine, they were dispensing with the clearing services of Merrill Lynch's Broadcort and going to self-clearing. "We have heard from people that they would like to deal with us on a direct basis," said Chris Pento, a managing director for Knight. At that time, management estimated the immediate benefits of the self-clearing would be $20 million a year. However, they went to self-clearing for the same reason other brokerages were considering it: it would give them greater control over trades.[12]

Joyce, as always, didn't let this go through. The spin he used was that Sadoff really had two jobs: global head of operations, services & technology, and growing the "corresponding clearing part of our business and technology and services area." Now, he said, Knight had a more focused Sadoff working on a very important initiative for the firm. "We are giving our best executives a chance to focus on an important initiative." Not even Jack Welch could have said it better.

For Coleman, doing it right meant fixing the way things were done at Knight, not the computers the firm used to trade high volumes of stock at fractions of seconds. "I just want to differentiate between some science fiction notion of a machine gone crazy, and a problem that ultimately could have been caught and resolved probably more quickly than it was."

Asked about potential regulatory action after the incident, Stifel Financial's Kruszewski said that he didn't believe that more regulation was in and of itself the answer. He claimed that the best regulator he knew was the free market. "The free market worked here. There was a loss. It was settled. Capitalism stepped in and did the right thing. Shareholders lost money, but it worked. And I think that we just need to just not be trying to get trades done in milliseconds."

Stephen's Bradbury wasn't pushing for more regulation either. "I think that the rapidity of trading and the speed is something that the regulators are looking at and probably need to. I think as Tom said on TV this morning they need to look at the specific situation, and make their own decisions about what needs to be done. But I think if I back up and look at this from what I think is an important aspect of it, from the country's point of view, from the regulator's point of view, from everybody's point of view, this is a good day for American capital markets. There was not a bailout needed by the government. Private investors came together, and fixed this company with cash. And, in fact, what happened is the American capital markets worked, as they should work, and the situation was remedied within the American capital market structure, free enterprise had a good day."

Bradbury also questioned the speed with which Knight reacted, not the speed its computers were trading at. The issues of why the software failed, of what failsafe should have been in place, and what its traders did before and after they recognized there was a problem, are going to need to be addressed, he said. "Did [Joyce's] people respond quickly enough? When they saw they had a problem, what happened?" Didn't he know Joyce was not even in the office that fatidic morning?

"Once the internal review of the trading error is completed, we would expect the board and management to re-evaluate the model and strategic direction," Christopher Allen, an analyst at Evercore Partners in New York, wrote in an e-mail. "We would not be surprised if there was increased scrutiny of any businesses that generate only marginal profitability relative to their capital usage."

One Knight trader said, "It's a very, very complex world that we're talking about. It's just not an on-off switch." However, when the very experienced Cantor Fitzgerald's Lutnick was asked by FOX Business Network's Liz Claman if something like the Knight's incident could happen in any of his firms, he plainly said it couldn't.

"You would figure every three second you would have an alarm that goes off; fifteen seconds after, there's a problem, it would be deafening in the place. You have to build in things in your systems where they turn themselves off. It should just be core and inherent in the system. If something goes wrong, it shuts itself down and kills itself. If you don't build that in, it is impossible to think how you wouldn't build that in 2012. Everything about our system is designed to check, double check, triple check and quadruple check itself all the time. That's why we were able to survive 9/11, '08, '09. It is a way of thinking; it is a way of processing. You can't make fundamental mistakes like that. If you do make a mistake, you'd darn well better catch it in one minute. One minute could have cost him a million dollars, he would be embarrassed; but this is someone who was picking on Bob Greifeld and then two weeks later does the same thing".[13]

Just as everything seemed to be coming together for management, the most important task was still pending. How to reclaim the leading positions in electronic trading Knight had enjoyed for the last years? While some customers were already back, there were still institutional clients who held reservations about redirecting their flow to Knight.

In August, Joyce agreed he wouldn't receive a bonus for the year and would waive a change-in-control provision triggered by the cash infusion after the incident that would have extended his contract for another two years. CFO Bisgay and market-making head Sohos had also waived these payments.

Previously in May 2012, shareholders had voted against the firm's compensation structure by a margin of about 2-to-1, prompting Knight to hire consulting firm Pay Governance to advise on pay matters.

Executives had seen their awards reduced, though some "discretionary bonuses" were made for helping the firm navigate the August trading debacle. Bisgay and Sohos received such discretionary awards, which included cash awards of $1.7 million and $2.9 million, respectively.[1]

In addition to those payments, Bisgay had made $1.5 million in overall compensation in 2012, while Sohos had collected $3.4 million. In 2011, Bisgay was paid $2.9 million overall and Sohos was paid $9 million. Joyce's annual salary was set at $750,000; in 2011, Joyce received $6.4 million including incentive-plan compensation and stock awards. In 2012, his pay fell by about 41 percent to $3.7 million. On the afternoon of August 7, it was revealed that Knight was in talks with external advisers to augment an internal review of the wayward trading episode that nearly drove it out of business the week before. Additional safeguards had been put in place in recent days to guard against more trades going off-course, and the firm planned further steps to strengthen controls on trading.

In an email to clients, Joyce had attached communications from the Depository Trust & Clearing Corp. and the Options Clearing Corp., showing that Knight remained in good standing with both trade-processing institutions.

Nonetheless, employees were still nervous; an industry recruiter who had reached out to 30 Knight employees, ranging from managing directors down the chain, confirmed that some people were saying they were going to stick it out, while half gave him their resumes.

In June 2012, NASDAQ retained IBM to review the bungling of Facebook's flotation in late May, which drove hundreds of millions of dollars in losses for Wall Street firms. IBM was to conduct "a thorough review of the current state of processes for designing, developing, testing, deploying and operating market systems."[2] The review was essentially completed by mid-October.

IBM "has given us the recommendations and we are implementing them. They are to make sure that we don't have any glitches again in the future," Meyer Frucher, vice chairman at NASDAQ, had indicated on the sidelines of a four-day annual meeting of the World Federation of Exchanges being held in Taipei. "We are going to look at [the systems] constantly, reappraise, reappraise and reappraise. It's an ongoing process."[3]

Following on NASDAQ's experience, Knight also hired IBM to look into the August 1 trading glitch. IBM began its third-party review of Knight's product development lifecycle processes on August 27.

Knight had been IBM's customer for a long time. On October 21-25, Knight's Ken Nelson was scheduled to appear at the Business Analytics Forum @Information On Demand 2012 in Las Vegas, Nevada, to present "How Integrated Financial Management Applications TM1, Controller, and BI Help Knight Capital Drive Insight." The session intended to showcase attendees Knight's application of IBM business intelligence tools in the finance organization.

"At times of economic uncertainty there are always opportunities for revolutionary changes. Leading enterprises are charting a new course that uses both high efficiency and expanded technology to provide business analytics and insights to meet new challenges and opportunities. In this session you'll see how organizations are navigating uncertainty by integrating financial information, analyzing it and converting it to a competitive asset. This session will explore how one such company, Knight Capital Group, replaced their previous system and has stepped up to a new role to help the finance organization make closing, consolidation and reporting better and faster with IBM Cognos Controller, IBM Cognos TM1 and IBM Cognos Business Intelligence."

Retaining IBM was an admission that the firm needed a fresh set of eyes reviewing its application development process. Perhaps Sadoff, the sponsor of the study, hoped IBM's feedback would help him maintain his job.

Days after the rescue, Joyce said the brokerage firm expected to reclaim nearly all lost business by mid-August. "Given what our clients have witnessed over the past week, we're unbelievably encouraged by how quickly they're coming back."[4]

On August 8, Knight in fact retook leading positions in the trading of shares included in the Russell 2000 index and exchange-traded funds, though its presence in blue-chip stocks remained below typical levels, according to data from Thomson Reuters' Autex service, to which brokers reported trading activity.

Joyce said also on Thursday August 9 that market making, Knight's core business of buying and selling shares directly with customers and on exchanges, was "85 percent to 95 percent" back to levels seen ahead of the August 1 trading incident. Knight's institutional sales and trading division, which includes bonds and currencies, was then at 65 percent to 70 percent of its normal strength.

Other firms, however, had continued holding back. Investment firm Edward Jones was routing its trades to other market makers following Knight's calamity and continued to "monitor the situation".

Tradeking Group, a retail brokerage with about 500,000 accounts, resumed doing business with Knight on August 7 and as of August 9 was back to its usual level of trading with the firm. "Everything's going perfectly fine."

In the days after the deal, Knight confirmed it had selected three new directors, including the chief executive officer of TD Ameritrade, Fred Tomczyk, and private-equity firm representatives Martin Brand, managing director of Blackstone, and Matthew Nimetz, advisory director of General Atlantic. The three additional directors brought Knight's board membership to ten.

"Oxford math genius" Brand had started his Blackstone career in 2003 in London and transferred to New York in 2005. Before joining Blackstone, Brand worked as a derivatives trader with the FICC division of Goldman Sachs in New York and Tokyo and with McKinsey & Company in London. He had received bachelor and master's degrees in mathematics and computation from Oxford University, where he graduated with first class honors, and an MBA from Harvard Business School. Brand served on the Advisory Board of the Hudson Union Society and the board of directors of the Harvard Business School Club of New York.

Nimetz served as managing director and Chief Operating Officer of General Atlantic from 2000 through 2011. Prior to that, he had been a partner and former chair of Paul, Weiss, Rifkind, Wharton & Garrison in New York, where he practiced corporate, securities, financing and international law from 1980 to 2000. Nimetz had worked at Simpson Thacher & Bartlett from 1969 to 1977 where he rose to partner. Nimetz once served as President Clinton's Special Envoy to mediate the resolution of the Macedonia naming dispute. Nimetz served as a member of the Council on Foreign Relations and a trustee of the National Committee on American Foreign Policy. He received a bachelor of arts in political science from Williams College, a master of arts in philosophy, politics and economics from Balliol College, Oxford University, where he was a Rhodes Scholar, and a JD from Harvard Law School, where he was president of the Harvard Law Review.

Speaking at the Barclays Global Financial Services Conference in New York on September 11, Joyce predicted that the SEC would likely reexamine rules on how errors were dealt with by trading firms and exchanges, as well as the circuit breakers that were tripped by unusual volume and so-called "kill switches" which could shut down order flow. But adopting rules to prevent errors, even big ones, wouldn't be simple.

"To insulate yourself against somebody, or some team, making a stupid move is going to be hard to do," Joyce said. "I don't know if there's any great way that you can unearth somebody's mistake ahead of time."

"The silver lining is that, at the end of the day, I believe some regulatory changes will be made and there are probably only two or three of them that need to be considered, but it will make the system stronger," Joyce said.

"In effect, we kicked the beehive," Joyce said. "We began generating orders unrestricted by volume caps."

As orders accumulated, the New York Stock Exchange was "hamstrung" by SEC rules that prevented it from breaking trades that did not fall under specific circumstances, Joyce said.

"We haven't exactly given the retail investor a reason to have confidence," the Knight CEO said. Joyce acknowledged Knight was "completely embarrassed" to bring about the next high-profile market "debacle."

"People do stupid things," he said of his own company's software errors, which he said stemmed from mistakes by a handful of Knight employees. "A small team of people made a grievous mistake."

In the same conference, Joyce had criticized the rules that guided the SEC's handling of Knight's accidental August 1 trades. Knight had urged the SEC to authorize "breaking," or canceling, many of the trades, but the SEC instead stuck to its guidelines and allowed only a handful to be canceled. The decision saddled Knight with losses it could have avoided had more trades been broken, forcing the firm to scramble for emergency capital.[5] Furthermore, time spent by Joyce trying to reverse NYSE's decision by appealing to the SEC worked against his firm; his traders hadn't touched their positions accumulated through the morning hoping the SEC would acquiesce to their demand.

"We have proven that's a bad rule," Joyce had said that Tuesday morning. "There is no reason to put a firm at risk because some knucklehead, or a series of knuckleheads at the firm, made a big mistake. If it's an error, you should be able to fix an error," he said.

By then, exchanges were already plotting fixes for potential glitches. The biggest U.S. stock exchanges had met with some of their largest customers to hatch a plan they hoped would convince regulators that the industry could prevent the kind of technology snafus that have dogged the stock market this year.[6]

Officials at the New York Stock Exchange held a call with big brokerage customers in August to hash out steps for curbing out-of-control trades. On Monday September 10, NASDAQ executives held a similar meeting with bank and brokerage customers at NASDAQ's Lower Manhattan headquarters. More meetings and calls were planned.

In response to the wave of technology problems, BATS Global Markets and rival electronic exchange Direct Edge, like NASDAQ and NYSE, were also talking with customers about potential new risk controls.

At the same time officials at these competing stock exchanges planned to work together to draw up joint recommendations for the SEC, their marketing teams were busy plotting plants to leverage their competitors' mistakes in their sales pitches.

Exchanges contend with one another intensely over listings, which bring much-needed fees as well as commissions from trading the instruments. Trading activity in NYSE- and NASDAQ-listed stocks exhibit an inclination to concentrate on the marketplace where those instruments are listed at the open and close of markets each day. Officials at exchanges will often woo firms by glorifying the virtues of their market model and proposing ways to promote the firms, through marketing efforts and high-visibility venues like the front of the NYSE's New York City headquarters.[7]

The NYSE was using the Facebook debacle to say that the NASDAQ system could not be trusted. NASDAQ was fighting back saying that the Knight meltdown occurred on the NYSE's watch, implying the NYSE's trading system could not be trusted either. To say that neither Joyce nor Niederauer appreciated NASDAQ's pitch is an understatement; they went ballistic when they learned about it. To be fair, the NYSE had a better case to present to potential clients: the Knight fiasco didn't start in its systems.[8]

On September 18, it was announced that Knight's Wald, the overseer of trading programs sold to institutions, was leaving the firm. Wald was well respected throughout the firm; he could speak confidently on high-frequency trading and algorithms, so he was usually invited to meetings with clients. As always, he was very articulate and well spoken.

This was the first senior executive departure after the trading incident on August 1, although his unit was not behind it. Knight named Brendan McCarthy as its new head for the Knight Direct algorithmic trading unit, reporting to senior managing director David Lehmann, head of electronic execution services. Lehmann had been partner with Montgomery Securities (one of the "Four Horsemen") in San Francisco. Previously, he also served as a vice president of Salomon Brothers as well as of Merrill Lynch. Lehmann had received a bachelor's of science from University of Illinois and an MBA from Columbia Business School.

McCarthy, a six-year pro, had been the business manager and head of relationship management for Knight Direct. He would continue to work alongside managing director Ray Ross, who oversaw the technology side of Knight Direct.[9] McCarthy became very vocal and eager to set the record straight about his group's involvement in the trading incident.

"It had nothing to do with any of our algorithmic trading. Knight Capital's algorithmic trading group is completely separate from the market-making unit. We don't share any of the same technology. We don't even share the same resources. We have a completely independent team of 40 people in development, and none of them are shared or do any work between the two businesses." McCarthy's group was part of the electronic execution services unit, not the market-making unit.[10]

McCarthy would later become embroiled in a lawsuit brought up by Robert Milloul, an Orthodox Jew of Syrian descent, who had joined Knight from EdgeTrade. Milloul alleged that McCarthy displayed anti-Semitic views and "at times had a piece of paper in his hands that he waived around the trading floor, stating that it was a list of people he was going to fire." Milloul claimed he was fired in January 2013 because he was a religious Jew and in retaliation for complaining to the trading firm's human resources department about being persecuted by McCarthy for his religious beliefs.[11]

The way Joyce handled the immediate questions of why Wald was leaving so soon after and whether this was connected in any way to the issue on August 1 left doubts about his commitment to the job. Joyce was attending the 79th Annual Conference & Business Meeting hosted by the Security Traders Association in Washington D.C. alongside a number of industry luminaries such as Virtu Financial's Concannon, the partner behind the firm's approaches to Knight, Fidelity Capital Markets' president Brian Conroy and NYSE's Leibowitz, as well as members from congress. On the sidelines of the conference on September 21, Bloomberg Television's Ruhle asked him how he was going to keep the team intact and save the firm from poaching. "I know you lost a senior member this week," she said.

Joyce faked a surprised face and promptly answered with a hedge, "I don't believe we lost anybody to any competitors this week." Do people leaving the firm have to say which competitor they are going to work for? What about if people agree to hold on to that information until everybody forgets about it? Ruhle, who had misplaced her notes about Wald's announcement, had to initially admit that she was mistaken. It turned out she wasn't.

Joyce didn't want to speak about Wald, so he savored the moment. "We lost several second and third tier players who I guess weren't happy with whatever was going on in their careers. But we haven't lost anybody important." Aren't "second" and "third-tier" players important? Joyce was forgetting that it wasn't a member of the top management who messed up with the update installation prior to August 1; wasn't this person's role crucially important to the firm?

Ruhle just couldn't believe Joyce's poker face; she was still looking for her notes because she had a point to make. He continued preaching. "Stephanie, we have a lot of employees, if somebody several layers down who was unhappy with their career left, God bless them in their new career. We have not lost anyone important to our organization." Then he went into PR mode, "I would like to think that is because we have a terrific culture. We have a client-oriented culture. We have a culture of compliance. And people kind of like working in places like that. So, we are continuing to grow the company in a fashion that we think is attractive to talented people."

Joyce was slightly off describing Knight's culture and trying to cover up the recent departures. Plainly said, Knight displayed a competitive environment and a sales-oriented culture, a place where everybody was a salesman. A culture where salesmen were 100 percent commission-based; they were getting zero, repeat, zilch, for salary, so there was always hustling; they had to be hustling. It was competitive, it was individualistic. Salesmen had to look out for themselves. A client-oriented culture? A culture of compliance? It was "me" first.

Joyce was hopeful he had been saved by the bell. Unfortunately for him, they went to the break and Ruhle had to come back. "I had thought that you lost some people. Just this week on the 18th, it was reported that Knight Capital's head of trading algorithms, Joseph Wald has left the firm. To me, that doesn't seem like someone who is a second or third tier down person. Your algo business is among the most important businesses at Knight and this guy runs it."

It didn't have to go this way. Joyce could have acknowledged that Wald was leaving when Ruhle first asked about it; now he had to try to put things in perspective.

"Joe started a company, 10-12 years ago, that we bought. Joe did very well, God bless him, when we bought the company in 2006, and he had been running a lot of our businesses. There was a management shift in that company, sorry, in that division internally. Joe decided it was better situation for him to go fishing for a little while I guess. But, as far as I know, he has not gone to a competitor. Joe decided that it was better time after a very successful career as both an independent entrepreneur and as part of Knight Capital Group to do something different and I would wish him nothing but the best."

Only four months later, it was publicly disclosed that Wald was going to Gain Capital, a provider of retail foreign exchange trading services, to GTX, the firm's electronic communications network used by hedge funds and institutions for currency trading. He would report to Glenn Stevens, chief executive officer of the Bedminster, New Jersey-based company, and would work from the New York office.[12]

As the weeks and months passed, Joyce stated on a conference call that the firm was open to exploring "any and all alternatives" to rebuild shareholder value, favoring retaining the U.S. electronic trading group's diverse line of businesses to help rebuild profits, which he said was his priority. "If we had a yard sale, we could have a little bit more of this and a little bit more of that. But as an organization, we believe there is an interrelatedness amongst all of our business lines." That meant Knight was able to sell Forex or bond-trading services to customers who came to Knight looking to deal in stocks. "We are better off having them all than becoming a siloed kind of one-product firm," Joyce said. "We came back as well as we came back because of the broadness of our organization."

However, he pointed out, "If we can't restore the valuation the way we expect to restore valuation, we will have to investigate any and all alternatives to make sure our shareholders get rewarded for investing in this company."[13]

Was Joyce already shopping the company? Joyce sounded optimistic, saying momentum was returning to Knight's core business of trading with its clients, which included major retail brokerages. For the quarter, the company had posted a $389.9 million loss compared with a profit of $26.9 million in the quarter the year prior. The per-share loss of $3.22 followed a 29-cent profit a year earlier. The firm also acknowledged that the August 1 trading errors drove a $461.1 million loss for Knight.

Some of the private equity investors were certainly interested in scrutinizing some businesses that had struggled in recent years, such as its institutional sales and trading division. The future of a reverse-mortgage unit acquired in 2010 was also under scrutiny and ultimately would be shopped around.

Repetto, the analyst for Sandler O'Neill, had told clients in a note that he saw logic in Knight sticking to its strategy as it recovers from the trading blunder. Still, Repetto ventured to suggest that Knight's shareholders could benefit if the firm looked at selling "parts or possibly the entire firm" in the next 6 to 18 months. "Knight's business is more stable now. I don't think Knight needs to do an acquisition but it may help speed a recovery after the technology mishap that occurred." He said he considered GETCO a "possible partner, especially once they participated in Knight's recapitalization."

In hindsight, it was clear to see some of the private equity firms behind Knight's highly-dilutive rescue on August 6 in an effort to sell the company. Blackstone and General Atlantic had made a shrewd deal by acquiring a trading powerhouse at its darkest hour. If Blackstone was prepared to pay more than a billion dollars to take Knight private before the trading incident, why wouldn't they want to enter into a deal now that the company was back on its feet? Naturally, Joyce was concerned about his prospects as a potential new acquirer wouldn't be able to guarantee his position.

Class action lawsuits were on the radar of Knight's legal team. Law firm Ryan & Maniskas announced on October 2 that a class action lawsuit had been filed in the U.S. District Court for the Western District of Tennessee on behalf of purchasers of Knight Capital common stock during the period of February 29, 2012, through August 1, 2012. The complaint alleges that Knight misrepresented and/or failed to disclose that the firm knowingly introduced unproven electronic trading software packages into the NYSE that "destabilized the global equity markets", and that Knight knew or should have known that its new electronic trading technology had the potential to engage in "large-volume erroneous trading." Only in a litigious society like the U.S. could a suit of this type have been allowed to be filed.

Saxena White P.A. had also announced that it had filed a securities fraud class action lawsuit against Knight Capital on behalf of investors who purchased or otherwise acquired the common stock of the company during the period from January 19, 2012 through August 1, 2012. The complaint alleged that Knight had made materially false and misleading statements regarding Knight's business, operational and accounting practices. Again, management had shown confidence that while they would need to spend more money on lawyers, they would ultimately prevail.[14]

It was no secret that trading volumes were unusually low over the summer of 2012. U.S. stock trading volume was 40 percent below its peak volume in 2009, falling from an average of 12 billion trades a day to 6 billion to 7 billion in 2012.

Average daily trading levels in August clocked in at their lowest levels since 2007. Dark pools across the board saw month-over-month volumes decline. Platforms operated by Credit Suisse and Goldman Sachs saw volumes decline by 14 percent and 2 percent, respectively, while BIDS Trading and Liquidnet each experienced 17 percent declines in August.

Knight Match, one of the two dark pools operated by Knight Capital, saw volume plunge 44 percent, outpacing declines which other dark pools suffered in a sluggish month overall. Knight Match, a registered ATS, was an anonymous source of non-displayed liquidity, through which clients had access to Knight's liquidity that consisted of institutional, retail and algorithmic order flow. Knight Match received both passive (resting) and flow orders of liquidity. This, in addition to the small- and mid-cap flow orders originating from Knight's retail broker-dealer clients, provided increased fulfillment opportunities for Knight Match clients.

While Knight had $300 million in excess capital, the firm had announced that it couldn't rule out more losses from lawsuits and diminished business, a reason why it considered selling its currency platform, Hotspot FX, and its stake in Direct Edge, a firm where Joyce was once a director. Hotspot FX, the foreign-exchange trading system acquired in 2006, would get as much as $300 million in a sale, based on the valuations of its competitors and taking into account increased trading volume, which had tripled since 2006 when Knight bought the business for $77.5 million, according to J.P. Morgan analyst Kenneth B. Worthington. Its 19.9 percent of Direct Edge may be worth $80 million, according to Raymond James & Associates. Overall, analysts agreed that businesses Knight had acquired over the last seven years might have been worth $600 million.

Sandler O'Neill's Repetto had estimated that Hotspot FX's value could be about half Worthington's figure. The currency platform reported $28 billion in average daily volume in the first half of 2012, he wrote. Assuming this could lead to about $48 million in revenue and $10.3 million in post-tax profit this year, Repetto said Hotspot FX would be worth $155 million after applying a 15 times multiple on earnings. Even NASDAQ would be later rumored to be interested in Hotspot FX.

Knight's stake in Direct Edge may be worth as much as $100 million in cash, Repetto wrote. The exchange had been valued at $390 million in 2008 when International Securities Exchange Holdings bought a 31.5 percent stake in the company.

On October 24, 2012, Joyce had a controversial message for fellow directors: other companies were interested in discussing potential job openings with him. He had had preliminary talks regarding the CEO post at online brokerage ETrade.

With his employment contract expiring at year's end and negotiations to extend his tenure dragging on, private conversations regarding Joyce's willingness to discuss other potential jobs showed the heartburn both Knight and its CEO were feeling after August 1.[15]

Directors generally preferred to reach agreement well before expiration of an executive's term. However, Joyce's employment contract talks had extended to near deadlines before; in 2008, the company announced his employment-contract renewal on December 24, a week before the prior contract expired.

Laurie Shahon headed the compensation committee and was on the nominating committee. Shahon, a Knight director since 2006, was president of Wilton Capital Group. She had previously held investment banking positions with Morgan Stanley and Salomon Brothers, where she scoured the landscape for leveraged buyouts (LBOs), the industry popularized in the 1980s by such big buyout firms as KKR or Forstmann Little.[16]

Focused on making principal investments in later-stage ventures and medium-sized buyouts, Shahon founded Wilton in 1994. She was board member of several private companies, including the Life Insurance Company of Boston & New York and Lux Beauty Group; she had served as a director of more than twenty public and private companies since 1988, including Eddie Bauer Holdings, The Bombay Company, and Kitty Hawk. Shahon had received a bachelor's degree in English and political science from Wellesley College in 1974 and an

MBA in finance and international business from Columbia Business School, where she later taught as adjunct professor.

Shahon had participated in talks with Joyce about his contract and interest from other companies. Publicly through, Joyce was looking forward to continuing discussions with the board as he had said he did "expect to work at Knight for the next several years."

Just days after Knight's trading malfunction, SEC lawyers were already trying to determine if Knight had violated a new rule designed to protect the markets from rogue algorithmic computer trading programs, despite Joyce's insistence that he didn't believe any market rules had been broken in the trading mishap.

The SEC's probe became a formal investigation on August 29. SEC investigators had been looking into whether Knight had failed to adequately test its systems after installing code on computer servers, paving the way for the August 1 error. Regulators were looking into whether the size and volume of the orders showed that Knight lacked "reasonable" risk-management procedures; the SEC was also looking at whether the same programmers who wrote code tested it.

The SEC was deepening its probe into whether Knight did enough to police its trading systems before computer errors nearly destroyed the firm. The probe was broadened to look further at the company's risk-control procedures. Certainly, the SEC's decision to intensify its investigation was seen as a setback for a brokerage eager to put the episode behind it.

In her introductory remarks on October 2 at SEC's Market Technology Roundtable, Schapiro seemed to move away from that question and pointed to infrastructure and technology as deeper reasons behind Knight's trading malfunction.

"Consider as well the events this summer with Knight Capital– a trading firm that had just installed trading software that was intended to send orders to the NYSE's new RLP. Instead, the software wound up sending 'a ton of orders' into the market. As the market data that morning revealed, the software did not create patterns of rapid orders and cancels. Rather, the data showed a massive amount of orders resulting in executed trades that caused Knight Capital to accumulate significant and unwanted positions. This type of problem, as with the IPO mishaps, was the result of basic technology 101 issues. Events like these demonstrate that core infrastructure and technology issues can be problematic in any market structure."

Knight had separated its processes for developing software and installing it to ensure they were now done by different people, Joyce had said on a conference call October 17. It had instituted more checks and balances to reduce the chance of a similar mistake occurring and implemented controls on systems that send orders to markets "so we can get to the router faster and stop it from creating problems sooner," he had said.

The SEC's market access rule "has been widely cited in discussions of the Knight Capital disaster of August 1, when erroneous orders from the market maker inundated the New York Stock Exchange for 40 minutes," said David Zinberg, financial services and insurance principal at software provider Infosys. "The rule requires broker-dealers to implement risk controls that would block erroneous orders from reaching exchanges and other market centers."[17]

As a result, between September and October, Knight directors had agreed in private deliberations that indeed the firm violated their capital thresholds, which was a component of the market-access rule. Knight's board had gone so far as to vote in favor of a settlement with the SEC, with a framework based on preliminary conversations with regulators. But when Knight notified the SEC of the board approval ahead of the company's third-quarter earnings in mid-October, the regulator didn't respond.[18] At some moment during the conversations, Joyce thought Knight was "close to having resolution" with the SEC about its August 1 trading incident.

As if Knight didn't have enough headaches in what amounted to a more than challenging 2012, the firm had to ask clients on Wednesday morning, October 31, to route all stock orders away from the brokerage, out of fear that its backup power generator in Jersey City would run out of fuel. This was the second such request in less than three months as the effects of massive hurricane Sandy were being dramatically felt in the area. The letter sent to Knight's clients at 11:51 A.M. didn't specifically mention the reason behind the request.

Dear Clients:

Due to a building emergency (power issues), Knight Capital Americas is asking you to seek an alternate destination for the order handling and execution of your OTC, Options and Listed orders until further notice. This includes Knightlink and Knightmatch clients.

All computer interfaces with Knight will be shutdown with no new orders, both by phone or electronic, being accepted at this time.

Please continue to e-mail Help@Knight.com with any questions.

Thanks

Tonya Walker, managing director

The brokers were already relaying the information to their own clients:

Dear Valued Client,

As per Knight's request below, please route away from Knight. If a client routes an order to Knight, the order will be rejected by our system. Information on existing orders will still flow back from Knight.

If you have any questions or concerns, please feel free to contact us.

Regards,

InstaQuote | Bank of America Merrill Lynch

All stock markets in the country had been shut down on Monday and Tuesday in response to suggestions from firms worried about employee safety during Sandy, as well as concerns about financial markets functioning effectively on contingency plans with relatively light staffing in place. It was the first time in 27 years that exchanges closed because of weather conditions.

Like many other firms in the New York metro area, the company had been operating on backup energy after Sandy hit late on Monday, only to have their main generator failing before midday, affecting its institutional equities sales and trading, as well as market making businesses. Hotspot FX, which electronically matches up currency trades, was also affected.

Knight was in communication with NYSE and confirmed it had a backup in Purchase, New York. When asked why Knight had opted to operate from Jersey City rather than from Purchase, Knight's Fitzsimmons said, "Our preference is to remain with our primary site when possible. With our Jersey City headquarters intact, we proceeded accordingly."[19]

NYSE was also operating on backup generators. COO Leibowitz had said NYSE had multiple backups in place; while he was told it might have power by Friday, NYSE was ready to run on generators through the weekend and beyond. "Many people are operating from some contingency place, and often that works fine, but sometimes there are hiccups. But as a whole, it's actually going quite well. We haven't heard of widespread problems," Leibowitz said.

Knight would have lost some trading capabilities if switched all business operations there to its backup center. Later in the day, it decided against switching data centers in the middle of the trading session because it feared operational risks.

On the other hand, Direct Edge, which operated out of the same Jersey City building as its shareholder Knight, had moved its base to a backup facility in Secaucus, New Jersey, run by Equinix. By the end of Thursday trading schedule, Knight was processing stock orders as usual after its regular power supply had been restored, as was communicated to clients in a note sent at 4:20 P.M. Explaining the contingency on Wednesday, the memo said, "Out of abundance of caution and to protect our clients, a decision was made to instruct clients to route away."

"Honestly, what I believe happened at Knight is that they didn't have a clear-cut decision making process for managing when to switch over," Rachel Dines, senior analyst at Forrester Research, commented. If those business policies aren't clear, "people will stall" when it comes to implementing fail-over in the event of an actual disaster, she said.[20]

"It is a little disconcerting for things like backup generators to not be working because these are relatively basic disaster recovery things to have in place," Noah Hamman, chief executive officer of AdvisorShares, had said. As a result of the Knight issue, AdvisorShares had seen a few of its ETFs, such as its Global Echo ETF and its Accuvest Global Long Short ETF, start trading at wider spreads than usual for a few hours.

Mitch Hodus, SVP of Information Technology at ViningSparks, pointed out that while companies with good disaster recovery practices often test their fail-over capabilities, many do not test their ability to run their business for an extended period of time at the backup site so they don't really know if their systems and network have the necessary horsepower to drive the business. He had seen many disaster recovery designs where companies spent only enough money to have the bare minimum number of systems to run in a disaster, fully knowing that they need to add more systems to truly handle the full load. "I could see where Knight could have been concerned about handling their processing load if this was the case," he added. "I could see where companies might choose not to fail-over if they felt they might only have to be down for 24 hours. DR testing can be a risky proposition when done correctly."

IBM had not been hired to do a forensic analysis of the trading glitch; that was PricewaterhouseCoopers' role, which was also investigating the computer meltdown that affected millions of RBS customers in the U.K. IBM had been hired to provide an assessment on Knight's product development lifecycle processes, and that's what they set out to do starting in mid-September. It took them around ten weeks to prepare their report.

The IBM team interviewed everybody who was involved that terrible morning. Joyce wasn't interviewed; he wasn't there that morning so probably he would have added much anyway. His excuse was that he wanted the board to be in charge of leading the review. They did interview Sang though; how did this man behave in the interview? Very contrite, very apologetic.

IBM found out that Knight's technology wasn't as modern as they had tried to get the markets to believe. They learned that Knight's different lines of business had different processes in place to implement new developments. They learned that Knight relied on people that had been with the firm for a long time and were given a lot of leeway. More importantly, they identified the firm needed a lot more controls in place.

The market-making team was a particular case of concern. Quants were working with programmers together on developing and launching new algorithms; they quickly had to figure out from the data how to make money quickly too because they were competing with firms with the same sophisticated models and bright scientists. Launching new algorithms was the priority; testing was not.

IBM's report was ultimately presented to the board around Thanksgiving time. How seriously they took IBM's recommendations remains a question mark, as the board was already concentrated on evaluating deal proposals to acquire the firm.

Chapter Sixteen

Barbarians at the Gate?

After a sumptuous breakfast at the terrace of the luxurious Ritz-Carlton Beach Resort in Naples, Florida, the hundreds of attendees at the annual CME Group's Global Financial Leadership Conference walked back to the conference room as the panelists in the lead-off session about "Evolving Capital Market Dynamics: Volatility, Liquidity and High-frequency trading" stepped up to the gigantic and certainly impressive stage put together by Jack Morton Worldwide, the American multinational brand experience agency.

The conference had been the brainchild of charismatic CME Group's executive chairman and president Terry Duffy, avid golfer and hockey-loving father of twin boys with hair as blonde as his. It had become the most exclusive event for futures traders eager to run away from their trading rooms for a week of sun at this beach-front luxury complex. Attendees got the opportunity to rub shoulders with decision-makers from the world's leading financial institutions and hear them discuss emerging geopolitical trends and critical economic issues, as well as provide perspectives on future developments in the financial marketplace.

The day before, attendees had attentively listened to former U.S. Secretary of State Condoleezza Rice's calls for President Obama to get America's fiscal house in order. She spent most of her speech fighting a mischievous fly that somehow had challenged the strong security contingent by the door; Duffy would commend Rice for staying focused on her speech despite such a freakish distraction. Later in the day, traders would be treated to a rather unconventional presentation by Virgin Group's founder, Sir Richard Branson. His entrance was worthy of a Hollywood movie: six Virgin flight attendants dressed in their red uniforms walked through the hallways from the front all the way to the back pushing their carts and offering drinks and refreshments to surprised comfortably-seated attendees pulling out their iPhones and Blackberries to catch the unexpected treat.

Open only to a few media organizations, this high-level schmoozing wasn't unusual at all. Additional featured speakers at the November 12-14 gathering included former U.S. Secretary of State Madeleine Albright, strategist James Carville (the brains behind President Clinton's re-election), award-winning journalist Ted Koppel, Republican star strategist Karl Rove and Wikipedia's founder Jimmy Wales.

Past speakers at the forum had included opinion leaders and luminaries such as Presidents Bill Clinton and George W. Bush, award-winning journalist and author Katie Couric, new media liberal symbol Arianna Huffington, Nobel Prize of Economy winners Robert Merton and Myron Scholes, legendary hedge fund manager and philanthropist Paul Tudor Jones and bestselling author Michael Lewis.

Michael Mackenzie, U.S. markets editor of the Financial Times, was leading the panel, which also included Jeff Jennings, the outgoing global head of listed derivatives at Credit Suisse, Richard Prager, the cerebral global head of trading and capital markets at BlackRock, Edgar Perez, the globe-trotting author of *The Speed Traders*, and Coleman.

Mackenzie discussed with his fellow panelists the perceptions, realities and possible regulatory outcomes for high-speed electronic trading. Coleman of GETCO addressed the idea of uncertainty around high-speed trading, and shared his view that the industry was better off when compared to past eras.

"Large technological changes always lead to these kinds of uncertainties because they're really hard to get your arms around.

And it happens a lot in different industries over history, and it's happening now in ours. But I was also in this business before we had these changes, and as crazy as it is now, it's better. It's better from an execution point of view, it's better from a competitive point of view with trading venues, in my view, and it's better for the end client."

While Coleman was not giving away any hint of the move his firm was set to make, GETCO's biggest investor had already set its eyes on Knight. Just a week after the rescue deal, General Atlantic had started discussions with Joyce about a possible combination with GETCO. Due diligence started and soon terms for a merger were presented to Knight; however, Joyce let Coleman know that he didn't find the terms particularly attractive. The stage was set for GETCO's outright attempt to acquire the whole company.

As soon as Coleman was back in the office, GETCO would announce that it could consider transactions with Knight including buying or selling their shares, something it hadn't mentioned in its filing on August.

According to an amended 13D filed on November 15 with the Securities and Exchange Commission, GETCO had said it might evaluate its investment in Knight, as it owned convertible securities representing a 23.8 percent of Knight's outstanding common stock (it previously had held a 37.4 percent stake). The new language was similar to passages in filings by Blackstone and Stephens but not Jefferies, three other Knight investors who had helped save the firm in August.

Entities were required to file an amendment to schedule 13D when any material change occurred in the facts set forth previously including, but not limited to, any material increase or decrease in the percentage of the class beneficially owned; an acquisition or disposition of beneficial ownership of securities in an amount equal to one percent or more of the class of securities was deemed "material"; even acquisitions or dispositions of less than those amounts might be material, depending upon the facts and circumstances.

Something was up with Knight then, despite Joyce's denial. "This is really GETCO's story to tell, not ours," he had commented.[1] Shares had already moved up almost 9 percent for the day. On Monday November 19, Knight had set a special shareholder meeting for December 27 to decide a new stock-based incentive plan for executives, following the tragic dilution in August. The firm needed the approval of investors to boost the number of shares allotted to executive incentive plans by about 54 million shares.[2]

Knight's equity incentive plan, approved in 2010, had held about 10.6 million shares able to be granted to executives as an incentive for delivering good performance. Would overseeing the August 1 catastrophe count as good performance? That number of shares was apparently no longer enough for the executives, as the firm's share count had ballooned under the rescue deal. Conversion of the preferred securities granted to Knight's new investors in the deal had boosted Knight's share count to about 356 million from its prior level of about 89 million shares outstanding. Knight was seeking to boost the number of shares available to grant to executives to 64.6 million.

"A failure to increase the number of shares of stock under the Amended 2010 Plan would likely require the use of less-efficient compensation strategies or result in an inability to pay our executives market rates of compensation, which could compromise the company's ability to retain key members of management," Knight added. Would any key member of management really be able to find a better place after August 1?

GETCO's move was now being precipitated by its interest in Knight as a whole and a capital markets event three days before that not many people in the investing world had paid attention to.

Knight's largest shareholder, Jefferies, was getting its own capital injection by way of a sale to Leucadia National, which valued the investment bank at roughly $3.6 billion. The low price of the deal signaled that Jefferies' investment banking and trading units were in dire need of a balance sheet injection to withstand pressure from a weak economic outlook, the burden of expansion efforts and new regulations that made it more costly to do business.

Just a year before, trading firm MF Global had filed for bankruptcy after an outsized position in European government bonds caused ratings agencies to question Jefferies' capital and cut its bond ratings to junk. In the aftermath of MF Global's demise, investors and some analysts questioned whether Jefferies would be next. Shares had plummeted 20 percent and prompted Jefferies to liquidate the firm's European debt position by the end of the year.

After taking a 22.8 percent stake in and advising Knight on its rescue efforts, Jefferies posted record third quarter results in September. Still, underlying the firm's record profit, largely due to its Knight Capital stake, were weak results in its core trading and investment banking business that augured poorly for its future. Leucadia National's move might have left little room for Jefferies but to unload its successful investment in Knight.

Smart market analysts certainly were able to see the writing on the wall. William Tuttle, a Washington D.C.-based lawyer who focused on corporate and securities matters at Dechert reasoned that GETCO might have been contemplating or signaling to the market that they were more open to acquisition-type transactions. Elizabeth Nowicki, a mergers and acquisitions professor at Tulane University Law School, had said that the change in GETCO's filing suggested they were thinking of expanding their holding and going for more control."[3]

Not surprisingly, Knight shares rallied 6.6 percent to $2.52 as of early afternoon on the day of the announcement, in what was their biggest advance in almost two months. The rally was not missed by the major investors who had bailed out Knight in August; they owned 70 percent of the firm and had provided the cash in exchange for $400 million in preferred stock that they could convert into common stock at a price of $1.50 a share. Given where shares of Knight traded amid the takeover talk, many of those investors would have liked to walk away with their profits immediately.

These were the investors pushing Joyce to do a deal. Over Thanksgiving weekend, Joyce sent a message to employees saying capital levels were strong and, in a tacit acknowledgement of the upcoming moves, no deal would be done unless it made sense for the company. Joyce wrote in his message, which included talking points for clients, that he expected business as usual with no need for additional cash and that the company was operating at full capacity.[4] Bottom line, Knight was waiting for proposals to materialize over the following week.[5]

While initial conversations focused on selling just Knight's market making business, it was clear that the remaining parts of the firm would have trouble as a going concern, because market making was the mainstay. For Sandler O'Neill's Repetto, "if they sold the market-making business, it would make sense to sell simultaneously the other assets to them or somebody else. They don't have a company once they sell that business. It's the mainstay."

On Tuesday November 27, in a bid to keep the firm's integrity, Joyce approached a number of large Wall Street firms in an attempt to get them interested in an acquisition; this option seemed much more attractive for him than the prospect of being taken over by a direct competitor. Joyce was also planning to discuss a deal with money management powerhouse BlackRock; chief executive Larry Fink (who had sold a chunk of BlackRock to Merrill Lynch in 2006 when Joyce worked there) had yet to be briefed on the matter.[6]

Joyce's contract with Knight was ending at the end of the year, and it was unclear if the board would be willing to extend it. Wanting to keep control over Knight's future and, more importantly, his own,

Joyce was not interested in selling the firm but instead on finding a much bigger acquisition partner that could take over all of the firm's businesses.

Seemingly out of nowhere, Virtu Financial was readying to display its ambitions to dominate the market making space. On November 27, Virtu privately submitted an unsolicited bid for Knight. The electronic trading firm accounted for more than 5 percent of U.S. equities volume and had about 150 employees. Virtu, which had traded only stocks listed in the U.S. when it started, handled shares on six continents, along with government bonds, foreign currencies, contracts in energy and metals, and futures. Virtu traded through regional offices, with its Singapore office handling Australia and Asia, while the Middle East and Europe were managed from Dublin. Employees in New York and Santa Monica, California, were responsible for trading energy products and currencies in North and South America.[7]

Virtu, which provided bids and offers on 205 venues around the world in products from U.S. equities to silver and copper futures, was seeing its fastest growth opportunities in currency trading as well as providing liquidity to stocks in Asian markets including Japan and Australia. It certainly expected rapid growth in new products that would become available when over-the-counter derivatives started trading electronically under rules mandated by the Dodd-Frank Act. Virtu was also committed to stay faithful to its roots and boost its market-making operations even as some rivals mightily struggled.

The enterprising firm had been founded by Vincent Viola[8] and had grown from a proprietary-trading firm investing its own capital to one of the biggest electronic trading firms, expanding in the U.S. and abroad. Virtu operated on more than 25 exchanges globally including NYSE Euronext, NASDAQ and the Chicago Mercantile Exchange. Virtu's other co-founders included Doug Cifu, a former partner at law firm Paul, Weiss, Rifkind, Wharton & Garrison, and Graham Free, Virtu's head trader who had earlier worked the same job at Madison Tyler.[9]

In May 2011, Virtu merged with proprietary trading firm Madison Tyler, based in Santa Monica, California, with the backing of Silver Lake. Both had been co-founded by Viola, respectively in 2008 and 2002. Viola had co-founded Madison Tyler with David Salomon, a former arbitrage trader at Goldman Sachs and an early developer of algorithmic trading.

The same year, Virtu had bought the market making unit of Cohen Capital, making it a prominent counterparty in trading of shares listed on NYSE MKT, formerly known as Amex, and expanding its clout in trading of NYSE-listed stocks more broadly.

Viola, whose family comes from the city of Sanza, in the Salerno province of Italy, had been born in Brooklyn in 1956 where he went to local schools, St. Cecilia's elementary school in Williamsburg and Brooklyn Tech High School. He had received an appointment to the U.S. Military Academy at West Point, graduating with a bachelor's degree in 1977 as well as from U.S. Army Ranger School. He had served as an officer in the 101st Airborne following West Point. Viola and his wife, Teresa D'Angelo, lived in Manhattan after raising three sons in Chatham, New Jersey, John, Michael and Travis.

"Vinnie is for Vinnie," said a former colleague.[10] "He is a master at leveraging people; he's very smart and he's very charismatic. It is very difficult to not want to be on Team Vinnie. But if you think you're going to be the one person who he'll need past your utility for him, shame on you."

After leaving the Army, where he had achieved the rank of major, Viola joined the New York Mercantile Exchange (NYMEX), the world's dominant energy and metals market, as a "local" trader, becoming a member of the exchange in 1982. That same year, he graduated from New York Law School with a J.D. degree. During his career, Viola served in various positions of leadership at NYMEX, serving as the chairman from 2001 to 2004. He helped the exchange through the turmoil of the 9-11 attacks and took NYMEX public later in 2006.

Viola was chameleonic and irascible, a master of both disguise and reinvention. "Vinnie is not a details guy," a fellow trader who watched Viola execute his first trade at NYMEX said in the same Fortune profile; it had been for five platinum futures contracts. "He is a macro thinker. He finds the best people in the business to carry out his vision and he pays them well. If Vinnie gets Knight, he'll literally be the largest trader in the world. And he's very, very aware of that. He is not a technology guy and he's not into this as a technology play. He will be focused on the trading and the intelligence it will give him. The true underlying value of Knight isn't its platform. It's the macro view of the market it will give to anyone who owns it. Whoever gets it will be able to see huge sections of the market and trade on it."

Viola, a kung-fu fighter, cloaked himself in a Mafia-esque mystique, according to a number of NYMEX traders, and was counted as one of the most fearsome traders in the history of the exchange. He was also a devout Roman Catholic and committed philanthropist, most recently giving $2 million to Fordham University to establish the Avery Cardinal Dulles, S.J., Chair in Catholic Theology. He had also co-founded the National Children's Educational Reform Foundation, which was dedicated to the fundamental reform and improvement of inner-city education with an emphasis on bilingual programs in immigrant communities.

On Tuesday November 27, Virtu had offered to pay $3.20 a share in its all-cash bid. Virtu had initially proposed to pay at least $3 a share in a deal that valued Knight at more than $1.5 billion, including debt. Under this deal, Knight would have become a private company, Joyce would have remained as the chief executive, Viola would have been chairman of the combined company, and co-founder Cifu would have continued as president and chief operating officer. Behind the scenes, former NYSE chief Dick Grasso was acting as "unofficial adviser".[11]

The proposal would be financed by a loan commitment of at least $1 billion led by Credit Suisse; Barclays Capital and Citigroup would participate as well. Virtu was in talks with three other banks and could have raised an additional $100 million. The bid also included a commitment of new equity financing from Silver Lake, which owned a stake in Virtu and was discussing contributing additional equity, Cerberus Capital Management, and management of the market-making company.

Cerberus's participation in the Knight takeover talks with at least a $200 million commitment would have marked the latest in a string of recent high-profile deal discussions involving the private equity firm, which had sought to stay out of the headlines since the financial crisis. Before the crisis, Cerberus had gained majority control of Chrysler Group and Ally Financial, General Motors' former financing arm; both firms had nearly collapsed and been bailed out by the federal government. Eventually, Cerberus turned the deals into moneymakers. For a period afterward, the firm had refocused on lower-profile distressed companies, some so small they couldn't raise money in the junk-bond market. In addition to the Knight conversation, Cerberus was talking with Best Buy founder Richard Schulze about a potential bid to take the struggling electronics giant private, and weighing a bid for troubled grocery chain Supervalu, one of the largest supermarket owners in the U.S.

Virtu had asserted in talks with Knight that its offer was more attractive than GETCO's because it was for all of Knight's shares and was more likely to be completed. Virtu had sought to convince directors that Knight and its employees would be better off if the firm was restructured as a private company. Virtu would go public later.

General Atlantic, the private equity firm that owned a minority stake in GETCO, had figured prominently in pushing for a takeover of Knight to create an opportunity to realize its investment without having to publicly float GETCO.

To understand the logic of submitting an unsolicited bid for Knight, it was important to know that GETCO had already eliminated about 40 jobs in June 7 amid an industry slowdown in transactions that impacted even the biggest firm of all in the high-frequency trading world. Half the cuts, which had followed the company's first strategic review of its businesses, were in the U.S. GETCO had about 450 employees before the layoffs. Something needed to be done. The more transformational the deal, the better, Coleman thought.

Back on October 15, 1999, former floor traders Stephen Schuler and Dan Tierney recognized the beginning of a paradigm shift in the financial markets and founded Global Electronic Trading Company, GETCO, in a small office at the Chicago Mercantile Exchange. They believed technology would fundamentally change the way markets functioned, and usher in a new era of efficiency, transparency, and competition. GETCO traded across three continents, in four asset classes, and on over 50 markets around the world.

Since its founding, the firm had risen to become one of the five biggest traders measured by volume in stocks and other instruments that traded electronically on exchanges, such as Treasury bonds and currency futures. GETCO depended on the success of its proprietary complex algorithms to help it make money on the transactions more often than not. It also could pick up tiny rebates that exchanges offered to firms willing to take the other side of trading orders. The company focused on hiring top computer programmers and technicians, as well as traders.[12]

On April 16, 2007, General Atlantic invested about $300 million in GETCO, a deal which then valued it at around $1.5 billion. CEO Bill Ford and managing director Rene Kern joined GETCO's board of directors.[13] General Atlantic had demonstrated a long-term investment horizon and an active, value-added approach to investing in both public and private companies on a global basis. The firm had been an active investor in the financial services sector, with a number of investments in innovative, technology-driven companies including ETrade, Computershare, NYSE Euronext, NYMEX, Saxo Bank, Sharekhan, National Stock Exchange of India Limited and RiskMetrics. From that standpoint, GETCO was General Atlantic's bet on the growth of electronic, global and multi-asset class trading.

In 2008, the NYSE transformed its specialist system, which had become obsolete in the age of superfast trading. The specialists were replaced by designated market makers. While designated market makers maintained a presence on the trading floor, ready to step in during chaotic markets, most of the order flow was handled electronically. GETCO became the first high-frequency-trading firm to go after that role, taking over the assignments from Barclays Capital; the other designated market makers were still big Wall Street firms and former specialists. GETCO was already making markets for about 500 NYSE stocks under the exchange's special liquidity provider program. For Dave Babulak, a GETCO managing director, this was an "opportunity for us to leverage what we've been doing and bring that technology to the floor" of the NYSE.

UBS's Coleman had met for lunch with Ford. Coleman remembers discussing his desire to move from his role as managing director and head of U.S. equity trading for the Americas. Coleman had become dispirited after losing dozens of employees in 2009, when UBS paid its bankers significantly less than Wall Street and European rivals. He had first mooted the possibility of leaving the bank a year before.[14]

Coleman had joined UBS in 1986 as a graduate trainee at its Chicago-based O'Connor & Associates business, which had 200 or 300 people back then. They were bought by Swiss Bank Corp. and later became part of UBS. Coleman, based later in Stamford,

Connecticut, was instrumental in building UBS's equities platform and played a key role in the integration of some of its big acquisitions, including the Paine Webber merger.

Coleman had been with UBS Investment Bank and its predecessor firms as head of convertible trading, risk manager, maker and specialist on equity and index derivatives. Later, he was the head of client trading at the firm. He was appointed joint global head of equities in 2005 and global head of equities in 2008. Coleman was also the joint global head of equities and director of UBS Investment Bank's asset management arm.

With his rapid ascension up the corporate ladder, Coleman and wife Brooke Hartzog found time to restore the Swann House, which they had bought in 2003 to begin an extensive renovation and conservation project in 2005. The Theodore Swann residence, also called Chaucer Hall or Swann Castle, was an English Tudor-style mansion located on the crest of Red Mountain at 3506 Redmont Road in Birmingham. It had been constructed from 1927 to 1930 for industrialist Theodore Swann and was the largest and most highly-ornate residence in Birmingham when it was constructed. During the Great Depression, the Swanns lost the house to foreclosure. Over the years various misfortunes befell the occupants of the house, inspiring superstition.[15]

After interviewing several firms, the Colemans selected Jack Pyburn Architects of Atlanta to oversee a large-scale restoration of the house's exterior. The slate roof was replaced in its entirety with the huge chimney-pots carefully repaired in situ. The exterior stonework was repointed while flashings and trim were replaced where necessary. The window sashes were sent to New Jersey for re-leading and the terrace pavers were taken up to allow for new waterproofing membranes to be installed before they were meticulously re-laid.

Thanks to their work restoring the Swann House, the Colemans received in 2009 the Thomas Jefferson Award from the Jefferson

County Historical Commission; this award was presented each year to outstanding Jefferson County individuals and organizations whose works had contributed significantly to the knowledge and conservation of their historic resources. Continuing with the service tradition, on April 22, 2012, the Colemans had the Birmingham Historical Society hold a Gathering at the Swann House. On November 1, 2012, Friends of Birmingham Botanical Gardens held its annual Fall Donor Appreciation Event at the house, where the Colemans hosted nearly 100 donors for cocktails and hors d'oeuvres at the Magic City landmark.[16]

At UBS, Coleman was ultimately responsible for overseeing trading and risk management for cash equities, derivatives, convertible bonds, proprietary, and program trading operations. UBS's equities franchise had been one of the bright spots for an institution that had lost hundreds of senior investment bankers during the downturn, when it was forced to write down billions in impaired mortgage related assets and take a $59.2 billion bail-out from the Swiss government. However, the business had ceded ground to rivals amid concerns about the extent of its problems and whether it would continue to be able to retain and attract top equities talent. According to a recent report from Morgan Stanley and Oliver Wyman, the consultancy, UBS had lost the most market share in global equities over the crisis as measured in revenues, dropping from a nearly 10 percent share in the first half of 2007 to 6.4 percent in the second half of 2009.

It was this wealth of Wall Street experience for Coleman, who had earned a bachelor of arts from Yale University and an MBA from the University of Chicago, that led Ford to introduce him to GETCO's co-founders. They had both been looking to grow beyond their equity roots by bringing somebody from the outside; they decided to get Coleman on board as managing director with a focus on business development extending the company's trading services to mutual funds and other asset managers. The company offered a set of algorithms called GETAlpha designed to help institutions save money and minimize their impact on prices as they traded. Coleman would split his time between his home in Birmingham, Alabama, and GETCO offices in New York and Chicago, where the firm had just moved its headquarters in 2011.

"We've had success bringing broker-dealer customers on to the router and bringing buy-side as well as broker-dealers on to the GETAlpha [algorithm] product. We're not looking to service thousands of clients, it may be less than 200 over time. We're well on our way to signing up the number we're looking for. On the sell-side, it's possible that at some point we will do a white-labeling deal with one or more broker-dealers there. That would enable us to reach clients that need a higher-end service.

"We fit into the landscape as an execution-only broker. We have to go to clients that have an execution-only budget or are prepared to pay for execution, unlike the banks, that use execution to get paid for many different services. Our product itself is a bit different than what's out there. It's built on our infrastructure for market making and built using the models we use so it's continuously being updated. When a client uses our product, it would most likely make the client's order look like market noise, or a little more random, or a little more like a market-making type of firm, a lot less noticeable and a lot more difficult to figure out the client's trading footprint."[17]

This potential growth of GETCO's business servicing asset managers had followed its decision in 2010 to become a so-called designated market maker on the New York Stock Exchange. The company had agreed to buy Bank of America's NYSE market-making business in 2011. It had created GETCO Execution Services' dark pool, called GETMatched, in 2008.

Coleman became first global head of equities and client services and managing director at GETCO on September 29, 2010. "We were fortunate enough to bring Daniel Coleman to GETCO," said Schuler, co-founder and executive director; "we had a sense that he might be the right person to lead us into the next phase of our evolution, and we are pleased to see our instincts borne out. Since joining GETCO, Daniel's leadership and insights have greatly contributed to our continued growth, success, and most importantly, our culture."

"Daniel is perfectly aligned with our long-term vision of utilizing technology to transform how investors transfer risk," said GETCO co-founder Tierney. "His unique combination of professional experiences, leadership ability and business acumen make him the ideal leader for the next stage of our growth." "He has a demonstrated track record of success on a larger scale," had said Doug Hanslip, a managing director in Chicago at Baltimore-based recruiting firm Allegis Partners.

Bringing Coleman in said some important things about the firm. Not least important of these was GETCO's realization that its longstanding aversion to public attention wasn't appropriate for a worldwide business that was now one of the biggest market makers in U.S. equities. Coleman was bringing an outsider's perspective, wide-ranging experience in global markets and executive skills honed at one of the world's largest financial firms.

A more open approach would have helped also advance GETCO's efforts to diversify into new lines of business. The company was trying to develop businesses that depended less on trading volumes, which had declined in recent years, hurting its market making operation. "Our openness grows because we have clients now, and because we're building new businesses," Coleman had said. GETCO realized that if it didn't define itself to the public, "other people were going to define GETCO for us."[18]

In certain ways, the market had already defined GETCO. The firm was highly respected in financial circles. "GETCO is terrific," was a usual comment. "Their trading group is highly sophisticated and their infrastructure is probably industry-leading". Some considered GETCO as the best technologists in the industry. "They scalp us frequently; their trading is so good that we lose money competing with them," a trader at a major financial firm had commented. Coleman's challenge was to build on their widely admired expertise and capabilities.

In July 2011, GETCO made its first foreign acquisition, buying Automat Ltd., a London-based proprietary trading firm; the purchase, for an undisclosed price, extended its reach into currency and derivatives markets. The prior year, GETCO had become a Singapore Exchange trading member and was also using an office in that city to trade on the Tokyo Stock Exchange. GETCO additionally revealed that it had decided to connect to the London Stock Exchange's Turquoise venue, which would let it pursue its penchant for trading in a variety of asset classes.[19]

Coleman was ultimately named CEO on February 27, 2012; only a few months later, he was ranked 12th in Institutional Investors' The 2012 Tech 50 (he would be ranked 15th in the 2013 list). Coleman's appointment coincided with a third straight annual slowdown in American equities trading. In 2012, stock volume had dropped to an average 6.81 billion shares a day in the U.S. versus 7.80 billion in 2011, 8.52 billion in 2010 and 9.77 billion in 2009. Full-year net income had fallen to $16.2 million in 2012, down from $162.7 million in 2011, as quieter stock and derivatives markets left traders with fewer opportunities to make money. However, Virtu was going against this depressing trend; the firm had earned about $240 million before interest, taxes and other expenses in 2012.

The fourth quarter of 2012 was particularly rough: GETCO reported $24.6 million in net income for the first nine months of 2012. Later, it would have been revealed that GETCO had lost more than $8 million in the fourth quarter. These numbers compared with the peak of $430 million earned in 2008 as GETCO traded through that year's intense market swings. In general, the trends hadn't been favorable for the marketplace, especially for those firms that relied on volume for revenue (such as all trading shops) and volatility (all high-frequency trading shops).[20]

The proposed merger was Coleman's answer to the squeeze on profits from falling volume and tighter spreads in the equity and derivative markets as well as the rising costs of technology and compliance. Under GETCO's initial proposal, submitted to Knight's board on November 28, Coleman would head the new company and Joyce would be non-executive chairman, with more distance from the day-to-day operations. The board would include four directors nominated by GETCO shareholders and three directors currently serving on the Knight board of directors. GETCO's bid valued Knight at between $1.4 billion and $1.8 billion including debt, depending on the value of shares in the combined entity, which would remain publicly traded. The bid was being backed by $950 million financing from Jefferies, another Knight investor.

GETCO was proposing a two-step reverse merger in which Knight would be reorganized as a holding company with GETCO receiving 242 million newly issued shares and warrants to buy 69 million more. As a result of this first step, the 57 million shares of Knight currently owned by GETCO would be retired. The company then would make a tender offer for up to 154 million Knight shares, about half those outstanding, excluding GETCO's current stake, at $3.50, or about $539 million. It would have been fair to assume that GETCO's offer was taking into account Knight's expected $118 million tax refund from the carryback portion of the August trading loss and the related net operating losses (NOLs).[21]

"In addition to creating an industry leader in market making and agency execution that is well positioned across multiple product lines globally, the work completed by our respective management teams to date indicates that there are large and achievable cost and revenue synergies attainable through a merger. The integration of our firms' operations would generate substantial earnings accretion going forward. Moreover, the larger

capital base and higher regulatory capital of the combined company would
provide strong support for existing customer operations as well as an
attractive currency for potential future acquisitions."

Coleman pointed out in his letter that he believed the merger
offered Knight's shareholders a clear path to reaping the benefits of
their investment. "In addition, by structuring the transaction with
both cash and equity components, Knight shareholders are able to
realize an immediate return on investment, as well as preserve the
opportunity to participate in the future growth of the combined
company."

"They think there's long-term value in the company because
they're making a bid and because of how the warrants are
structured," Keith Ross, CEO of PDQ Enterprises (a Chicago-based
dark pool operator), had said. He had been head of GETCO from
2002 to 2005. "The warrants give them an incentive to help the
company be profitable. This is an additional carrot."

For Nagy, the acquisition of Knight was now "all GETCO's to
lose'. GETCO would be aggressive in pursuing Knight, because it
had next-generation technology for making electronic markets that
could use Knight's network for pulling in order flow effectively.
"Pairing GETCO's cutting-edge technology and trading speeds with
Knight's extensive sales force and broad electronic customer network
would let the combined company grab a bigger part of the market
more efficiently." Nagy called it the kind of "transformation" that
GETCO's Coleman had been seeking.[22]

Joyce clearly favored Virtu's offer not only because he was expected,
at least initially, to continue as CEO of the company, but also because
Virtu was a more profitable company. Perhaps out of loyalty to Joyce,
some in the rank and file were signaling their preference for Virtu's
offer as well. Some trading teams were less sanguine about the
upcoming deal and had been shopping around themselves; these
traders expected job cuts regardless of whether the firm remained

independent or merged with some non-core assets expected to be divested.

The ensuing bidding pushed Knight to its biggest rally in nine years as shares rose 37 percent to $3.42 in the three days ending November 28, when the offers were submitted.

GETCO, Knight and Virtu were all DMMs on the New York Stock Exchange or NYSE MKT. GETCO became a Big Board market maker in 2010. Virtu had the most companies on NYSE MKT, formerly known as the American Stock Exchange. Barclays Capital represented 12 NYSE-listed companies in the DJIA, followed by GETCO with 10 and Goldman Sachs with 5, according to data from NYSE.

"If you're involved in a share deal, then you're betting that their market is going to continue to grow and there is an upside after the deal, whereas in a cash-only deal the upside is you're taking cash, and cash now," had said Sang Lee, managing partner at Boston-based Aite Group. "It really depends on how the shareholders look at the market that all these firms are in."[23]

On Thursday November 29, directors evaluated the two bids submitted the days before, without establishing a timeline for a decision. The group was considering its alternatives and hadn't ruled out keeping the company independent. The board meeting had concluded late Thursday with no decision on whether to accept either one of two buyout offers.

The bids from closely held GETCO and Virtu represented differing structures and would force Knight to choose between cash and a value that depended in part on the stock market's view of GETCO, as Joyce's discussions with other Wall Street firms had failed. The cash-and-stock bid from Chicago-based GETCO valued Knight at $3.50 a share and retained its public listing. Virtu was pursuing a deal to buy Knight for about $3.20 a share in cash, after increasing its first offer of $3.

"It's a very competitive marketplace," Sang Lee, managing partner at Aite Group in Boston, said. "The equities trading market has not been great the last three years. Given the issues Knight went through and the offers at hand, they have to make a decision. They're viable offers."

Virtu's cash offer was widely seen as a backstop bid floor while the GETCO's cash and stock merger recapitalization proposal as an attempt to paper price the implied consideration at the mid-point of the bid/ask range. A $4 or $5 share offer price reflected hopes from Joyce for a strongly competitive jousting contest with a frothy price outcome, driven potentially by the emergence of a white knight such as the always befuddling and feared Citadel.

In fact, Joyce was convinced he could walk away from either offer. His logic was that the firm was making money at the moment as well as before the trading snafu, so he felt justified in claiming that perhaps the firm was worth more, much more.

Knight's board met again on December 3 to resume assessing takeover offers from GETCO and Virtu, its second gathering in five days. On Thursday December 6, employees congregated at the Lighthouse at Chelsea Piers in Manhattan overlooking the Hudson River for their last holiday party as an independent company and pondered their future with as much excitement as they experienced when the trading error was unfolding on August 1.[24] Over the weekend, Virtu executives were already declaring victory, based on support from part of Knight's management. Weren't GETCO and Jefferies persuasive enough for fellow investors to follow their lead?

Knight's board met again on Monday the 17 at 8 A.M. While no decision was reached, the board was to meet again Tuesday at 3 P.M. It was clear the board was aiming for an after-the-bell decision. Indeed, by the afternoon the winner was well known on the Street. Knight's board had ultimately decided to accept the offer coming from the Windy City over the competing offer from Virtu, ending the

17-year independence of Knight, a company that had been propelled by the explosion in electronic trading in American stock markets.

The Knight board had agreed with Joyce's recommendation and concluded that a merger between Knight and GETCO would provide the best possible value creation opportunity for Knight's shareholders. "The transaction provides near-term certainty in the form of cash, while also allowing shareholders to benefit from participation in the future success of the firm."

GETCO, the most successful high-frequency trader in Chicago, had succeeded after raising its offer from initially $3.50 to $3.60, and again to $3.75 a share for Knight, one-third of it in stock, for a total value of $1.4 billion, according to a statement released by both companies in the morning of Wednesday December 19. The offer represented a 13 percent premium to Knight's closing stock price of $3.33 on Tuesday December 18; it was also a 51 percent premium to Knight's closing price on November 23, when reports surfaced that the company was looking for buyers, and a 18 percent premium from the November 27 close, when both offers were in place. If the merger was terminated, Knight or GETCO might have been required to pay the other party a $53 million fee.

Under the terms of the agreement, existing shareholders could receive the price per share in cash or instead one share in the combined firm. The payout would be pro-rated if shareholders elected to receive more than $720 million in cash. Jefferies, which had provide financing to GETCO, agreed to limit the cash portion to 50 percent of their Knight shares.

GETCO would receive 233 million shares in the new company and retire the 57 million shares of Knight it currently owned. It would also receive warrants for 75 million additional shares with staggered strike prices. While merging with GETCO preserved Knight's equity listing and expanded its reach, it also meant the combined company's value would depend on the view of markets, where GETCO had never traded.

"After a thorough evaluation, the Knight board of directors unanimously concluded that a merger between Knight and GETCO provides the best possible value creation opportunity for Knight's shareholders," said Joyce. "The transaction provides near-term certainty in the form of cash, while also allowing shareholders to benefit from participation in the future success of the firm. Broker-dealers and institutions will continue to experience the same industry-leading execution quality and client service they've come to expect from Knight, with the additional liquidity-enhancing capabilities of GETCO's renowned technology.

"The combination of Knight and GETCO will create a powerful, dynamic firm with an unmatched ability to deliver results for clients," said Coleman, GETCO's chief executive officer. "Market participants will benefit from industry-leading services, and our larger capital base will provide strong support for existing operations, as well as an attractive currency for growth. We are looking forward to bringing the talented employees of both companies together and beginning to realize the full potential of the combined organization."

The decision by the board of Knight to pursue GETCO's offer gave its investors an opportunity for stock appreciation while surrendering the certainty of cash. Pasternak had expressed his preference for this type of offer, which provided some upside in a publicly traded security. "If you didn't want to continue with GETCO you could take the cash and sell the stock and probably get as much as Virtu is giving you."

Pasternak, who was recently involved in distressed real estate, understood GETCO's advantage going into the bidding. "GETCO was one of the six that bought Knight and they probably have insights into the company as part of that due diligence. An acquirer always thinks the acquired company is undervalued and they could do things differently that could enhance the value of the enterprise."

GETCO was committed to being a large DMM on the NYSE floor and maintaining Knight's market-making business for over-the-counter equity securities. The takeover was now making GETCO the largest DMM on the New York Stock Exchange, with more than 1,400 companies, surpassing Barclays Capital, which has 1,200, according to data from October 31.

According to Larry Tabb, founder of the data firm the Tabb Group, if the new company managed indeed to maintain their individual market share, the combined company could be larger than any other participant in the stock market and involved in more trades each day than the nation's largest stock exchange, the NASDAQ. "The two 800-pound gorillas are getting together, and they will be a 1,600-pound gorilla," said Professor Angel.[25]

Joel Hasbrouck, a professor at New York University who advised exchanges and trading firms, had said that the size of the new company worried him because it could give the company too much influence with regulators, as it had happened when companies have grown large in other corners of the financial markets. "Sometimes, just by virtue of sheer size, an organization can have a bit more weight with regulators."

Similarly, Davis Polk & Wardwell's Nazareth had said that given the recent disruptions that had hit the stock markets the size of the company was "something you have to think about in this deal". "It is a factor if you have a very large player that could have an impact on the market if it had a problem."

Coleman couldn't have been more excited about the prospects of the combined company. "This represents the opportunity to build out what Knight has put together over the years on a global scale. We think we are going to be the largest or close to the largest liquidity provider in the market and have the opportunity to price risk in a way that will not make us reliant on government back stops."

Coleman would be expected to spend more of his time in Jersey City, where the "vast majority" of the new firm's staff would be, although the combined firm would maintain a "major presence" in Chicago; exactly how "major" its presence would be was a question mark that people in the Windy City detested. Coleman had said the deal negotiations were "long and complicated", and in the end, GETCO had wanted Joyce to be active in the new company, "explaining the new story to the clients." How long and how happy that made Joyce would be clear right after the completion of the merger.

This was an impressive feat for the members of the consortium that had invested $400 million on the longest weekend ever for Knight back in August. The ultimate price was more than owners would have received had no bidding contest occurred.[26]

Predictably, on December 26, TD Ameritrade had pledged its support for the brokerage firm's acquisition by rival GETCO, in the latest sign that the deal was likely to win shareholder approval. As of late August, TD Ameritrade's stake in Knight translated to about 7.1 percent of the firm's common stock. The architects of the rescue deal in early August, Jefferies, with an approximately 22 percent stake, had already signaled support for the transaction.

While a majority of Knight shares had to be voted in favor of the deal, Knight's ten-member board had voted already unanimously to back the GETCO proposal.

The new board was to be composed of nine members: five from the GETCO side, and four from the Knight side; Joyce plus three other current Knight directors would be joining the new company's board. GETCO's co-founders Schuler and Tierney would serve as two of five board members selected by GETCO.

Knight had agreed to extend Joyce's term, slated to become executive chairman of the new company, until the GETCO deal closed or the last day of 2014, whichever was sooner; his current contract was set to expire at the end of December. Was Joyce considering an exit as soon as the deal closed? Indeed, Joyce was already telling board members that he didn't intend to remain with the combined company past the completion of the merger. However, he wouldn't let outsiders know about his plans; he was the long-standing liaison to major customers like online brokerage firms that had been responsible for the bulk of the revenue at Knight; knowing of their departure would have scared them away.

This was still a remarkable turn of events for Joyce who only a few weeks before faced the prospect of losing his job if Virtu succeeded; while Virtu's proposal included him as CEO, he knew he would have eventually been pushed out after a transition period. Now, as part of the merger deal, Joyce was on his way to the bank to cash a $7.5 million retention bonus payout when the GETCO deal closed in return for his previously agreed severance terms with Knight. This time, Knight employees were incensed by this more than generous package for Joyce.

Once again, Sandler O'Neill acted as the financial advisor; Edward D. Herlihy and Nicholas G. Demmo of Wachtell, Lipton, Rosen & Katz acted as legal advisors to Knight. GETCO was advised by Jefferies as financial advisor and H. Rodgin Cohen and John P. Mead of Sullivan & Cromwell as legal advisors; Bank of America Merrill Lynch had provided a fairness opinion to the board of directors of GETCO. Matthew W. Abbott of Paul, Weiss, Rifkind, Wharton & Garrison acted as legal advisor for General Atlantic, GETCO's outside investor.

The acquisition agreement had just been announced when a number of law firms sprang into action to contest the terms of the deal, alleging possible breaches of fiduciary duty by the board of directors of Knight and other violations of state law.

For Block & Leviton, a Boston-based law firm, the offer from GETCO to acquire Knight in a deal for approximately $3.75 per share represented a paltry 13 percent premium to the previous day's closing price. This price failed to take into account the fact that

Knight common stock was poised to recover from the losses it suffered in August 1, 2012 due to a one-time, non-repeating technological glitch. Indeed, said Block & Leviton, the company had already begun to recover from the one-time loss, increasing well over 20 percent from the time of the glitch through the announcement of the proposed transaction. As such, they conclude, it appeared that the proposed transaction premium offered insufficient recognition of Knight's growth potential. Moreover, there appeared to be significant conflicts of interest arising out of the interrelationships between GETCO and Knight.

For Levi & Korsinsky, a firm with offices in New York, New Jersey, and Washington D.C., their investigation concerned whether the Knight board of directors breached their fiduciary duties to stockholders by failing to adequately shop the company before entering into this transaction and whether GETCO was underpaying for Knight shares, they claimed, thus unlawfully harming Knight stockholders.

Similarly, Rigrodsky & Long, P.A., another firm with offices in Wilmington, Delaware and Garden City, New York, announced their investigation concerned whether Knight's board of directors failed to adequately shop the Company and obtain the best possible value for Knight's shareholders before entering into an agreement with GETCO. Rigrodsky was advising shareholder Ann Jimenez McMillan who claimed that the price was "unfair and grossly inadequate", and would deny investors "their right to share proportionately and equitably in the true value of the company's valuable and profitable business, and future growth." McMillan was asking for class-action, or group status, on behalf of all outside stockholders, unspecified damages, and an order to stop the deal under its present terms.[27]

Surprisingly, Rosen Law, another firm that specializes in prosecuting securities litigation, didn't immediately launch an investigation. Were they sleeping at the wheel? Not really. On August 25 of 2011, the firm announced that a class action lawsuit had been filed on behalf of investors who purchased the common stock of Penson Worldwide seeking to recover damages for apparent violations of federal securities laws. The following year Knight acquired Penson Futures, a unit of Penson Worldwide; it would have looked rather strange had Rosen Law jumped in favor of Knight shareholders when they were already fighting the firm.

Chapter Seventeen

The End of the Independent Knight

A significant sign of consolidation in the industry came on December 19 when IntercontinentalExchange (ICE), a derivatives trading powerhouse in the U.S., offered to buy the parent company of the New York Stock Exchange for $8.2 billion; this happened to be the same day Knight and GETCO announced their deal. The ICE and NYSE deal would give 12-year old commodities and energy bourse ICE a powerful presence in Europe's lucrative financial derivatives market through control of NYSE Liffe, Europe's second-largest futures exchange, and a major advantage over U.S.-based rivals CME Group and NASDAQ. The rationale of the acquisition was that regulatory changes, in the wake of the financial crisis, were forcing banks to channel derivatives business through clearing houses and regulated exchanges to ensure that their risk positions could be better monitored than they were when bank dealers were trading complex contracts directly among themselves. Once again, scale was the name of the game.

The deal between Knight and GETCO spurred also from the continuing struggles of equity trading, as total volume had fallen and competition had driven down profit margins. Ford had told the Financial Times before, "We've done a lot of strategic thinking at GETCO. The way you react to lower trading volumes is to actively globalize the business, grow into multiple asset classes and try to gain scale to become more efficient." For him, the deal was motivated by a strong positive view towards value creation with no plans for a short-term exit.

Coleman wanted to combine with the U.S. market maker to grow by trading new products and markets around the world and obtain a stock market listing and potential currency for further deals. "This is about creating a new type of market making firm that's publicly traded, like Knight, but it's going to have a bigger scale around the world."

GETCO and Knight had already outlined expected cost savings from the deal at between $90 million and $110 million annually, though they had noted this could have taken three years to achieve. Within the first year of the deal closing, the firms expected to save $20 million to $30 million; GETCO intended to slash costs by streamlining the technology that both used to trade shares and derivatives while cutting duplicated positions and operations such as trade processing. Together, the two companies' expenses amounted to $1.8 billion in 2012, compared with $1.3 billion in combined revenue.

Once the transaction was made public, Coleman, chief executive officer, and Joyce, executive chairman, started leading the integration of the former rivals' operations and technology. Coleman had thought long and hard about the potential of the two firms together. "Knight has some great business that from time to time people want to buy, but that's because they're great businesses." Acquiring Knight had sped up by five years GETCO's plans to expand into new businesses; these plans had been hatched during a strategic review earlier in the year.

Joyce agreed on the takeover uniting complementary businesses; however, it was clear that he was no longer running the show as he had for more than 10 years at Knight. "There's certainly going to be an element of me being Mr. Outside, if you will, on the road a little more often, out in front of clients," Joyce had said. Coleman as CEO would be "Mr. Inside", running the company's day-to-day business.

That Joyce was no longer running the show could have been easily appreciated by checking the proportion of GETCO executives who were part of the new management team unveiled in February 20. While the chief financial officer post was retained by Knight's Bisgay, the remaining top positions were largely filled with GETCO executives, at a four-to-one ratio.

The only other Knight executives were Maasland, head of global execution services and platforms, and Sohos, global head of client market making. From GETCO, top executives included Darren Mast, chief operating officer and interim head of fixed income, currencies & commodities; Nick Ogurtsov, chief risk officer, Robert Smith and Farid Moslehi, heads of Europe and Asia, respectively; John DiBacco, global head of equities trading; Jon Ross, chief technology officer; Sophie Sohn, chief communications & marketing officer; John McCarthy, general counsel, and Jerry Dark, chief human resources officer.

"The senior management team that we are announcing today possesses the expertise to successfully integrate our two organizations, develop new and innovative products and, most importantly, serve the needs of our clients across multiple asset classes and time zones," Coleman had said.

GETCO's new management team brought to the spotlight a number of executives who had been shining under the radar. An executive that had demonstrated an exquisite ability to get things done in Washington D.C., an ever important skill as of late, was John McCarthy. GETCO's general counsel since 2006, he had served before as an associate director at the SEC; there he led the Office of Compliance Inspections and Examinations Market Oversight unit, which was responsible for regulatory oversight of trading on stock and options exchanges. Before joining the SEC in 1992, McCarthy had clerked for the United States Attorneys' office and the Court of

Special Appeals of Maryland. McCarthy had degrees in engineering and economics from the University of Michigan, a master in finance from the London School of Economics, and a J.D. with Honors from the University of Maryland.

McCarthy had engineered one of the most significant SEC employee poaching cases. In June 2010, Elizabeth King, a seventeen-year SEC veteran and associate director in the Division of Trading and Markets, accepted a job offer from McCarthy to join GETCO. King was then reporting to Cook, the director of the Trading and Markets Division who played an important role during Knight's darkest hours. While at the SEC, King had contact with the firm at least a few times per year. She also had a "long-standing relationship" with McCarthy, whom she considered a personal friend.[1]

Over coffee three months before departing, McCarthy proposed that she come to work for GETCO. That same afternoon, King contacted the SEC's ethics office, which advised her the next day to recuse herself from three rulemaking projects: one for options fees, another for high-frequency trading, and a third with a "specific GETCO nexus", because she was considering the offer. Furthermore, during her cooling-off period, King was prohibited from lobbying SEC employees on matters involving GETCO, though she was allowed to work behind the scenes. She hadn't represented GETCO at meetings with the SEC during that period.

An internal report by the office of SEC Inspector General H. David Kotz would find later that King did not violate conflict of interest rules when she negotiated her new job with GETCO. Her move (and similar moves by other SEC staffers) directly from the regulatory agency to a company that it oversaw had sparked questions from lawmakers, in particular, Senator Charles Grassley, R.-Iowa, who had written to Kotz in June regarding his concern over King's employment and the "revolving door" between the private sector and the SEC.

John DiBacco, who would oversee equities trading, was the banker who supervised Kweku Adoboli at UBS at the time the rogue trader engaged in what the Swiss investment bank said was unauthorized trading. The incident cost UBS $2.3 billion, not as much as J.P. Morgan's loss in early 2012 but not pocket change either. DiBacco, who had received a bachelor's degree in mechanical engineering from Massachusetts Institute of Technology, was terminated by UBS for failing to properly supervise Adoboli.[2]

DiBacco, a thirteen-year veteran at the bank, had said in a testimony at Adoboli's criminal trial that he was "surprised" at the large positions traders in the British capital were taking. DiBacco, who ran the exchange-traded funds desk, said at the time that he had no idea Adoboli had been faking transactions for as long as three years.[3]

Jon Ross was the affable and outgoing personality who took the top technology role at GETCO from Michael Rauchman in July 2012. Ross had previously been head of GETCO Execution Services (GES) in Europe and had overseen order management, execution and technology solutions for the company's European clients.[4]

Prior to joining GETCO, Ross was the CTO of NASDAQ after it acquired Inet ATS from Instinet in December of 2005. While at NASDAQ, Ross led the "Single Book" integration of INET, Brut and NASDAQ's SuperMontage into a single platform and oversaw NASDAQ's initial Regulation NMS implementation. Prior to his position at NASDAQ, Ross was the CTO of the INET ATS, in charge of development and maintenance of INET's core trading platform. He held the same role at Island ECN, which was acquired by Instinet in 2002.

Only a few days later, Coleman was able to snatch 13 years of experience accumulated as global head of electronic trading from Goldman Sachs wrapped around the face of Greg Tusar's humanity;[5] he had joined Goldman Sachs through its SLK acquisition to become involved in a number of market structure investments pursued by the infamously called "great vampire squid."[6] The new hire would become co-head of global execution services and platforms and join Maasland to assume co-responsibility for the firm's sales, products and platforms globally by August 20, 2013.[7]

Knight had 1,524 employees at the end of December, according to a regulatory filing. In February, the firm had announced that it would lay off about 5 percent of its workforce.[8] GETCO, conversely, had slightly more than 400 employees in September after having eliminated 40 jobs earlier that year. Whether the combined company maintained units not involved in stock trading depended on where cost reductions lay and how important diversification was to the firm. Certainly having almost 2,000 employees in the combined payroll wouldn't last long.

On potential staff reductions, Coleman had said that while any merger had overlaps, "this is more about the revenue potential than it is about ripping out cost synergies." However, industry veteran Buzzy Geduld, the chief executive officer of Cougar Trading in New York who had sold his firm Herzog, Heine & Geduld to Merrill Lynch, suggested the combined total of more than 1,900 employees could shrink to 1,500 or less. Geduld, who owned 55,000 shares of Knight as of September 30, had said that the combined company was likely to lower expenses through job cuts and other measures. "You'll see a contraction in personnel, perhaps an increase in sales personnel because that's revenue. Anything that drives revenue they'll keep or enhance, and anything that doesn't drive revenue or is duplicated you'll see them say goodbye and good luck." He was on to something; by the end of the second quarter, the combined headcount had passed that number and was on the way down.

Knight's new owner wanted to carve up and sell parts of the trading and financial services firm to reduce debt used to pay for the acquisition. The firms were reviewing the dark pools, or private venues that didn't display orders and quotations; each would continue to operate in the next few months and management would decide later whether clients would benefit if they were combined. Knight's and GETCO's platforms were already among the most heavily used, according to data from Rosenblatt Securities. Together, they would be significantly larger than the next biggest dark pool operator, Credit Suisse's Crossfinder.

On March 15, 2013, Stifel would acquire Knight's U.S. and European institutional fixed-income sales and trading business, beating rivals Guggenheim Partners, Canaccord Financial and Sterne Agee & Leach in the process.[9]

Knight had indeed been shopping the unit out with Bank of America Merrill Lynch's advice. Defections to rivals had already thinned out the credit team at Knight; traders who had recently stormed out included Anthony Guido, Richard Mercante, Kevin Smyth, William Murphy and Nestor Cybriwsky.[10]

The group, led by Lhota and Bob Lyons in New York, covered high-yield and investment-grade corporate bonds, asset-backed and mortgage-backed securities, emerging markets and fixed-income research. Knight planned to retain BondPoint, the electronic system for corporate, municipal and government debt.[11]

Knight was among several firms which had bolstered their debt unit, following the worst financial crisis since the Great Depression, by hiring in 2009 Lhota as head of high-yield, distressed and bank loan sales. Knight started a European credit trading and sales group led by Neil Robertson that included 14 people. At least half of them had previously worked at UBS. Chapdelaine & Co., Citadel and Ticonderoga Securities had shuttered or scaled back credit units since 2010 as the biggest banks regained their dominance over debt markets.

Trading on Hotspot FX had remained intact over the past years despite the challenges Knight had faced; its platform had recorded year-on-year volume increases in recent months. In May 2013, its average daily volume was $33.7 billion, up 19 percent from $28.2 billion in May 2012.

"Hotspot FX is a very successful venue that has been steadily growing market share relative to its peer group. It has very good people and very good technology, which is consistent with what KCG is about. The platform is obviously now part of a bigger company, which could help it to acquire new clients, but the venue itself doesn't change in any material way," confided Maasland. Jointly with Joseph Mazzella, head of institutional equities, Maasland commanded over Hotspot FX electronic communication network's management team, including business manager Bill Goodbody and head of sales John Miesner.

"One of Hotspot FX's strengths is that it has found a way of providing useful services to banks and buy-side firms without trying to be everything to everyone. In addition to our core activity, we have developed capabilities such as our wholesale initiative, which caters to the retail broker community, for example, and we provide good quality services to regional banks that wish to extend distribution in their home currencies, but need access to liquidity across all currencies," explained Maasland.

Following the formal merger announcement on July 2, 2013, GETCO and Knight combined their designated market-maker units under one identity on the floor of the New York Stock Exchange. The new unit was called Knight Capital Americas, and would trade 1,551 NYSE and NYSE MKT securities, making it the largest designated market maker on the two exchanges, ahead of Barclays Capital, Goldman Sachs, Virtu Financial, J. Streicher & Co., and Brendan E. Cryan & Co. Knight's designated market-making unit traded approximately 512 NYSE and 139 NYSE MKT-listed securities. GETCO's unit traded approximately 900 NYSE-listed securities.[12]

GETCO, arguably once the biggest name in Chicago high-speed trading firms, was gone for the Windy City. It wasn't only that the firm was moving its headquarters to Jersey City; since the announcement of the merger, the company had been cutting back as trading and the markets slowed. By the completion of the merger, GETCO employed between 200 and 250 workers in Chicago, down from 400 the year before.[13]

There was an unhappy man left in Chicago. Mayor Rahm Emanuel had always been quick to embrace good news anytime a Chicago employer added a few dozen jobs. Statements would frequently fly out and TV cameras would often be invited to press conferences featuring the mayor himself. Emanuel had spoken with GETCO owners in early January and had indicated that Chicago was willing to work closely with the company. But the mayor always knew that keeping the headquarters "was an uphill battle; the majority of the company's business interests are in New York."[14]

The rite of passage in modern capitalism would not be passed up by KCG. On July 8, CEO Coleman rang the opening bell at the New York Stock Exchange, marking the completion of the Knight and GETCO's merger and the unveiling of its new corporate logo, the three interweaving rings that characterized GETCO next to the word "KCG."

With the birth of KCG Holdings, there was somebody who considered there was nothing else for him to do. This person had lived the most tumultuous 11 months of his life arranging the bailout of his firm and spearheading its acquisition by GETCO; this executive had gotten tired and bored at work, despite his now coming daily to the office.[15] There was no CEO hat he could wear anymore. Moreover, with $7.5 million getting into his bank account just days before, why stay?

Joyce announced on July 3 that he was quitting his executive chairman role at KCG, being replaced by GETCO co-founder Schuler, who had been CEO until Coleman's appointment. Joyce's bio, which had debuted in KCG's brand new corporate website, was removed almost as promptly. His communication to the board of directors was broadcast to employees and friends and read like an epitaph.

"Over the course of the last eleven years, I have been fortunate to be the CEO of Knight Capital Group. Together we achieved a wide variety of the business goals we had established. With the transaction with GETCO completed, and after careful consideration, I have decided that now is the right time for me to resign as Executive Chairman and leave the organization.

As you know, it was my recommendation to the board that Knight remain independent. That said, I remain confident that, once the issue of independence was taken off the table, the merger with GETCO was the best alternative available to Knight shareholders and other key stakeholders – including clients and employees.

I take great pride in the fact that 'legacy Knight' is operating so well as it moves into KCG Holdings. And I am gratified that the values at the core of Knight's DNA – client service, integrity and maintaining the highest standard of business ethics – will continue to be core values of KCG going forward. Our business success is dependent upon relationships built on trust, and it is due to the committed and hardworking employees of Knight that our company has been successful through the years. Similarly, it has been an honor to work closely with Knight's clients. They have been remarkably loyal to the firm and have been rewarded with consistently outstanding market making, institutional sales and trading, and electronic execution services.

I wish my fellow directors and KCG's employees every success as they move forward.

All the best,

Tom Joyce"[16]

"Tom Joyce has always put clients first. His focus on client service continues to influence every aspect of our new organization," Daniel Coleman, chief executive of KCG, said. "Tom played an important role in the creation of KCG and we thank him for his leadership."[17]

The man who once claimed he had succeeded in making a small hedge fund even smaller was not able to succeed in making Knight much bigger, not even remotely close to its heights during the late 1990s. Joyce's dream had been to see Knight acquired by a top financial conglomerate; it never happened.

"I've known Tommy for 25 years and he's as honest as the day is long," had said Cougar Trading's Geduld. "If you want to be in the market-making business, they've got a real franchise," he said.

"He was able to turn it around," said Andresen, then co-CEO at Headlands Technologies. "When he took over that company, they were essentially a manual trading operation. He overhauled that firm into a real electronic trading powerhouse. There's not a lot of precedent for doing that."

"T.J. was able to shift the firm to become more like an institutional broker," said Baez. "Whereas the prior Knight needed to have a gigantic scale of operations to make money, in the wholesale business you needed scale in your systems and the ability to squeeze every single penny out of every order that comes through."

Shpilberg believed that Joyce had lost his sense of direction in the last couple of years. Joyce always wanted to merge or sell, but none of the advances he made turned out successful. Shpilberg said he never understood why.

"Joyce was a good leader, he had a clear vision of what to do, yet he was not a hands-on manager. He relied on people and trusted people a lot. Normally that would work, but in this industry it's kind of tough to verify. He was a good CEO. He did a very good job. Until he didn't."

While Raquet and Pasternak were the founders of the firm, it was Joyce who helped the firm transition from the Internet boom and bust cycle through the worst financial crisis to its acquisition by GETCO.

However, he will be forever remembered by the trading error that his strategic timing and management style allowed to happen.

About the Author

Edgar Perez is widely regarded as the preeminent global speaker in electronic, algorithmic and high-frequency trading. He is author of The Speed Traders, An Insider's Look at the New High-Frequency Phenomenon That is Transforming the Investing World, published in English by McGraw-Hill Inc. (2011), 交易快手：透视正在改变投资世界的新兴高频交易, Chinese by China Financial Publishing House (2012), and Investasi Super Kilat: Pandangan Orang dalam tentang Fenomena Baru Frekuensi Tinggi yang Mentransformasi Dunia Investasi, Bahasa Indonesia by Kompas Gramedia (2012).

Perez is course director of The Speed Traders Workshop, How High Frequency Traders Leverage Profitable Strategies to Find Alpha in Equities, Options, Futures and FX (Hong Kong, Sao Paulo, Seoul, Kuala Lumpur, Warsaw, Kiev, New York, Singapore, Beijing, Shanghai) and was Adjunct Professor at the Polytechnic Institute of New York University, where he taught Algorithmic Trading and High-Frequency Finance. He contributes to The New York Times and China's International Finance News and Sina Finance.

Perez has been interviewed on CNBC, Bloomberg TV, FOX Business, CNN, BNN Business Day, CCTV China, Bankier.pl, TheStreet.com, Leaderonomics, GPW Media, Channel NewsAsia Business Tonight and Cents & Sensibilities. He has been globally featured on FXFactor, Columbia Business, OpenMarkets, Sohu, News.Sina.com, Yicai, eastmoney, Caijing, ETF88.com, 360doc, AH Radio, CNFOL.com, CITICS Futures, Tongxin Securities, ZhiCheng.com, CBNweek.com, Caixin, Futures Daily, Xinhua, Chinese Financial News, ifeng.com, International Finance News, hexun.com, Finance.QQ.com, Finance.Sina.com, The Korea Times, The Korea Herald, The Star, The Malaysian Insider, BMF 89.9, iMoney Hong Kong, CNBC, Bloomberg Hedge Fund Brief, The Wall

Street Journal, The New York Times, Dallas Morning News, Valor Econômico, FIXGlobal Trading, TODAY Online, Oriental Daily News and Business Times.

Perez has been engaged to present at the Council on Foreign Relations, Vadym Hetman Kyiv National Economic University (Kiev), Quant Investment & HFT Summit APAC 2012 (Shanghai), U.S. Securities and Exchange Commission (Washington D.C.), CFA Singapore, Hong Kong Securities Institute, Courant Institute of Mathematical Sciences at New York University, University of International Business and Economics (Beijing), and Hult International Business School (London and Shanghai), among other public and private institutions.

In addition, Perez has spoken at a number of global conferences, including Emerging Markets Investments Summit 2013 (Warsaw), CME Group's Global Financial Leadership Conference 2012 (Naples Beach), Harvard Business School's Venture Capital & Private Equity Conference (Boston), High-frequency Trading Leaders Forum (New York, Chicago, London), MIT Sloan Investment Management Conference (Cambridge), Institutional Investor's Global Growth Markets Forum (London), Technical Analysis Society (Singapore), TradeTech Asia (Singapore), FIXGlobal Face2Face (Seoul) and Private Equity Convention Russia, CIS & Eurasia (London).

Perez was a vice president at Citigroup, a senior consultant at IBM, and a strategy consultant at McKinsey & Company in New York City. Perez has an undergraduate degree from Universidad Nacional de Ingeniería, Lima, Peru (1994), a Master of Administration from Universidad ESAN, Lima, Peru (1997) and a Master of Business Administration from Columbia Business School, New York, with a dual major in Finance and Management (2002). He belongs to the Beta Gamma Sigma honor society. Perez resides in the New York City area and is an accomplished salsa and hustle dancer.

Index

Notes

Chapter One
The Lazy Morning that Wasn't

[1] "The Tradition Of The NYSE Bell," Investopedia, March 4, 2010
(http://www.investopedia.com/financial-edge/0310/the-tradition-of-the-nyse-bell.aspx)

[2] "Floor Traders Praise NYSE Officials' Handling of Trading Glitch," The Wall Street Journal, August 1, 2012
(http://blogs.wsj.com/marketbeat/2012/08/01/floor-traders-praise-nyse-officials-handling-of-trading-glitch)

[3] "The Climb: Doreen Mogavero", Forbes, November 14, 2008
(http://www.forbes.com/2008/11/06/056.html)

[4] "A NASDAQ Critic Takes Aim," The Wall Street Journal, July 4, 2012
(http://online.wsj.com/article/SB10001424052702303933404577504981772663406.html)

[5] "Stock traders' tough floor exercise," Los Angeles Times, January 8, 2009
(http://articles.latimes.com/2009/jan/08/business/fi-trader8)

[6] "Greed Never Left," Vanity Fair, April 2010
(http://www.vanityfair.com/hollywood/features/2010/04/wall-street-201004)

[7] "Wall Street: Money Never Sleeps," Wikipedia, July 24, 2013
(http://en.wikipedia.org/wiki/Wall_Street:_Money_Never_Sleeps)

[8] "Nanex ~ 01-Aug-2012 ~ Knightmare on Wall Street," August 3, 2012
(http://www.nanex.net/aqck2/3522.html)

[9] "Professional athletes and knee injury," Brown University, 2004
(http://biomed.brown.edu/Courses/BI108/BI108_2004_Groups/Group06/Group6project/Sports/SProathletesandinjuries.htm)

Chapter Two
The Biggest Risk for Financial Markets

[1] "Dark Pools Win Record Stock Volume as NYSE Trading Slows to 1990s Levels," Bloomberg, February 29, 2013

(http://www.bloomberg.com/news/2012-03-01/dark-pools-capture-record-share-of-declining-u-s-equity-volume.html)

[2] "Exchanges Say Dark Pools 'Degrade' Public Markets," MarketWatch, December 18, 2012 (http://rblt.com/news_details.aspx?id=217)

[3] "Wall Street sees Knight as software risk wake-up call," Chicago Tribune, August 3, 2012 (http://articles.chicagotribune.com/2012-08-03/business/sns-rt-us-knightcapital-loss-dealerresponsebre87300h-20120803_1_bats-global-markets-glitches-systems)

[4] "Errant Trades Reveal a Risk Few Expected," The New York Times, August, 2, 2012 (http://dealbook.nytimes.com/2012/08/02/errant-trades-reveal-a-risk-few-expected)

[5] "High-Speed Traders' Technology Controls Are Focus of Finra Probe," BloombergBusinessweek, July 18, 2013 (http://www.businessweek.com/news/2013-07-18/high-speed-traders-technology-controls-are-focus-of-finra-probe)

[6] "Infinium fined $850,000 for computer malfunctions," Financial Times, November 25, 2011 (http://www.ft.com/intl/cms/s/0/f97e0668-1783-11e1-b157-00144feabdc0.html#axzz2Zi89b1Vv)

[7] "Getco Fined $450,000 for Failing to Supervise Equity Trading," Bloomberg, March 22, 2012 (http://www.bloomberg.com/news/2012-03-22/getco-fined-450-000-for-failing-to-supervise-equity-trading-1-.html)

[8] Letter of Comment from John J. Rapa, President/Chief Executive Officer, Tellefsen and Company, SEC, April 19, 2013 (http://www.sec.gov/comments/s7-01-13/s70113-9.pdf)

[9] Letter of Comment from Raymond M. Tierney Ill, President and Chief Executive Officer, Bloomberg Tradebook LLC, SEC, June 19, 2013 (http://www.sec.gov/comments/s7-01-13/s70113-26.pdf)

[10] "Impact of Reg SCI: Q&A with Jim Angel," Traders Magazine, May 17, 2013 (http://www.tradersmagazine.com/news/impact-of-reg-sci-qa-with-jim-angel-111194-1.html)

[11] "The CEO/CFO Certification Requirement," The CPA Journal, 2003 (http://www.nysscpa.org/cpajournal/2003/0703/features/f073603.htm)

Chapter Three
Flash Crash, Pipeline, BATS and...

[1] "Traders Navigate a Murky New World," The Wall Street Journal, April 9, 2012

(http://online.wsj.com/article/SB10001424052970203889904577199114267593518.html)

[2] Cease and Desist Proceedings, Securities and Exchange Commission, October 24, 2011 (http://www.sec.gov/litigation/admin/2011/33-9271.pdf)

[3] "Bats: the Epic Fail of the Worst IPO Ever," Bloomberg Businessweek, March 23, 2012 (http://www.businessweek.com/articles/2012-03-23/bats-all-folks-the-epic-fail-of-the-worst-ipo-ever)

[4] "Speedy New Traders Make Waves Far From Wall St.," The New York Times, May 16, 2010 (http://www.nytimes.com/2010/05/17/business/17trade.html)

[5] "IPO Preview: BATS Global Markets," Seeking Alpha, March 22, 2012 (http://seekingalpha.com/article/451901-ipo-preview-bats-global-markets)

[6] "BATS Receives Funding from GETCO and Wedbush", BATS Trading, October 14, 2005 (http://www.batstrading.com/resources/press_releases/BATS percent20Receives percent20Funding percent20from percent20GETCO percent20and percent20WEDBUSH.pdf)

[7] "Get Briefed: Joe Ratterman", Forbes, October 17, 2009 (http://www.forbes.com/2009/08/14/ratterman-bats-tradebot-intelligent-investing-exchange.html)

[8] "IPO software behind BATS' failure," Financial Times, March 26, 2012 (http://www.ft.com/cms/s/0/1f4ccaaa-774c-11e1-93cb-00144feab49a.html#axzz2YU8s4Kco)

[9] "BATS Global Markets: The 'spectacularly botched' IPO," The Week, March 26, 2012 (http://theweek.com/article/index/226041/bats-global-markets-the-spectacularly-botched-ipo)

[10] "BATS Chief on Friday's Troubles: 'My Stomach Sank'," The New York Times, March 26, 2012 (http://dealbook.nytimes.com/2012/03/26/bats-chief-on-fridays-meltdown-my-stomach-sank)

[11] "Bats CEO Cedes Chairman Role as Board Said to Delay IPO," Bloomberg, March 28, 2012 (http://www.bloomberg.com/news/2012-03-27/bats-ceo-ratterman-to-give-up-chairman-s-role-after-failed-ipo.html)

[12] "BATS appoints ex-SEC commissioner as non-executive chairman," Reuters, July 17, 2012 (http://www.reuters.com/article/2012/07/17/us-bats-chairman-idUSBRE86G0ZV20120717)

[13] "BATS exchange withdraws IPO after stumbles," March 24, 2012, Reuters (http://www.reuters.com/article/2012/03/24/us-batsglobal-idUSBRE82M13A20120324)

[14] "BATS Faced Revolt Over IPO," The Wall Street Journal, March 26, 2012 (http://online.wsj.com/article/SB1000142405270230417710457730390422876909 4.html)

Chapter Four
The Men Behind Knight

[1] "Tax-fraud case began with tip I.R.S. got in '81," The New York Times, November 23, 1983 (http://www.nytimes.com/1983/11/23/nyregion/tax-fraud-case-began-with-tip-irs-got-in-81.html)
[2] "Net Entrepreneurs Only," Gregory K. Ericksen, John Wiley & Sons, Inc., 2000

Chapter Five
The Ascendance of Knight

[1] "Doll House in limbo," Daily Freeman, April 21, 2013 (http://www.dailyfreeman.com/articles/2013/04/21/life/doc51730ec8270ad767 969677.txt?viewmode=fullstory)
[2] "Are These Reader Submitted Comments For Real Or Are They Saire For Two Very Public Persons," Greenwich Roundup, October 2, 2008 (http://greenwichroundup.blogspot.com/2008/10/100208-are-these-reader-submitted.html)
[3] "Lakefront home on Via Del Mar fetches $19.5M," Palm Beach Daily News, May 24, 2011 (http://www.palmbeachdailynews.com/news/news/lakefront-home-on-via-del-mar-fetches-195m/nMDPx)
[4] "Steve Mnuchin, Meet Rose Gudiel," The Huffington Post, October 3, 2011 (http://www.huffingtonpost.com/peter-dreier/steve-mnuchin-meet-rose-g_b_992940.html)
[5] "Billion-Dollar Blunders", Forbes, August 20, 2013 (http://www.forbes.com/2003/08/20/cz_nw_0820blunder.html)
[6] "The Stealth Superstar of Online Trading Knight/Trimark is the biggest Wall Street firm you've never heard of. It came from nowhere four years ago and caught the cyberwave just right. Can it keep on winning?," Fortune, September 27, 1999 (http://money.cnn.com/magazines/fortune/fortune_archive/1999/09/27/26616 8/index.htm)

Chapter Six
Knight in Free Fall

[1] "Wall St. Is Flush With Cash But Also Green With Envy," The New York Times, December 14, 1999
(http://www.nytimes.com/1999/12/14/business/the-markets-market-place-wall-st-is-flush-with-cash-but-also-green-with-envy.html)

[2] "John Phelan, N.Y.S.E. Chief Who Ushered In New Technology, Is Dead at 81," The New York Times, August 6, 2012
(http://dealbook.nytimes.com/2012/08/06/john-phelan-81-n-y-s-e-chief-who-ushered-in-new-technology-is-dead)

[3] "Fear, Greed And Technology," Forbes, May 15, 2000
(http://www.forbes.com/forbes/2000/0515/6511170a.html)

[4] "Dark Pools: High-Speed Traders, A.I. Bandits, and the Threat to the Global Financial System," Scott Patterson, Crown Business, 2012

[5] "Matthew Andresen," Crain's New York Business, 40 Under Forty Class 2000 (http://mycrains.crainsnewyork.com/40under40/profiles/2000/matthew-andresen)

[6] "TD's Nagy Starts New Firm," Traders Magazine, June 15, 2012
(http://www.tradersmagazine.com/news/chris-nagy-kor-ameritrade-110088-1.html)

[7] "Knight/Trimark warns due to lower trading volume," October 11, 2009
(http://www.marketwatch.com/story/knighttrimark-warns-due-to-lower-trading-volume)

[8] "Venture capitalist Efi Gildor breaks his "no interviews" rule," GLOBES Israel's Business Arena, July 1, 2002
(http://www.globes.co.il/serveen/globes/docview.asp?did=598325)

[9] "Money Honey riles viewers with her Trimark grilling," New York Post, April 23, 2000
(http://www.nypost.com/p/item_Sbsun6OW2OiFYYDqIAYrSJ)

[10] "Forbes 2001 Executive Pay List," Forbes.com, December, 2001
(http://www.forbes.com/lists)

[11] "Company News; Knight Trading Names Different Interim Chief," The New York Times, January 17, 2002
(http://www.nytimes.com/2002/01/17/business/company-news-knight-trading-names-different-interim-chief.html)

[12] "After Pasternak, Knight Trading Juggles CEOs," Waters Technology, March 1, 2012

(http://www.waterstechnology.com/waters/feature/1610897/position-keeping)

[13] "John A. Mulheren," Wikipedia, April 25, 2013
(http://en.wikipedia.org/wiki/John_A._Mulheren)

[14] "Knight Trading Group finally honing the ax," Investment News, May 13, 2002 (http://www.investmentnews.com/article/20020513/SUB/205130720)

Chapter Seven
New CEO on Board

[1] "High-Frequency Trading Provides Essential Liquidity," The Wall Street Journal, January 4, 2013
(http://online.wsj.com/article/SB1000142412788732382010457821166317077708 52.html)

[2] "The Bitter and the Sweet Flavor Sports Seasons," The Harvard Crimson, June 12, 1975 (http://www.thecrimson.com/article/1975/6/12/the-bitter-and-the-sweet-flavor)

[3] "Harvard Baseball '77: A Tale of What's Coming," The Harvard Crimson, July 8, 1977 (http://www.thecrimson.com/article/1977/7/8/harvard-baseball-77-a-tale-of)

[4] "Joe Restic, 85, an Innovator in Football at Harvard, Dies," The New York Times, December 11, 2011
(http://www.nytimes.com/2011/12/12/sports/ncaafootball/joe-restic-an-innovator-in-football-at-harvard-dies-at-85.html)

[5] "COMMONWEALTH vs. EDWARD J. SOARES," Commonwealth of Massachusetts, March 8, 1979
(http://masscases.com/cases/sjc/377/377mass461.html)

[6] "Private Sector; A Mild-Mannered Mr. Fix-It," The New York Times, December 8, 2002 (http://www.nytimes.com/2002/12/08/business/private-sector-a-mild-mannered-mr-fix-it.html)

[7] "Darien Woman Of Distinction Works To Teach Life Lessons," The Darien Daily Voice, January 15, 2013
(http://darien.dailyvoice.com/neighbors/darien-woman-distinction-works-teach-life-lessons)

[8] "Six to be named 'Women of Distinction' by YWCA Darien/Norwalk," Norwalk Citizen, June 1, 2011
(http://www.norwalkcitizenonline.com/news/article/Six-to-be-named-Women-of-Distinction-by-YWCA-1400856.php)

[9] "STRATFOR," Dazzlepod, February 23, 2013 (https://dazzlepod.com/stratfor)

Chapter Eight
Stabilizing the Ship

[1] "Glitch Slams Knight Trading Shares," Los Angeles Times, June 4, 2002 (http://articles.latimes.com/2002/jun/04/business/fi-knight4)
[2] "Knight Trading stock slammed on report of probe," USA TODAY, June 4, 2002 (http://usatoday30.usatoday.com/money/general/2002/06/04/knight-hurt.htm)
[3] "Knight Faces Allegations It Cost Investors Millions," The Wall Street Journal, June 4, 2002 (http://online.wsj.com/article/0,,SB1023120495675734240-search,00.html)
[4] "SEC Formalizes Probe at Knight Trading Group," Los Angeles Times, November 13, 2002 (http://articles.latimes.com/2002/nov/13/business/fi-wrap13.3)
[5] "Bank integrating acquired businesses, in-house systems," Securities Technology Monitor, January 14, 2008 (http://www.securitiestechnologymonitor.com/issues/19_44/21863-1.html)
[6] "Two Independents Left Now That Knight Obtains Attain ECN," Securities Technology Monitor, May 16, 2005 (http://www.securitiestechnologymonitor.com/issues/20050515/15554-1.html)
[7] "Newly Rebranded ValuBond Is More Open, Says Knight," Securities Technology Monitor, January 28, 2008 (http://www.securitiestechnologymonitor.com/issues/19_46/21932-1.html)
[8] "Knight Appoints Albert C. Maasland As Senior Managing Director, Head Of International," Knight Capital, May 1, 2012 (http://www.knight.com/investorRelations/pressReleases.asp?releaseID=1689397)
[9] "Knight Capital Group Completes Acquisition of Libertas Holdings, LLC," Knight Capital, July 11, 2008 (http://www.knight.com/newsRoom/pressReleases.asp?compid=105070&releaseID=1174012)
[10] "Knight Capital's Deephaven to sell fund's assets," Reuters, January 27, 2009 (http://www.reuters.com/article/2009/01/28/knight-deephaven-idUSN2748755920090128)

[11] "Deephaven to Sell Flagship Fund," The New York Times, January 27, 2009 (http://dealbook.nytimes.com/2009/01/27/deephaven-to-sell-flagship-fund-and-exit-business)

[12] "Knight Capital Group Announces Agreement To Acquire The Futures Division Of Penson Financial Services, Inc." Knight Capital, May 29, 2012 (http://www.knight.com/investorRelations/pressReleases.asp?compid=105070&releaseID=1700195)

Chapter Nine
Unfriending Facebook

[1] "The Facebook Effect: the Inside Story of the Company That Is Connecting the World," David Kirkpatrick, June, 2010.

[2] "Top Bank Lawyer's E-Mails Show Washington's Inside Game," Bloomberg, September 5, 2012 (http://www.bloomberg.com/news/2012-09-05/top-bank-lawyer-s-e-mails-show-washington-s-inside-game.html)

[3] "Tennis' loss is lacrosse's gain for Greyhounds," The Baltimore Sun, April 23, 1996 (http://articles.baltimoresun.com/1996-04-23/sports/1996114113_1_sye-arnett-lacrosse)

[4] "U.S. approves Nasdaq payback plan for Facebook IPO, UBS unhappy," Reuters, March 25, 2012 (http://www.reuters.com/article/2013/03/25/us-sec-nadsaq-facebook-idUSBRE92O0DL20130325)

Chapter Ten
What Made Knight Tick and Profit

[1] "Battle for Tech Geeks: Street vs. Silicon Valley," The Wall Street Journal, January 18, 2011 (http://online.wsj.com/article/SB10001424052748704637704576082512439373244.html)

[2] "High-Speed Traders Race to Fend Off Regulators," The Wall Street Journal, December 27, 2012 (http://online.wsj.com/article/SB10001424127887324001104578165842110484364.html)

[3] "Citadel's Sentinel: CIO Tom Miglis Aims to Do the Impossible," Waters Technology, November 26, 2012 (http://www.waterstechnology.com/waters/feature/2227450/citadels-sentinel-cio-tom-miglis-aims-to-do-the-impossible)

[4] "NYSE Computer Issue Led to No Closing Auction in 216 Stocks", Bloomberg, November 13, 2012 (http://www.bloomberg.com/news/2012-11-12/nyse-computer-issue-means-no-closing-auction-in-216-securities.html)

[5] "Add Pretend Pets to Mom's Duties," The New York Times, July 22, 2007 (http://www.nytimes.com/2007/07/22/fashion/22webkinz.html)

[6] "Help is on the way," TimeOut New York, January 1, 2007 (http://www.timeout.com/new-york-kids/new-york-families/help-is-on-the-way)

[7] "A Day Before its Massive Tech Glitch, Knight Had Another Flub," FOX Business Network, August 8, 2012 (http://www.foxbusiness.com/industries/2012/08/08/day-before-its-massive-tech-glitch-knight-had-another-flub)

[8] "Draft Interagency White Paper on Sound Practices to Strengthen the Resilience of the U.S. Financial System," Board of Governors of the Federal Reserve System, Office of the Comptroller of the Currency and Securities and Exchange Commission, August 30, 2002 (http://www.federalreserve.gov/boarddocs/press/bcreg/2002/20020830/attachment.pdf)

[9] "Disaster Recovery Planning - How Far is Far Enough?," CIO Update, March 25, 2010 (http://www.cioupdate.com/trends/article.php/3872926/Disaster-Recovery-Planning---How-Far-is-Far-Enough.htm)

[10] "Interagency Paper on Sound Practices to Strengthen the Resilience of the U.S. Financial System," Board of Governors of the Federal Reserve System, Office of the Comptroller of the Currency and Securities and Exchange Commission, April 8, 2003 (http://www.sec.gov/news/studies/34-47638.htm)

[11] "SEC Was Looking at Knight in Midst of Errant Trade," FOX Business Network, August 14, 2012 (http://www.foxbusiness.com/investing/2012/08/14/sec-was-looking-at-knight-in-midst-errant-trade)

Chapter Eleven
The Fight for the Firm's Survival

[1] "Knight Cap CEO: Regulators Did Their Job," CNBC, August 6, 2012 (http://video.cnbc.com/gallery/?video=3000107479)

[2] "Knight Capital obtains credit line after IT glitch causes $440m loss," The Telegraph, August 3, 2012

(http://www.telegraph.co.uk/finance/markets/9449856/Knight-Capital-obtains-credit-line-after-IT-glitch-causes-440m-loss.html)

[3] "Knight Capital Faces Pressure to Find Savior After Loss," Bloomberg, August 2, 2012 (http://origin-www.bloomberg.com/apps/news?pid=conewsstory&tkr=INGP:US&sid=aeS WJYbaj.EA)

[4] "The Actual Details of the Knight Capital Error," Kid Dynamite's World, August 9th, 2012 (http://kiddynamitesworld.com/the-actual-details-of-the-knight-capital-error)

Chapter Twelve
Surviving One More Day

[1] "Knight Talks Deal With Virtu, Seeks J.P. Morgan Funding," The Wall Street Journal, August 2, 2012 (http://online.wsj.com/article/SB10000872396390443866404577565112003062548.html)

[2] "Knight Deal May be Raw Deal for Shareholders," FOX Business Network, August 5, 2012 (http://www.foxbusiness.com/business-leaders/2012/08/05/knight-capital-ceo)

[3] "Loyalty, Profit Drive Knight Rescue," The Wall Street Journal, August 7, 2012 (http://online.wsj.com/article/SB10000872396390444246904577572752865497064.html)

[4] "Knight Capital former CEO Pasternak says company can rebound," Reuters, August 2, 2012 (http://www.reuters.com/article/2012/08/02/us-knightcapital-loss-pasternak-idUSBRE8711BR20120802)

[5] "Searching for a Speed Limit in High-Frequency Trading," The New York Times, September 8, 2012 (http://www.nytimes.com/2012/09/09/business/high-frequency-trading-of-stocks-is-two-critics-target.html)

[6] "SEC closely reviewing Knight Capital trading glitch," Reuters, August 2, 2012 (http://www.reuters.com/article/2012/08/02/us-knightcapital-glitch-sec-idUSBRE8711W620120802)

[7] "Burned by MF Global, futures watchdogs eye Knight," Reuters, August 2, 2012 (http://www.reuters.com/article/2012/08/02/knightcapital-regulators-idUSL2E8J26R720120802)

[8] "Knight Capital 'has 48 hours' to save itself after IT glitch causes $440m loss," The Telegraph, August 3, 2012 (http://www.telegraph.co.uk/finance/markets/9448893/Knight-Capital-has-48-hours-to-save-itself-after-IT-glitch-causes-440m-loss.html)

Chapter Thirteen
90 Interested Parties
[1] "US SEC examining risk controls at Knight Capital," Reuters, August 4, 2012 (http://in.reuters.com/article/2012/08/03/sec-knight-idINL2E8J33FU20120803)
[2] "No 'White Knight' Needed for Knight: Co-Founder," CNBC, August 3, 2012 (http://www.cnbc.com/id/48489033)
[3] "Knight Capital heads into make-or-break weekend," Reuters, August 4, 2012 (http://uk.mobile.reuters.com/article/usTopNews/idUKBRE8710PG20120804)
[4] "The Amazing Life Of The Guy Apple Tried To Poach: Blackstone CFO Laurence Tosi," Business Insider, January 6, 2011 (http://www.businessinsider.com/laurence-tosi-2011-1)
[5] "Before Trading Debacle, Blackstone Wanted to Take Knight Private," FOX Business Network, August 6, 2012 (http://www.foxbusiness.com/industries/2012/08/06/before-trading-debacle-blackstone-wanted-to-take-knight-private)
[6] "Griffin's Overtures to Knight Were Hampered by Distrust," Bloomberg, August 8, 2012 (http://www.bloomberg.com/news/2012-08-09/griffin-s-overtures-to-knight-were-hampered-by-distrust.html)

Chapter Fourteen
Enjoying the Light of a New Day
[1] "Stewart v. Leibowitz: Will "Daily Show" Host Go After His NYSE-Exec Brother?," The Wall Street Journal, May 7, 2010 (http://blogs.wsj.com/deals/2010/05/07/stewart-v-leibowitz-will-daily-show-host-go-after-his-nyse-exec-brother)
[2] "Jon Stewart's Unfunny Brother Is Testifying About the 'Flash Crash' Right Now," New York Magazine, May 11, 2010 (http://nymag.com/daily/intelligencer/2010/05/jon_stewarts_unfunny_brother_i.html)

3 "Jon Stewart's brother says mom 'pretty happy with both'," Reuters, March 29, 2010 (http://blogs.reuters.com/summits/2010/03/29/jon-stewarts-brother-says-mom-pretty-happy-with-both)

4 "White Knights for Knight Capital," CNBC, August 7, 2012 (http://video.cnbc.com/gallery/?video=3000106996)

5 "Knight's Shining Armor: Getco, Blackstone, TD, Stifel, Stephens, Jefferies," Securities Technology Monitor, August 6, 2012 (http://www.securitiestechnologymonitor.com/news/knight-capital-rescuers-31076-1.html)

6 "Happy to Help Knight: Stifel CEO," CNBC, August 6, 2012 (http://video.cnbc.com/gallery/?video=3000107466)

7 "Knight Investor: Knight Suffered Unique Event, Easily Fixable," CNBC, August 6, 2012 (http://video.cnbc.com/gallery/?video=3000107365)

8 "Knight's Joyce gets reprieve but new owners want answers," Reuters, August 10, 2012 (http://www.reuters.com/article/2012/08/10/knighttrading-loss-joyce-idUSL2E8J6CMK20120810)

9 "NYSE Shifts Knight's Stocks Temporarily to GETCO," Bloomberg, August 6, 2012 (http://www.bloomberg.com/news/2012-08-06/nyse-shifts-knight-companies-temporarily-to-getco-s-market maker.html)

10 "Hush-Hush Investor Added to Knight Bailout Team," FOX Business Network, August 21, 2012 (http://www.foxbusiness.com/industries/2012/08/21/knight-bailout-team-scottrade)

11 "Knight CEO Joyce says has full support as firm in flux," Reuters, August 6, 2012 (http://www.reuters.com/article/2012/08/07/knightcapital-joyce-idUSL2E8J668P20120807)

12 "Knight Capital's Latest Loss," Traders Magazine, March 2013 (http://www.tradersmagazine.com/issues/26_348/knight-capital-getco-closes-clearing-110902-1.html)

13 "Lutnick: Knight Capital Error Doesn't Make Sense," FOX Business Network, August 6, 2012 (http://video.foxbusiness.com/v/1773935872001/lutnick-knight-capital-error-doesnt-make-sense)

Chapter Fifteen
Rebuilding the Business

[1] "Knight executives took pay cuts for 2012", Financial News, April 18, 2013 (http://www.efinancialnews.com/story/2013-04-18/knight-executives-pay-cuts-2012)

[2] "NASDAQ Retains IBM to Review Market Systems," Securities Technology Monitor, June 6, 2012 (http://www.securitiestechnologymonitor.com/news/nasdaq-retains-ibm-review-market-systems-30699-1.html)

[3] "NASDAQ: Systems Review 'Essentially' Complete," The Wall Street Journal, October 16, 2012 (http://online.wsj.com/article/SB1000087239639044367540457805992035412528 6.html)

[4] "Knight Capital CEO: 'Close to 100 percent'," The Wall Street Journal, August 9, 2012 (http://online.wsj.com/article/SB1000087239639044340400457757943332520698 6.html)

[5] "Knight CEO: Regulatory Changes Likely Following Trading Glitch", FOX Business Network, September 11, 2012 (http://www.foxbusiness.com/industries/2012/09/11/knight-ceo-regulatory-changes-likely-following-trading-glitch)

[6] 'Exchanges Plot Fixes for Their Glitches", The Wall Street Journal, September 11, 2012 (http://online.wsj.com/article/SB1000087239639044369660457764596018217639 8.html)

[7] "Oracle to Switch Shares to NYSE From Nasdaq Stock Market," The Wall Street Journal, June 20, 2013 (http://online.wsj.com/article/BT-CO-20130620-711545.html)

[8] "NASDAQ Blames NYSE for Knight's Implosion," FOX Business Network, June 7, 2013 (http://video.foxbusiness.com/v/2449752550001/nasdaq-blames-nyse-for-knights-implosion)

[9] "Knight Names McCarthy as New Algo Chief," Traders Magazine, September 18, 2012 (http://www.tradersmagazine.com/news/knight-mccarthy-algo-110306-1.html

[10] "Knight Capital Sets the Record Straight on Algo Testing," Advanced Trading, November 26, 2012 (http://www.advancedtrading.com/algorithms/knight-capital-sets-the-record-straight/240142501)

[11] "Knight Sued by Ex-Sales Trader for Discrimination and Wrongful Termination," Traders Magazine, July 1, 2013

(http://www.tradersmagazine.com/news/knight-sued-by-ex-sales-trader-for-discrimination-and-wrongful-Termination-111316-1.html)

[12] "Gain Capital Hires Ex-Knight Executive Wald for Institutions ECN," Bloomberg, January 17, 2013 (http://www.bloomberg.com/news/2013-01-17/gain-capital-hires-ex-knight-executive-wald-for-institutions-ecn.html)

[13] "Knight Capital CEO vows to rebuild value," Financial News, October 18, 2012 (http://www.efinancialnews.com/story/2012-10-18/knight-capital-ceo-voes-rebuild-trust)

[14] "Saxena White P.A. Files Securities Fraud Class Action Against Knight Capital Group Inc.," Reuters, October 26, 2012 (http://www.reuters.com/finance/stocks/KCG/key-developments/article/2631080)

[15] "Knight Capital's Chief Ponders His Options," The Wall Street Journal, October 25, 2012 (http://online.wsj.com/article/SB1000142405297020389740457807692134093786.html)

[16] "Talking Deals; Small Buyouts Are Booming," The New York Times, July 2, 1987 (http://www.nytimes.com/1987/07/02/business/talkng-deals-small-buyouts-are-booming.html)

[17] "Why the SEC's Market Access Rule is the Critical Test for Compliance," October 19, 2012 (http://marketsmedia.com/market-access-rule-the-critical-test-for-compliance)

[18] "SEC Expands Knight Probe," The Wall Street Journal, November 13, 2012 (http://online.wsj.com/article/SB1000142412788732459590457811725353457138 8.html)

[19] "Generator Problems Hit Knight," The Wall Street Journal, October 31, 2012 (http://online.wsj.com/article/SB1000142405297020370760457809085179344589 8.html)

[20] "Knight Capital Punts on Using Backup Center," The Wall Street Journal, November 1, 2012 (http://blogs.wsj.com/cio/2012/11/01/knight-capital-punts-on-using-backup-center)

Chapter Sixteen
Barbarians at the Gate?

[1] "GETCO May Consider Boosting Knight Capital Shares," Bloomberg TV, November 16, 2012 (http://www.bloomberg.com/video/getco-may-consider-boosting-knight-capital-shares-m7~FAkXdSaSe~M8Oe3RQtQ.html)

[2] "Knight Capital sets meeting for stock awards", MarketWatch, November 20, 2012 (http://www.marketwatch.com/story/knight-capital-sets-meeting-for-stock-awards-2012-11-20)

[3] "GETCO to Consider Buying Knight Shares, Evaluate Investment," BloombergBusinessweek, November 16, 2012 (http://www.businessweek.com/news/2012-11-16/getco-to-consider-buying-knight-shares-evaluate-investment)

[4] "Knight CEO Said to See Business as Usual Amid Unit Sale Report," Bloomberg, November 25, 2012 (http://www.bloomberg.com/news/2012-11-25/knight-ceo-said-to-see-business-as-usual-amid-unit-sale-report.html)

[5] "Knight to Take Acquisition Proposals," Traders Magazine, November 26, 2012 (http://www.tradersmagazine.com/news/knight-to-take-acquisition-proposals-110558-1.html)

[6] "Knight's Joyce Looking for White Knight," FOX Business Network, November 27, 2012 (http://www.foxbusiness.com/industries/2012/11/27/knight-capital-ceo-looks-to-wall-street-for-merger)

[7] "Market-Maker Virtu Expands Globally as It Mulls Public Offering", Bloomberg, May 2, 2013 (http://www.bloomberg.com/news/2013-05-02/market-maker-virtu-expands-globally-as-it-mulls-public-offering.html)

[8] "Who is Vincent Viola?," NETSDAILY, June 26, 2009 (http://www.netsdaily.com/2009/6/26/1346761/who-is-vincent-viola)

[9] "Two large US proprietary trading firms to merge," Financial Times, May 28, 2011 (http://www.ft.com/intl/cms/s/0/a9345d52-893e-11e0-b342-00144feab49a.html)

[10] "The mysterious man behind the bid for Knight Capital," Fortune, December 12, 2012 (http://finance.fortune.cnn.com/2012/12/12/vincent-viola-virtu-knight)

[11] "Virtu Submits All-Cash Counter for Knight," Traders Magazine, November 28, 2012 (http://www.tradersmagazine.com/news/virtu-preparing-all-cash-offer-for-knight-110577-1.html)

[12] "Meet GETCO, High-Frequency Trade King," The Wall Street Journal, August 27, 2009 (http://online.wsj.com/article/SB125133123046162191.html)

[13] "GETCO Announces Investment by General Atlantic," General Atlantic LLC, April 16, 2007 (http://www.generalatlantic.com/en/news/article/730)

[14] "UBS blow as global equities chief quits," Financial Times, March 22, 2010 (http://www.ft.com/intl/cms/s/0/bb90238c-35e3-11df-aa43-00144feabdc0.html)

[15] "Theodore Swann residence," Bhamwiki, January 29, 2013 (http://www.bhamwiki.com/w/Theodore_Swann_residence)

[16] "Friends of Birmingham Botanical Gardens hosts Fall Donor Appreciation event," All Alabama, November 27, 2012 (http://www.al.com/living/index.ssf/2012/11/scribblers_photos_friends_of_b.html)

[17] "Q&A with GETCO's new CEO Coleman: WSJ," MarketWatch, February 27, 2012 (http://www.marketwatch.com/story/qa-with-getcos-new-ceo-coleman-wsj-2012-02-27)

[18] "Quiet giant Getco opens up," Crain's Business Chicago, May 21, 2012 (http://www.chicagobusiness.com/article/20120519/ISSUE01/305199981/quiet-giant-getco-opens-up)

[19] "Getco goes global as U.S. margins shrink," Crain's Business Chicago, September 19, 2011 (http://www.chicagobusiness.com/article/20110917/ISSUE01/309179977/getco-goes-global-as-u-s-margins-shrink)

[20] "GETCO Profit Slumps," The Wall Street Journal, April 15, 2013 (http://online.wsj.com/article/SB10001424127887324485004578424253648843778.html)

[21] "KCG Seeks Healthy Knights for Jousting Tournament," Oscar Gruss & Son, November 30, 2012 (http://ogru.com/ssblog/2012/11/30/KCG+Seeks+Healthy+Knights+For+Jousting+Tournament.aspx)

[22] "Merger would bring more transparency, New York focus to Getco," Crain's Business Chicago, December 17, 2012 (http://www.chicagobusiness.com/article/20121215/ISSUE01/312159982/merger-would-bring-more-transparency-new-york-focus-to-getco)

[23] "GETCO Proposes Buying Knight Capital With Cash, Stock," Bloomberg Businessweek, November 28, 2013 (http://www.businessweek.com/news/2012-11-28/getco-proposes-buying-knight-capital-at-3-dot-50-a-share)

[24] "Knight Capital Sale Only a Matter of Time," FOX Business Network, December 6, 2012 (http://www.foxbusiness.com/industries/2012/12/06/knight-capital-sale-only-matter-time)

[25] "High-Speed Trade Giants to Merge," The New York Times, December 20, 2012 (http://www.nytimes.com/2012/12/20/business/knight-capital-announces-sale-to-getco.html)

[26] "Knight Gets a Key Nod; $7.5 Million for CEO," The Wall Street Journal (http://online.wsj.com/article/SB1000142412788732353040457820374115256674.html)

[27] "Knight Capital shareholder sues over GETCO merger," New Jersey On-Line, December 31, 2012 (http://www.nj.com/business/index.ssf/2012/12/knight_capital_shareholder_sue.html)

Chapter Seventeen
The End of the Independent Knight

[1] "No Ethics Breach In SEC Staffer's Job Change: Report," Law360, March 7, 2011 (http://www.law360.com/articles/230112/no-ethics-breach-in-sec-staffers-job-change-report)

[2] "GETCO Executives Dominate Knight Takeover," Traders Magazine, February 21, 2013 (http://www.tradersmagazine.com/news/getco-executives-dominate-knight-takeover-110899-1.html)

[3] "Getco Names John DiBacco as Head of Equities Trading," Bloomberg, February 21, 2013 (http://www.bloomberg.com/news/2013-02-21/getco-names-john-dibacco-as-head-of-equities-trading.html

[4] "Getco Taps Jon Ross for CTO Role," Wall Street & Technology, July 2, 2012 (http://www.wallstreetandtech.com/career-management/getco-taps-jon-ross-for-cto-role/240003062)

[5] "Getco hires Goldman Sachs electronic trading head," Financial News, February 28, 2013 (http://www.efinancialnews.com/story/2013-02-28/getci-hires-goldman-electronic-trading-head-greg-tusar)

[6] "The Great American Bubble Machine," Rolling Stone, July 9, 2009 (http://www.rollingstone.com/politics/news/the-great-american-bubble-machine-20100405)

[7] "Tusar Lands at KCG Holdings," Traders Magazine, July 16, 2013 (http://www.tradersmagazine.com/news/ex-goldman-exec-greg-tusar-lands-at-kcg-holdings-111359-1.html)

[8] "Knight Capital Group cutting 5 pct of workforce," AP News, February 5, 2013 (http://www.businessweek.com/ap/2013-02-05/knight-capital-group-cutting-5-pct-of-workforce)

[9] "Stifel Agrees to Acquire Fixed-Income Group From Knight," Bloomberg, March 15, 2013 (http://www.bloomberg.com/news/2013-03-15/stifel-agrees-to-acquire-fixed-income-group-from-knight.html)

[10] "Knight Capital seeks buyers for its credit sales, trading team," New Jersey On-Line, January 18, 2013 (http://www.nj.com/business/index.ssf/2013/01/knight_capital_seeks_buyers _fo.html)

[11] "Knight Selling Bond Unit to Stifel," Traders Magazine, February 25, 2013 (http://www.tradersmagazine.com/news/knight-selling-bond-unit-to-stifel-110935-1.html)

[12] "GETCO and Knight Merging NYSE Market Maker Units," Traders Magazine, June 28, 2013 (http://www.tradersmagazine.com/news/getco-and-knight-merging-NYSE-market maker-units-111315-1.html)

[13] "GETCO goes away," Crain's Chicago Business, July 2, 2013 (http://www.chicagobusiness.com/article/20130702/NEWS01/130709944/getco-goes-away)

[14] "GETCO takes a piece of Emanuel with it to New Jersey," Crain's Chicago Business, July 3, 2013 (http://www.chicagobusiness.com/article/20130703/BLOGS02/130709921/getco-takes-a-piece-of-emanuel-with-it-to-new-jersey)

[15] "Gasparino: Joyce Quits Knight Capital," FOX Business Network, July 3, 2013 (http://video.foxbusiness.com/v/2524727774001/gasparino-joyce-quits-knight-capital)

[16] "Knight Capital's CEO Tom Joyce Quits, Here's His Resignation Letter," Business Insider, July 3, 2013 (http://www.businessinsider.com/knight-capitals-tom-joyce-quits-2013-7#ixzz2Xzkbp1fU)

[17] "Knight brokerage exec leaves a year after trading meltdown," Los Angeles Times, July 3, 2013 (http://www.latimes.com/business/money/la-fi-mo-knight-capital-brokerage-chief-departs-20130703,0,2737268.story)

AN INSIDER'S LOOK AT THE NEW
HIGH-FREQUENCY PHENOMENON
THAT IS TRANSFORMING
THE INVESTING WORLD

THE SPEED
TRADERS

FEATURING INTERVIEWS WITH TODAY'S
TOP HIGH-FREQUENCY TRADERS

EDGAR PEREZ

CPSIA information can be obtained at www.ICGtesting.com
Printed in the USA
LVOW06*1434021213

363566LV00002B/15/P